EERDMANS COMMENTARIES ON THE DEAD SEA SCROLLS

The Eerdmans Commentaries on the Dead Sea Scrolls series marks a milestone in scroll studies. The sixteen volumes in the ECDSS series, each one written by a world-renowned scrolls scholar, bring together for the first time expert translations, critical notes, and line-by-line commentary for every translatable manuscript found at Qumran. Produced with scholarly rigor yet accessible to non-specialists and students, these volumes are essential to the study of the Dead Sea Scrolls and also provide crucial background for research into both the New Testament and rabbinical Judaism

EERDMANS COMMENTARIES ON THE DEAD SEA SCROLLS

Martin G. Abegg Jr. and Peter W. Flint, General Editors

*Now available

LITURGICAL WORKS

JAMES R. DAVILA

WILLIAM B. EERDMANS PUBLISHING COMPANY
GRAND RAPIDS, MICHIGAN / CAMBRIDGE, U.K.

Wm. B. Eerdmans Publishing Co.

255 Jefferson Ave. S.E., Grand Rapids, Michigan 49503 /
P.O. Box 163, Cambridge CB3 9PU U.K.

Printed in the United States of America

05 04 03 02 01 00   7 6 5 4 3 2 1

Library of Congress Cataloging-in-Publication Data

Davila, James R., 1960-
Liturgical Works / James R. Davila.

p.   cm.   — (Eerdmans commentaries on the Dead Sea scrolls)
Includes bibliographical references and index.
ISBN 0-8028-4380-8 (pbk: alk. paper)
1. Dead Sea scrolls — Liturgical use.
2. Dead Sea scrolls — Criticism, interpretation, etc.
3. Judaism — Liturgy.
I. Dead Sea scrolls. English. Selections. 2000.
II. Title.   III. Series.

BM487.D35 2000
296.1'55 — dc21
                        00-049471

www.eerdmans.com

For Rachel and Teddy

Contents

Special Abbreviations, Symbols, and Primary Sources

Baraita di Maaseh Bereshit   A Jewish cosmological tractate in Hebrew, closely related to the *Seder Rabba di Bereshit* (see below). Versions A and B are cited according to the lineation of Nicolas Séd, "Une cosmologie juive du haut moyen age: la Běraytā dī Maʿaseh Berēšīt," *REJ* 123 (1964) 259-305 and 124 (1965) 23-123.

BDB   Francis Brown, S. R. Driver, and Charles A. Briggs, eds., *Hebrew and English Lexicon of the Old Testament* (London: Oxford University Press, 1907).

BH   Biblical Hebrew

3 Enoch   A Hekhalot text comprising §§1-80 of *SH-L* (see below) and translated by Philip Alexander in *OTP* 1:223-315. Passages not included in *SH-L* are cited according to the edition of Hugo Odeberg, *3 Enoch, or the Hebrew Book of Enoch* (1928; rpt. New York: Ktav, 1973).

EVV   English version (when the verse numbering of a biblical passage differs from that of the Hebrew text in the MT).

G   A Geniza fragment of the Hekhalot literature. Cited according to the numeration and lineation of the edition by Peter Schäfer, *Geniza-Fragmente zur Hekhalot-Literatur* (Tübingen: Mohr Siebeck, 1984). For example, "G11 2b:2-4" means lines 2-4 of column 2b, text 11 in this edition.

HB   Hebrew Bible

HDSS   Elisha Qimron, *The Hebrew of the Dead Sea Scrolls* (HSS 29; Atlanta: Scholars Press, 1986). Cited by paragraph number.

Hekhalot Rabbati   A Hekhalot text comprising roughly *SH-L* §§81-121, 152-54, 156-73, 189-96, 198-277.

Hekhalot Zutarti   A Hekhalot text comprising roughly *SH-L* §§335-74, 407-26.

HL   Hekhalot literature

Jan. Jamb.   *Jannes and Jambres.* Cited according to the edition of Albert Pietersma, *The Apocryphon of Jannes and Jambres the Magicians* (Leiden: Brill, 1994). Also translated by Pietersma and R. T. Lutz in *OTP* 2:427-42.

Jastrow   Marcus Jastrow, *A Dictionary of the Targumim, the Talmud Babli and Yerushalmi, and the Midrashic Literature* (2 vols.; New York: Pardes, 1950).

Jos. Asen.   *Joseph and Aseneth.* Always cited from the long version: Christoph Burchard, "Ein vorläufiger griechischer Text von Joseph und Aseneth," in *Gesammelte Studien zu Joseph und Aseneth* (SVTP 13; Leiden: Brill, 1996) 161-209. Translated by Burchard in *OTP* 2:177-247.

KCG   *Ketubbot* from the Cairo Geniza, according to their numbering in Mordechai Akiva Friedman, *Jewish Marriage in Palestine: A Cairo Geniza Study* (2 vols.; Tel Aviv and New York: Jewish Theological Seminary of America, 1980-81).

Ma'aseh Merkavah   A Hekhalot text comprising §§544-96 of *SH-L* (see below).

Massekhet Hekhalot   A Hekhalot text. Cited according to the edition of Klaus Hermann, *Massekhet Hekhalot: Traktat von den himmlischen Palästen. Edition, Übersetzung und Kommentar* (TSAJ 39; Tübingen: Mohr Siebeck, 1994). In my citations, chapter and verse are separated by a period, not a comma (i.e., §20,1 in Hermann's edition = §20.1).

Merkavah Rabba   A Hekhalot text comprising §§655-708 of *SH-L* (see below).

NHC   Nag Hammadi Codex

PAM   Palestine Archaeological Museum

QH   Qumran Hebrew

QL   Qumran literature

RH   Rabbinic Hebrew

Sar Panim   A Hekhalot text comprising §§623-39 of *SH-L* (see below).

Sar Torah   A Hekhalot text comprising §§281-306 of *SH-L* (see below).

Seder Rabba di Bereshit   A Jewish cosmological tractate in Hebrew, closely related to the *Baraita di Maʿaseh Bereshit* (see above). Published by Shlomo
Aharon Wertheimer and Abraham Joseph Wertheimer in *Batei Midrashot:
Twenty-Five Midrashim Published for the First Time from Manuscripts Discovered in the Genizoth of Jerusalem and Egypt with Introductions and Annotations* (2nd ed.; Jerusalem: Ktab Yad Wasepher, 1968) 3-48 (in Hebrew).
Cited according to the paragraphing of this edition and according to the
paragraphing of *SH-L* (see below; roughly §§428-67, 518-40, 714-853).

Sepher HaRazim   A Jewish magical tractate in Hebrew. Cited according to the
lineation in the edition of Mordechai Margoliot, *Sepher Ha-Razim: A Newly
Recovered Book of Magic from the Talmudic Period* (Jerusalem: Yediot
Achronot, 1966) (in Hebrew). Translation by Michael A. Morgan, *Sepher
Ha-Razim: The Book of the Mysteries* (SBLTT 24; SBLPS 11; Chico, Calif.:
Scholars Press, 1983).

SH-L   Peter Schäfer, et al., *Synopse zur Hekhalot-Literatur* (TSAJ 2; Tübingen:
Mohr Siebeck, 1981). Hekhalot texts published in the *Synopse* are cited by
the traditional name of the given "macroform" (*Hekhalot Rabbati, Hekhalot
Zutarti*, etc.) followed by the relevant paragraph number(s) in *SH-L*. Passages not found within the boundaries of the traditional named texts are
cited as "*SH-L*" followed by the relevant paragraph number(s).

Songs I-XIII   The thirteen *Songs of the Sabbath Sacrifice*.

<text>   Text written above the line as a scribal correction. Supralinear text too
badly damaged for translation is ignored.

<<text>>   Text marked for deletion with dots above and below the letters.

~~text~~   Text marked for deletion by being crossed out or erased.

text(!)   The translation corrects a mistake in the Hebrew text.

//   Marks a parallel passage found in two different texts or manuscripts. For
example, Ps 105:8 // 1 Chron 16:15.

Introduction

I. The Qumran Library and Its Liturgical Texts

The story of the discovery more than half a century ago of a large cache of scrolls in caves overlooking the Dead Sea near the Wadi Qumran is too well known to require a detailed rehearsal here. The Dead Sea Scrolls are one of the greatest archaeological treasures ever recovered, and although all too often preserved only in small pieces, they have added immeasurably to our knowledge of pre-rabbinic Judaism and the cultural background of early Christianity. They include our earliest manuscripts of most books of the Hebrew Bible, copies in the original Aramaic and Hebrew of Jewish books that had survived otherwise only in translations (such as *1 Enoch* and *Jubilees*), and numerous previously unknown Jewish compositions, mostly in Hebrew and Aramaic, some of which show a sectarian consciousness that defines itself in contrast to other contemporary forms of Judaism.

The Dead Sea Scrolls have been and remain a focal point of controversy, with even the most basic questions about them still subject to debate. It is agreed that they were hidden in the caves around the turn of the era, probably in response to the invasion of the Roman military forces in 68 CE. Some doctrines, precepts, and ideas in the sectarian texts resemble those of the Essenes, a Jewish group described by a number of writers in the first century CE, including the Jewish historian Flavius Josephus, the Jewish philosopher Philo of Alexandria, and the Roman author Pliny the Elder. Many but not all specialists in Qumran studies see a close relationship between the sectarian scrolls and the

1

Essenes. Many also think that the scrolls were copied and sometimes composed in the buildings that now lie in ruins next to the Wadi Qumran, but this is not entirely certain either. The nonsectarian compositions are also of great interest, since they seem to give us information on the elements of Judaism that were widely accepted in the Second Temple period by the various competing Jewish groups.[1]

The focus of this volume of the Eerdmans commentary series on the Dead Sea Scrolls is the liturgical texts from the Qumran library. The main criterion for inclusion is that the text show evidence of composition for use in the ritual life of ancient Judaism, whether pertaining to the cycle of festivals and holy days, to daily prayer in various situations, to ceremonial purification, or to rites of passage such as marriage.[2] Apart from the Scrolls, most of our information about such matters comes from the Hebrew Bible, so a few words should be said about the study of liturgical and ritual elements in the Bible.

Although the Bible is a book, a selective library of the literature of ancient Israel, it is important to regard it not only as theologically authoritative text or as great literature, but also as a repository of ritual and liturgical traditions. Literary analysis is indeed a key to understanding the Hebrew Bible, but many of the works it includes pertain to concrete ritual contexts that must be investigated if we are to gain a full and balanced comprehension. Jewish tradition has generally been much more sensitive to this aspect of the Bible than has Christian theology. Even modern critical biblical scholarship has to some degree tended to emphasize textual analysis over study of the ritual background of the Bible, a tendency attributable to the origins of biblical criticism in the Protestant Reformation, with its accompanying bibliocentrism.[3] Happily, in recent years much has been done to correct this bias, thanks to the work of Jewish

---

1. For good overviews of the discovery and significance of the Scrolls, see the following introductory works: Cook, *Solving the Mysteries of the Dead Sea Scrolls;* Schiffman, *Reclaiming the Dead Sea Scrolls;* VanderKam, *The Dead Sea Scrolls Today;* and Vermes, *An Introduction to the Complete Dead Sea Scrolls.* The following comprehensive translations of the Scrolls are also recommended: García Martínez, *The Dead Sea Scrolls Translated;* Vermes, *The Complete Dead Sea Scrolls in English;* and Wise et al., *The Dead Sea Scrolls.*

2. Separating the liturgical texts from the others was not always a straightforward process. One could make the case, for example, that exorcism rituals (4Q510-11 and 11Q11) belong in this volume, but in the end other considerations led to their being assigned to the volume of psalms and hymns.

3. For a look at how its Protestant origins has affected the exegetical approach of modern biblical criticism, see Kugel, "The Bible in the University." The distorting effect of Protestant assumptions on ritual studies has also been explored by Smith in *To Take Place,* esp. chap. 5.

scholars sensitive to the centrality of ritual in the biblical and Jewish traditions, and the work of researchers drawing on insights from cultural anthropology.

This textual bias in biblical studies may help explain the history of interpretation of the Qumran texts covered in this volume. Those documents that illuminate later mystical traditions (especially the *Songs of the Sabbath Sacrifice* and the *Berakhot*) have received considerably more attention than those (such as the "Wedding Ceremony," the "Daily Prayers," the "Words of the Luminaries," the "Festival Prayers," and the "Purification Liturgies") that focus mainly on matters of prayer, the celebration of festivals, and ritual purification. Of course, other factors have been at work as well. Many liturgical texts, such as 4Q501-509, 4Q512, survive only in exceedingly badly damaged copies, mostly published in volume 7 of the Discoveries in the Judaean Desert series, a volume well known for its laconic French commentary. Others (e.g., 4Q409, 4Q434a, 4Q414) have been published only recently and sometimes incompletely in advance of the official editions. Yet whatever the reasons for the previous relative neglect, a thorough new look at many of these fascinating documents is in order, and it is hoped that this volume will advance our understanding of them.

II. Cult, Covenant, and Purity

It is important to grasp a number of basic terms and concepts when working with the liturgical texts from Qumran. One of these is "cult," a word used colloquially in a negative sense to mean any religion of which the speaker disapproves. However, scholars use the term "cult" in a neutral and technical sense to mean any set of rituals used in a given religious tradition. "Cult" is essentially any ritual actions marking out and taking place in sacred space and sacred time. Thus, for example, a Catholic Mass, a Protestant sermon, a Jewish Shabbat meal, or a Japanese ritual observance of an ancestor's "death day" are all living examples of cult.[4] Likewise the sacrifices, temple services, and observations of religious festivals in ancient Israel are cultic acts.

A second crucial idea is that of "covenant." In the ancient Near East, contracts or treaties were signed between a so-called great king, who ruled over a large empire, and lesser kings, who ruled as vassals under his overlordship. The biblical concept of covenant is modeled on these vassal treaties, with God functioning as the great king and the people of Israel as his vassal. The basic outline of the vassal treaties went something like the following.

---

4. For the last in the list, see Earhart, *Religions of Japan*, 59-63.

1. A title or preamble.
2. A historical prologue recording the past relations between the great king and the vassal.
3. The treaty stipulations, describing what the vassal agrees to do in exchange for the overlord's loyalty and support.
4. Provisions for the deposit of a copy of the treaty in a temple and its regular public reading.
5. A list of gods who act as witnesses to the agreement.
6. A series of blessings and curses that the gods would bring on the obedient or disobedient vassal.

The covenant between God and Israel ratified at Sinai is the central theme of the books of Exodus to Deuteronomy, and much of the material describing this covenant is based on elements in this outline (e.g., the covenant blessings and curses in Leviticus 26). The entire book of Deuteronomy can be read as an exemplar of a vassal treaty adapted to the cultural and religious parameters of ancient Israel. This notion of "covenant," with its accompanying literary conventions, survived beyond the biblical period and formed part of the theology of the Qumran sectarians (see below).[5]

A third essential concept for understanding Judaism in general and the liturgical texts from Qumran in particular is that of ritual or ceremonial "purity." This is a rather foreign idea for modern people in the Western world. It bears some similarity to our concept of hygiene but is based on a very different set of assumptions. For the ancient Israelites, ritual purity was delineated by a panoply of rules covering proper foods to eat, clothes to wear, sexual conventions, requirements concerning bodily health and soundness, and other factors, some within and some beyond human control. According to Israelite belief, God was the central locus of sacredness and he dwelt in a realm of perfect purity, unapproachable by normal human beings (Isa 6:1-5). The center of purity on earth was the innermost room of the temple in Jerusalem, the so-called holy of holies, into which only the high priest could enter on the Day of Atonement (see below). Progressively less pure zones surrounded the holy of holies: the rest of the temple, in which the priests offered sacrifices; the temple precincts, which were maintained by the Levites; the shadowy realm of the average Israelite, where ritual purity was more often than not an ideal rather than a reality; and the defiled reaches outside the camp or the city wall, to which the chronically impure were banished: lepers, demons, and the other nations.

---

5. For an introduction to the biblical idea of covenant in its ancient Near Eastern context, see Hillers, *Covenant.*

Anthropology has shown that human beings rely on cultural conventions and structures to grow up into a normal adulthood, and that such conventions and structures are often more or less arbitrary, although they are parts of a coherent whole in the given culture.[6] The concept of ritual purity and impurity is one such convention, one that helps people to divide the world into a hierarchical web of relationships in which they can find a proper place. Such ideas are ubiquitous: the Israelite polluted by touching a lizard suffers the same sense of impurity as a child who has acquired "cooties" by being touched by a member of the opposite sex on the playground, or a modern Western adult who has arrived at a social occasion in inappropriate dress. Only the culture of the last offers no straightforward rite of cleansing for the inadvertent defilement!

Means of purification from uncleanness are also conventional and vary widely from culture to culture. This process typically involves set rites that move a person or thing from a state of defilement into a marginal or liminal state, usually presided over by a cultic functionary such as a priest, and from there into a state of purity. In ancient Israel such rites included a visit to the sanctuary, where a priest would offer sacrifices on behalf of the defiled person. Or the priest might visit the person to perform a ceremonial sprinkling or supervise an immersion. These rituals, which figure prominently in the books of Leviticus and Numbers, are also presented in the Qumran "Purification Liturgies" (4Q512 and 4Q414) covered in this volume.[7]

III. The Ritual Cycle in Ancient Israel

The reconstruction of the history of ancient Israel is an exceedingly complex problem, and there is no widespread consensus concerning its details or even its broad outlines. Thus it is often very difficult to work out the date or historical context of ritual instructions and liturgical material preserved in the Hebrew Bible. In general, we can assume that most of this material was preserved in circles associated with the temple in Jerusalem and its priesthood, although some of it may come from rival priestly groups in competition with them. Some of the liturgical traditions go back to the period of Solomon's temple in preexilic

---

6. See Geertz, "The Impact of the Concept of Culture on the Concept of Man," in *The Interpretation of Cultures*, 33-54; "The Growth of Culture and the Evolution of Mind," *ibid.*, 55-83.

7. For a discussion of ritual purity and sacrifice in the biblical world, see Malina, *The New Testament World*, chap. 6.

times (586 BCE and earlier) or even before, but these must have been edited and adapted in the period of the Second Temple. The ritual cycle was not static during the biblical period, and something like the following seems to have been the history of the development of the main series of festivals and sacred times.

The most fundamental holy day in the life of an ancient Israelite was the Sabbath, a weekly holiday mandated as one of the Ten Commandments (Exod 20:8-11; 23:12; 34:21; Lev 23:3; Deut 5:12-15). According to this custom, each Saturday was a day of rest, and no work was to be done on it on pain of death (Num 15:32-36). Special offerings were made on the Sabbath (Num 28:9-10; Ezek 46:4-5). Observation of the Sabbath became one of the basic dividing lines that marked a person as an Israelite or a Jew. The destruction of Solomon's temple in 586 BCE may have made this custom all the more important to the exiles as a way of preserving self-definition while they were deprived of the socially unifying temple cult. The Sabbath was already a major feature of the cult by the early Second Temple period, and it has maintained this importance in many Jewish circles to the present.

In the spring (the first month of the year — Aviv or Nisan, corresponding to March-April) the seven-day Festival of Unleavened Bread, or *Maṣṣot* (מצות), was celebrated at the beginning of the barley harvest (Exod 23:15; 34:18). At some point early on, the day of the Festival of Passover or *Pesaḥ* (פסח) was set immediately before Unleavened Bread (Exodus 12; Lev 23:5-8; Num 28:16-25; Deut 16:1-8; Ezek 45:21-24). Passover celebrated the exodus of the Israelite tribes from slavery in Egypt. Leviticus 23:9-14 prescribes an additional ceremony involving the waving of the sheaf of the firstfruits (the *Omer*) "on the morrow after the Sabbath," traditionally on the sixteenth day of the first month, although celebrated on the twenty-sixth of this month according to the Qumran calendar. If an Israelite was unable to participate in the Passover celebration because he was ceremonially defiled or on a journey, he was permitted to celebrate it exactly one month later, on the fourteenth day of the second month (Num 9:6-14).

In the late spring, the Festival of Weeks, *Shavuot* (שבועות), marked the wheat harvest. It is called Weeks because seven weeks were counted between it and Passover (Deut 16:9-12) or the *Omer* offering (Lev 23:15), a total of fifty days — hence the alternate name Pentecost (Acts 2:1). It is also discussed in Deut 26:1-11 and is known by the alternate name the Festival of the Harvest of Firstfruits (Exod 23:16; 34:22; cf. Num 28:26-31). In postbiblical tradition this holiday became associated with the revelation of God's Torah ("instruction" or "law") on Mount Sinai (e.g., *Jub.* 6:17).

In the fall, beginning on the fifteenth day of the seventh month (September-October), the Festival of Booths or Tabernacles, *Sukkot* (סכות), marked the

6

olive harvest (Lev 23:33-36; Num 29:12-38; Deut 16:13-15; Ezek 45:25). During this holiday, the custom was to live outdoors in "booths" of woven branches (Lev 23:39-43). It was also known as the Festival of Ingathering (Exod 23:16; 34:22).

These were the three "pilgrimage-festivals" (חגים) that formed the backbone of the Israelite cultic year, and in which every male Israelite was required to participate (Exod 23:14, 17; 34:23; Deut 16:16-17). In addition, a number of other festivals were also in vogue at various times in the history of ancient Israel.

Evidently there were conflicting views in Jewish tradition on when to begin the year. Most biblical texts assumed a spring New Year commencing in March-April, although relatively little was made of its observance (Exod 12:1-2; Ezek 45:18-20). Reckonings of dates were generally given according to this calendar. Some passages, however, seem to place the Festival of Booths or Ingathering near the end of the year (Exod 23:16; 34:22), and indeed, just before Booths, Priestly tradition celebrated another festival called the "trumpet-blast memorial," which took place on the first day of the seventh month (September-October) and which was observed as a day of solemn rest accompanied by the blowing of trumpets and by sacrifices (Lev 23:23-25; Num 29:1-6). In later Jewish practice up to the present, this sacred convocation is the New Year celebration or Rosh Hashanah (ראש השנה).

There are some indications that in the preexilic era, in the time of the Davidic monarchy, the king was reenthroned after ceremonially defeating the enemies of Israel in a ritual drama that took place at the (autumnal) beginning of the year. Some of the psalms in the Psalter seem to have been recited during this ritual (e.g., Psalms 2, 89, 110).[8] The Day of Atonement, Yom Kippur (יום כפור or יום הכפורים), may be a postexilic adaptation of this festival after the monarchy ceased to exist. Everyone in Israel fasted during the Day of Atonement, an annual priestly ritual enacted on the tenth day of the seventh month, and the high priest entered the holy of holies in the temple and there offered sacrifices to atone for the sins of the whole nation (Exod 30:10; Lev 16; 23:26-32; Num 29:7-11; Heb 9:6-7).

Besides these ancient annual rituals, sacrifices were offered on the first day of each lunar month in the New Moon celebration (e.g., Num 10:10; 28:11-15; Ezek 45:17; 46:3). Two other annual rituals seem to have been added to the Jewish calendar late in the Second Temple period. According to the book of Esther, the Festival of Purim (פורים), on the thirteenth and fourteenth days of the twelfth month (Adar, in February-March), commemorates the victory of the Jewish people over their enemies with the help of Queen Esther during the

---

8. See Eaton, *Kingship and the Psalms.*

reign of King Ahasuerus (Esther 3:7-15; 8:9-14; 9:1-32). But 1 Macc 7:26-49 and 2 Macc 14:11–15:37 refer to a festival on the thirteenth of Adar commemorating the defeat of the Syrian general Nicanor by Judah the Maccabee in 161 BCE. This double explanation may mean that the Jewish celebration of an older Babylonian or Persian holiday was justified with more than one rationale.

The other annual ritual celebrates the rededication of the temple in 165 or 164 BCE, on the twenty-fifth day of the ninth month (Chislev, in December), after it had been defiled by Antiochus Epiphanes some years before (1 Macc 4:52-58; 2 Macc 10:1-8). The traditional name of this eight-day festival is Hanukkah (חנוכה), a Hebrew word meaning "rededication."

In addition to these annual, monthly, and weekly holy days, two multiyear cycles are described in the Hebrew Bible. Every seventh year was a special sabbatical year or year of rest, probably originally a rotating fallow year for the land (Exod 23:10-11), but by the time of the writing of Deuteronomy it had become a time marked by the remission of all debts (Deut 15:1-11). According to the (probably later) Priestly traditions recorded in the book of Leviticus, the entire land of Israel was to lie fallow during the seventh year (Lev 25:1-7). Furthermore, only in the Priestly tradition do we find the Jubilee year: every seven cycles of sabbatical years was followed by a fiftieth year in which all debts were canceled, all sold property was returned to its original owners, and the land was left to lie fallow (Lev 25:8-55). It is difficult to imagine how either the sabbatical year or the Jubilee could have been implemented in practice, but there is good evidence from antiquity into the Middle Ages that at least the former actually was observed.

IV. Liturgical Traditions in the Qumran Documents[9]

One of the challenges in working with the Qumran texts is determining which were composed by the sectarians and which were included in their library but composed outside the group. A number of clues can be of some help. The most direct of these are the content and technical terminology of the various works. The sectarian texts share a similar set of terms and doctrines and a similar hostility toward other forms of Judaism. These texts include the *Community Rule*, the *Damascus Document*, the *War Scroll*, *the Pesharim*, and so forth. However, even these works have significant differences from one another, and some sur-

9. Recent monographs on the Qumran liturgical texts include Nitzan, *Qumran Prayer and Religious Poetry;* and Falk, *Daily, Sabbath, and Festival Prayers in the Dead Sea Scrolls.*

vive in multiple editions. It is perhaps more useful to think of a broad movement with different subgroups than of a well-defined sectarian community. A particular style of spelling (orthography) is also especially associated with these documents and may be an indicator that a given work was composed in sectarian circles (although this orthographic system may also have been adopted by the Qumran community from one of a number of Palestinian scribal schools, and thus may have been practiced outside the group as well). Most scholars agree that the Qumran sectarian movement was not well developed before the middle of the second century BCE at the earliest, so scrolls that can be dated earlier than this by the style of the Hebrew script used in them (paleography) should not be considered sectarian.

A major liturgical controversy revolved around which calendar to follow, and this debate seems to have been defined at least partially along sectarian lines. The system traditionally used in rabbinic Judaism to the present is a "lunisolar" calendar, which has twelve lunar months totaling 354 days but which is supplemented every three years or so with a thirteenth month to bring the average total of days up to the 365¼ of the solar year. Something like this system may have been in use in the Second Temple period, or even before the exile, although the evidence is not clear and there is no mention of a thirteenth intercalary month in the Hebrew Bible.

Another system was built entirely around a solar year of 364 days. It was first clearly explicated in the Astronomical Book of *1 Enoch* 72–82, datable to the third century BCE at the latest, and it is strongly advocated by the second century BCE book of *Jubilees* (6:32-38). This calendar too may have been used as early as the preexilic period. It has the advantage of being divisible by seven, so that each festival day comes on the same day of the week every year. The disadvantage, of course, is that unless intercalary corrections are made (which would spoil the harmonic relationship with the week), the reckoning of this calendar would depart from the true solar year by one and a quarter days per year. The Astronomical Book and the book of *Jubilees* are too old to be sectarian compositions, but multiple copies of both were recovered from the Qumran library, and it is clear that the sectarians used the solar calendar and considered its use a point of differentiation from other, competing forms of Judaism. We are told in the Qumran *Pesher on Habakkuk* that the Wicked Priest, an opponent associated with the priestly power structure in Jerusalem, engaged in a hostile act against the sect on the Day of Atonement, an action that would hardly have been possible if he had been following the same calendar (1QpHab xi:4-8).

Another distinctive sectarian liturgical practice was a covenant renewal ceremony celebrated during the Festival of Weeks, a holy day that in the book of *Jubilees* and in later rabbinic Judaism was associated with the revelation of the Torah on Mount Sinai. The details of this ceremony are described in the *Community Rule* (1QS cols. i-ii) and the *Berakhot*. The latter work is included in this volume.

Apart from the solar calendar, whose relationship with biblical traditions is debatable, the liturgical practices attested in the Qumran library are based on the biblical ritual cycle and generally conform closely to it. The Sabbath is important in the Qumran texts, and they also probably refer to the celebration of all the holy days mentioned in the previous section except Purim and Hanukkah. It is sometimes unclear, however, whether the relevant liturgical texts are sectarian compositions or works composed outside the community but adopted by it.

There are a few festivals attested primarily or only in Qumran literature. Two more festivals of Weeks appear: the second is the Festival of Firstfruits of New Wine, which is celebrated seven weeks after the original Festival of Weeks, and the third is the Festival of Firstfruits of Oil, which occurs seven weeks later. The observance of these new holy days is outlined in the *Temple Scroll* (11Q19 xix:11-xxii:16 +?), a work that is probably presectarian but that was kept in multiple copies by the sectarians. The Wood Offering is mentioned in the biblical text and elsewhere (e.g., Neh 10:35 [EVV 10:34]), but it is explicitly placed in the annual cycle of festivals only by the *Temple Scroll* and by a calendar found in one manuscript of 4QMMT (the latter may have been an early sectarian manifesto, but it is not at all clear that the calendar in question was meant to be part of it). For more on the Wood Offering Festival, see the chapter on 4Q409, "Times for Praising God."

The question of the relationship between the Qumran sectarians and the temple in Jerusalem is a matter of great interest, but one about which we have frustratingly little data. As noted above, the *Pesher on Habakkuk* presents the priestly authorities in Jerusalem in an exceedingly unfavorable light (cf. 1QpHab viii:8-13; xii:7-10), a view coherent with the hostility of some of the earlier Enoch literature toward the Second Temple. See, for example, the condemnation of the temple (allegorically called the Tower) by the Animal Apocalypse in *1 Enoch* 89:73-77, copies of which were recovered from the Qumran library. The *Community Rule* speaks of the sectarian community itself as the true temple that atones for sin without animal sacrifice (1QS viii:1-10; ix:3-6). This evidence seems to imply a serious breach between the community and the Jerusalem temple. However, although the *Damascus Document* refers to the desecration of the temple by its opponents (CD iv:15-19; v:6; vi:11-12), it also speaks reverently of the city of the temple and orders sect members to take steps to avoid defiling it (CD xii:1-2). It also seems to assume casually that the sectarian brethren would sometimes offer sacrifices there (CD xi:17-23). It may be that relations between the Qumran sect and Jerusalem varied over time, sometimes improving and sometimes deteriorating, but we are unable at present to chronicle this process.

V. The Later Jewish Liturgy

The destruction of Jerusalem and the Second Temple by the Romans in 70 CE brought an end to the traditional temple cultus and forced the sages who gradually rebuilt Palestinian Judaism to rethink the ritual and liturgical underpinnings of their religion. Unlike the early Christians, whose theology put Jesus' atoning death in the place of the sacrificial system of the temple (e.g., Hebrews 9), the early rabbinic sages had no obvious theoretical structure with which to replace the sacrificial cult. At some point, probably before the end of the first century, they reached a consensus that acts of piety could effect atonement for sin in the place of sacrifice (*'Abot R. Nat.* A 4), a solution perhaps not so different from that of the earlier but now defunct Qumran group.

Jewish worship in the Diaspora had long since had to adapt to the unavailability of the temple in everyday life, and from 70 CE to the present this has been the reality for Judaism everywhere. We have no systematically preserved information on the development of the Jewish liturgy in late antiquity, although a fair amount can be culled from the rabbinic literature, including the Mishnah (early third century), the Jerusalem Talmud (late fourth century), and the Babylonian Talmud (sixth century). The Jewish liturgical poetry (the Piyyutim) of the early centuries CE onward also preserves valuable data. Although trends of systematization can be discerned early on, a fixed liturgy was a very late development, and the earliest complete Jewish prayer books are products of the ninth and tenth centuries. However, some elements of the later Jewish liturgy can be found already in the Qumran texts in this volume, showing that the process of development was a conservative one that drew reverently on earlier traditions. In the commentaries I have noted parallels to the sources mentioned here, whenever they seemed interesting.[10]

Another corpus of Jewish ritual texts is less well known, since it never attained the formal or informal canonical status of the Jewish liturgy, but it is important for our purposes. The Hekhalot literature is a motley collection of Hebrew and Aramaic documents, preserved mainly in medieval manuscripts, which purport to describe the adventures of a number of rabbis of the second century CE who were able to ascend to heaven to participate in the heavenly liturgy and to call down angels and compel them to reveal heavenly secrets, and which give detailed instructions for the reader to accomplish the same feats. The term *hekhalot* is a Hebrew word meaning "palaces" or "temples," so called

---

10. For a good general introduction to the content and historical development of the Jewish liturgy, see Schauss, *The Jewish Festivals.* More technical monographs on the subject include Elbogen, *Jewish Liturgy;* and Reif, *Judaism and Hebrew Prayer.*

because these texts concern themselves with the ascent to the heavenly temple and its ancillary palaces.[11] The supposed experiential basis behind this literature is often called merkavah mysticism, since one of its goals is the ascent to heaven to gaze on the *merkavah,* God's celestial throne-chariot described in the first chapter of the book of Ezekiel. Merkavah mysticism is a religious tradition rooted in late antiquity, although it draws on much earlier antecedents in Jewish esotericism. Its texts continued to be collected, edited, and perhaps even composed well into the Middle Ages.

Two of the liturgical works in the Qumran library have many parallels to the Hekhalot literature. The *Songs of the Sabbath Sacrifice* describes the worship and sacrificial cult of the angels in the heavenly palaces and before the throne-chariot of God, anticipating many details of terminology and theology in the Hekhalot texts. Likewise, the *Berakhot* includes hymns about the celestial realm with many similarities to the merkavah hymns sung by mystics and angels in the Hekhalot literature. A detailed analysis of these parallels can be found in the chapters on these two Qumran works.

Thanks to the fortuitous survival of these scraps of leather and papyrus in the Judean desert, there is a fascinating new chapter to be written in the history of the Jewish liturgy, and indeed in the history of Judaism as a religion and cultural system. Scattered light is now shed on a period of Jewish history whose ritual life formerly lay almost entirely in darkness, and its outlines are gradually coming into focus. Much has been lost, but we must be grateful for what has survived, for even in ruins the ancient library of Qumran offers treasures and mysteries that will occupy scholars, and indeed anyone interested in the biblical world, well into the twenty-first century.[12]

11. Many of the most important Hekhalot manuscripts have been edited by Peter Schäfer, who has shown that the texts of the individual works can vary widely from manuscript to manuscript. Traditionally, a number of Hekhalot documents have been identified, and they are cited in this volume by their conventional names (see the list of "Special Abbreviations, Symbols, and Primary Sources") and according to Schäfer's paragraphing, or the paragraphing of the relevant edition if they are not included in Schäfer's edition, *Synopse zur Hekhalot-Literatur.* For a good basic introduction to this material, see Schäfer, *The Hidden and Manifest God.*

12. I am very grateful to my wife, Rachel, for her tireless editorial help with this volume, and to Professor Martin Abegg, Jr., whose careful reading of the manuscript saved me from many errors. Any that remain are, of course, my responsibility alone.

BIBLIOGRAPHY

Baillet, Maurice. *Qumrân Grotte 4.III (4Q482-4Q520)*. DJD 7. Oxford: Clarendon, 1982.

Cook, Edward M. *Solving the Mysteries of the Dead Sea Scrolls: New Light on the Bible*. Grand Rapids, Mich.: Zondervan, 1994.

Earhart, H. Byron. *Religions of Japan*. San Francisco: HarperSanFrancisco, 1984.

Eaton, John Herbert. *Kingship and the Psalms*. London: S.C.M., 1976.

Elbogen, Ismar. *Jewish Liturgy: A Comprehensive History*. Philadelphia: Jewish Publication Society; New York: Jewish Theological Seminary of America, 1993.

Falk, Daniel. *Daily, Sabbath, and Festival Prayers in the Dead Sea Scrolls*. STDJ 27. Leiden: Brill, 1998.

García Martínez, Florentino. *The Dead Sea Scrolls Translated: The Qumran Texts in English*. Leiden: Brill, 1994.

Geertz, Clifford. *The Interpretation of Cultures*. N.p.: HarperCollins, 1973.

Hillers, Delbert R. *Covenant: The History of a Biblical Idea*. Baltimore: Johns Hopkins University Press, 1969.

Kugel, James L. "The Bible in the University." In *The Hebrew Bible and Its Interpreters,* edited by William Henry Propp, et al., 143-65. Winona Lake, Ind.: Eisenbrauns, 1990.

Malina, Bruce J. *The New Testament World: Insights from Cultural Anthropology*. Rev. ed. Louisville, Ky.: Westminster/John Knox, 1993.

Nitzan, Bilhah. *Qumran Prayer and Religious Poetry*. STDJ 12. Leiden: Brill, 1994.

Reif, Stefan C. *Judaism and Hebrew Prayer: New Perspectives on Jewish Liturgical History,* Cambridge: Cambridge University Press, 1993.

Schäfer, Peter, et al. *Synopse zur Hekhalot-Literatur*. TSAJ 2. Tübingen: Mohr Siebeck, 1981.

———. *The Hidden and Manifest God: Some Major Themes in Early Jewish Mysticism*. Albany, N.Y.: State University of New York Press, 1992.

Schauss, Hayyim. *The Jewish Festivals: A Guide to Their History and Observance*. New York: Schocken, 1996.

Schiffman, Lawrence H. *Reclaiming the Dead Sea Scrolls: The History of Judaism, the Background of Christianity, the Lost Library of Qumran*. Philadelphia and Jerusalem: Jewish Publication Society, 1994.

Smith, Jonathan Z. *To Take Place: Toward Theory in Ritual*. Chicago and London: University of Chicago Press, 1987.

VanderKam, James C. *The Dead Sea Scrolls Today*. Grand Rapids, Mich.: Eerdmans, 1994.

Vermes, Geza. *The Complete Dead Sea Scrolls in English*. London and New York: Penguin, 1997.

————. *An Introduction to the Complete Dead Sea Scrolls*. London: S.C.M., 1999.

Wise, Michael, et al. *The Dead Sea Scrolls: A New Translation*. San Francisco: HarperSanFrancisco, 1996.

Festival Prayers

(1Q34 + 1Q34*bis*, 4Q507, 4Q508, 4Q509 + 4Q505)

INTRODUCTION

I. Contents

As noted in the general introduction to this volume, the cycle of festivals in the ritual year was a major component of Israel's religion as far back as we can trace it. Although the Hebrew Bible gives fairly detailed instructions for the celebration of the festivals, it is remarkably reticent about the liturgies that must have accompanied them. The collection of Festival Prayers from Qumran rectifies this omission. Despite its poor state of preservation, enough of this work survives to show that it contained prayers to be recited on the Day of Atonement, at the monthly New Moon celebration, at the Festival of Weeks, and probably at the fall New Year as well as Passover. We cannot be sure, but it seems likely that the full annual cycle of festivals was covered. Most, but not all of the prayers seem to be given in chronological order, starting with those for the New Year.

II. The Manuscripts

Four manuscripts of this work survive, one of which was formerly treated as two separate works.

- 1Q34 and 1Q34^{bis} is a single manuscript that was published in two batches.
- 4Q507 consists of a few fragments, probably of the same work, whose handwriting the editor dates to the beginning of the first century CE.
- 4Q508 is preserved in forty-three small fragments, a few of which overlap with 1Q34 + 1Q34^{bis}, and was written about the same time as 4Q507.
- 4Q509 and 4Q505. 4Q509 is found on the recto of a large papyrus manuscript that bears writing on both sides (an "opisthograph"). The verso contains a copy of the *War Scroll* (4Q496) and a copy of the "Words of the Luminaries" (4Q506). Maurice Baillet thought that the ten fragments he assigned to 4Q505 also belonged to a copy of the "Words of the Luminaries," but as Florentino García Martínez pointed out in his review of DJD 7, this is quite unlikely. These fragments on the recto of the same manuscript in the middle of 4Q509 are written in the same script, of the late Hasmonean period (about the middle of the first century BCE). Though they have similarities to the "Words of the Luminaries," it makes more sense to regard 4Q509 and 4Q505 as a single work now preserved in a total of 313 fragments.

Overlaps between the manuscripts are indicated in the translation by underscoring.

III. Structure and Genre

The Festival Prayers are formally very similar to the "Words of the Luminaries." If we can generalize from the surviving fragments, it appears that each prayer began with a title in the form "A Prayer for," followed by the name of the festival in question. Next came an invocation in the form "Remember, O Lord . . ." It ended with a closing benediction for God's blessings in the form "Blessed be the Lord . . . ," followed by a double amen. Sometimes the content of a given prayer seems directly relevant for the festival at which it is to be recited (e.g., the prayers for the Day of Atonement refer to God's mercy), but sometimes the surviving content has no obvious connection with the festival (such as the final

16

prayer for the Festival of Firstfruits or Weeks). Given the fragmentary state of the prayers, little can be said about their genre.

IV. Life Situation

Two elements of the Festival Prayers give us some small insight into their life situation. First, the titles of some of the prayers mark them for use in specific festivals. This use is sometimes confirmed by the content of the prayers themselves. Second, these prayers are couched in the first-person plural, presumably the "we" of a community. Although there is no doubt this community was Jewish, it is difficult to say more about it.

For the most part, the language lacks the technical terminology of the sectarian scrolls. However, the word "lot" (גורל) in 1Q34 + 1Q34[bis] 3i:2 and "period" (קץ) in 1Q34 + 1Q34[bis] 3ii:5 may be used in the sense attested only in the sectarian texts. However, we have so little information on the Hebrew of this era that we cannot assert that these technical senses were never used outside the Qumran sectarian literature. Nothing in the surviving content is specifically sectarian, but neither are there elements that would be objectionable to the sectarians. Overall it seems more likely than not that the Festival Prayers were composed outside the Qumran community and were adopted for use by its members.

V. Literary Context

The Hebrew Bible gives directions for the celebration of the festivals in Exod 23:14-19; 30:10; 34:18-19, 22-26; Leviticus 16, 23; Num 9:1-14; 10:10; 28-29; Deut 16:1-17; 26; Ezek 45:13-25. Sometimes the festivals are alluded to or particular celebrations of specific festivals are described (e.g., Josh 5:10-12; 1 Sam 20:5, 24-27; 2 Kgs 23:21-23; Isa 1:13-14; Amos 8.5; Zech 14:16-19; Ezra 3:1-6; 6:19-22; Neh 8:14-18; 2 Chron 30; 35:1-19). The book of *Jubilees* gives instructions for and accounts of the festivals (6:17-31; 15:1-2; 16:20-31; 22:1-9; 32:4-9, 27-29; 34:18-19; 44:1-4; 49), and they are sometimes mentioned in the New Testament (Matthew 26; Mark 14; Luke 2:41; 22; John 2:13, 23; 6:4; 7:2, 10, 14, 37; 10:22; 11:55, etc.; Acts 12:3-4; 20:6; Col 2:16). A whole order of the Mishnah *(Mo'ed)* is devoted to them, much of which is elaborated on in the Babylonian and Palestinian Talmuds. Nevertheless, although it is clear that singing and liturgical recitations were elements of the celebration (e.g., Lev 16:21; Neh 8:18; 2 Chron 30:21, 27; 35:15; Mark 14:26; Philo, *Spec. Leg.* 2.148), only a few scraps of liturgies or prayers are included in the earlier texts (e.g., Deut 26:3-10, 13-15; *Jub.* 22:6-9; 2 Macc 1:18, 24-29).

According to the heading of the Greek translation, Psalm 29 (LXX 28) was recited during the Festival of Booths and Psalm 30 (LXX 29) during a feast of dedication (Hanukkah?). The passage on David's compositions in 11QPs[a] (xxvii:7-8) lists festival songs attributed to David but does not give the text of the songs themselves. A few other Qumran documents (the *Berakhot*, the *Songs of the Sabbath Sacrifice*, possibly 4Q409, and the "Daily Prayers") preserve prayers meant for various festivals and holy days. Whether any of the Qumran prayers preserve liturgical traditions used in the Second Temple or even the First Temple is impossible to determine with our current evidence. The fixed liturgies for the festivals were composed many centuries later, but a number of parallels between them and the Festival Prayers at Qumran show that the official liturgies sometimes drew on very ancient traditions.

The Festival Prayers sometimes allude to or echo scriptural passages, but their language is not steeped in biblical tradition to the same degree as some of the other liturgical texts from Qumran, such as the "Words of the Luminaries."

BIBLIOGRAPHY

Baillet, Maurice. "Débris de textes sur papyrus de la grotte 4 de Qumran." *RB* 71 (1964) 353-71, plates xiv-xv.

———. "505. Paroles des Luminaires (deuxième exemplaire: DibHam[b])." In *Qumrân Grotte 4.III (4Q482-4Q520)*, 168-70, plate xxiii. DJD 7. Oxford: Clarendon, 1982.

———. "507. Prières pour les fêtes (premier exemplaire: PrFêtes[a])." In *Qumrân Grotte 4.III (4Q482-4Q520)*, 175-77, plate xxviii. DJD 7. Oxford: Clarendon, 1982.

———. "508. Prières pour les fêtes (deuxième exemplaire: PrFêtes[b])." In *Qumrân Grotte 4.III (4Q482-4Q520)*, 177-84, plate liv. DJD 7. Oxford: Clarendon, 1982.

———. "509. Prières pour les fêtes (troisième exemplaire: PrFêtes[c])." In *Qumrân Grotte 4.III (4Q482-4Q520)*, 184-215, plates ix, xi, xiii, xv, xvii, xix, xxi, xxii. DJD 7. Oxford: Clarendon, 1982.

Carmignac, J. "Le recueil de prières liturgiques de la grotte 1 (I Q 34 et 34 [bis])." *RevQ* 3/14 (1963) 271-76.

Charlesworth, James H., et al. *The Dead Sea Scrolls: Hebrew, Aramaic, and Greek Texts with English Translations*, vol. 4A: *Pseudepigraphic and Non-Masoretic*

Psalms and Prayers, 46-105. Tübingen: Mohr Siebeck; Louisville: Westminster John Knox, 1997.

Falk, Daniel K. *Daily, Sabbath, and Festival Prayers in the Dead Sea Scrolls.* STDJ 27. Leiden: Brill, 1998. All citations of Falk followed by page numbers refer to this work.

García Martínez, Florentino. Review of DJD 7. *JSJ* 15 (1984) 157-64.

Milik, J. T. "34. 'Recueil de prières liturgiques'" and "34bis. 'Recueil de prières liturgiques.'" In *Qumran Cave I,* edited by D. Barthélemy and J. T. Milik, 136, 152-55, plate xxxi. DJD 1. Oxford: Clarendon, 1955.

Nitzan, Bilhah. *Qumran Prayer and Religious Poetry.* STDJ 12. Leiden: Brill, 1994.

Trever, J. C. "Completion of the Publication of Some Fragments from Qumran Cave I." *RevQ* 5/19 (1965) 321-36, plates i-vii.

Weinfeld, Moshe. "Prayer and Liturgical Practice in the Qumran Sect." In *The Dead Sea Scrolls: Forty Years of Research,* edited by Devorah Dimant and Uriel Rappaport, 241-58. STDJ 10. Leiden: Brill, 1992.

FESTIVAL PRAYERS

(1Q34 + 1Q34[his], 4Q507, 4Q508, 4Q509 + 4Q505)

I. 1Q34 + 1Q34[bis]

1Q34 + 1Q34[his] 2 + 1 + 4Q509 3:15-23

A prayer for the New Year celebration?

[. . . und her wealth[a] . . . You have . . .] [1][. . .] the festival of [our] peace [. . . us from our grief and You have gathered our outcast men] [2]for the festival of [. . . and] our [disper]sed women for the cyc[le . . . on our congregation like raindrops on] [3]the land in the seas[on of [b]. . .[b] and] like copious showers on [herbage in seasons of greenery . . . Your wondrous acts] [4]for generation after generation. Blessed be the Lord who makes u[s] happy [. . .] [5][. . .] BLANK [. . .]

A prayer for the Day of Atonement

[6]A prayer for the Day of Atonement.
Reme[mber, O L]ord, the fe[stival of . . .] [7]..[. . .].[. . .]..[. . .].[. . .]

Notes

[a]וֹאונה The word could also be translated "and her wickedness."
[b-b]Inexplicably, 4Q509 3:20 has a blank space corresponding roughly to the lacuna in line 3.

Commentary

Lines 1-5. Ancient Israel used two systems to reckon the cycle of the year. In one, the year began in the spring (see Exod 12:2; Num 28:11-15; 11Q19 xiv:9-18), and in the other, in the fall (see Exod 23:16; 34:22; Lev 23:23-25; Num 29:1-6). The latter holiday is never explicitly called the New Year in the Bible, but it functions as such in postbiblical Judaism to the present day under the name Rosh Hashanah (ראש השנה), the "Head of the Year." Since it comes immediately before the Day of Atonement, it is probably the festival being celebrated in this prayer.

Line 1. Compare the phrase "[fes]tivals of pea[ce]" in 4Q512 17:2, which occurs in a broken context. The gist of the next phrase was probably that God restored the speakers' happiness in place of their grief (cf. Jer 31:13; Esther 9:22). The end of the line is restored from Isa 11:12.

Line 2. The word translated "and our dispersed women" is from Isa 11:12, a passage that speaks of the ingathering of the exiles (cf. line 1). There is a similar echo of this verse in the Jewish liturgy in the prayers of the Additional Service for the festivals (Weinfeld, "Prayer and Liturgical Practice," 245).

In BH the word translated "cycle" can refer either to the cycle of the year (Exod 34:22; 1 Sam 1:20; 2 Chron 24:23) or to the daily cycle of the sun (Ps 19:7 [EVV 19:6]). Compare 1QS x:2-3, 6; 1QH[a] ix:24; xx:5-6, 8; 1QM x:15. The first meaning fits the likely context here better.

Lines 2-3. Reconstructed with the help of Deut 32:2. The autumn New Year would have come in the rainy season.

Lines 3-4. Here the speakers probably promise to recount God's wondrous acts to posterity (cf. Ps 71:18; 78:3-4, 6; 79:13; 145:4; 1QH[a] xiv:11).

Line 5. A blank space marks the end of the prayer.

Line 6. The same title may have been found in 4Q508 2:2. The rites for the Day of Atonement are described in Exod 30:10; Lev 16; 23:26-32; Num 29:7-11;

and 11Q19 xxv:11-xxvii:10. This holy day is also mentioned in 1QpHab xi:7; 11Q13 ii:7, and the Mishnaic tractate *Yoma* is devoted to it.

1Q34 + 1Q34^bis 3i + 4Q508 1:1-3

A prayer for the Day of Atonement or the Passover Festival?

[1][. . .]...[. . .]..[. . .]. [2][. . .]. in the lot of the righ[te]ous, but for the wicked a l[o]t of [3][. . .]. in their bones a reproach to all flesh. But the righteous [4][. . . to fa]tten [themselves] on the clouds of heaven and the produce of the earth, to dis[cer]n [5]between righ]teous and wicked. And You have made the wicked our [at]onement, but with [the upri]ght[a] [6][. . .]annihilation among all who afflict us. And we give thanks to Your name forever [7][. . .]since for this You created us and this is wh[at we return to You. Blessed be [8][. . .] BLANK

The beginning of another prayer

[9][. . .]...[. . .]

Note

[a]וּבֹֽ[שׁ]יִם This word is badly damaged. Another possible reading is וּבֹֽ[וגֹ]דִים, "and the treacherous." Either reading could be supported by Prov 21:18 (see the commentary).

Commentary

Lines 1-8. Baillet takes this as a prayer for the Day of Atonement (DJD 7: 178), but Falk suggests tentatively that it may belong to Passover (pp. 177-78).

Line 2. Compare Ps 125:3. In the sectarian usage, a "lot" means someone's eternal destiny. It is unclear whether this technical meaning applies here or whether the word is being used in a more general sense.

Line 3. Compare Isa 66:24; Jer 29:18. This may be a general statement about the fate of the wicked, but it is also possible that it refers specifically to the generation that perished in the wilderness (cf. Num 14:29; Heb 3:17).

Lines 3-4. A description of the fate of the righteous. Compare Gen 27:28; Deut 32:13-15; Isa 55:2; Prov 28:25. Line 4 may refer to the feeding of the Israelites with manna until they were able to eat of the produce of the land (cf. Josh 5:12; Ps 78:23-25), in which case this prayer may have been intended for Passover.

Lines 4-5. Compare the first (reconstructed) clause to Mal 3:18. The second clause echoes Prov 21:18. The reference to atonement may indicate that this prayer was used on the Day of Atonement, although it would be unusual to associate this holiday with the idea of the wicked being a substitutionary atonement for the righteous.

Line 6. Perhaps a reference to the destruction of the Egyptians at the Sea of Reeds. Compare the first clause to Zeph 3:19 (the Targum to Zephaniah includes the word "annihilation," as here) and the second clause to Ps 44:9 (EVV 44:8).

Line 7. Compare Isa 43:7.

Lines 7-9. A closing benediction begins in line 7 and presumably concluded with a double amen in the first part of line 8, the rest of which is blank. Unreadable traces of another prayer survive in line 9.

1Q34 + 1Q34^bis^ 3ii + 4Q509 97-98

A prayer for the Day of Atonement or the Festival of Weeks?

[1][. . .] a greater light for the appointed time of the [. . .] [2][. . .].[. . .]. and there is no transgressing their laws and all of them [. . .] [3][. . .]. and their realm in the whole inhabited world. And h[uman] [s]e[e]d has not understood everything You have bequeathed it, and they do not know You [4][so as to carry out] Your word. And they have acted more wickedly than anyone, and they have not understood Your great strength. But You have rejected them, for You do not delight [5]in in[iqui]ty, and the wicked shall not be established before You. But You have chosen a people for Yourself in the period of Your favor, for You have remembered Your covenant [6]and You have [set] them apart for Yourself as holy out of all the peoples, and You have renewed Your covenant for them [a]with the vision of gl[o]ry[a] and the words of [7]Your holy [prophets], by the works of Your hands and the writing of Your right hand, so as to make known to them the foundations[b] of glory and the steps[c] of eternity [8][. . .].[ ]. faithful shepherd ..[. . .]. afflicted man and .[. . .]...

Notes

[a-a]מראת כבֿ[ו]ד This phrase echoes "the appearance of the glory of the Lord" (מראה כבוד יהוה) in Exod 24:17, which refers to God's fiery manifestation on Mount Sinai. But the word "vision" is used in the HB specifically to refer to revelatory visions or auditions to human intermediaries (Gen 46:2; Num 12:6; 16; 1 Sam 3:15; Ezek 1:1; 8:3; 40:2; perhaps 43:3; Dan 10:7-8). The slight change in wording may hint that the

sectarians gave their visions of the divine glory an authority comparable to the traditional revelation at Sinai.

[b]יסודי One could also read יסורי, "admonitions of."

[c]מעלי According to the original editors (DJD 1: 155), this reading fits the traces better than מעשי, "the works of." The photograph seems to bear this out, although Falk has argued against this on paleographical grounds (p. 179 n. 76). The word appears in the plural in the HB with the meaning "steps" (of a staircase) (Ezek 40:31, 34, 37 *qere*). For a possible interpretation, see the commentary.

Commentary

Lines 1-3. A reference to the heavenly luminaries. Compare Gen 1:16-18; Ps 74:16-17; 104:19-20; 136:7-9; 148:3-6.

Line 3. The phrase "human seed" (without the definite article) appears in Jer 31:27.

Lines 4-6. In the Jewish liturgy, the Closing Prayer for the Day of Atonement asserts, addressing God, that "You have set mortal man apart from the beginning," and that "You do not delight in the destruction of the world." The sentiment is similar to this passage in 4Q508 but more universalistic (Weinfeld, "Prayer and Liturgical Practice," 247).

Line 4. The phrase "Your great strength" appears in Deut 9:29; Jer 32:17; Neh 1:10. For God's rejecting the wicked, see Jer 6:30; Ps 53:6.

Line 5. God's choosing of Israel as his people is a common biblical theme (e.g., Deut 7:7; 14:2; 1 Kgs 3:8; Isa 44:1-2; Ezek 20:5; Ps 33:12), as is his remembering of his covenant (Gen 9:15, 16; Exod 2:24; 6:5; Lev 26:45; Ezek 16:60; Ps 105:8 // 1 Chron 16:15; Ps 106:45; 111:5). The word "period" (קץ) is a sectarian term with eschatological connotations. The closest biblical phrase is "a time of favor" in Isa 49:8; Ps 69:14 (EVV 69:13).

Line 6. Echoes Lev 20:26. The HB never speaks of "renewing" the covenant, although Jeremiah does refer to a "new covenant" (31:31; cf. CD vi:19; viii:21; 1QpHab ii:3). The renewal of the covenant is a theme traditionally associated with the Festival of Weeks.

Lines 6-7. Milik reads "the words of His holy [spirit]" (DJD 1: 154), but the Hebrew word translated "spirit" seems too short to fit the break at the beginning of line 7, and I cannot find reference to "words of" the holy spirit elsewhere. "Words of the prophets," however, are mentioned in 1 Kgs 22:13; Jer 23:16; 26:5; 27:14, 16; 2 Chron 18:12; 1QpHab ii:9; vii:5; Bar 1:21; Acts 15:15; and "holy prophets" are mentioned in Luke 1:70; Acts 3:21; Eph 3:5; 2 Pet 3:2.

Line 7. "The works of Your hands" is a biblical phrase signifying the creation (e.g., Ps 8:7 [EVV 8:6]; 19:2 [EVV 19:1]; 92:5 [EVV 92:4]; 143:5). There is a reference to a "writing of the hand of the Lord" (1 Chron 28:19) containing instructions for the building of the temple and given to Solomon by David. It may be that the "foundations of glory" and the "steps of eternity" refer to the architecture of the celestial temple, which is described in detail in the *Songs of the Sabbath Sacrifice* and the *Berakhot,* two documents that also have connections with the Feast of Weeks. But as far as I can determine, neither phrase is used elsewhere.

Line 8. Perhaps a reference to David, who was a shepherd before he became king (see 1 Sam 16:11; 17:15; Ps 78:70; 1 Chron 17:6; 11QPs^a xxviii:3-4), and as king was considered the shepherd of his people (Ps 78:71-72; 2 Sam 5:2 // 1 Chron 11:2). The psalmist, writing in the name of David, presents himself as afflicted (Ps 25:16, 18; 40:18 [EVV 40:17]; 69:30 [EVV 69:29]; 70:6 [EVV 70:5]; 109:22).

II. 4Q507

4Q507 1

A prayer for the Day of Atonement?

^{1}.[. . .].. ...[. . .]...[ ]our [. . .].. ...[. . .] ^{2}and we are iniquitous from the womb, and from the breasts gu[ilty . . .] ^{3}as long as^a we exist, our steps with defilement ..[. . .]

BOTTOM MARGIN

Note
^{a}עד This preposition usually means "until," "as far as," but Baillet notes that it has the meaning "as long as" in Exod 33:22; Judg 3:26; Jon 4:2 (DJD 7: 176).

Commentary

Line 2. Compare 1QH^a xii:29-30 and the sentiment in Ps 51:7 (EVV 51:5).

4Q507 2

A closing benediction

¹[. . .] all the [. . .] ²[. . . Bl]essed be the Lord [. . .] ³[. . .] BLANK [. . .]

The beginning of another prayer

⁴[. . .].. ... ...[. . .]

4Q507 3

A closing benediction

¹[. . .] your [. . . Bl]essed be the Lo[rd . . .] ²[. . .] eternal [gener]ations. Amen. Amen[. . .]

An opening invocation

³[. . .].. Reme[mber, O Lord . . .]

III. 4Q508

4Q508 1

See 1Q34 ⊢ 1Q34ᵇⁱˢ 3i above

4Q508 2

The conclusion of a prayer for the New Year?

¹[. . .]. and [Yo]u have dwelt in o[ur] midst [. . . Amen. Amen.]

A prayer for the Day of Atonement

[2][Prayer for the Day of Atonemen]t.

Remember, O Lord, the festival of Your mercies and the time of return[. . .] [3][. . .] and You raised ~~them~~ <it> over us as a festival of fasting, an ete[rnal] law [4][. . .]and You know the secret things and t[he] r[e]v[ealed things . . .] [5][. . .]You [kn]ow our nature .[. . .] [6][. . .]. our ... ..[. . .]

Commentary

Line 1. Perhaps the end of a prayer for the New Year, since the prayer that begins in the next line seems to be for the Day of Atonement. This fragment may overlap with 1Q34 + 1Q34[bis] frag. 2 + 1:4-6, although the apparent second-person form in the concluding benediction is uncharacteristic of the Festival Prayers. God's dwelling in the midst of the Israelites is a common biblical theme (see Exod 25:8; 29:45-46; Num 5:3; 35:34; 1 Kgs 6:13; Ezek 43:9; Zech 2:14-15; 8:3, 8; cf. 11Q19 xlv:13-14; xlvi:4; xlviii:18; li:7-8).

Line 2. Compare 1Q34 + 1Q34[bis] 2 + 1:6.

Line 3. The word "fasting" occurs in the HB only in Ezra 9:5. The phrase "festival of fasting" is found in 4Q171 1-2ii:9; 3-4iii:3, but the context implies a meaning more along the lines of "appointed time of affliction" (cf. the usage in 4Q509 16:3 and the plural in 4Q510 1:7-8; 4Q511 8:5; 121:2; 11Q11 iv:12). The Day of Atonement is called "the day of fasting" in CD vi:19. Precepts in the Pentateuch are often presented as an "eternal law" (e.g., Exod 29:28; Lev 7:34; Num 18:8, 11, 19; cf. 1QS viii:10; CD xv:5).

Line 4. Compare Deut 29:28. A similar statement is found in the Jewish liturgy in the Confession for the Day of Atonement: "Do You not know all the secret things and the revealed things?" (Weinfeld, "Prayer and Liturgical Practice," 246).

Line 5. Echoes Ps 103:14 (cf. Deut 31:21). Compare 1QH[a] xv:13, 16; 1Q18 1-2:3 (*Jub.* 35:9). The question of human "nature" or "inclination" (יצר) and its good and bad aspects is a matter of interest in rabbinic literature (e.g., *Gen. Rab.* 9.7).

4Q508 3

A prayer for the Day of Atonement?

¹[. . .]. we have acted wickedly [. . .] ²[. . .]. on account of their multitude, [and] You established for Noah [a covenant . . .] ³[. . . for Is]aac and for Jacob an agreem[ent . . .] ⁴[. . .]. You have ... periods of [. . .]

Commentary

Line 1. Probably a confession of sin; the surviving phrase (a single word in Hebrew) appears in such a context in Ps 106:6; Dan 9:5; Neh 9:33. However, one could also restore and translate "[He has no]t condemned us" (cf. Ps 37:33). In the vicinity of the confession of God's omniscience (see the commentary to frag. 2:4, above), the Confession for the Day of Atonement in the Jewish liturgy has exactly the same word (Weinfeld, "Prayer and Liturgical Practice," 246-47).

The content is appropriate for the Day of Atonement, but nothing explicitly connects this fragment to that particular holiday. Other fragments that may pertain to the Day of Atonement include 4, 5, 30, 39, 40, 41.

Line 2. Compare Gen 6:1, 18; 9:9, 11, 17.

Line 3. Compare Ps 105:8-10 // 1 Chron 16:15-17; CD iii:3-4.

4Q508 4

A fragment of a prayer

TOP MARGIN?

¹[. . .].[ ] her desolate daughters [. . .] ²[. . .] who chose us. And His covenant [. . .] ³[. . .].[. . .]

Commentary

Line 1. Baillet plausibly suggests that the reference is to the daughters of Jerusalem (DJD 7: 180). Compare Isa 3:16-17; 4:4; 4Q179 2.

4Q508 5

A fragment of a prayer

[1][. . .]. us and You [. . .] [2][. . .] o[ur] sins [. . .]

4Q508 13

A prayer for the Festival of Weeks?

[1][. . . Lo]rd, for by Your love [2][. . .] Your [. . .]. in the festivals of glory and to sanc[tify] [3][. . .].. g[rain and] new wine and oil

Commentary

Line 2. "Festivals of glory" are also mentioned in CD iii:14-15; 4Q286 1ii:10; 4Q503 4-6:4.

Line 3. Baillet suggests that this fragment could pertain to the Festival of Weeks, which is associated with the wheat harvest, when the firstfruits of grain, new wine, and oil might be gathered (cf. Deut 18:4). But he also notes that the *Temple Scroll* includes two additional festivals, the Festival of Firstfruits of New Wine (11Q19 xix:11–xxi:10) and the Festival of Firstfruits of Oil (11Q19 xxi:12-xxii:16) (DJD 7: 181).

4Q508 15

A fragment of a prayer

[1][. . .] and to sacrifice an o[x . . .]

Commentary

Line 1. An ox might be sacrificed as an "offering of well-being" (traditionally, "peace offering") at any of the major festivals (Lev 4:10; 7:11-36; Num 29:39).

28

4Q508 20

The end of a prayer

¹[. . .] us. Amen. Amen. [. . .]

The beginning of a prayer

²[. . .] us to be happy before [You . . .]

4Q508 21, 22-23

See below under 4Q509 8

4Q508 30

A fragment of a prayer

¹[. . .].. to You to atone [ ].. on ..[. . .] ²[. . .]from before You .. .., in the festivals of [. . .] ³[. . .]...[. . .]

4Q508 32

A fragment of a prayer for the New Moon celebration

¹[. . .] ,[. . .]... ²[. . . beg]innings of the month[s . . .] ³[. . . to y]ou for a mem[orial . . .]

Commentary

Line 2 The beginnings of months (new moons) were celebrated as festivals, according to Num 10:10, 28:11-15; Isa 1:13-14; Ezek 45:17; 46:3; Amos 8:5; Ps 81:4 (EVV 81:3); Neh 10:34 (EVV 10:33); 1 Chron 23:31; 2 Chron 2:3 (EVV 2:4); 8:13; 31:3. Compare 1QS x:4-5; 1QM ii:4; 11Q19 xiv:1-8. According to 11QPsª xxvii:7-8, David composed songs for the New Moon celebration along with songs for other festivals.

29

Line 3. Restored with Num 10:10. The word "you" is a plural form.

4Q508 39

A fragment of a prayer

[1][. . .] as for us, our lives are with a heart of grief by d[ay . . .] [2][. . .] we are not faithful in our lives [. . .] [3][. . .].[. . .]

Commentary

Line 1. Compare Ps 13:3 (EVV 13:2); 31:11 (EVV 31:10). Perhaps restore "[and by night]" (cf. Deut 28:66 and the commentary to line 2, below).
Line 2. Echoes Deut 28:66 (cf. Job 24:22).

4Q508 40

A fragment of a prayer

[1][. . .]which You have given to ..[. . .] [2][. . .]. those who hate us and ...[. . .] [3][. . .].. all [. . .]

4Q508 41

A fragment of a prayer

[1][. . .] corresponding to all our sins[. . .] [2][. . .].. by day and night[. . .] [3][. . .]... ...[. . .]

IV. 4Q509 + 4Q505

4Q509 col. i

4Q509 i:1-2 + 4

A fragment of a prayer?

[1][...] our [...].. [2]... [3][... mi]re of the streets of [...] [4][...]. we pour out [our] co[mplaint ...]... to all ..[...] [5][...].[...]. us in the period of the [...]. ... and He made us happy[...] [6][...]...[...]..[... Blessed be the L]or[d wh]o makes us understand .[...][7][...]...[ ]...[... forever and] ever. Amen. Amen. BLANK [...]

A prayer for the New Year celebration?

[8][...]...[...].....[...] [9][...] Mo[ses.] And You spoke to [...] [10][...]... ... which is over [...] [11][... wh]ich you commanded [t]o[...] [12][...].. with You .[...] [13][...].[...]

Commentary

Lines 1-13. These lines seem to come just before frag. 3 below, whose parallel in 1Q34 + 1Q34[bis] should probably be assigned to the New Year. Thus lines 8-13 probably belong to the same prayer, although their content apparently has to do with God's revelation to Moses. The prayer in lines 1-7 is too badly damaged for its occasion to be clear, but it may be another prayer for the New Year.

Line 3. This phrase is also found in 2 Sam 22:43 // Ps 18:43 (EVV 18:42); Mic 7:10; Zech 9:3; 10:5.

Line 4. Compare Ps 102:1 (EVV 102 title); 142:3 (EVV 142:2).

Lines 6-7. If the reconstruction is correct, the prayer concludes with a closing benediction and the double amen.

4Q509 i:3 + 1Q34 + 1Q34[bis] 2 + 1

[15][...]and her wealth ..[...] [16][...] You have [...] the festival of our peace [...] [17][...]us from our grief and Yo[u have] gath[ered our outcast men for the festival of ...] [18]... and our dispersed women [for the cycle ...].[...] [19][...]... on our congregation like ra[indrops on the land in the season of ...] [20]BLANK

[21][and like copious showers on her]bage in seasons of greenery .[. . .] [22][. . .]
Your [wo]ndr[o]us acts for generation after generat[ion . . .] [23][. . . Bless]ed be
the Lord who makes [us] happy [. . .] [24][. . .]...[. . .]

Commentary

Lines 16-23. This passage corresponds to 1Q34 + 1Q34[bis] 2 + 1:1-4, where
it is followed by a prayer for the Day of Atonement. For additional comments,
see the commentary to this passage.

Lines 22-23. There appears to have been additional text (not found in
1Q34 + 1Q34[bis] 2 + 1:4) in the break before the benediction.

4Q509 col. ii

A prayer for the Day of Atonement?

4Q509 5-6

[1][. . .]... ...[. . .] [2][. . .]. our blood[a] in the period of [. . .].[. . .] [3][. . .]... to meet us,
al[l . . .] [4].[ ].. ...[. . .]. You know everything[. . .] [5]You apportioned and You have
told[. . . a]ll the imprecations[. . .] [6][. . .].. as You spoke[. . .].[. . .] [7][Behold,]
you are about to lie down with [your] fath[ers . . .] [8][. . .].[. . .]

Note

ᵃדֹּמֵנוּ One could also translate "we were silent" (from the root דמם√).

Commentary

Line 5. The "imprecations" are the covenant agreements or covenant
curses (the word has both meanings) mentioned in Deut 29:11, 13, 18, 19, 20
(EVV 29:12, 14, 19, 20, 21).

Line 7. This is a quotation from Deut 31:16, addressed to Moses.

4Q509 7

[15][. . .].[. . .] [16][and] in the abysses and in all .[. . .] [17][fo]r of old You have hated .[. . .] [18][ ]unique before You .[. . .] [19]at the end of days[. . .] [20][. . .].. holy ones .[. . .] [21][. . .].. to take care .[. . .] [22][. . .]..[ ]...[. . .]

Commentary

Line 16. Compare 1QH[a] v:15.

4Q509 iii

4Q509 8 + 4Q508 22 + 23, 21[a]

TOP MARGIN?

[1][. . .] the work[. . .] [2][. . .] Your [. . .]..,[. . .] [3][. . . Blessed be the Lord who has mercy on us in , , Amen. Amen.]

A prayer for the Festival of Booths?

[4][A prayer for the pilgrimage-festival of Booths
Remember, O Lord, the multitude of Your mercies . . .] [5][. . . the produce of] our [lan]d for a wa[ve] o[ff]eri[ng . . .] [6][. . .]in the beginning .[. .] [7][. . . v]ery ...[. . .] [8][. . . and our despised and our wayfarers] and our poor ones [. . .] [9][. . . and there is no . . . in all . . . re]alm of ...[. . .] [10][. . .]...[. . .]

Note
[a]The overlap of 4Q508 22 + 23 with 4Q509 8:3-5 is highly likely. I follow Falk's proposed reconstruction of the passage, which is speculative but plausible (pp. 166-67). The proposed overlap between 4Q508 21 and 4Q509 8:7-8 is more speculative. The proper location of the words reconstructed in line 8 is very uncertain.

Commentary

Line 3. The content of this line is compatible with the Day of Atonement.
Line 4. The next festival after the Day of Atonement is Booths (Lev 23:26-

36, 39-43), so, given the probable placement of frag. 8 in 4Q509, Falk's reconstruction of the title of this prayer is reasonably likely, although the prayer could also be for the Day of Atonement. For the reconstruction of the opening line, compare 1Q34 + 1Q34^{bis} 2 + 1:6; 4Q507 3:3; 4Q508 2:2.

Line 5. The mention of "produce" fits the Festival of Booths (Lev 23:39), although the "wave-offering" is mentioned in the context of festivals in the HB only in association with the offering of firstfruits on the *Omer,* the day after the concluding Sabbath of the Festival of Unleavened Bread (Lev 23:9-12), and with the Festival of Weeks (Lev 23:17-20). It is also associated with the ordination of priests (e.g., Exod 29:24), which the *Temple Scroll* makes an annual institution at the beginning of the first month of the year (11Q19 xv:3-xvii:5). The *Temple Scroll* also includes two additional festivals, of Firstfruits of New Wine (11Q19 xix:11–xxi:10) and of Firstfruits of Oil (11Q19 xxi:12-xxii:16). None of these occasions can be ruled out as a possible context, but if these festival prayers are given in the order in which they are recited, Booths is the most likely here.

4Q509 9-10i

[21][. . . in o]rder that ... [22][. . .] and You have blessed [23][. . .] their [. . .]. which [24][. . .] Your [. . .]. [25][. . .]...[. . .] [26][. . .]..[. . .] [27][. . .]..[. . .] [28][. . .].[. . .] [29][. . .]. ..[. . .] [30][. . .]our mercy[. . .]

4Q509 12i-13

[36]the banished[a] who wander with no [one to return them . . .] [37][wi]thout valor, the fallen with n[o one to raise them . . .] [38]with no one who understands, the broken with no [one to bind them up . . .] [39]in iniquity [and] there is no healer [. . .] [40]who comforts ones who have stumbled in their transgressions [. . . Rem]ember [41]grief and weeping. You are a friend of prisoners[. . .].

BOTTOM MARGIN

Note

[a]המנודחים The Pual participle of the root נדח√ appears in the HB only in Isa 8:22.

Commentary

Lines 36-41. Baillet (DJD 7: 190) points out that these lines resemble biblical verses describing how God comforts the suffering (e.g., Ps 145:14; 146:7-8; 147:3; Jth 9:11). Such material seems more appropriate for the Day of Atonement rather than for Booths.

Line 36. Reconstructed on the basis of 4Q501 1:3.

Line 37. For the reconstruction, compare Jer 50:32.

Line 38. For the reconstruction, compare Ezek 34:4 and 4Q501 1:3.

4Q509 10ii + 11

²..[...] ³You have shepherded and .[...] ⁴in Your .[ ]. ⁵and Your angels[...] ⁶and Your inheritance .[... Blessed be] ⁷the Lord [who ... Amen. Amen.]

Another festival prayer

⁸[A pra]yer for the Festival of [...
...] ⁹Your [...].. whi[ch ...] ¹⁰[...].. ...[...] ¹¹[...]. all [...] ¹²[..]..,..[...]

Commentary

Line 3. For God as shepherd, see Isa 40:11; Ezek 34:13-16; Hos 4:16; Ps 23:1; 28:9.

Lines 5-6. Falk notes that early traditions (*Jub.* 32; 11Q19 xxix:8-10) associate Booths with the covenant God made with Jacob at Bethel, as recounted in Gen 28:10-22, and he suggests very tentatively that this story could provide a context appropriate for references to inheritance and angels (p 172).

Lines 6-7. I reconstruct a concluding benediction followed by the double amen.

Line 8. The surviving fragments of the prayer that begins in this line and continues in the rest of the column are too poorly preserved for us to be sure which festival it celebrated. The content is similar to the previous prayer, which, along with its place in the manuscript, would tend to indicate it was associated with Booths or the Day of Atonement. The spring New Year is also possible.

4Q509 12ii[a]

[1]we know .[. . .] [2]because ..[. . .] [3]Y[ou] have done [. . .] [4]Yo[u . . .] [5]and ..[. . .]

Note

[a]According to Baillet's reconstruction (DJD 7: 191), frag. 12ii probably overlaps with frag. 16, but the exact relationship between the two fragments is unclear.

4Q509 16

[1][. . .].[ ].[. . .] [2][. . .]with every pain[. . .] [3][. . .]He has had mercy on them because of their affliction [4][. . .]the grief of our elders and [our] honored [ones] [5][. . .]youths have made fun of them [6][. . .] they have [n]ot looked, because [7][. . .] our wisdom ...[ ]. [8][. . .]and we ...[. . .]

Commentary

Lines 4-5. Compare Isa 3:5.

4Q509 97-98i (+ 1Q34 + 1Q34^bis 3ii:3-7)

A prayer for the Day of Atonement or the Festival of Weeks?[a]

[2][. . .] And human seed [has not understood] [3][everything You have bequeathed it, and they do not know You] so as to carry out ~~so as to carry out~~ [4][Your word. And they have acted more wickedly than anyone, and they have not under]stood Your [great] strength. [5][But You have rejected them, for You do not deligh]t in iniquity, [and the wicked] [6][shall not be established before You. But You have chosen a people for Yourself in the period of Your favor,] [7][for You have remembered Your covenant and You have set them apart for] Yourself as holy [8][out of all the peoples, and You have renewed] Your [covena]nt for them with the vision of [9][glory and the words of Your holy prophets, by the] works of Your hands and the writing of

Note

[a]See 1Q34 + 1Q34^bis 3ii:3-7 for commentary.

4Q509 97-98ii

A fragment of a prayer

¹[ ]..[. . .] ²a crown of right[eousness . . .] ³a beaut[iful] diadem [. . .]
⁴righteousness ...[. . .] ⁵[. . .].[. . .] ⁶.[. . .] ⁷.......[. . .] ⁸[. . .]...[. . .]...[. . .] ⁹...[. . .]

Commentary

Line 2. The word "crown" appears in the HB only in Esther 1:11; 2:17; 6:8. The writer of 2 Tim 4:8 refers to the "crown of righteousness" as an eschatological reward, and crowns as a reward for the righteous are a recurrent theme in contemporary literature (Wisd 5:15-16; *4 Ezra* 2:45; *2 Apoc. Bar.* 15:7-8; *Odes Sol.* 17:1).

Line 3. Compare Wisd 5:16. The word "diadem" is not found in BH, but it is used in RH (Jastrow, 893a).

4Q505 124

A prayer for the Festival of Weeks?[a]

¹[. . .] ...[. . .] ²[. . .].[ ].[ ]. the e[arth . . .] ³. . . and because [we believe . . .]
⁴[. . . forev]er, and You established [a covenant] for [us at Horeb . . .] ⁵[. . .]...
..[. . .] ⁶[. . . to Abraham] and to Isaac and to Ja[cob . . .] ⁷[. . .]holiness standing
be[fore . . .] ⁸[. . .]. [. . .]

Note

[a]This fragment has some parallels to passages in the "Words of the Luminaries" (4Q504 3ii:11-13 and 5ii:1-2), from which some of the restorations have been taken. Yet the parallels are not exact, and, for reasons explained in the introduction to this chapter, 4Q505 is more likely to be from the same copy of the "Festival Prayers" as 4Q509. The content of this fragment has to do with the giving of the covenant at Mount Horeb, which would fit the Festival of Weeks. Given the probable order of the fragments, this would place the prayer for Weeks out of chronological order, before a prayer for Passover, but there are other indicators that not all the prayers in the work appear in the order of their recitation.

4Q505 125

A prayer for Passover?[a]

[1][A prayer for the Night of] Vigils.

Reme[mber . . .] [2][. . . Yo]u [have passed] over our houses [. . .] [3][. . .] He has not delivered y[ou . . .] [4][. . .]all the nations [. . .]

Note

[a]4Q505 125 and 127 represent the left side and right side, respectively, of adjoining columns, as is shown by the text on the other side (4Q506).

Commentary

Line 1. In the HB the word "vigils" occurs only in Exod 12:42 (x2). I follow Falk's tentative reconstruction, which interprets this line as the title and beginning of a prayer (pp. 175-76). Directions for the celebration of Passover are found in Exod 12; 23:15; 34:18; Lev 23:5-8; Num 28:16-25; Deut 16:1-8; 11Q19 xvii:6-16.

Line 2. Compare Exod 12:7, 13.

Line 4. Compare 4Q504 1-2iii:3, 5 and iv:8.

4Q505 127

A prayer for Passover?

[1][ ].... ..[. . .] [2]Your wondrous acts[. . .] [3]You are declared mighty[. . .] [4][ ]...[. . .]

Commentary

Line 2. God's wondrous acts figure in accounts of the Exodus (Exod 3:20; Ps 78:11, 32; 106:7, 22; Neh 9:17).

4Q509 131 + 132i

A prayer for Passover?[a]

[4][...]... [5][...]Your holiness [6][...]... [7][...].. [8][...].. months of [9][...] his [to]ngue [10][...]. to hear [11][...]with all [12][...] our [...].. [13][...] Your [wond]rous acts [14][...]You sent us [15][...]... [16][...] Your [ ]... [17][...] You have [h]ated [18][...] was [19][...]before [20][...] [21][...].

Note

[a]This prayer is too poorly preserved for its subject to be clear, but the fact that it comes immediately before the prayer for Firstfruits raises the possibility that it may be for Passover.

Commentary

Line 13. Compare Exod 3:20; Ps 78:11, 32; 106:7, 22; Neh 9:17.
Line 14. Compare Exod 3:20; 4:23; 5:1 etc.
Line 17. Compare Deut 12:31.

4Q509 131 + 132ii

[1][...].[ ].[ ].[ ].[...] [2][...] Your [gl]ory ..[...] [3][...] His [...]. Amen. Am[en.] [4][...] BLANK [...]

A prayer for the Day of Firstfruits (the Festival of Weeks)

[5][A prayer for the Day of] Fi[rs]tf[ru]its.
    Remember, O L[or]d, the f[e]s[t]i[v]a[l of] [6][...] and the freewill offerings of Your favor which You commanded [7].[...] before You the finest of [Your] works [8]to .[...]. on earth to be ..[ ] [9].[...].. Your .[ ]. because on the day of the ..[ ] [10].[...]. You have sanctified [...] [11][...] offspring[a] [...] [12].[...] [13].[...] [14]...[...] [15]with [...] [16]hol[iness ...] [17]in all [...] [18].[...] [19]..[...] [20]..[...]

Note

[a]The Hebrew word שׁגר is always used of the offspring of animals.

Commentary

Lines 3-4. Apparently the prayer concluded with a closing benediction followed by the double amen, as usual. A blank line separates it from the next prayer.

Line 5. The Day of Firstfruits is the name given to the Festival of Weeks in Num 28:26; 4Q365ᵃ 2i:2 (cf. Exod 23:16; 34:22; Lev 23:17, 20; *Jub.* 22:1; 11Q19 xi:11; xviii:14; xix:5-6, 9, 12; xliii:3, 6-7).

Line 6. Freewill offerings are commanded for the Festival of Weeks in Deut 16:10.

Line 7. Compare Deut 26:2, 4-5, 10.

4QBerakhot

(4Q286-90, 4Q280?)

INTRODUCTION

As noted in the general introduction, the covenant ratified at Sinai between God and Israel was central to the theology of the Qumran sectarians. They saw themselves as the true Israel in opposition to other forms of Judaism that they considered apostate. This sharp contrast is well illustrated by 4QBerakhot, a liturgy for a ritual the sect celebrated annually to reaffirm their covenant with God. No title survives in the manuscripts, but by convention the work is called the *Berakhot*, Hebrew for "blessings." In fact, curses on apostates and on the evil spirits who lead them figure every bit as prominently as blessings.

I. Contents

The *Berakhot* is one version of the sectarian community's annual covenant renewal liturgy. It is similar to the description of this ritual in the *Community Rule* (1QS i-ii) and shares much of its wording, but it seems to be an expanded account that describes in detail what the *Community Rule* only alludes to or mentions in passing. It also develops the liturgy in a somewhat different direction, shifting the emphasis from the opposition between the sect and outsiders or apostates to the opposition between God and the evil angel Belial or Melchiresha.

41

II. The Manuscripts

Five, or possibly six, manuscripts are preserved in very fragmentary form. The manuscripts 4QBerakhot[a-e] (4Q286-90) are written in scripts that date them to roughly the middle of the first century CE. 4QBerakhot[f]? (4Q280) is written in a somewhat earlier hand, dating to sometime in the first century BCE. There are overlaps between 4Q286 and 4Q287 and between 4Q286 and 4Q288, indicated in this translation by underscoring. The other manuscripts are linked with these on the basis of close similarity in content. Much of the work is lost, but enough survives to give us a general idea of what was in it.

III. Genres and Prosody

The *Berakhot* is clearly a work composed for communal recitation. Units of thought end with the phrase "Amen. Amen." God and the chief of the evil angels are addressed directly. A number of phrases are directions for either the leader of the ceremony (e.g., 4Q289 1:4) or the group participating in it (e.g., 4Q286 7i:8; 7ii:1-2). The main genres of the surviving material are also associated with ritual recitation. These are curses and blessings, hymns, and legal instruction.

Cursing rituals are directed against the evil angel and his minions (4Q286 7ii:1-13; 4Q289 1:1-7; 4Q290 1:1-3?; 4Q280 1:1-3?; 2:1-7). No corresponding blessings survive, but a number of passages bless God (4Q286 7i:7-8; 4Q287 3:1-5). We must be cautious due to the fragmentary state of the work, but the best biblical parallels seem to be found in the covenant curses and blessings that derive ultimately from ancient Near Eastern vassal treaties. This pattern, in which a great king made a treaty with a vassal king, included a list of blessings and curses that would come upon the vassal depending on whether he was obedient to the great king or rebellious. This genre is adapted in the Hebrew Bible to apply to God's covenant with Israel, with God as the great king and Israel as the vassal; the blessings and curses of this covenant are found mostly in Leviticus 26 and Deuteronomy 27–28. The covenant renewal ceremony carried out by the Qumran sectarians during the Festival of Weeks or *Shavuot* (see the general introduction) was an adaptation of this tradition to meet the needs of the community.

In the Hebrew Bible the closest formal parallel to the cursing rituals in the *Berakhot* is Deut 27:12-26, a liturgy in which the assembled tribes bless the people (although none of the blessings are given) and curse malefactors. Led by the

Levites, the people recite the curses and conclude with an "Amen." In the *Berakhot*, however, the double amen is always used (cf. the ritual curse of the suspected adulteress in Num 5:16-20), and the recipients of the curse are either referred to in the third person, as in Deuteronomy 27, or addressed directly, as in Deut 28:15-20. The curses appear to be recited by the "council of the Community" (4Q286 7ii:1), which probably means the whole assembled group. The most illuminating parallel is the account of the sect's covenant renewal ritual in the *Community Rule* (1QS cols. i-ii). Much of the language of the *Berakhot* seems to be borrowed from this ceremony, although some of the curses on the "men of the lot of Belial" are applied to the evil angel himself. The curses in 1QS ii:4b-18 are recited by the Levites, with the other members responding "Amen. Amen" at the end of the ceremony. Thus the rituals in the *Berakhot* and the *Community Rule* are extremely similar yet not identical.

Perhaps we should assume there was a short liturgy of blessings on the sectarian group as well, even though no trace of it survives on the leather. Blessings are an integral part of the covenant renewal ceremony going back to the second millennium BCE; although they received less emphasis as time went on, it is hard to imagine that they were ever dropped entirely. They are found in the corresponding ceremony in 1QS ii:1-4a. It is also possible that some of the hymns of praise functioned in part as blessings on the group. God is explicitly blessed in the *Berakhot*.

The *Community Rule* (1QS i:18b-22) states that the priests and Levites shall recite God's faithful, righteous, and mighty deeds. The content of the praise is not recorded, but apparently we have fragments of it in the songs of the *Berakhot*. These seem to come under the form-critical category "hymns" (songs of praise to God), which can be divided into further subcategories.

The first is hymns praising God for his work in nature (4Q286 3:1-8; 4:1-4?; 5:1-8, 9-13; 6:1-3; 4Q287 1:1-4; 3:1-5; 4Q289 2:1-4). They address God and praise him for his acts of creation and for the natural world, and they conclude with the double amen. Biblical hymns with a similar theme include Psalms 65 and 104. Although the beginnings of all the hymns in the *Berakhot* are lost, they may have started with some form of call to praise or invocation (cf. Ps 65:2; 104:1).

The second, nonbiblical subcategory (although it does have biblical antecedents) is what we may call "merkavah hymns." These are hymns set in the heavenly realm and sung by heavenly beings and mystics. (The Hebrew word *merkavah* is a technical term in Jewish literature for God's heavenly throne-chariot, especially as described in the first chapter of Ezekiel. The word is used in this technical sense in the *Songs of the Sabbath Sacrifice*.) These hymns praise God and his works, describe the heavenly throne room and its inhabitants, and include lists of God's attributes. Some biblical traditions describe the angelic praise (e.g., Isa 6:1-3; Ps 103:19-22) or celebrate the heavenly realm (Ps 104:1-4), but merkavah hymns are a postbiblical phenomenon. The book of Revelation frequently quotes hymns sung by angels and exalted saints in heaven. These hymns address God (or Christ), list his attributes, and praise him for his mighty acts. A typical example is found in Rev 15:2-4. John sees the victorious saints in heaven standing by the sea of glass mingled with fire, holding harps of God and singing the following song:

> Great and wondrous are Your works,
> Lord God Almighty!
> Righteous and true are Your ways,
> King of eternities!
> For You alone are holy.
> Who will not fear You, Lord,
> And glorify Your name?
> For all the nations shall come
> and they shall bow down before You,
> For Your righteous acts have been revealed.

The Hekhalot literature (see the general introduction) contains numerous hymns of this sort, often in a developed and baroque form. A short example at the beginning of the *Ma'aseh Merkavah* is similar to some of the hymns in Revelation:

> You are blessed forever on the throne of glory.
> You dwell in the chambers on high and in a majestic palace.
> For You revealed the mysteries and the mysteries of mysteries,
> The compulsions and compulsions of compulsions
> To Moses and Moses to Israel,
> In order for them to carry out the Torah by means of them
> And multiply the teaching (or "the Talmud").
>
> (*Ma'aseh Merkavah* §544)

Another hymn from the *Ma'aseh Merkavah* is closer to what we find in the *Berakhot*.

> YHWH my God,
> You are declared holy everlastingly,
> You are declared majestic over the living creatures

And over the chariots of Your power.
You are adorned, You are declared blessed
For there is none like You.
You are declared holy
For there are none like Your works.
For the uppermost heavens declare Your righteousness;
Fearsome ones tell Your glory;
Seraphim above and below prostrate themselves before You.
For You are great and fearsome
And there is no perversion or forgetfulness before Your throne of glory.
Blessed are You, YHWH, He who forms all the creatures in truth.

(*Ma'aseh Merkavah* §585)

The *Berakhot* contains a number of songs that show many similarities to the songs in Revelation and the Hekhalot hymns, and it seems legitimate to term them merkavah hymns (4Q286 ii:1-13; 2:1-7; 4Q287 2:1-13; 7:1-2?). Detailed discussion of the parallels may be found in the commentary. The two subcategories are not mutually exclusive; merkavah hymns often celebrate God's creation.

The poetic structure of the hymns in the *Berakhot* is difficult to work out due to their fragmentary condition. The best-preserved ones, 4Q286 1ii and 5, give a long list of features and beings in the celestial realm and on earth, often in pairs but not really in poetic couplets. The structure might be better termed rhythmic prose rather than poetry, much like parts of the *Songs of the Sabbath Sacrifice*.

The third category of material preserved in the *Berakhot* manuscripts consists of legal precepts and instructions. These are expansions of biblical laws that seem to have been adapted to the sect's life situation. A fragment of the rules for the half-shekel tax (cf. Exod 30:11-16) is preserved in 4Q287 17. The law regarding reproof of a neighbor (Lev 19:17-18) is a theme addressed frequently in the Qumran sectarian literature, and a passage from 4Q286 13-14 + 20 + 4Q288 1 reconstructed by Bilhah Nitzan seems to have dealt with it.

IV. Life Situation

A reasonable idea of the life situation of the *Berakhot* may be worked out with some confidence. The frequent echoes of the *Community Rule* and *Damascus Document*, and the explicit mention of the sectarian "Community" (יחד) in

4Q286 7ii:1 leave no doubt that it is a sectarian composition. These same parallels, especially to 1QS col. ii, also make the cultic context clear. The *Berakhot* is another formulation of the sectarian covenant renewal ceremony celebrated during the Festival of Weeks. Like later Jewish tradition, the *Berakhot* associates this festival with the Sinai covenant and with exegesis of Ezekiel's merkavah vision. The similarities to the merkavah hymns in the book of Revelation and the Hekhalot texts raise the possibility that the songs sung in the *Berakhot* were considered to be angelic hymns of mystical significance — perhaps some of the hymns referred to frequently in the *Songs of the Sabbath Sacrifice* but whose texts are never given.

Any attempt to reconstruct the order of the ceremony from the scattered surviving fragments is highly speculative, but it appears to have contained the following elements, perhaps in something like the following sequence.

1. The laws of the covenant (4Q286 13-14 + 20 + 4Q288 1; 4Q286 15:1-4; 4Q287 8:1-2; 9:1-2; 4Q288 1:1-3; 4Q280 3:1-2).

2. A communal confession or review of the sect's history (typical of the older covenant formularies but surviving, if at all, only in the small fragment 4Q286 1i:7-8 in the *Berakhot*).

3. Hymns praising and blessing God (4Q286 ii:1-13; 2:1-7; 3:1-8; 4:1-4?; 5:1-8, 9-13; 6:1-3; 7:1-7, 8-9; 8:1-3; 11:1-3; 4Q287 1:1-4; 2:1-13; 3:1-5; 7:1-2; 4Q289 2:1-4).

4. Blessings recited over the sectarian community (?). (We would expect these from the structure of the covenant formulary, but none appear in the surviving fragments of the *Berakhot*.)

5. Curses on Belial and his followers (4Q286 7ii:1-13; 4Q289 1:1-7; 4Q290 1:1-3?; 4Q280 1:1-3?; 2:1-7).

6. A census of the sect (4Q286 17), placed at this point in the ceremony on the basis of 1QS ii:19-23.

V. Literary Context

The main scriptural influences on the *Berakhot* are the legal traditions in Leviticus and Deuteronomy, the structural elements of the covenant formulary in both, the vision of the divine chariot in the first chapter of Ezekiel, and the general psalmic theme of the praise of God for his creative acts. There are numerous allusions to scripture, but for the most part these are thoroughly reworked according to the interests of the composer.

There is a very close relationship to the Qumran sectarian literature that pertains to the covenant and the covenant renewal festival. Much of the language is drawn directly from the *Community Rule,* and some also from the *Damascus Document.* The *Berakhot* shares exegesis of Ezekiel's merkavah vision with the *Songs of the Sabbath Sacrifice,* a work that reaches a climax around the time of the Festival of Weeks, when the sect's covenant renewal festival was held.

This merkavah exegesis is also closely related to the hymns found in the much later Hekhalot literature. These parallels are discussed in the commentary to the *Berakhot* and in the commentary and introduction to the *Songs of the Sabbath Sacrifice.*

VI. The Problem of 4Q280

In 1972, J. T. Milik published frags. 1 and 2 of 4Q280 (as 4QTeharot, "Règle de la Pureté" — 4QPurifications, "The Purity Rule"), but in more recent years it has been identified with the *Berakhot* on the basis of similarities in content.[1] Questioning this identification, Nitzan has suggested that 4Q280 may be a source of the *Berakhot* rather than another manuscript of it.[2] Indeed, it is odd that two somewhat different versions of the same set of curses (4Q286 7ii and 4Q280 2) should be found in the same composition. Nevertheless, 4Q280 is clearly a sectarian liturgy for the covenant renewal ceremony, and it is legitimate to include it in this chapter whether it is from the same composition as the *Berakhot* or an alternate version of the ceremony. It has as much claim to belong to the *Berakhot* as 4Q289 and 4Q290, which are tied to it only on the basis of similar content. Many of the sectarian texts survive in multiple versions.

BIBLIOGRAPHY

Baumgarten, Joseph M., and Jósef T. Milik, *Qumran Cave 4.XIII, The Damascus Document.* DJD 18. Oxford: Clarendon, 1996.

Collins, John J. *The Scepter and the Star: The Messiahs of the Dead Sea Scrolls and Other Ancient Literature.* New York: Doubleday, 1995.

Eshel, Esther. "4Q477: The Rebukes by the Overseer." *JJS* 45 (1994) 111-22.

Kobelski, Paul J. *Melchizedek and Melchireša*. CBQMS 10. Washington, D.C.: Catholic Biblical Association of America, 1981. When Kobelski is cited without

---

1. Milik, "Milkî-ṣedeq et Milkî-reša'," 115, 126-30.
2. Nitzan, "4QBerakhot (4Q286-290): A Covenantal Ceremony," 489-90.

other identification in the body of the commentary, the reference is to his comments on the relevant passage in 4Q280 or 4Q286 in this volume.

Kugel, James L. "Hatred and Revenge." In *In Potiphar's House: The Interpretive Life of Biblical Texts*, 214-46. San Francisco: HarperSanFrancisco, 1990.

Milik, J. T. "Milkî-ṣedeq et Milkî-reša' dans les anciens écrits juifs et chrétiens." *JJS* 23 (1972) 95-144. When Milik is cited without other identification in the body of the commentary, the reference is to his comments on the relevant passage in 4Q280 or 4Q286 in this article.

————. "4Q Visions de 'Amram et un citation d'Origène." *RB* 79 (1972) 77-97.

Nitzan, Bilhah. "4QBerakhot (4Q286-290): A Preliminary Report." In *New Qumran Texts and Studies: Proceedings of the First Meeting of the International Organization for Qumran Studies, Paris 1992*, edited by George J. Brooke with Florentino García Martínez, 53-71. STDJ 15. Leiden: Brill, 1994.

————. "Harmonic and Mystical Characteristics in Poetic and Liturgical Writings from Qumran." *JQR* 85 (1994) 163-83.

————. "4QBerakhot[a-e] (4Q286-290): A Covenantal Ceremony in the Light of Related Texts." *RevQ* 16/64 (1995) 487-506.

————. "The Laws of Reproof in 4QBerakhot (4Q286-290) in Light of Their Parallels in the Damascus Covenant and Other Texts from Qumran." In *Legal Texts and Legal Issues: Proceedings of the Second Meeting of the International Organization for Qumran Studies, Cambridge 1995*, edited by Moshe Bernstein et al., 149-65. Leiden: Brill, 1997.

————. *Qumran Cave 4.VI, Poetical and Liturgical Texts, Part 1*, edited by Esther Eshel et al., 1-74. DJD 11. Oxford: Clarendon, 1998. The official edition of the *Berakhot* is included in this volume. When Nitzan is cited without other identification in the body of the commentary, the reference is to her comments on the relevant passage in 4Q286-90.

Wacholder, Ben Zion. "The Calendar of Sabbatical Cycles during the Second Temple and Early Rabbinic Period." *HUCA* 44 (1973) 153-96.

Wertheimer, Shlomo Aharon, and Abraham Joseph Wertheimer. *Batei Midrashot: Twenty-five Midrashim Published for the First Time from Manuscripts Discovered in the Genizoth of Jerusalem and Egypt with Introductions and Annotations* (in Hebrew). 2 vols. 2nd ed. Jerusalem: Ktab Yad Wasepher, 1968.

4QBERAKHOT

(4Q286-290, 4Q280?)

4Q286 (4QBerakhot^a)

4Q286 1i^a

A liturgical fragment

⁷[, . .] our . . . ⁸[. . .] Amen.

Note
^aThe line numbers of this column are determined by those of column ii of the same fragment.

Commentary

Lines 7-8. The word "our" in line 7 and the word "Amen" in line 8 may place this fragment in a liturgical context, but little else can be inferred about its content. Nitzan suggests that it may have been part of a communal confession or a historical review.

4Q286 1ii

A hymn recounting the scene of the heavenly throne room, God's wisdom, and the sacred cycles he ordained

TOP MARGIN

^{1a}Your worthy seat^a and the footstools of Your glorious feet in the [he]ights of Your station and the flo[or of]^b ²Your holiness and the chariots of Your glory, their cherubim and their ophannim, and all [their] foundations,^c ³foundations of fire and sparks of brightness and radiances of effulgence, ^driv[er]s of fires^d and luminaries^e of wonder, ⁴[effulg]ence and adornment and exaltation of glory, foundation of holiness and so[urce of] radiance and exaltation of orna-

49

ment, wo[nder of] ⁵than[ksgivings] and a reservoir of mighty acts, adornment of praises and greatness[f] of fearsome acts and ac[ts of] healing[g] ⁶and a work of wonder, a foundation of wisdom and a structure of knowledge and a source of <<from>> understanding, a s[o]u[r]c[e of] p[ru]d[en]ce ⁷and counsel of holiness and a foundation of truth, a treasury of insight, [h]constructions of righteousness,[h] and groundworks of uprigh[tness, abundant[i]] ⁸kind acts and humility of goodness and kind acts of truth and eternal mercies and mysteries of wo[nders] ⁹when [th]ey ap[pear] and weeks of holiness in their measure and divisions of new moons [. . .] ¹⁰[beginnings of yea]rs in their circuits and festivals of glory in [their] set per[iods . . .] ¹¹[. . .]and Sabbaths of the land in [their] allo[tments and fest]ivals of lib[erty . . .] ¹²[. . .] [j]everlasting [li]berations[j] and .[. . .] ¹³[. . .][k]light and dar[kness[k] . . .]

Notes

[a-a]In the HL the phrase "His worthy seat" is found in Aramaic (מושב יקריה) in *SH-L* §376, and in Hebrew (מושב יקרו) in *Massekhet Hekhalot* §7.2 (cf. "His glorious seat" [מושב כבודו] in *SH-L* §373).

[b][ס]מדֹרֹ The word "floor" should be restored here, rather than Nitzan's "treading place" ([ך]מדֹרֹ). The former is used for the celestial floor in Songs XI 4Q405 19:2.

[c]Although the word translated "foundation" (סוד) always means "council" or "secret" in BH, in QH it is often a synonym of the more common word for "foundation" (יסוד), so its meaning must be determined here by the context. The subject of the passage is the architecture and inhabitants of the heavenly realm, so "their foundations" makes better sense.

[d-d]I translate "rivers of fires," reading נה]רֹי אֹורים. One could possibly also translate "rivers of lights" (vocalizing the second word אֹורים rather than אֹורים). For parallels in the HB, QL, and HL, see the commentary to Songs X 4Q405 15ii-16:2, where the nearly identical phrase "rivers of fire" (נה]רֹי אֹור) is found.

[e]The word "luminary" (מאור) normally takes a feminine plural ending, but the masculine plural form is found here and in Ezek 32:8; 4Q287 1:1; Songs XI 4Q405 19:5; *m. Ber.* 8.5.

[f]In classical Hebrew the word translated "greatness" (גדול) would mean "great," or "Great One," but it is unclear what the antecedent of the adjective would be in this context. Either this word is an error for "greatness" (גודל) or a variant spelling of a sort found elsewhere in QH (*HDSS* 200.24).

[g]The word רפאות, "acts of healing," appears in the HB (Ezek 30:21; Jer 30:13; 46:11), in 4Q511 20i:4; 11Q11 ii:7 (both exorcism texts), and often in reference to spells of healing in the later Jewish magical literature.

[h-h]The word "construction" (מבנה) is found in the HB in Ezek 40:2 (cf. the related word מבנית, which has the same meaning in a similar context in Songs VII 4Q403 1i:41, 44; IX 4Q405 14-15i:6, etc.). Another possible reading of the consonantal text of the phrase translated "constructions of righteousness" (מבני צדק) is "from the sons of righteousness," but the architectural meaning fits the context and parallelism much better than an unexpected mention of the members of the sectarian community.

ᶦFor this restoration compare Exod 34:6; 4Q381 46:2.

ʲ⁻ʲ[ד]רׄורׄי נצח I read "everlasting [lib]erations," although Nitzan's suggestion "everlasting generations" (דׄורׄי נצח) is possible as well.

ᵏ⁻ᵏאׄור וחש[ך] In the phrase "light and dark[ness]" we would expect the second word to have a plene spelling (חושך), but shorter spellings also occur in this manuscript (e.g., בחדשים in 5:7). The phrase "light and darkness" appears in Songs XIII 11Q17 x:4 in a similar cosmological context; light and darkness are also mentioned as part of the sacred cycle in 1QS x:1-2 and 1QHᵃ xx:5-7. Nitzan reconstructs "light and reck[onings of]" (אׄור וחש[בוני]) here, but this seems unnecessarily complicated.

Commentary

Line 1. "Your worthy seat" refers to the seat of God's throne (cf. Ezek 28:2, "the seat of the gods"). Other heavenly seats are mentioned in Songs XI 4Q405 20ii-21-22:2, 4. The word "footstool" never appears in the plural in the HB or elsewhere in the QL (but cf. *2 Enoch* 19:6?), and it is not clear why it is plural here. The divine footstool is mentioned in Songs VII 4Q403 1ii:2 and XIII 11Q17 x:7.

Line 2. Multiple divine chariots appear in the HB (e.g., Isa 66:15), the *Songs of the Sabbath Sacrifice*, and the HL, and cherubim and ophannim figure in Ezekiel's visions in chaps. 1 and 10, in the *Songs of the Sabbath Sacrifice,* and in the HL. See the commentary to Songs VII 4Q403 1ii:15 for details. The phrase "their cherubim and their ophannim" appears in the latter passage, again with chariots as the referent of the pronoun "their." The "four foundations of the firmament of wonder" are mentioned in Songs XII 11Q17 viii:5-6; Newsom suggests that they refer to foundations for the cherubim.

Line 3. This line begins with a different and unambiguous word for "foundation" (see note c). The phrase "sparks of brightness" echoes "sparks of fire" in Dan 7:9 (cf. 3:22). Compare also "the sparks of His brightness" in 1QHᵃ xiv:18.

Line 4. The word pair "effulgence and adornment" is used frequently to describe the heavenly realm. See the commentary to Songs VII 4Q403 1i:45 for details.

Line 6. The word translated "a work of" could also be translated "works of," but since the other elements of this line are singular, the first translation fits the meaning better. The word "structure," meaning a pattern or copy or form in BH, is applied to structures in the heavenly realm in the *Songs of the Sabbath Sacrifice.* For details, see the commentary to Songs VII 4Q403 1i:44.

Lines 9-13. Compare 1QS x:1-10 and 1QHᵃ xx:4-11 for similar celebrations of the sacred cycle of festivals and holy times.

Line 9. The word "division" is used in the sense of (human or angelic) military divisions in the *Songs of the Sabbath Sacrifice,* the *War Scroll,* and the *Temple Scroll* (see the commentary to Songs XII 4Q405 20ii-21-22:14) and in the sense of divisions of the month into periods of light and darkness in 4Q503.

Line 10. "Festivals of glory" are also mentioned in CD iii:14-15; 4Q503 4-6:4; 1-3:14; 4Q508 13:2.

Line 11. The phrase "Sabbaths of the land" refers to the sabbatical year, mandated every seventh year, in which the land was to be left to lie fallow (Exod 23:10-11). According to Deut 15:1-18; 31:10, debts and contracts of bonded servitude were canceled at each sabbatical year, and this institution is developed in more detail in Leviticus 25 (cf. 26:34-35), culminating in the tradition of the Jubilee year, a cancellation of debts, property sales, and slavery every fiftieth year. The sabbatical year and the Jubilee are mentioned fairly often in the literature of the Second Temple period, including the QL, and the Jubilee cycle is central to the chronology of the book of *Jubilees.* It appears that the sabbatical year was still being celebrated in this period since Josephus refers to it as an active institution in the second and first centuries BCE (*Ant.* 12 §378; 13 §234; 14 §475) and an Aramaic promissory note discovered in the Wadi Murabbaʿat (Mur 18) is dated in a sabbatical year that fell in 55/56 CE. Documents from the period of the Bar Kokhba revolt also refer to this institution. See Wacholder, "The Calendar of Sabbatical Cycles," for more details.

The word "liberty" is usually used in the HB in association with the sabbatical year (Jer 34:8, 15, 17) or Jubilee year (Lev 25:10; Ezek 46:17). The phrase "festival of liberty" appears just after the mention of the sabbatical years in 1QS x:8, and the word "liberty" in the context of the eschatological Jubilee in 11Q13 ii:6 (the Melchizedek document).

4Q286 2

Fragments of two hymns that describe the heavenly realm

TOP MARGIN

[1][. . .]. in the power of Your adornment.[a] And all spirits of the or[a]c[l]es of the sanctu[ary . . .] [2][. . .]in [their] counc[ils and in] their [r]ealms, mighty ones of gods in strength [3][. . .]. zeal of judgment in power. BLANK

[4][. . .].. all of them . . . Your holy name [5][. . . ho]ly of holies and [they] c[ur]se [6][. . .]knowledge, und[erstan]ding [7][. . .]. chanting .[. . .].

Note

ªSurely read הדרכֹה, "Your adornment," rather than הדרֹמֹה, "their adornment" (Nitzan). The tick at the top of the penultimate letter appears to lean right, as with *kaph*, rather than left, as with *mem*. This reading also makes better sense in context.

Commentary

Lines 1-3. Nitzan finds echoes of the biblical poetic tradition about the divine revelation at Sinai in this fragment, especially in these lines ("4QBerakhot [4Q286-290]: A Preliminary Report," 71), but it must be said that such echoes are very faint. 4QBerakhot describes the power of God and his angels alongside a mention of the sanctuary, but this corresponds at most to the general sentiment of Ps 68:34-36 and Deut 33:2-4, 26b-27. No phrases from these passages are borrowed.

Line 1. The phrase "spirits of the oracles of the sanctuary" is odd. Assuming the damaged reading "oracles" is correct, it seems to be used in the sense of "utterance, oracle," that is, the heavenly and perhaps revelatory words spoken by the angels in the celestial temple. This usage is known from the *Songs of the Sabbath Sacrifice* (e.g., Songs XII 11Q17 viii:6, 8, 9). Songs VII 4Q403 11:11 also has a reference to celestial objects that I have tentatively translated "load-bearing pillars," perhaps the heavenly analogues to the two pillars that stood before the earthly temple. An indirect reference to the same objects may be possible here, since the word translated "load-bearing" is the same as that translated "oracle" elsewhere. Yet the first possibility seems more likely.

Line 2. On the term "council," see note c to 4Q286 1ii:2, above. Angelic councils also appear in the *Songs of the Sabbath Sacrifice* and the *Songs of the Sage* (4Q510-511). Note the expression "in the council of the gods" in Songs I 4Q400 1ii:9; 4Q511 10:11. For angelic "realms," see the commentary to Songs II 4Q401 14i:6.

The "mighty ones of gods in strength" are angels. Compare "[m]ighty ones of gods" (1QM xv:14), "mighty ones of power" (Songs IV 4Q402 1:4), "mighty ones of strength" (1QIIª xvi:11; xviii:34-35; SH-L §372; *Ma'aseh Merkavah* §§558, 587; G23 1a:4), and "mighty ones of valor" (CD ii:17; 1QM x:6). For the term "mighty ones" in general, see the commentary to Songs IV 4Q402 1:4.

Line 3. The blank space at the end of the line seems to indicate that one hymn ended here and another began on line 4.

Line 4. The phrase "Your holy name" appears in liturgical contexts in Ps 106:47 // 1 Chron 16:35; 1 Chron 29:16; 1QM xi:3; 4Q287 3:1; 11Q14 1ii:4, 15.

Line 5. Either "[ho]ly of holies" or "most [ho]ly . . ." are possible translations.

4Q286 3

A fragment of a hymn that mentions angels and describes a storm

[1][. . .]. ..[. . .] [2][. . .]. [a]atte[nding] angels[a] [. . .] [3][. . .].. [. . .] in [a]ll their service [. . .] [4][. . .].. and lightning bolts [b]... rain ... [misty cl]ouds[c] of water,[b] thick [5][. . .] and droplets of dew .[. . .].. and spirits of realms [6][. . .] w[hen] th[ey were cre]ated [7][. . .].. one to another.[. . .] [8][. . .].[. . .]

Notes

[a-a]מלאכי [מש]רת Or possibly read [מלאכי מש]חית, "angels of destruction" (cf. 1 Chron 21:15), or מלאכי [מש]תמות, "angels of animosities" (cf. 4Q225 2ii:6?; 4Q387 3iii:4; 4Q390 1:11; 2i:7). This word "attending" is from the root √שרת, "to attend, serve" (cf. 4Q381 1:10-11), not the root √שרר, "to be prince, rule." The former is applied frequently to angels in Jewish esoteric literature.

[b-b]Nitzan reads [מ]לאכי עַנ[נ] י מטר [ו]עֲרפלי מים, "angels of rain c[lou]ds [and] misty clouds of water" (cf. *Jub.* 2:2 [4Q216 vi:6-8]). The words she interprets as "angels" and "c[lou]ds" are badly damaged.

[c]The word ערפל, "misty cloud," is found only in the singular in the HB, where it refers to the gloom around Mount Sinai during the revelation of the Torah (Exod 20:21; Deut 4:11); to the abode of God in heaven or the temple (e.g., 1 Kgs 8:12; Job 22:13); or to gloom as a natural phenomenon (e.g., Ezek 34:12; Job 38:9). It is used frequently in the HL to describe the heavenly realm (e.g., *3 Enoch* 37:2 [*SH-L* §55]; *Hekhalot Rabbati* §198; *Ma'aseh Merkavah* §590).

Commentary

Lines 2-5. The God of Israel is the storm god and god of fertility in the HB and is often pictured as riding in a storm, frequently in the company of the lesser gods or angels (e.g., Exod 15:1-18; Deut 33:2-3; Hab 3:3-15; Zech 14:1-9; Ps 18:7-16 // 2 Sam 22:7-16; Ps 29; 68:8-11, 17-18; 74:12-17; 89:6-18). The tradition about the storm god inspires these lines.

Line 2. Compare "attending angels" to "attendants of the Presence" in Songs I 4Q400 1i:4, 8. See note a above for the meaning of the term "attending."

Lines 4-5. Warrior angels are compared to a thunderstorm in 1QM xii:8-9 // xix:1-2 in language similar to that of this passage.

Line 5. The phrase "droplets of dew" is found elsewhere only in Job 38:28. For angelic realms, see 2Q286 2:2 and the commentary to Songs II 4Q401 14i:6.

4Q286 4

Perhaps a fragment of the same hymn as frag. 3

¹[. . .]..[. . .] ²[. . .]...[. . .] ³.[. . .]. on the face of [. . .] ⁴[. . .]and all the[. . .]

Commentary

Line 3. Perhaps, as Nitzan suggests, a reference to rain falling on the face of the land (cf. 4Q286 3:4-5).

4Q286 5

*Fragments of two hymns that recount the wonders of nature*ᵃ

TOP MARGIN

¹... the earth and all ..[. . .] its inhabitants, land, and all its depths .[. . .] ²[the earth and al]l that exists on it [. . . al]l hil[l]s, valleys, and all streams, dr[y] land [. . .] ³[. . .] its [ce]dar, shady places*ᵇ* of forests, and all wildernesses of desola[tion . . .] ⁴[. . .]. and its wastes and the supports of its structure, jackals [. . .]. ⁵. . . th[ei]r fruit, exalted trees, and all the cedars of Leba[non . . .] ⁶[. . . grain and ne]w wine and oil and all its products [. . .] ⁷[. . .] and all wave offerings of the inhabited world in the tw[elve] months[. . .] ⁸[. . .]. Your word. Amen. Amen. BLANK [. . .]

⁹[. . .]...ᶜ seas, fountains of the deep[. . .] ¹⁰[. . .].. all wadis, watercourses of the depths [. . .] ¹¹[. . .]... ... seas [. . .] ¹²[. . . al]l their foundations .[. . .] ¹³[. . .]...[. . .]

Notes
ᵃSome of the readings of this badly damaged fragment are conjectural. Nitzan fills in schematic reconstructions to try to recover the parallelism, and I have followed her in cases where her reconstruction seems very likely. The (feminine singular) "it" throughout seems to refer to the earth (הארץ).

[b]The word translated "shady places of" (מצולי) should apparently be distinguished from "depths" (מצולות, perhaps from the root √צול, "to be deep"); it appears to be derived from a root meaning "to be shady" (√צלל). Nitzan suggests it is a Pual participle. This word may appear in Zech 1:8 and 1QH[a] xvi:19.

[c]Nitzan reads this badly damaged word as וֹמֹצוּר, which she translates as "and creatures of." This word, with the meaning "formation" (from a putative root √צור; cf. √יצר, "to form"), may be used in 1QS xi:21 // 4Q264 1:9.

Commentary

Line 1. The word "depth" is unattested outside QH, but it is used in this sense here and in 1QH[a] xi:32-33; 4Q504 1-2vii:7; 4Q511 37:4.

Line 3. The word translated "desolation" can refer to a desolate region (e.g., Isa 61:4) or the condition of dryness or drought (e.g., Jer 50:38). It is spelled the same way as (Mount) Horeb, but nothing in the context ties the passage to the Exodus or to a particular region, and Horeb is not associated with multiple deserts in the HB (cf. Exod 3:1; Deut 1:1, 19).

Line 4. The word translated "wastes" is attested only in the singular in the HB (e.g., Gen 1:2; Deut 32:10). The word translated "jackals" could also be translated "coastlands."

Line 5. This phrase seems to be inspired by Ps 148:9. "Cedars of Lebanon" are mentioned frequently in the HB.

Line 6. The three words "grain," "new wine," and "oil" occur together frequently in the HB as symbols of blessing and fertility (e.g., Hos 2:10) or as produce especially associated with the cult (e.g., Deut 12:17). They also appear together in the former sense in 1QH[a] xviii:24 and 11Q14 1ii:10 (cf. *Sib. Or.* 3:745), and in the latter sense in the *Temple Scroll* (11Q19 xliii:3-9; lx:6).

Line 8. The end of a song. The double amen appears in the HB in Num 5:22; Ps 89:53; Neh 8:6 (cf. "Amen and Amen" in Ps 41:14; 72:19). In 1QS i:20; ii:10, 18 it appears in a liturgical context of blessing and cursing similar to that in 4Q286 7ii. Note also the curse in *Jub.* 33:12 (4Q221 4:2), which is seconded by the angels with a double amen. In the Gospel of John, Jesus uses the double amen as an emphatic opening to his pronouncements (e.g., John 3:3), and the same usage is found in *T. Abr.* 20:1-2 (long recension) in the mouth of Death.

Line 9. The phrase "fountains of the deep" is closely paralleled by the similar phrase with the same meaning but a feminine plural ending in Gen 7:11; 8:2. The latter phrase is found in the HL in *SH-L* §515; G8 2a:7.

Line 12. For "their foundations," see note c to 4Q286 1ii:2 above.

4Q286 6

A fragment mentioning God's creation and the festivals

TOP MARGIN

[^1][. . .].. for Y[ou] have created [. . .] [^2][. . .]in their festivals and from month[a] [to month . . .] [^3][. . .]to satisfy them [. . .]

Note
    [a]One may translate either "and from month (ומחדש) [to month]" as above, or (with Nitzan) "(He) renews" (Piel participle). Compare 4Q287 3:4 and 4Q381 1i:8-9.

Commentary

Lines 1-3. A fragment celebrating God's creation of the world and his sustaining of it in the sacred cycle of the year.
    Line 1. God is frequently praised in the second person for his creation (e.g., 1QH[a] v:14; vii:18-21, 26; ix:7, 13, 27; xii:38; 4Q287 3:2 4; 4Q289 2:1; cf. Rev 4:11).

4Q286 7i

The end of a hymn that exalts God's kingdom, and the beginning of a communal blessing of God

TOP MARGIN

[^1][. . .]the lands [^2][. . .]. their chosen ones [^3][. . .] and all of those who have [kn]owledge with psalms of [^4][. . .]and blessings of truth in periods of .[. . .] [^5][. . .] Your [. . .] and for Your kingdom to be lifted up in the midst of .[. . .]. [^6][. . .].. gods of purity with all eternal knowing ones to ps[alm] [^7][. . . to ble]ss Your name of glory with all [. . .].[. . .] Amen. Amen. BLANK
    [^8][. . .]again they bless the God of [. . . a]ll ...[. . .] His truth [^9]..[. . .]

Commentary

Line 2. The term "chosen one" is used in the HB of the people of Israel (e.g., Isa 45:4; Ps 105:6, 43; 106:5), the Davidic king (Ps 89:4), Moses (Ps 106:23) and Deutero-Isaiah's servant of God (Isa 42:1), always with God as the chooser. In the QL, the chosen ones can be the members of the sect (e.g., 1QS viii:6; xi:16; CD iv:3-4; 1QH^a vi:15; x:13), but also the angels (e.g., 1QM xii:4-5). The word usually modifies another noun. The context here is not clear; the word may refer either to Israel or to angels.

Line 3. The word translated "those who have knowledge" is used of the sectarian sages in 1QSa i:28; 1QH^a xix:14; 4Q298 1i:3; 3-4ii:4, and of angels in Songs I 4Q400 3ii + 5:5; II 4Q400 2:9; V Mas1k i:4; VI Mas1k ii:2. It is not found in the HB apart from the proper name Jaddua in Neh 10:22; 12:11, 22.

Line 4. The word translated "period" (קץ) has the meaning "end" in time (e.g., Gen 8:6; Esther 2:12) or, rarely, space (e.g., 2 Kgs 19:23 // Isa 37:24) in BH. Sometimes it refers to a climactic or eschatological end (e.g., Amos 8:2; Hab 2:3; Dan 8:17, 19), which no doubt explains the meaning in QH. In QH the word has the sense of a predestined period or era ordained by God (e.g., 1QS iii:15; iv:13; 1QpHab vii:12-13; 4Q180 1-4).

Line 5. This line echoes Num 24:7.

Line 6. Angels are frequently called gods in the QL (for discussion, see the commentary to Songs I 4Q400 1i:4). For the purity of the angels compare Songs I 4Q400 1i:14-15; VI 4Q403 1i:13. The phrase "eternal knowing ones" is applied to angels in Songs VI Mas1k ii:26 // 4Q403 1i:11; Songs VIII 4Q403 1ii:19-20 // 4Q405 8-9:3-4; cf. also VI Mas1k i:11.

Line 7. God's "name of glory" is mentioned in the HB in Ps 72:19; Neh 9:5 (cf. Ps 29:2; 66:2; 79:9; 96:8 // 1 Chron 16:29), always in a liturgical context. The same phrase is found in 4Q286 11:1; 4Q287 2:8; Songs VI 4Q403 1i:29.

Lines 7-8. A double amen brings a song or liturgical unit to an end. A new unit begins in line 8, apparently the beginning of a liturgy of blessings and curses continued in col. ii of frag. 7.

4Q286 7ii (+ 4Q287 6:1-11)

A liturgy of imprecation against Belial and his minions

The end of a liturgical unit recited by the Community

TOP MARGIN

¹The council of the Community shall say, <u>all of them</u> in the Community, "Amen. Amen." BLANK

A curse on Belial and "the spirits of his lot"

And afterward [they] shall denounce Belial ²and his whole guilty lot and they shall answer and say, "Cur[se]d is [B]elial in his [pl]ot of animosity ³and he is denounced for his guilty service and cursed are <u>all the spi[rits of]</u> his [lo]t in their plot of wickedness ⁴and they are denounced for the plots of the defilement of their [im]purity, fo[r they are a lo]t of darkness and their visitation ⁵is to an eternal pit. Amen. Amen." BLANK

Another curse, apparently on both Belial
and his human servants

"And cursed is the wick[ed one in all the periods of] <u>his realms</u> and denounced are ⁶all the sons of Beli[al] in all the seasons^a of their station until their termination^b [forever. Amen. <u>Amen."</u>] BLANK

Another curse on Belial

⁷And [again they say, "Cursed are you, ange]l of the pit and spir[it of destru]ction in al[l] plots of <u>your</u> nature of ⁸g[uilt and in all schemes of abomin]ation and [your] counsel of wicked[ness. And den]ounced are you, in the r[ea]l[m of] ⁹[your iniquity] <u>and in [yo]ur</u> [service of wickedness and guilt], with all ^cthe de[filements of Sheo]l^c and wi[th the taunts of the pi]t ¹⁰[and with the humi]liations of annihilation, with [no survivor and with no acts of for]<u>giveness, with the anger</u> of the rage of [Go]d [for al]l [eterniti]es. Amen. A[men."]

A curse on wicked human beings

[11]["And cursed are a]ll who do <u>their</u> [plots of wick<u>edness] and who establish</u> your schemes [in their hearts to scheme] [12][against the covenant of Go]d and to [reject the words of] His [fait]hful [visionaries] and to alter <u>the judgme[nts of the Torah"]</u>[d] [13][. . .].. .[. . .]

Notes

[a]עוּנֹת From the noun עוֹנָה. One could also translate "the iniquities of" (from the noun עָוֹן), but one would expect the spelling עוונות. The word "season" appears with this meaning (i.e., "period of time") in RH (Jastrow, 1054) and in 4Q177 5-6:13; 4Q491 1-3:15, 16; 4Q493 8, 10. In 4Q502 1-3:9 it seems to have the meaning "conjugal duty."

[b]For use of the root "to be sound, complete, whole" (√תמם) in the sense of "to terminate," see Ps 73:19; 1QM xiv:7; 1QH[a] iv:21; 4Q185 1-2i:14.

[c-c]ל[שאול אולי]ג Restoring with Nitzan (the first word is found in Neh 13:29 and CD xii:16). Milik reconstructs ג[שאול לולי]ג, "the i[dols of Sheo]l" ("les hu[miliations du Sheo]l" in his French translation).

[d][התורה] Restored with Milik (cf. 1QH[a] xii:10), who notes that the restoration ["God"] ([אל]) is equally possible.

Commentary

Line 1a. The term "Community" (יחד) is a technical use of a word whose basic meaning is "together." A neologism found only in the Qumran sectarian literature, it appears frequently in 1QS, in many of the biblical commentaries (the *pesharim*), and in some other texts. Its use in this liturgical context in 4QBerakhot confirms that this document should be grouped with the other sectarian texts. The phrase "the council of the Community" is also found frequently in the *Community Rule* (1QS) and in 1QpHab xii:4. It usually refers to the sectarian community as a whole, although 1QS viii:1-5 seems to envisage a smaller group within this community. The phrase "in the Community" in this line can also be translated simply "together."

The double amen marks the end of the liturgical unit.

Lines 1-5. With minor variations in wording, this curse is found in 1QM xiii:1-2a, 4-6, where it is delivered by the priests, Levites, and elders. The latter text inserts a blessing on God in lines 2b-3.

Line 1b. Belial (בליעל) is never the name of a demon in the HB; rather, it is a concrete noun meaning "worthlessness" or the like, applied especially to persons in phrases like "a worthless man" ("a man of *beliʿal*") (e.g., 2 Sam 16:7) and "sons of worthlessness (*beliʿal*)" (1 Sam 2:12). Presumably the idea of a demonic figure named Belial arose from a personalized understanding of such terms. The word almost always refers to the chief of the fallen angels in the QL, both sectarian and nonsectarian texts. It appears sometimes in literature outside Qumran in the form Beliar (2 Cor 6:15; *Mart. Isa.* 2:4; 4:2, 4; *Sib. Or.* 3:63, 73; *Vita Proph.* 4:6, 20; 17:2; often in the *Testaments of the Twelve Patriarchs*; *Ques. Bart.* 1:11, 16-17, 18; 4:17, 25, 38, 47). Key Qumran passages for the sectarian theology of the evil angel include 1QS iii:13–iv:1 (although the name Belial is not used); 1QM i:1-17; xiii:11-12; 1QHª xi:28-32.

Lines 2-3. The roots "to curse" and "to denounce" appear together in Num 23:7 and 1QS ii:7; 1QM xiii:4-5; 4Q280 2:2-5.

Line 2. The phrase "they shall answer and say" is a common rubric for introducing a communal recitation. It introduces priestly curses on Belial in 1QS ii:5, 4Q280 2:1-2 (reconstructed); and priestly blessings of God in 1QM xiii:2, xiv:4, xviii:6; and of Israel and God in 11Q14 1ii:3. Note also 11Q19 lxiii:5 and the formula "and they shall bless and they answer and say," used frequently in 4Q503.

The word "animosity" is found in the HB only in Hos 9:7-8. It is used in the QL as an attribute or title of the evil angel (1QS iii:23; CD xvi:5; 1QM xiii:4, 11) and also as a regular noun (e.g., 4Q177 9:5). The "prince of animosity" appears in 4Q225 2i:9; 2ii:13, 14 (alongside Belial in line 14) as well as, perhaps, "the angels of an[imosities]" (2ii:6). The latter phrase also occurs in 4Q387 3iii:4; 4Q390 1:11; 2i:7. In *Jubilees*, Mastema (the transliteration of the Hebrew word "animosity") is the name of the chief of the fallen angels (e.g., 10:7-8).

Line 3. The word translated "service" is translated "attending" in 4Q286 3:2 (see note a to that passage). The phrase "all the spirits of his lot" is also found in 1QS iii:24; 1QM xiii:4, 11-12; 4Q491 14-15:10. The word "lot" (גרול) is a technical term in the sectarian literature, referring to the unchangeable fates of the righteous and the wicked (see, e.g., 1QS iii:13–iv:1; iv:15-26).

Line 4. For angelic and demonic impurity, see the commentary to Songs I 4Q400 1i:14-15. The phrase "lot of darkness" also appears in 1QM i:11, 16; xiii:5. Contrast the "lot of light" in 1QM xiii:9.

Line 5. Those who follow the spirit of iniquity are banished "to an eternal pit" in 1QS iv:12. A double amen marks the end of the liturgical unit.

The term "the wicked one" seems to refer to Belial here rather than to a generalized wicked humanity (see the discussion of Melchiresha in the commentary to 4Q280 2:2, below). The "realm" (singular) of Belial is mentioned in lines 8-9 and elsewhere in the sectarian literature (e.g., 1QS i:18, 23-24; 1QM xiv:94); the phrase "the prince of the realm of wickedness" occurs in 1QM xvii:5-6. For angelic realms in general, see the commentary to Songs II 4Q401 14i:6.

Line 6. A double amen marks the end of the liturgical unit.

Line 7. Both "pit" and "destruction" are used consistently in the HB to refer to the realm of death. According to Rev 9:11, the demonic king of the locust-spirits who ascend from the abyss is "the angel of the abyss, whose name in Hebrew is Abaddon" (the word translated "destruction" here). This word is also used in the QL (e.g., 1QH[a] xi:32; 4Q504 1-2vii:8). Belial is associated with the pit in 1QM xiii:11-12. The pit and Abaddon also appear together in the late Jewish cosmological treatise *Seder Rabba di Bereshit* §27 (*SH-L* §447 // §754), §28 (*SH-L* §448 // §755).

Lines 7-8. The phrase "plots of your nature of guilt" is reminiscent of Gen 6:5 (cf. CD ii:16; 4Q370 1i:3). Belial's "plots" are mentioned in 1QH[a] x:16-17; xii:12-13; 4Q174 1-2i:8 (singular), and his "schemes" in CD v:18-19; 1QH[a] x:16 (cf. 1QH[a] xii:13); and 4Q280 2:6 (of Melchiresha).

Line 10. A double amen marks the end of the liturgical unit. No blank space follows, since the second amen is at the end of the line.

Lines 11-13. Compare 4Q280 2:5-7, which, however, is addressed to the evil angel Melchiresha (evidently the same being as Belial).

4Q286 8

Perhaps a fragment of a hymn

TOP MARGIN

[1][. . .] their [. . .] to the eter[nal] God [. . .] [2][. . .] eternal ...[. . .] [3][. . .] their [. . .]

Commentary

Line 1. The phrase "eternal God" is also found in Gen 21:33; 1QH[a] xv:31; *Merkavah Rabba* §708 (one ms).

4Q286 9

A liturgical fragment

[1][. . .]. [2][. . .]. Amen. Amen.
  [3][. . . and] they [answ]er and say [4][. . .] our [father]s[a]

Note

ªAlternatively, reconstruct this word as "our [iniquit]ies."

Commentary

Line 2. A double amen at the end of the line marks the end of a lost liturgical unit or hymn.

Line 3. Part of a rubric introducing a communal recitation. See the commentary to frag. 7ii:2 above.

4Q286 10

An unidentifiable fragment

¹[. . .]in every .[. . .] ²[. . .].[. . .]

4Q286 11

Perhaps a fragment of a hymn

¹[. . .]. name of glory[. . .] ²[. . .] Your [. . .]..[. . .] ³[. . .]. of ho[liness . . .]

Commentary

Line 1. For this phrase, see the commentary to 4Q286 7i:7.

4Q286 12

See 4Q287 2, with which this fragment overlaps

4Q286 13-14

See the reconstruction of the laws of reproof below (frag. 20)

4Q286 15

A fragment that mentions a widow

¹[. . .]widow ..[. . .] ²[. . .]. ...[. . .] ³[. . .]...[. . .]

Commentary

Line 1. The word "widow" is also used in CD vi:16-17; 4Q269 9:5 // 4Q270 5:19 // 4Q271 3:12; 11Q19 liv:4. The context here is uncertain.

4Q286 16

A fragment of what may have been an eschatological passage

¹[. . .]. .[. . .] ²[. . .]with a visitation of[. . .]

Commentary

Line 2. In the QL the word "visitation" refers to God's decisive intervention in the world, usually at the eschaton (e.g., frag. 7ii:4; 1QS iv:26).

4Q286 17

The half-shekel tax

¹[. . .] ᵃ[the] mina and the tenth of the [mina . . . a half shekel by the shekel of the sanctu]ary. The sons of A[aron]ᵃ ²[. . .]. ᵇthe chiefs of [. . .] shall registerᵇ [. . . for they are in charge of] judgment and of wealth and ..[. . .]

BOTTOM MARGIN

Notes

ᵃ⁻ᵃAll the readings in line 1 are badly damaged.

ᵇ⁻ᵇOr translate as "they shall register [their] heads" (i.e., they shall register them individually, by their names or the like).

Commentary

Lines 1-2. I follow the tentative reconstruction of Nitzan, who associates this fragment (actually two fragments) with Exod 30:11-16; 38:26. These passages prescribe a half-shekel tax on each Israelite in support of the sanctuary when a census is taken, as an atonement to avert plague (cf. 2 Samuel 24). The collection of this tax is mentioned in 2 Chron 24:4-14; Matt 17:24-27; 4Q159 1ii:6-16; 11Q19 xxxix:7-11; the weight of the shekel is also mentioned in 4Q513 1-2i:1-2. According to 2 Chron 24:4-14, the priests and Levites were in charge of collecting and using the tax. Nitzan plausibly suggests that this census may have preceded the mustering ceremony mentioned in 1QS ii:19-23 and CD xiv:3-6 ("4QBerakhotᵃ⁻ᵉ [4Q286-290]: A Covenant Ceremony," 193).

4Q286 18

A fragment that mentions clans

¹[. . .] in the clans of[. . .] ²[. . .]...[. . .]

Commentary

Line 1. Perhaps this fragment is related to 4Q287 5.

4Q286 19

No translatable text survives

4Q286 20 + 4Q288 1 + 4Q286 13-14

A reconstruction of the laws of reproof[a]

[1]. . . [for a man to reprimand his neighbor with truth and with good humility and with a] righteous [purpo]se [2][in the Community of God. And as for him who] errs, when [he] retu[rns to the truth according to] their [commandments,] he shall reprimand him and shall have mercy [3][on him if he was faithl]ess. And no [man] shall hol[d it against his neighbor from day] to [da]y. [He shall] not [4][hate him in his heart, l]e[st he bring sin upon himself. And that which is revealed to the me]n of the Community [5][they shall give him insight into. With] his [k]ind [love] and with a spirit of [humility he shall turn him away from works of] slac[kne]ss. [6][The Inspector over the Many shall in]struct him in all [their customs in order to perfect his actions] [7][from all sin when repri]manding him before wit[nesses. Let no one take revenge for himself in any matter,] [8][for he shall be] fined . . . [And let no one seek vindication] [9][on his own, so as to rebel against the order of his neighbor. Let him not speak to him] in anger and in a jealous [10][spirit of wickedness, so as to weaken the discipline of his associate with . . . and ang]ry wrath and uprising without [11][justice . . .]

Note

[a]Nitzan's reconstruction arranges the fragments as follows: lines 1-5: 4Q286 20:1-5 (20a); lines 2-4: + 4Q286 13:1-3; lines 4-11: + 4Q288 1:1-8; lines 5-8: + 4Q286 14:1-4; lines 9-10: + 4Q286 20:9-10 (20b). For the Hebrew text and the details of the reconstruction, see DJD 11.

Commentary

Lines 1-11. Again I follow Nitzan's tentative reconstruction based on fragments from 4Q286 and 4Q288. If her understanding is correct, this passage describes a sectarian ritual elaboration of Lev 19:17-18. Passages in the sectarian texts that deal with reproof of a member by his associates or the authorities include 1QS v:24–vi:1; vii:8-9, 17-18; ix:17-18; CD vii:2-4; ix:2-8; ix:16–x:3;

xv:12-13; xx:3-13; 4Q477. The last seems to be the record of a series of rebukes delivered in the Community to particular members. Other texts referring to or developing the law of rebuke include Sir 19:13-17; *T. Gad* 6:1-7; Matt 18:15-17, 21-22; Luke 17:3-4; *Did.* 15:3; *Sipra* (a halakic midrash on Leviticus). Sirach advises questioning a friend or neighbor about rumored misdeeds before threatening him over them. Luke also enjoins only a private admonition, as do the *Testament of Gad,* the *Didache,* and *Sipra.* Matthew describes a more formal process that involves in sequence a private rebuke, a rebuke in front of witnesses, and a rebuke by the Church, followed by expulsion if the malefactor refuses to repent. Such a process may be assumed by Paul in 1 Cor 5:1, 13; 6:1-6; 2 Cor 2:5-11, although only rebuke by the Church and potential expulsion are mentioned. The Qumran material also has a more formal process codifying the brotherly private rebuke in a legal proceeding that can result in the calling of witnesses and an official, recorded rebuke by the leader of the group.

Line 2. Nitzan suggests that the word "errs" means to sin unintentionally in contrast to the verb "to be faithless" restored in line 3. The verb "to err" is used with this technical sense in Lev 4:13; Num 15:22; Ezek 45:20; but one can also err or go astray because of deliberate sin (e.g., 1 Sam 26:21; Prov 5:23). Likewise, the verb "to be faithless" can be used of unintentional sin (e.g., Lev 5:15). The subject of the verbs "to reprimand" and "to have mercy on" at the end of this line is presumably the Overseer (see line 6). Other references to having mercy on a rebuked and repentant sinner include Matt 18:21-22; Luke 17:3-4; 2 Cor 2:5-11.

Lines 3-4. Rebukers are admonished not to hold a private grudge in *T. Gad* 6:2-3.

Line 5. The word "him" in this line refers to the erring member, while "his" and "he" probably refer to the Inspector (see line 6).

Line 6. The word "Inspector" (מבקר) is a technical term used of a sectarian official only in the QL, from a root meaning "to seek, inquire after." This official is mentioned in the *Community Rule* (1QS vi:12, 20); the *Damascus Document* (CD ix:18-19, 22; xiii:6, 7, 13, 16, xiv:8, 11, 13; xv:8, 11, 14; 4Q266 5i:14; 7iii:2, 3; 11·16; 4Q267 8:4; 4Q271 3:14); and elsewhere (4Q275 3:3; 4Q513 4:1). This office seems to be the highest in the sectarian hierarchy; the Inspector convenes the meetings of the group, controls its finances, enrolls new members, instructs the priests regarding Torah, teaches the members of the group, mediates disputes, and oversees accusations and rebukes of the members (CD ix:17–x:2). It is plausible but not certain that he should be mentioned in this context.

Line 7. For reprimanding before witnesses compare Matt 18:16. It is a New Testament theme that one should not take revenge for oneself (e.g., Matt

5:38-42), but there the remedy is God's judgment, not a human judicial process.

Line 8. For fines levied on the group members for transgressions, see 1QS vi:24–vii:25 and 4Q266 10ii:1-15.

Lines 9-11. Angry rebukes are discouraged in Sir 19:17; *T. Gad* 6:3, 6.

4Q287 (4QBerakhot[b])

4Q287 1

A *fragment of a hymn that mentions celestial bodies and festivals*

TOP MARGIN

¹[. . .] and luminari[es]ᵃ ²[. . .] their [. . .]. in their constellationsᵇ ³[. . .] their [.
. .]. in all the festivals of ⁴[. . .]all of them. Amen. Amen.
⁵[. . .]. ...[. . .]

Note

ᵃמאורׄׄׄׄׄׄם The reading מאורות (the normal biblical form with the feminine plural ending) is not possible: the lower right-hand corner of the final *mem* is visible on the photograph. For this form of the word "luminaries," see note e to 4Q286 1ii:3.

ᵇThe word "constellations" (מזלות) appears only in 2 Kgs 23:5 in the HB (but cf. the similar word מזרות in Job 38:32). It is also found in 8Q5 1:3. In RH it can mean constellations in general or specifically the signs of the zodiac (Jastrow, 755). Two merkavah hymns (*Hekhalot Rabbati* §105; *SH-L* §320 // §653) mention the constellations in their praise of God as creator. The *Baraita di Mazzalot* (External Tractate on the Constellations) is a treatise in Talmudic Hebrew on the practice of astrology (Wertheimer, *Batei Midrashot*, 2:7-37).

Commentary

Lines 2-3. The heavenly bodies were important for the sect because they marked the appropriate times for the celebration of the festivals. Compare 1QS i:13-15; x:1-11; 1QHᵃ xx:4-11; *1 Enoch* 72–82; *Jub.* 4:17; 6:32-38.

Lines 4-5. The double amen at the end of the line ends a hymn. Presumably a new hymn or liturgical unit began in line 5, but only part of a few letters toward the end of this line survive.

4Q287 2 (+ 4Q286 12:1-3a)

*A hymn that describes the heavenly temple
and its angelic attendants*

TOP MARGIN

¹[. . .] their [. . .] and [. . .]. their lavers[a][. . .] ²[. . .] their .[. . . struc]tures of their adornment [. . .] ³[. . . walls of the vestib]ules of glory, their doors of wonder [. . .] ⁴[. . .] their [. . .]. angels of fire and spirits of cloud .[. . .] ⁵[. . .]..[b] colorful spirits of the holy of hol[ies . . .] ⁶[. . .]...[. . .]. and firmaments of holiness [. . .] ⁷[. . . holy of] holies in all festival[s of . . .] ⁸[. . .] the name of the glory of Yo[ur] godhood[c] [. . .] ⁹[. . . th]eir [. . .] and all the attendants of h[oliness . . .] ¹⁰[. . .]in the integrity of th[eir] works [. . .] ¹¹[. . .]. in the palaces of [Your] ki[ngdom and ....].. ¹²[. . .]all [Your] attendant[s in the ornamentation of] their adornment, angels of ¹³[. . .] Your holiness in the dwell[ing of . . . a]ngels of Your righteousness

BOTTOM MARGIN

(4Q286 12:3b-4) [d]in . . . ⁴. . . [mo]st hol[y ones][d] . . .

Notes

[a]כיור The consonantal text of this word is not in doubt, but it could represent two different words depending on how it is vocalized. If vocalized כִּיּוֹר, it should be translated "laver," but if vocalized כִּיּוּר, it should be translated "panel work, tablature." See the commentary for details.

[b]Reconstruct the word before "colorful" as either הר[וז], "radiance of" (supported by Nitzan) or הר[וט], "purity of" (cf. Songs XI 4Q405 19:4-5; XII 4Q405 20ii:21-22:11; XIII 11Q17 ix:7).

[c]The word "godhood" (אֱלוֹהוּת) is also found in Songs I 4Q400 1i:2; VII 4Q403 1i:33; and RH (Jastrow, 67a), but not in BH.

[d-d]4Q286 12:3b-4 may overlap with the beginning of 4Q207 3, below.

Commentary

Line 1. There are two possible understandings of the word translated "laver," depending on how the consonants of the word are vocalized (see note a). The laver was a large washbasin used by priests for ablutions before offering sacrifices. According to the HB, a bronze laver stood with its bronze base between the tent of meeting and the altar (Exod 30:17-21), and ten bronze lavers stood with their bronze bases in Solomon's temple, five on the north side and five on the south (1 Kgs 7:30, 38-39, 43). The lavers in this passage may be part of the paraphernalia of the heavenly temple, and if so, they imply that sacrifices were carried out there (cf. the commentary to Songs XII 4Q405 23i:5-6 and XIII 11Q17 ix:3-4). The laver and the "house of the laver" in the earthly temple of the *Temple Scroll* are described in 11Q19 xxxi:10-xxxiii:15; the laver is mentioned again in xxxv:8 (cf. 11Q21 1:2 // 11Q19 iii:14-15). However, there is a nonbiblical word with the same consonantal spelling that means "panel work, tablature," and that is used of the temple architecture in the *Temple Scroll* (11Q19 vi:5; xxvi:10) and in RH (Jastrow, 631b). Either word could be the one meant in this line.

Line 3. The doors to the inner chamber and the nave of the earthly temple are described in 1 Kgs 6:31-35 and 7:50 (cf. Ezek 41:21-25; Mal 1:10; 2 Chron 3:7; 4:9, 22; 28:24; 29:3, 7, which mention these doors as well as doors to the vestibule). The Aramaic *New Jerusalem* text mentions "the doors that are in front of the temple" in 11Q18 19:1. The *Temple Scroll* (11Q19) mentions a number of doors in the temple complex. The gates of the seventh celestial palace are called "doors" in *3 Enoch* 48C:4 (*SH-L* §72); *Hekhalot Rabbati* §§244, 247. Presumably the doors mentioned in this line also belong to the heavenly temple.

Line 4. The text echoes Ps 104:3-4. For more on the word "angels," see the commentary to Songs VI 4Q403 1i:1. "Angels of fire" are mentioned in *SH-L* §785 // §805; §972.

Line 5. The term "colorful" also appears in celestial contexts in the *Songs of the Sabbath Sacrifice* (see the notes and commentary to Songs V 4Q402 2 + 3i:7). Colorful spirits are probably mentioned in Songs XI 4Q405 19:5 (cf. the phrase in the singular in Songs VII 4Q403 1ii:1). An alternative translation is "colorful most ho[ly] spirits."

Line 6. Multiple firmaments are also found in Songs XII 11Q17 viii:2; XII 4Q405 23i:6-7; XIII 11Q17 x:5, 8.

Line 9. Angels are called "attendants" in the HB, the QL, and the HL. For details, see the commentary to Songs I 4Q400 1i:4. The phrase "attendants of holiness" is also found in the HL in G4 1a:12.

Line 11. Celestial palaces also appear in Songs I 4Q400 1i:13 (see the commentary to this line); XIII 11Q17 x:8; and often in the HL.

Line 13. For the term "dwelling," see the commentary to Songs II 4Q400 2:5.

4Q287 3

A fragment of a hymn that celebrates God's creation

TOP MARGIN

¹[. . .] their ...ᵃ and they shall bless Your holy name with blessings [. . .]ᵇ ²[and] all creatures of flesh [shall ble]ss You, all of them that [You] created [. . .] ³[. . . c]attle and fowl and creeping things and fi[sh of the s]eas and all ..[. . .] ⁴[. . .]ᶜ[Y]ou create all of them, renewingᶜ[. . .] ⁵[. . .].[. . .]

Notes

ᵃPerhaps 4Q286 12:3b-4 overlaps with line 1. Nitzan restores בנור[אותמה], "[with] their [fear]some acts," at the beginning of the line (assuming an overlap with 4Q286 12:3b).

ᵇPerhaps read "with blessings [of the most holy ones]" if the text of 4Q286 12:4 overlaps with the end of this line.

ᶜ⁻ᶜCompare line 4 to the phrase "(You are He who) renews Your creatures each and every day" (מחדש בריותיך ברל יום ויום) in a merkavah hymn (*Hekhalot Rabbati* §269).

Commentary

Line 3. The text echoes Gen 1:24-26 and 9:2.

Line 4. Nitzan takes this to be a reference to living creatures born after the Flood (cf. Gen 8:17), but there is no tradition in the Bible of God creating the animals anew. Rather, this line probably echoes Ps 104:30, which describes God's ongoing creation of life and renewal of the earth.

4Q287 4

The end of one liturgical unit and the beginning of another

¹[. . .] year by year ...ᵃ[. . .] ²[. . .] their [stiff] neck, and You make humanity rule[. . .] ³[. . .]Amen. Amen. BLANK [. . .]
    ⁴[. . .].. in all ..[. . .]

Note

ᵃNitzan reads "in order" after "year by year," which is possible but uncertain. The word "order" (סרך) can also be a technical term meaning a written "rule" or "constitution" of the sect.

Commentary

Line 1. In the HB the phrase "year by year" is used of annual contracts (Lev 25:53), annual rituals or festivals (Deut 15:20; 1 Sam 1:7; Zech 14:16; Neh 10:35, 36), and annual supplies, taxes, or tribute (1 Kgs 5:25; 10:25; 2 Kgs 17:4; 2 Chron 9:24; 24:5). It is used in a liturgical context in 1QS ii:19 (cf. *Jub.* 6:17) and of the annual examination of the sect's members in 1QS v:24.

Line 2. For God assigning humanity rule over the other creatures, see Gen 1:28; for this wording compare Ps 8:7; Sir 17:2; 4Q381 1:7; 4Q504 8:6.

Line 3. The double amen ends a hymn. Presumably a new hymn or liturgical unit began in line 4.

4Q287 5

The end of one liturgical unit and the beginning of another.
Both seem to pertain to Israel and the nations

⁷[. . .]..[. . .] ⁸[. . .]... nations to .[. . .] ⁹[. . .]their clans ..[. . .] ¹⁰[. . .] in the truth of Your righteousness, when[. . .]ᵃ is lifted [up . . .] ¹¹[. . .] Your [. . .] in the Commu[nity], all of them. Amen. A[men . . .]

¹²[. . .] ones approa[chin]g You and se[ed . . .] ¹³[. . .]clans of the land to be[. . .]

BOTTOM MARGIN

Note

ᵃPerhaps restore "[Your kingdom]" with Nitzan (cf. 4Q286 7i:5 and Num 24:7).

Commentary

Lines 11-12. The double amen ends a song. Presumably the rest of line 11 was blank and line 12 began a new song or liturgical unit.

4Q287 6

See 4Q286 7ii, with which this fragment overlaps

4Q287 7

A fragment of a cosmological passage?

TOP MARGIN

[1][. . .]their dark regions[a] [. . .] [2b][. . .]. [. . .].[b]

Notes

[a]According to a merkavah hymn (*Hekhalot Rabbati* §256 // §265 // §418), God is

רואה במעמקים
צופה במסתרים
מביט במחשכים

the one who sees into the depths,
who gazes at the secret things,
who looks into the dark regions.

[b-b]Nitzan reads the traces in this line as "[Ame]n. [Ame]n," followed by a blank space, indicating the end of a unit.

Commentary

Line 1. In the IIB the "dark regions" are where the wicked plot (Isa 29:15; Ps 74:20) as well as their eternal abode (Ps 88:7, 19). They can also be the abode of all the dead (Ps 143:3; Lam 3:6). God delivers the righteous from this darkness when he comes in the storm (Isa 42:16). These regions are the place of eternal damnation in 1QS iv:13 and 4Q491 8-10i:15; they seem to be mentioned in 4Q525 21:1 in the context of a rebuke to the wicked.

4Q287 8

A fragment describing wickedness

[1][. . .]. .[. . .]..[. . .] [2][. . . of gu]ilt and eyes of prostitution and work of [. . .]

BOTTOM MARGIN

Commentary

Line 2. The phrase "eyes of prostitution" is not found in the HB, but it does occur in the QL in the phrases "a heart of guilt and eyes of prostitution to do everything evil" (1QS i:5-6) and "a nature of guilt and eyes of prostitution" (CD ii:16).

4Q287 9

A fragment that mentions God's precepts

[1][. . .]...[. . .] [2][. . .]. the precepts of Yo[ur] righteousness [. . .]

BOTTOM MARGIN

4Q287 10

A fragment that mentions "anointed ones"

[1][. . .].[. . .] [2][. . .]. against the anointed ones[a] of [His] hol[y] spirit [. . .]

BOTTOM MARGIN

Note

[a]משיחי One could also take the final letter as a singular suffix, translating "on My anointed one," or reading משיחו, "His anointed one." The phrase could be a reference to the placing of the holy spirit "upon" (על, rather than "against") the anointed one or ones (cf. CD ii:12?), but this interpretation is more difficult to fit into the context of the surviving fragments of the *Berakhot*.

Commentary

Line 2. This phrase occurs in 4Q270 2ii:14 in a list of sinners who will be judged by God, including those who speak (?) "apostasy against the anointed ones of His holy spirit." The word "anointed" usually refers to the king of Israel in the HB (e.g., 1 Sam 24:7, 11; Ps 2:2; 89:39, 52; 132:17), although it can also refer to the high priest (e.g., Lev 4:3, 5, 16; cf. 4Q374 1:9; 4Q376 1i:1) or a non-Israelite king (Isa 45:1). The closest biblical parallel to this line is Ps 105:15 // 1 Chron 16:22, where the word seems to apply to both the patriarchs and prophets. Prophets are called "anointed ones" in CD ii:12; v:21–vi:1; 1QM xi:7-8.

Individual anointed ones or messiahs are mentioned in the QL, so it is not impossible that the word should be taken as singular here. The speaker in a hymn in 4Q381 15:17 calls himself "Your anointed one." The messiahs of Aaron and Israel (1QS ix:11; CD xii:23-xiii:1; xiv:19; xix:10-11; xx:1; cf. 1QSa ii:11-21) figure in the sectarian theology, albeit in a way that is not entirely clear: evidently both an anointed priest and an anointed king of the line of David are expected in the sect's eschatology. The latter may also be alluded to in 1QSb v:20-23; 4QpIsa^a 8-10; 4Q174 1-2i:7-13; 4Q252 v:3-4; 4Q285 5:1-5; 4Q382 16:2; 4Q521 2ii + 4:1 9:3. Since exegesis of Isaiah 11 figures frequently in those texts, it may be that this fragment refers to the resting of the holy spirit on the Davidic messiah (cf. Isa 11:2). For a detailed discussion of the messianic figures in the QL, see Collins, *The Scepter and the Star*, chaps. 3-4.

4Q288 (1QBerakhot^c)

4Q288 1

See the reconstruction of the laws of reproof, above under 4Q286 20

4Q288 2

A fragment that may refer to repentance or banishment

TOP MARGIN

^1[...]^a with his neighbors [...] ^2[...] when he turns back [...] ^3[...]....[...]

Note

[a]Perhaps reconstruct with Nitzan "[a man] with his neighbors," a common phrase in the QL (1QS v:25; vi:2; viii:20; ix:19; CD viii:6; xvi:15; cf. Mal 3:16; Ps 12:3).

Commentary

Line 2. This line may refer to the repentance of a sectarian (cf., e.g., 1QS v:13-14; 4Q286 13:1), the banishment of a member from the group (1QS vii:1-2), or a return in a more general sense (1QM iv:8, 13).

4Q288 3

A fragment referring to the "poor" and to knowledge

[1][. . .]poor ones of [. . .] [2][. . .]knowledge ..[. . .] [3][. . .].[. . .]

Commentary

Line 1. The word "poor" is a common self-designation of the sectarians, appearing either alone (e.g., 1QH[a] x:32; 1QpHab xii:3, 6; 4Q171 1-2ii:9) or modifying another word as here (e.g., 1QM xi:9; 1QH[a] xiii:22).

4Q289 (4QBerakhot[d])

4Q289 1a-b

Fragment of a liturgy of cursing and blessing[a]

The end of a liturgy of curses

[1][. . . a cou]nsel of wickedness [. . .] their [se]rvice in ..[. . .] [2][. . . eve]rlasting curses, [humilia]tions of annihilation[. . .] [3][. . .] for the truth of God and to bless His name and ..[. . .]

A liturgy of blessing led by a priest

⁴[. . .]then the priest [app]ointed at the head of [the many]ᵇ shall ... [. . .] ⁵[. . .]holiness in the midst of all [. . .] ⁶[. . .].. before Him [and they answer and say,] Blessed beᶜ [. . .] ⁷[. . .]all [. . .].[. . .]

Notes
ᵃFragment 1a does not appear in a photograph in Nitzan's edition (DJD 11), but it can be found in PAM 42.419.
ᵇFor this restoration, see 1QS vi:14; 4Q267 9v:11.
ᶜThe phrase "blessed be" normally begins a benediction that blesses God.

Commentary

Line 2. The phrase "everlasting curses" also appears in 4Q525 15:4; 5Q16 1:3. Compare the "eternal curses" in 1QS ii:17.

Line 3. A reference to a blessing to be recited after the curses in lines 1-2.

Line 4. Apparently the introduction of a new liturgical unit presided over by a priest and recited by the congregation. The words of the blessing begin in line 6.

4Q289 2

A fragment of a hymn praising the creative activity of God

¹[. . .] You created .[. . .] ²[. . .]. all of them ...[. . .] ³[. . .]... «and» enter[ing . . .] ⁴[. . .]... Amen. Ame[n . . .]
⁵[. . .].[. . .]

Commentary

Line 4. The double amen marks the end of a liturgical unit. Presumably the end of line 4 was blank and a new unit began in line 5.

4Q289 3

A fragment mentioning angels

¹[. . .]. all ...[. . .] ²[. . . a]ngels of .[. . .]

4Q290 (4QBerakhotᵉ)

4Q290 1

*A liturgical fragment that probably refers
to the destruction of the wicked*

¹[. . .] Amen. [. . .]
    ². . . all ...[. . .] were terminated [. . .] ³[. . .].[. . .] wrath and since [. . .]
BOTTOM MARGIN

Commentary

Line 1. Presumably the end of a liturgical unit marked with (a double?) amen.

Line 2. For this use of the verb "to be sound, whole, complete" with this meaning, see note b to 4Q286 7ii:6.

4Q280 (4QBerakhotᶠ?)

*See the introduction to this chapter for a discussion
of the relationship of 4Q280 to 4Q286-90*

4Q280 1

Perhaps a fragment cursing the wicked or Melchiresha

¹[. . .]..ᵃ [. . .] ²[. . .]. to make clingᵇ[. . .] ³.[. . .]has becomeᶜ [. . .]

Notes

ªGiven the surviving letters of this line, perhaps we should restore "[and when he hears t]h[e words of this covenant]" (cf. 1QS ii:12-13).

ᵇלהדביק Milik reads להבדיק here, but this appears to be a typographical error. Perhaps restore "to make cling [to him all the imprecations of this covenant]" (cf. 1QS ii:15-16; CD i:17).

ᶜPerhaps the subject of the verb is something like "His spirit" (cf. 1QS ii:14). The photograph of this line is unreadable.

Commentary

Lines 1-3. Milik plausibly suggests that the content of this passage corresponds approximately to 1QS ii:13-16, in which case this fragment probably came just before frag. 2, since the latter begins with parallels to 1QS ii:16-17.

Line 2. Compare CD i:17 and the sense of Deut 28:60.

4Q280 2

A fragment cursing Melchiresha and his minions

The end of a unit of cursing

¹[... And God will single him out] for evil from among the sons of l[ight, since he turned back from following God.

A communal curse on Melchiresha

ªAnd they answer] ²[and say,ª

Cur]sed are you, Melchiresha,ᵇ in all the pl[ots of your nature of guilt. May] God [set you] ³to quaking by the hand of those who take vengeance. May God not be gracious to y[ou] [when] you call. [May He lift up His angry face] ⁴to you for denunciation and may there be no peace for you in the mouth of all who make interce[ssion.

A curse on Melchiresha and his followers

Cursed are you] ⁵with no survivor and denounced are you without escape, and cursed are those who d[o their plots of wickedness] ⁶and who establish your schemes in their heart to scheme against the covenant of God ᶜ[and to reject the Torah and] ⁷[the word]s ofᶜ all [His] fait[hful] visionaries [and a]ll who refuse to enter [the covenant of God so as to walk in the stubbornness of]

BOTTOM MARGIN?

Notes

ᵃ⁻ᵃRestoring with Kobelski on the basis of 1QS ii:5. Milik restores "[and again they say]" on the basis of 1QS ii:11.

ᵇMelchiresha (מלכי רשע), literally, "my king is wickedness," is the chief of the evil angels who corresponds to Melchizedek, chief of the good angels. For Melchizedek, see the "Excursus on the Melchizedek Tradition" at the end of the chapter on the *Songs of the Sabbath Sacrifice*. The name Melchiresha is clearly a formation analogous to Melchizedek (מלכי צדק), "my king is righteousness," but it is unattested outside the QL. A similar name, Melchira (מלכי רע, "my king is evil"?), is found in *Mart. Isa.* 1:8 (Sammael Malkira) and in the Coptic *Book of the Resurrection of Jesus Christ by Bartholomew the Apostle*. In the HL the evil angel Sammael, prince of Rome, is called "Sammael the wicked" (סמאל הרשע) (*3 Enoch* 14:2 [*SH-L* §17] and 26:12 [*SH-L* §42] in some manuscripts; *Hekhalot Rabbati* §§108, 109).

ᶜ⁻ᶜRestoring with Kobelski (cf. 1QpHab v:11-12; 4QpIsaᵇ ii:7-8; 4Q266 7iii:5; 4Q286 7ii:12). Other reconstructions of the first phrase are possible, for example, "[to speak rebellion against the Torah]" or "[to despise the Torah]" (Nitzan, DJD 11: 30, on 4Q286 7ii:12).

Commentary

Lines 1-7. This passage is closely related to 1QS col. ii, and the parallels are often helpful for filling in damaged spots.

Line 1. The imprecation in the *Community Rule* targets "all the men of the lot of Belial" (1QS ii:4-5), but it is directed at Melchiresha in 4Q280. Kobelski plausibly suggests that the writer of 4Q280 has taken over this set of curses on the followers of Belial and applied them to the arch-demon Melchiresha, sometimes with incongruous results (see below). The first clause of this line echoes Deut 29:20, which warns that God's curses will fall on the apostate Israelite. The phrase "sons of light" is a common self-designation for members of the sect (e.g., 1QS iii:13, 24-25; 1QM i:1; 4Q177 10-11:7; 4Q266 1:1; 4Q510 1:7).

Lines 1-2. For the phrase "and they answer and say" see the commentary to 4Q286 7ii:2 above.

Line 2. Melchiresha appears to be another name for Belial or the Angel of Darkness, titles used elsewhere in the QL. The only other place Melchiresha is

80

attested is in the damaged text 4Q544 (4QAmram^b) 2:3, where he may have been explicitly identified with Belial. In any case, the identification of Melchiresha with Belial is reasonably secure simply on the basis of a comparison of this passage to the parallel texts in 4Q286 7ii:7-8 (cf. lines 2, 6) and 1QS ii:4-6.

Line 3. Kobelski suggests that "those who take vengeance" are the angels on the side of the sons of light (cf. 1QS iv:12; 11Q13 ii:13; *1 Enoch* 62:11; *T. Levi* 3:2-3), which makes sense given that Melchiresha is the object of vengeance in this passage. However, human beings can also be the agents of God's vengeance (1QM iii:6-8; iv:12; vii:5; xv:6), and such agency may not be excluded, especially in view of the parallel curse directed against human beings in 1QS ii:4-6.

Lines 3-4. These lines seem to allow for the possibility of Melchiresha's repentance, an unusual idea for the QL and for Jewish and Christian thought in general (but cf. Songs I 4Q400 1i:16; XII 4Q405 23i:12). Kobelski is probably right in arguing that the phrases that imply that God might be gracious to him or that someone might intercede for him are taken thoughtlessly from 1QS ii:8-9, which applies to human beings.

Line 4. The phrase "who make intercession" (also in 1QS ii:9; cf. 4Q369 2:1), literally "those who hold on to the fathers," is derived from an Akkadian phrase whose idiomatic meaning is clear. See Milik, "Milkî-ṣedeq et Milkî-reša'," 129 and n. 47; Kobelski, 41 n. 4.

Line 5. The words "survivor" (or "remnant") and "escape" are also found together in the HB (Gen 45:7; 2 Kgs 19:31 // Isa 37:32; Isa 15:9; Ezra 9:14; 1 Chron 4:43) and elsewhere in the QL (1QS iv:14; CD ii:6-7; 1QM i:6; 4Q374 2ii:4). Compare Isaac's curse on the Philistines in *Jub.* 24:30.

Line 6. The phrase translated "covenant of God" does not occur in the HB (although similar phrases with the same translation are found in 1 Sam 4:4; 2 Sam 15:24; Ps 78:10; 1 Chron 16:6; 2 Chron 34:32), but it is common in the QL (e.g., 1QS v:8; x:10; CD iii:11; vii:5; 1QpHab ii:4; 4Q491 11ii:18; 5Q13 28:3).

Line 7. Kobelski is no doubt right to take "[His] fait[hful] visionaries" to be the prophets, since the term "visionary" is a synonym for "prophet" in the HB (e.g., 2 Sam 24:11; 2 Kgs 17:13); this phrase also seems to have this meaning in CD ii:12-13 (cf. the commentary to 4Q287 10:2).

The word "stubbornness" always appears in the HB in the phrase "stubbornness of heart" (e.g., Deut 29:18), usually after a form of the phrase "to walk in," as here, or "to walk after." Various grammatical forms of the phrases "stubbornness of heart" and "to walk in stubbornness of heart" are found in the QL.

4Q280 3

A fragment that mentions a paradigmatic sin[a]

¹[. . .]..[. . .].[. . .]ᵇ ²[. . . those who] move the boun[dary marker . . .]

BOTTOM MARGIN

Notes

ᵃBaumgarten includes this fragment without comment in DJD 18 (173, plate xxxvii) as frag. 1 of 4Q271, a manuscript of the *Damascus Document,* even though it is grouped with 4Q280 in the photograph PAM 43.327 and Milik mentions a third fragment of 4Q280 ("Milkî-ṣedeq et Milkî-rešaʿ," 129). Either identification seems possible. The handwriting of the two manuscripts is very similar, and both preserve bottom margins of a column. Baumgarten takes this fragment to be parallel to CD v:20, but the phrase could fit equally well in 4Q280 (note that it also appears in a cursing liturgy in Deut 27:17). One argument against including the fragment in 4Q271 is that nothing else survives in this manuscript from this early in the *Damascus Document,* and we would have to assume that a number of intervening columns have been destroyed entirely. Still, this is hardly impossible, and we must leave both possibilities open until new information — perhaps genetic analysis — determines in which manuscript the fragment belongs.

ᵇBaumgarten reads [יהו]חֹ[א] אֹ̊ת[ו], "[and] [his] [br]oth[er]," to correspond with CD v:18-19, but the letters are so badly damaged that the text cannot be restored with any certainty.

Commentary

Line 2. Moving a boundary marker is a particularly serious sin in the HB (Deut 19:14; 27:17; Hos 5:10; Job 24:2; Prov 22:28; 23:10). The *Damascus Document* charges with this sin, apparently metaphorically, those who strayed from the true teachings of the sect (CD i:15-16; v:20; xix:15-16; 4Q266 11:12-13). Presumably this fragment also comes from a context describing the transgressions of those who reject the sect's teachings.

Songs of the Sabbath Sacrifice

(4Q400-407, 11Q17, Mas1K)

INTRODUCTION

The belief that the human world is a microcosm of the heavenly or ideal realm is best known from Platonist philosophy and its intellectual progeny, but the idea is far more ancient than Plato. For example, the Mesopotamian creation myth (the *Enuma Elish*) treats the earthly temple of the god Marduk as a copy of his heavenly palace.[1] In the Bible, the earthly sanctuary is pictured as a shadow of the archetypal heavenly sanctuary (Exod 25:9; 26:30; Heb 8:5), and this idea continues in postbiblical literature.[2]

The *Songs of the Sabbath Sacrifice* is one of the most extended and striking examples from the Second Temple period of the theme of the archetypal temple. Purporting to describe the Sabbath worship and sacrifices carried out by the angelic priests in the heavenly temple, this work preserves motifs and

---

1. *Enuma Elish* v 119-30 (*ANET* 503).

2. Postbiblical references to the idea of the heavenly sanctuary as archetype of the earthly temple include *1 Enoch* 14–15 and *2 Apoc. Bar.* 4:5-6; 59:4. Plato's theory of a heavenly archetype behind the physical world is developed in his dialogue *Timaeus* and is picked up and harmonized with biblical traditions some centuries later by the Jewish philosopher Philo of Alexandria, especially in *De Opificio Mundi*. The traditional Christian hierarchy of angelic beings arrayed around God's throne was given its canonical shape in the fifth or sixth century CE in the *Celestial Hierarchy*, a Neoplatonist work by an unknown author generally known as Pseudo-Dionysius today.

terminology known from the later book of Revelation in the New Testament and the still later Jewish mystical literature.

I. Contents

This document consists of thirteen songs, one for each of the Sabbaths in the first quarter of the year. The first song describes the heavenly angelic priesthood. The second, which is badly damaged, compares the human priesthood unfavorably to the angelic one. Although almost completely destroyed, Songs III-V seem to have dealt with an eschatological conflict in heaven. Song VI, describing the praises and blessings recited by the seven chief angelic princes, is mirrored by Song VIII, which relates the analogous praises and blessings of the seven secondary princes. The actual songs of the angels are not given. Song VII, sandwiched between them in a climactic position, invokes the praise of angels and the animate furnishings of the celestial temple. Songs IX to XI are also poorly preserved but appear to take us through the vestibules and entryways of the temple, and past the living divinities carved there, to rivers of fire. The curtain isolating the holy of holies is visible, apparently embroidered with living beings who add their praise to that of the others. We reach the nave of the temple, whose floor of wondrous plates is carved with more living spirits, and at last the innermost sanctuary and throne room can be seen. Song XII, another climactic passage, covers this scene in detail: in the vicinity of the throne-chariot we encounter cherubim, ophannim, and other angels offering praise, and various gods and divinities going out on divine missions and returning. Song XIII describes the high-priestly apparel of the chief angels who administer the celestial sacrifices.

Given the poetic nature and fragmentary condition of the *Songs of the Sabbath Sacrifice*, extracting a coherent cosmology from it is difficult, although such a cosmology was doubtless in the minds of the composers. A possible reconstruction is that seven firmaments are envisioned, each of which has its own sanctuary containing its own inner chamber (holy of holies) and administered by its own high-priestly chief prince and secondary prince. Multiple chariots and thrones are mentioned as well (e.g., XI 4Q405 20ii-21-22:2-5; XIII 11Q17 x:7), so perhaps each sanctuary has one of these, presumably ridden or occupied by its chief prince.

The final inner chamber, the central throne room inhabited by God himself, is the subject of the first parts of Songs VII and XII. In this room we find the structure of the throne-chariot located above the firmament of the cherubim. It may be that the heavenly sacrificial cult is carried out in the tabernacle of the exalted chief (VII 4Q403 1ii:10), perhaps the angelic priest and warrior angel Melchizedek, who sits on a seat like the throne of God's kingdom (XI 4Q405 20ii-21-22:2).

II. The Manuscripts

Eight manuscripts of the *Songs of the Sabbath Sacrifice* have been recovered in the Qumran library, seven from Cave IV and one from Cave XI. In addition, another copy was excavated in the remains of the rebel encampment on Masada.

- The seven fragments of 4Q400 are written in a formal script dated to the late Hasmonean period (ca. 75-50 BCE) and preserve most of the first column of the work and parts of the next three columns (Songs I and II).
- 4Q401 survives in thirty-eight fragments written in a formal to semiformal early Herodian hand (ca. 25 BCE). Most or all of these small pieces appear to belong to the first six songs.
- Twelve fragments of 4Q402 survive in a formal script with some semiformal influence that is roughly contemporary with the script of 4Q401 but not identical to it. The few identifiable fragments come from Song V and possibly Song IV.
- 4Q403 survives in three fragments in an early Herodian formal script. The first and largest of these preserves one column and part of another containing text from Songs VI to VIII. The second and third fragments probably come from the second column.
- 4Q404 preserves twenty-five small fragments, some of which are assignable to Songs VI to VIII, in a formal late Hasmonean to early Herodian script.
- 4Q405 is the best-preserved copy, written in a late Hasmonean formal script heavily influenced by the semiformal tradition and containing approximately one hundred five fragments, twenty-three of which are substantial. Identifiable text comes from Songs VI to XIII in roughly thirteen columns.
- The script of the five small fragments of 4Q406 cannot be identified, although it appears that the manuscript wrote divine names in paleo-Hebrew letters. It is likely that these fragments come from the end of Songs V and VI.
- The two small fragments of 4Q407 seem to be written in a late Hasmonean formal script with semiformal influence. The content is sim-

ilar to that of the *Songs of the Sabbath Sacrifice,* but the fragments cannot be assigned with certainty to the work, let alone to a particular place in it.

- The manuscript from Cave XI, 11Q17, has been newly reconstructed by the editors of DJD 23. Written in a formal Herodian script influenced by the round semiformal hand from roughly the turn of the era, it preserves forty-two fragments, twenty-five of which can be reconstructed into the remains of ten successive columns containing material from Songs VII to XIII.
- The manuscript from Masada, Mas1k, which survives in a single fragment written in a late Herodian formal hand of about the middle of the first century CE, preserves material from Songs V and VI.

There is a great deal of overlap among these manuscripts, and this fact, combined with the techniques developed by Hartmut Stegemann, allows us to reconstruct the content and order of most of the work with a good deal of confidence.[3] Allowing some reasonable assumptions, Carol Newsom estimates that 4Q405 contained a total of twenty to twenty-one columns of twenty-five lines each.[4] If we estimate thirteen or fourteen words to the average line, it seems that the entire work was about seven thousand words long, give or take several hundred words.

I translate an eclectic reconstructed text that incorporates all the manuscripts. Where these overlap, the best preserved is treated as a base text, and the readings of the other manuscript or manuscripts are indicated by underlining, italics, or dotted underlining. The header of the fragment shows how each manuscript is indicated in the text.

III. Genre, Structure, and Prosody

Although we do have indications that songs were recited during the Sabbath sacrifices, few examples survive. The heading of Psalm 92 ties it to the Sabbath, as does that of Psalm 38 (LXX 37) in the Greek translation. Yet nothing in these psalms is especially reminiscent of the *Songs of the Sabbath Sacrifice.* Indeed, despite its title, the latter work contains descriptions of the angelic worship services for each Sabbath, but the actual songs sung by the angels are never given.

---

3. Newsom, "He Has Established for Himself Priests," 101-2; Stegemann, "Methods for the Reconstruction of Scrolls."
4. DJD 11: 311.

Sabbath songs also survive in 4Q504, the "Words of the Luminaries," frags. 1-2 col. vii recto and vii verso, and possibly in 4Q503, "Daily Prayers," in the prayer for the twenty-fifth day of the month (frags. 37-38:2-11) and in frags. 24-25 and 40-41. Angelic praise figures in most of these, as in the *Songs of the Sabbath Sacrifice*.

Not all the openings of the thirteen songs survive, but they probably shared the same structure, with only minor variations: a heading "For the Sage" (למשכיל), followed by an indication of the date in the form "The song of the holocaust offering of the *x*th Sabbath on the *y*th day of the *z*th month." A call to worship follows, always beginning with "Psalm the God of . . ." The bodies of the songs vary considerably in content, although all of them share a focus on the worship and cult of the angelic priesthood in the celestial temple. There is a closing benediction at the end of Song VI (4Q403 1i:28-29), the only song whose ending is preserved.

The number seven is used frequently as a structuring element. Newsom has pointed out that the overall structure of the document points toward the seventh song as a climax: coming in the middle of the work, its description of the heavenly sanctuary is sandwiched between accounts of the praises of the seven chief angelic princes in Song VI and those of the seven secondary princes in Song VIII.[5] However, C. R. A. Morray-Jones has argued that this is "no more than a preliminary crescendo," and that the true climax of the work is Song XII, which, describing the scene in the celestial throne room, would have been recited the day after the Festival of Weeks when the Qumran sectaries celebrated their annual covenant renewal ceremony (see the next section).[6]

The overall genre of the work remains elusive, but it does share a number of features with apocalypses containing otherworldly journeys (e.g., *1 Enoch 1–36*). Like some of these, it carries the reader on a revelatory journey through the heavenly realm.[7] The differences, however, are striking. There is no angelic interpreter guiding a human intermediary. (The figure of the Sage recurs in the *Songs of the Sabbath Sacrifice*, but his role is unclear.) We simply travel through the heavenly realm from week to week and learn its secrets without the explicit revelatory framework central to the genre apocalypse.

Even the very basic problem of whether these songs are prose or poetry

---

5. Newsom, *Critical Edition*, 16-17; "He Has Established for Himself Priests," 102-3, 107-10.

6. Morray-Jones, "The Temple Within," 417-20.

7. The genre "apocalypse," whose basic structure involves heavenly revelations to a human visionary, is surveyed in detail in Collins, *Apocalypse*. For this type of apocalypse, see Collins's "Introduction," p. 15.

does not have a clear answer.[8] This is partly because the text is often too broken to allow us to work out the details of the poetic structure, and reconstruction holds the danger of creating poetry out of damaged prose. There are some passages that show good parallelism typical of Second Temple Hebrew poetry such as the *Hôdāyôt*. As an example, we may lay out XII 4Q405 23i:6b-11a in poetic couplets as follows:

> Divinit[ie]s psalm Him when they [be]gin to stand,
> and all the s[pirits of] the firma[men]ts of [7]purity rejoice in His glory,
> and a voice of blessing from all its districts is recounting
>   the firmaments of His glory,
> and His gates are psalming [8]with a voice of chanting.
> At the entrances of the gods of knowledge in portals of glory
> and at all exits of angels of holiness to their realm,
> [9]the portals of His entrance and the gates of exit proclaim the glory
>   of the King,
> blessing and psalming all spirits of [10]divinities in exiting and
>   in entering by gat[e]s of holiness.
> And there is none among them who oversteps a law,
> nor against the words of [11]the King do they set themselves at all.

Other passages are highly structured, but not according to traditional poetic canons. For example, the praises and blessings of the chief princes in Song VI and of the secondary princes in Song VIII follow set forms that correspond to a large degree between the two songs. Still others (e.g., XI 4Q405 19:3-8; XIII 4Q405 23ii:7-12) have less structure but still are not simple prose.

IV. Life Situation

The surviving headings of the songs tie them unambiguously to the holocaust offerings made on each Sabbath during the first quarter of the year. Although the Sabbath holocaust offering is described in Num 28:9-10 and Ezek 46:4-5, neither passage indicates that singing accompanied the offering. However, 2 Chron 29:27-28 reports that the levitical singers did perform during Heze-

---

8. This problem is discussed in more detail by Segert in "Observations on Poetic Structures." Kittel provides an analysis of the poetics of the *Hôdāyôt* in *The Hymns of Qumran*.

kiah's holocaust offering for rededication of the temple, and it is reasonable to assume that similar performances accompanied the Sabbath holocaust offerings. According to 11QPsᵃ xxvii:5-9, David composed fifty-two songs for the Sabbath offerings. It is possible that the thirteen songs in the work we call the *Songs of the Sabbath Sacrifice* were understood to be included among them, but this work covers only the first quarter of the year, with no trace of songs for the other thirty-nine Sabbaths. Any interpretation of it must explain its limited scope.

It is debatable whether the *Songs of the Sabbath Sacrifice* was written by the same group or groups who composed the other sectarian works in the Qumran library. Certainly the work does display notable similarities to these texts. It follows the same solar calendar; the sectarian community (יחד) may be mentioned in V 4Q402 4:5 (although the context is broken and the meaning of the relevant word is ambiguous); the term "Sage" (משכיל) is a sectarian title of office, but it is also used in the more general sense of "wise person" in the Hebrew Bible (e.g., Dan 11:33-35). Other words and phrases that seem to belong to the technical vocabulary of the Qumran sectarians include "lot" (גורל); "turners from transgression" (שבי פשע); "those sound of way" (תמימי דרך); and "set period" (תעודה). There are also numerous parallels with the description of the heavenly realm in the sectarian *Berakhot*.

Nonetheless, we simply do not know how widespread the use of the solar calendar was in this period; it was also advocated by the book of *Jubilees* and the Enochic Astronomical Book (*1 Enoch* 72–82). Nor do we know how much of the terminology of the sectarian literature was part of contemporary Jewish religious jargon. The parallels with the *Berakhot* are general and show no more than a shared interest in speculation about celestial matters. The sectarian texts tend to avoid certain divine titles such as *Elohim*, a word meaning "God" that is used freely in the *Songs of the Sabbath Sacrifice*. However, the same word also appears in the *Songs of the Sage* (4Q510-511), a sectarian collection of exorcism hymns that shows a vital interest in angels and the heavenly realm, so it may be that the term *Elohim* was acceptable in texts with an incantatory function. Finally, the discovery of a fragmentary copy of the *Songs of the Sabbath Sacrifice* at Masada makes problematic (although not impossible) the claim that it was an esoteric sectarian composition.[9]

Whether or not the *Songs of the Sabbath Sacrifice* was composed by the Qumran sectarians, they did keep many copies of it and presumably used it in their liturgy. Given the hostility of the sectarians to the contemporary priestly

---

9. Newsom has at different times argued for and against this view. See *Critical Edition*, 59-72, 81-83, and "'Sectually Explicit' Literature," 179-85.

power complex in Jerusalem, their liturgical use of these songs may have served as a validation of their self-identification as a spiritual temple. By identifying themselves with the cult of the heavenly temple they could exalt their own rank above the priesthood of the mere earthly temple in Jerusalem.

We are still faced with the problem of the curiously truncated scope of the *Songs of the Sabbath Sacrifice,* but recent research has made progress in explaining why it covers only the first quarter of the year. David Halperin has demonstrated that by the time of the translation of Ezekiel into Greek (in the third or second century BCE) the exegesis of the first chapter of this book had been tied to Ps 68:17-20, thus connecting Ezekiel's vision of the divine chariot to the revelation at Sinai. He has also shown that by the third century CE, these two passages figured in the liturgy of the Festival of Weeks, which celebrated the giving of the Torah at Sinai.[10] Newsom in turn notes that both scriptural texts have influenced Songs XI and XII, which would have been recited on either side of the Festival of Weeks, the festival that marked the sect's annual covenant renewal ceremony.[11] Thus, it is reasonable to deduce that the eleventh and twelfth songs marked the climax of the work in association with the covenant renewal, while the thirteenth functioned as a kind of coda or denouement that described the heavenly cult of the high-priestly angels.

V. Literary Context

The composers of the *Songs of the Sabbath Sacrifice* were obviously immersed in the Hebrew Scriptures. Although the work does not quote the Hebrew Bible directly, many details and some of the structuring elements come from biblical texts. The book of Ezekiel exerts the strongest influence, especially chapters 1 and 10 (the visions of the living creatures and cherubim) and 40–48 (the tour of the ideal temple). The description of Solomon's temple in 1 Kings 6–7 probably inspired aspects of the architecture of the celestial temple. The angelology of the work, the descriptions of the contents and denizens of the heavenly throne room, and the liturgical terminology also draw on Numbers 1–2, 10; Isa 63:9-14; Ps 24:7-10; 68:17-20; 104:1-4; and 1 Chronicles 28–29.[12]

---

10. Halperin, "Merkabah Midrash"; *Faces of the Chariot,* esp. chaps. 4 and 8.

11. Newsom, "Merkabah Exegesis," 29. See also Morray-Jones, "The Temple Within," 417-20; Fletcher-Louis, "Heavenly Ascent," esp. 382-99; and the introduction to the *Berakhot* in this volume.

12. I do not exclude the very real possibility that the composers had access to

Two sectarian texts from Qumran have strong thematic parallels with the *Songs of the Sabbath Sacrifice*. The *Songs of the Sage* (4Q510-511) is a collection of hymns of exorcism that prefigure elements of later Jewish magic and theurgy. The *Berakhot* (4Q286-290, 280?) is a liturgy for the covenant renewal ceremony during the Festival of Weeks. Both works share with the *Songs of the Sabbath Sacrifice* its interest in the heavenly temple and its angelic attendants, frequently making use of some of the same scriptural passages mentioned in the previous paragraph. It is difficult to establish dependence in any direction among these three works, and they may draw independently on a fund of already existing esoteric traditions.

Outside the Qumran library, the book of Revelation shares many themes and ideas with the *Songs of the Sabbath Sacrifice*. There is a similar emphasis on the scene around God's throne (chaps. 4–5) and the heavenly temple and its angelic attendants, including a tradition about an eschatological war in heaven between the warrior angel and the forces of evil (12:7-9). The descriptions of the heavenly realm also incorporate numerous "merkavah hymns" (see the introduction to the *Berakhot*). As with the *Songs of the Sabbath Sacrifice*, the number seven permeates the book of Revelation as a structuring element: the seven golden lampstands represent the seven churches, and the seven stars the seven spirits of the churches through whom Christ sends his messages; Christ the Lamb has seven eyes and opens the seven seals; seven angels blow the seven trumpets and later pour out the seven bowls of the wrath of God, and so on. Revelation too quotes no scripture directly, although much of its content consists of a tissue of biblical allusions, including some of the same passages from Ezekiel. John's vision is explicitly set "on the Lord's day" (2:10), the Christian analogue to the Sabbath (cf. *Barn.* 15:1-9).

There are also significant differences. Revelation is a Christian work whose hero is Jesus, the Christ who will return at the last judgment. In form it is an apocalypse with cosmic and political eschatology that lacks a historical review or otherworldly journey. Its view of the heavenly realm is also informed by Isa 6:1-3, a passage that is never alluded to directly in the *Songs of the Sabbath Sacrifice*, the *Songs of the Sage*, or the *Berakhot*.

The Christian Gnostic corpus from late antiquity also has connections with the cosmology of the *Songs of the Sabbath Sacrifice*. According to the Gnostics, the true God dwells in the highest heaven in unapproachable light,

---

nonbiblical royal, sapiential, and apocalyptic traditions about the celestial temple that no longer survive. As noted above, the idea that the earthly sanctuary is a shadow of the archetypal heavenly sanctuary is a very ancient one; see Barker, *The Gate of Heaven*, for a discussion of traditions concerning the temple in Jerusalem and its heavenly archetype.

but one of this God's emanations — Sophia, goddess of wisdom — generated her own offspring, a botched abortion named Yaldabaoth, Sammael, or Saklas. This offspring is the demiurge, the biblical god of Genesis 1–3 who created the imperfect physical world. One of his children is Sabaoth, a repentant god who is enthroned in the seventh heaven upon a four-faced chariot called cherubim. Evidently Sabaoth is a version of the biblical God YHWH Sabaoth, the Lord of Hosts (יהוה צבאות). Gnostic mythology clearly draws on Jewish esoteric traditions like those found in the *Songs of the Sabbath Sacrifice,* although the content has been radically reinterpreted.[13] The Melchizedek tractate found in the Coptic Gnostic library from Nag Hammadi (NHC IX, 1), although it may not be a Gnostic work, depicts Jesus Christ as the warrior angel Melchizedek, who defeats the evil archontic powers in an eschatological war in heaven. The same figure also appears elsewhere in Gnostic myth (see "Excursus on the Melchizedek Tradition" at the end of this chapter).

Finally, the Hebrew and Aramaic corpus of mystical revelatory traditions known as the Hekhalot literature also has numerous parallels to the *Songs of the Sabbath Sacrifice.* Adequate analysis of these parallels would require a monograph; this commentary collects many of them, but space allows little discussion of their implications. Nevertheless, some generalizations can be made. The Hekhalot texts build on an exegesis of many of the same biblical passages as does the *Songs of the Sabbath Sacrifice,* but like Revelation, they include Isa 6:1-3 as an integral element. They describe the heavenly temple and throne room and their denizens in great detail and often in ways similar to the *Songs of the Sabbath Sacrifice,* sharing with it many technical terms. They both use seven as a structuring element; for example, the Hekhalot texts refer to seven concentric celestial palaces that are sometimes arrayed in seven layered firmaments. Some of the shared exegesis has a cultic life situation in the synagogue sermons for the Festival of Weeks, and echoes of this origin surface occasionally.

But again, there are many differences, both substantial and trivial, between them. In the Hekhalot texts, the four living creatures of Ezekiel 1 are taken to be separate beings from the cherubim of Ezekiel 10. The living creatures are not mentioned at all in the *Songs of the Sabbath Sacrifice,* and their attributes seem to be assimilated to the cherubim. The exegesis of Isa 6:1-3 in the Hekhalot documents has already been mentioned. Some eschatological material survives in Songs III-V, but there is little elsewhere in the work. Eschatology

---

13. The material summarized here can be found in the *Hypostasis of the Archons* and *On the Origins of the World,* two Coptic Gnostic treatises from Nag Hammadi. For additional details, see the commentary to the *Songs of the Sabbath Sacrifice,* below, and De Conick, "Heavenly Temple Traditions and Valentinian Worship."

is still more muted in the Hekhalot texts: the primary interest is in the eternal verities of the celestial world, and the angelic high priest Metatron (or the Youth) plays no eschatological role. The cultic context most often presented in the Hekhalot material is a set of rituals that an individual mystic can use to experience the ascent (or "descent") to God's chariot in the seventh celestial palace. The *Songs of the Sabbath Sacrifice* contains no such instructions and presents the tour of the heavenly realm without making clear how it is being experienced. The vision of God's gigantic and magnificent enthroned body is described in great detail in the *Shiʿur Qomah* texts (a subgroup of the Hekhalot corpus), whereas in Songs XII and XIII there is a strange reticence in the material about the figure presumably sitting in the great throne-chariot, almost as if its light has caused the writer to turn his eyes away so that all he can see is the reflected glimmer of the glory on the angelic armor around the throne. Lastly, the Hekhalot literature is filled with incantations and nonsense words and often makes clear its quest for raw magical power. Although the hypnotic rhythms of the *Songs of the Sabbath Sacrifice* may imply a certain incantatory power, these trappings of magic and theurgy are entirely missing in them.

BIBLIOGRAPHY

I. Editions and Translations

Charlesworth, James H., Carol A. Newsom, et al. *The Dead Sea Scrolls: Hebrew, Aramaic, and Greek Texts with English Translations*, vol. 4B, *Angelic Liturgy: Songs of the Sabbath Sacrifice*. Tübingen: Mohr Siebeck; Louisville: Westminster John Knox, 1999. (Became available to me only when this volume was at the proof stage.)

García Martínez, Florentino, et al. "11QShirot ʿOlat ha-Shabbat." In *Qumran Cave 11.II, 11Q2-18, 11Q20-31*, 259-304, plates xxx-xxxiv, liii. DJD 23. Oxford: Clarendon, 1998.

Newsom, Carol. *Songs of the Sabbath Sacrifice: A Critical Edition*. Atlanta: Scholars Press, 1985.

———. "Shirot ʿOlat Hashabbat." In *Qumran Cave 4. VI, Poetical and Liturgical Texts, Part I*, edited by Esther Eshel et al., 173-401, plates xvi-xxxi. DJD 11. Oxford: Clarendon, 1998.

Strugnell, J. "The Angelic Liturgy at Qumrân — 4Q Serek Širôt ʿOlat Haššabbāt." In *Congress Volume: Oxford 1959*, 318-45. VTSup 7. Leiden: Brill, 1960.

II. Studies

Baumgarten, Joseph M. "The Qumran Sabbath Shirot and Rabbinic Merkabah Traditions." *RevQ* 13/49-52 (1988) 199-213.

Davila, James R. "The Dead Sea Scrolls and Merkavah Mysticism." In *The Dead Sea Scrolls in Their Historical Context,* edited by Timothy H. Lim et al., 249-64. Edinburgh: T&T Clark, 2000.

Fletcher-Louis, Crispin H. T. "Heavenly Ascent or Incarnational Presence? A Revisionist Reading of the *Songs of the Sabbath Sacrifice.*" *SBLSP* 37. Vol. 1, 367-99. Atlanta: Scholars Press, 1998.

Franzman, M. "The Use of the Terms 'King' and 'Kingdom' in a Selection of Gnostic Writings in Comparison with the Songs of the Sabbath Sacrifice." *Muséon* 104 (1991) 221-34.

Morray-Jones, C. R. A. "The Temple Within: The Embodied Divine Image and Its Worship in the Dead Sea Scrolls and Other Early Jewish and Christian Sources." *SBLSP* 37. Vol. 1, 400-431. Atlanta: Scholars Press, 1998.

Newsom, Carol A. "Merkabah Exegesis in the Qumran Sabbath Shirot." *JJS* 38 (1987) 11-30.

————. "'He Has Established for Himself Priests': Human and Angelic Priesthood in the Qumran Sabbath Shirot." In *Archaeology and History in the Dead Sea Scrolls,* edited by Lawrence H. Schiffman, 101-20. JSPSS 8. Sheffield: Sheffield Academic Press, 1990.

Puech, Emile. "Notes sur le manuscrit des Cantiques du Sacrifice du Sabbat trouvé à Masada." *RevQ* 12/48 (1987) 575-83.

Qimron, Elisha. "A Review Article of *Songs of the Sabbath Sacrifices: A Critical Edition,* by Carol Newsom." *HTR* 79 (1986) 349-71.

Schiffman, L. "*Merkavah* Speculation at Qumran: The 4Q*Serekh Shirot 'Olat ha-Shabbat.*" In *Mystics, Philosophers, and Politicians: Essays in Jewish Intellectual History in Honor of Alexander Altmann,* edited by J. Reinharz et al., 15-47. Durham, N.C.: Duke University Press, 1982.

Segert, Stanislav. "Observations on Poetic Structures in the Songs of the Sabbath Sacrifice." *RevQ* 13/49-52 (1988) 215-23.

Smith, Mark S. "Biblical and Canaanite Notes to the *Songs of the Sabbath Sacrifice* from Qumran." *RevQ* 12/48 (1987) 581-88.

Tigchelaar, Eibert J. C. "Reconstructing 11Q17 *Shirot 'Olat Ha-Shabbat.*" In *The Provo International Conference on the Dead Sea Scrolls: Technological Innovations, New Texts, and Reformulated Issues,* edited by Donald W. Parry and Eugene Ulrich, 171-85. STDJ 30. Leiden: Brill, 1999.

III. The Figure of Melchizedek

Davila, James R. "Melchizedek, Michael, and War in Heaven." *SBLSP* 35, 259-72. Atlanta: Scholars Press, 1996.

————. "Melchizedek: King, Priest, and God." In *The Seductiveness of Jewish Myth:*

Challenge or Response? edited by S. Daniel Breslauer, 217-34. Albany: State University of New York Press, 1997.

Fitzmyer, Joseph A. "'Now This Melchizedek . . .' (Heb 7:1)." In *Essays on the Semitic Background of the New Testament*, 221-43. SBLSBS 5. N.p.: Scholars Press, 1974.

Horton, Fred L., Jr. *The Melchizedek Tradition: A Critical Examination of the Sources to the Fifth Century A.D. and in the Epistle to the Hebrews*. SNTSMS 30. Cambridge: Cambridge University Press, 1976.

Kobelski, Paul J. *Melchizedek and Melchireša'*. CBQMS 10. Washington, D.C.: Catholic Biblical Association of America, 1981.

Milik, J. T. "4Q Visions de 'Amram et un citation d'Origène." *RB* 79 (1972) 77-97.

Pearson, Birger A. "The Figure of Melchizedek in Gnostic Literature." In *Gnosticism, Judaism, and Egyptian Christianity*, 108-23. Studies in Antiquity and Christianity 5. Minneapolis: Fortress, 1990.

Pearson, Birger A., et al. "IX, 1: Melchizedek." In *Nag Hammadi Codices IX and X*, 19-85. NHS 15. Leiden: Brill, 1981.

Pearson, Birger A., and Søren Giverson. "Melchizedek (IX, 1)." In *The Nag Hammadi Library in English*, 3rd ed., edited by James M. Robinson, 438-44. New York: Harper & Row, 1988.

Puech, Émile. "Notes sur le manuscrit de 11QMelchîsédeq." *RevQ* 12/48 (1987) 483-513.

Robinson, S. E. "The Apocryphal Story of Melchizedek." *JSJ* 18 (1987) 26-39.

Schmidt, Carl, and Violet Macdermot, eds. *Pistis Sophia*, 68-75, 383-93, 573-83, 645-53, 665-73, 703-705. NHS 9. Leiden: Brill, 1978.

——— . *The Books of Jeu and the Untitled Text in the Bruce Codex*, 142-49. NHS 13. Leiden: Brill, 1978.

Van Der Woude, A. S. "Melchisedek als himmlische Erlösergestalt in den neugefundenen eschatologischen Midraschim aus Qumran Höhle XI." *Oudtestamentische Studiën* 14 (1965) 354-73.

IV. Related Studies and Texts

Barker, Margaret. *The Gate of Heaven: The History and Symbolism of the Temple in Jerusalem*. London: SPCK, 1991.

Collins, John J., ed. *Apocalypse: The Morphology of a Genre*. *Semeia* 14 (1979).

——— . *Daniel*. Hermeneia. Minneapolis: Fortress, 1993.

Dan, Joseph. "Anaphiel, Metatron, and the Creator" (in Hebrew). *Tarbiz* 52 (1982-83) 447-57.

Davidson, Maxwell J. *Angels at Qumran: A Comparative Study of 1 Enoch 1–36, 72–108 and Sectarian Writings from Qumran*. JSPSup 11. Sheffield: JSOT, 1992.

Davila, James R. "Heavenly Ascents in the Dead Sea Scrolls." In *The Dead Sea Scrolls after Fifty Years: A Comprehensive Assessment,* edited by Peter W. Flint and James C. VanderKam, 2:461-85. Leiden: Brill, 1999.

De Conick, April D. "Heavenly Temple Traditions and Valentinian Worship: A Case for First-Century Christology in the Second Century." In *The Jewish Roots of Christological Monotheism,* edited by James R. Davila et al., 308-41. Leiden: Brill, 1999.

Dimant, D., and J. Strugnell. "The Merkabah Vision in *Second Ezekiel (4Q385 4)."* *RevQ* 14/55 (1990) 331-48.

Eshel, Esther. *"4Q471B:* A Self-Glorification Hymn." *RevQ* 17/65-68 (1996) 175-203.

Falk, Daniel. *Daily, Sabbath, and Festival Prayers in the Dead Sea Scrolls.* STDJ 27. Leiden: Brill, 1998.

Glessmer, Uwe. "Calendars in the Qumran Scrolls." In *The Dead Sea Scrolls after Fifty Years: A Comprehensive Assessment,* edited by Peter W. Flint and James C. VanderKam, 2:213-78. Leiden: Brill, 1999.

Halperin, David J. "Merkabah Midrash in the Septuagint." *JBL* 101 (1982) 351-63.

———. *The Faces of the Chariot: Early Jewish Responses to Ezekiel's Vision.* Tübingen: Mohr Siebeck, 1988.

Kittel, Bonnie. *The Hymns of Qumran.* SBLDS 50. N.p.: Society of Biblical Literature, 1981.

Lee, Desmond. *Plato: Timaeus and Critias.* Rev. ed. New York and London: Penguin, 1977.

Levey, Samson H. "The Targum to Ezekiel." *HUCA* 46 (1975) 139-58.

Luibheid, Colm, et al. *Pseudo-Dionysius: The Complete Works.* Mahwah, N.J.: Paulist, 1987.

Naveh, Joseph, and Shaul Shaked. *Amulets and Magic Bowls: Aramaic Incantations of Late Antiquity.* Jerusalem: Magnes, 1987.

Newman, Carey C. *Paul's Glory-Christology: Tradition and Rhetoric.* NovTSup 69. Leiden: Brill, 1992.

Newsom, Carol A. "'Sectually Explicit' Literature from Qumran." In *The Hebrew Bible and Its Interpreters,* edited by William Henry Propp et al., 167-87. Winona Lake, Ind.: Eisenbrauns, 1990.

Nitzan, Bilhah. *Qumran Prayer and Religious Poetry.* STDJ 12. Leiden: Brill, 1994.

Robinson, James M., ed. *The Nag Hammadi Library in English.* 3rd ed. New York: Harper & Row, 1988.

Schiffman, L. *"Sifrut Ha-Hekhalot ve-Kitve Qumran"* ("The Hekhalot Literature and the Qumran Writings"). *Meḥqere Yerushalaym Be-Maḥshevet Yisra'el* 6 (1987) 121-38.

Scholem, Gershom G. *Jewish Gnosticism, Merkabah Mysticism, and Talmudic Tradition.* 2nd ed. New York: Jewish Theological Seminary of America, 1965.

Segal, Alan. *Two Powers in Heaven: Early Rabbinic Reports about Christianity and Gnosticism.* Leiden: Brill, 1977.

Stegemann, Hartmut. "Methods for the Reconstruction of Scrolls from Scattered Fragments." In *Archaeology and History in the Dead Sea Scrolls,* edited by Lawrence H. Schiffman, 189-220. JSPSup 8; JSOT/ASOR Monograph Series 2. Sheffield: JSOT, 1990.

SONGS OF THE SABBATH SACRIFICE

(4Q400-407, 11Q17, Mas1k)

Song I

(4Q400 1 [+ 4Q401 15], 3i + 5, 3ii:1-7, 4i)

*Calls the holy divinities to psalm God and describes the angelic
priests who serve in the celestial temple and who intercede
for those who repent. Bits of description of the angels'
praises are preserved as well.*

4Q400 1i:1-21 | 4Q401 15

Title, opening call to praise, and description of the angelic priests

TOP MARGIN

[1a][For the Sage. The song of the holocaust offering of][a] the first [Sabba]th on the fourth of the first month. Psalm [2][the God of . . .]. O divinities of all the most holy ones, and in His godhood [3][. . .] most holy ones among the holy ones of eternity. And they have become to Him priests of [4][. . .] attendants of the Presence in the inner chamber of His glory, in the assembly belonging to all the gods of [5][. . .]divinities. He engraved His laws for all spiritual works and judgments of [6][. . .]knowledge, a people of understanding, glorified[b] by God. For those who draw near to knowledge [7][. . .]eternal [. . .] and from the source of holiness to the [most] holy sanctuaries [8][. . .]priests of the interior,[c] attendants

of the Presence of the King of the [most] holy ones [9][. . .] His glory and law upon law they confirm[d] to the seven [10][. . . H]e founded them [for] Himself, for the [most] ho[ly ones . . . in the ho]ly of holies [11][. . .]they became great[e] among them according to the council of[. . .]... from knowledge of [12][. . .] holy of holies, pri[ests . . . th]ey are officers of [13][. . . sta]tioned in the palaces of the King [. . .] [f]in their border and in their territory[f] [14][. . .]... they do not endure any who are perv[erted] of way and there is nothing impure in their holy (places) [15][and] He engraved for them [laws of ho]liness; by them all the eternal holy ones are sanctified. And He purifies the pure ones of [16][. . .]for all who are perverted of way. [g]And they propitiate His favor[g] on behalf of all who repent of transgression. BLANK [17][. . .] knowledge among the priests of the interior and from their mouths are teachings of all holy ones with judgments of [18][. . .]..[. . .] His [acts of ki]ndness for eternally merciful acts of forgiveness. But with His zealous vengeance [19][. . .]... He established for Himself priests of the interior, most holy ones [20][. . .].[. . .] gods, priests of [h]exalted heights[h] who a[ppr]oach [21][. . .]...[. . . p]raises of

BOTTOM MARGIN

Notes

[a-a][למשכיל שיר עולת] This heading is restored on the basis of the beginnings of Songs II, IV, VI-VIII, and XII.

[b]כבוד With Qimron I take כבודי as an (otherwise unattested) passive participle ("Review Article," 358-59). This is a linguistically difficult solution, but if the phrase is taken as "a people of His glorious understanding" (reading כבודו), the word "God" does not fit well syntactically with the rest of the line.

[c]קרוב This word is the Qumran equivalent of a BH noun (קֶרֶב) (cf. *HDSS* 200.26; 11Q13 1ii:10) and is used here with the technical meaning of the holy of holies in the heavenly temple (cf. Ps 48:10). It appears frequently in the *Songs of the Sabbath Sacrifice*, usually in the phrase "priests of the interior." This meaning is made explicit in IX 4Q405 14-15i:4: "the interior of the holy of holies." This interpretation of the word may be inspired by Exod 23:20-23, in which God tells the Israelites that he is sending his angel before them and that they should obey this angel, "for My name is in his midst" (כי שמי בקרבו). The composers of the *Songs of the Sabbath Sacrifice* may have taken this phrase to mean "for My name is in his (the angel's) interior (sanctuary)" and taken the angel in question to be Melchizedek or the "exalted chief," whose tabernacle seems to be mentioned in Song VII. For discussion of the passages mentioning Melchizedek and the exalted chief, see note e-e to VII 4Q403 ii:10; the commentary to VIII 4Q403 1ii:21; and "Excursus on the Melchizedek Tradition" at the end of this chapter.

[d]I take the word "they confirm" (יגברו) as a Piel imperfect. An alternate translation would be "they strengthen, sustain" (cf. Zech 10:6, 12; Eccles 10:10; 1QSb v:28; RH [Jastrow, 208b]). The Hiphil has the meaning "to confirm" in Dan 9:27.

רבו One could also read "they have [dra]wn near" (ק]רבו[) with Florentino García Martínez, *The Dead Sea Scrolls Translated: The Qumran Texts in English* (Leiden: Brill, 1994), 419.

f-f בגבולם ובנחלתם This phrase is difficult, since angels are not normally associated with borders or territories. Qimron suggests that it echoes the original text of Deut. 32:8 (cf. 4QDeutʲ xii:13-14 and the LXX), which says that God gave the nations their territory (using the same verbal root, √נחל) and established the borders (גבולת) of the peoples according to the number of the sons of God, that is, the angels ("Review Article," 359). In other words, the various angels are each assigned a human territory to look after, and presumably these are the borders and territories mentioned in this line. There is also a reference to the "inheritance" or "territory" of Melchizedek in 11Q13 ii:5. Seven most holy borders are mentioned in VIII 4Q403 1ii:27; 4Q405 44:1; and seven wondrous territories in VIII 4Q403 1ii:21, but these are more difficult to connect with Deut 32:8.

g-g ויכפרו רצונו An unusual expression, since the verb normally means "to atone," not "to seek atonement." But the similar expressions "atonements of favor" כפורי רצון) and "atonement[s of] Yo[ur] favor" ([ה]רצונכ]י [כפור]י) occur in 4Q513 13:2 and 4Q512 4-6:6, respectively.

h-h מרומי רום A common term for the heavenly realm in the *Songs of the Sabbath Sacrifice*. The closest analogue in the HL is "heights of height" (מרומי מרום) in G8 1a:11.

Commentary

Line 1. According to Gen 1:14-19, the sun and moon were created on the fourth day of the first week (a Wednesday). In Jewish tradition this marks the beginning of calendrical reckoning (which can be based on the movements of the sun or the moon), so in the solar calendar used in the *Songs of the Sabbath Sacrifice,* the first Sabbath of the first month is on the fourth day of the month.

The heading "For the Sage" is evidently comparable to the various headings in the book of Psalms, and like many of them its meaning is not entirely clear. Indeed this very heading appears in Pss 32, 42, 44, 45, 52–55, 74, 78, 88, 89, 142 (cf. Ps 47:8), but meaning a type of psalm rather than the title of an office. The word translated "Sage" appears in the HB nineteen times. The most interesting passages for our purposes are (1) Dan 1:4; 11:33, 35; 12:3, 10, which apply the term to Daniel and his friends as well as to sages who will suffer persecution and martyrdom during the Maccabean revolt, but who will be resurrected in glory at the eschaton (cf. *1 Enoch* 100:6; 104:12); and (2) 2 Chron 30:22, which applies the term to the levitical singers in the time of King Hezekiah. In the QL the word can be used as a general term meaning "one who is insightful" or "one who gives insight" (1QM x:10), but usually it is a title for an office in the sectarian community. The heading "For the Sage" occurs at the beginning of a number of songs and prose units in the QL (e.g., 1QS iii:13; 1QHᵃ v:1; 4Q511 2i:1). The grammar of the heading permits it to indicate authorship ("by the Sage") or reference ("pertaining to the Sage"). This heading seems to have begun all thirteen of the *Songs of the Sabbath Sacrifice,* and I take the word Sage to be a title, perhaps of the same office as in the undoubtedly sectarian texts.

The holocaust offering was a sacrifice in which the carcass of an animal was completely consumed on the altar. The Sabbath holocaust offering is described in Num 28:9-10 and Ezek 46:4-5. In 2 Chron 29:27-28 (cf. Josephus *Ant.* 20 §§216-18), songs sung by the Levites during the holocaust sacrifice are mentioned, but their content is not given.

Line 2. The word translated God *(Elohim)* can also be taken as a plural noun due to a peculiarity of Hebrew morphology in which one type of singular abstract noun has the same ending as the masculine plural noun. In the HB this word usually refers to the one true God, but it can also be applied to pagan deities (e.g., Exod 20:3; Josh 24:20, 23) and perhaps to angels (e.g., Ps 97:7; 138:1). The QL tends to avoid this word, although the *Songs of the Sage* (4Q510 and 4Q511) uses it freely, as does the *Songs of the Sabbath Sacrifice.* In both the word can refer either to God (e.g., 4Q510 1:2, 8; 4Q511 2ii:6; I 4Q400 1i:6), in which case I have translated it "God," or to angels (e.g., 4Q511 8:12; Songs I 4Q400 1i:2), in which case I have translated it "divinities." When the context is ambiguous I have noted this in the commentary.

The title "holy ones" is used mostly of angels or divinities in the HB (e.g., Deut 33:3; Ps 89:6, 8; Job 5:1; Zech 14:5; Dan 4:14). The only clear exception is Ps 34:10, in which the holy ones seem to be human. The term is used of angels in, for example, *1 Enoch* 1:9 (cf. Jude 14); 14:23; 61:8; 106:19; *T. Job* 33:2; *Jub.* 31:14; *Pss. Sol.* 17:49; and frequently in the QL (e.g., 1QS xi:7-8; 1QM x:12; 1QHᵃ xi:22; 4Q510 1:2; 11Q13 ii:9; and often in the *Songs of the Sabbath Sacrifice*), although it is applied to human beings in Tob 8:15; *1 Enoch* 48:7, and often in early Christian literature (e.g., Acts 9:13; Rom 8:27; 1 Tim 5:10; Heb 6:10; *1 Clem.* 46:2; *Ign. Smyrn.* 1:2). In the *Songs of the Sabbath Sacrifice* the main reference seems to be to angels, although the inclusion of the proleptically glorified human worshipers may be implied as well.

Line 3. The ancient Jewish philosopher Philo of Alexandria describes the heavens as the holy of holies of the true temple of God, having "for priests, the subordinate ministers of His power, namely, the angels" *(Spec. Leg.* i:66). For Michael as the heavenly high priest, see the commentary to XII 4Q405 23i:5-6.

Line 4. The phrase "attendants of the Presence" is also found in I 4Q400 1i:8, and the term "His Presence" in X 4Q405 15ii-16:4; XI 11Q17 vii:2. Compare 2 Sam 1:18 and Esther 1:10. In the HB the word "attendant" is usually used in a cultic sense of priests and Levites, although it refers to angels in Ps 104:4. It is used of deified humans in the eschatological temple in 4Q511 35:4. Angels are frequently called "attendants" in the HL, although the phrase "attendants of the Presence" does not occur.

The term "Presence" (literally "Face") as a divine title is more typical of the later literature, but it has biblical roots (Exod 33:14-15; Ps 21:10; Lam 4:16). The phrase "the angel of His Presence" in Isa 63:9 is doubtless the inspiration for the idea of a class of ministering angels of the Presence (many terms and ideas in Isa 63:9-14 are picked up in the *Songs of the Sabbath Sacrifice*). In the QL "the Presence of God" is mentioned in 4Q511 73:2; the eschatological high priest is likened to the angel of the Presence in 1QSb iv:24-25; and the angel or angels of the Presence appear in 1QH^a xiv:13; 1QSb iv:26; 3Q7 5:3. The phrase also appears in singular or plural in nonbiblical texts (e.g., *Jub.* 1:27, 29; *T. Judah* 25:2; *T. Levi* 3:5-7). The divine title "the Presence" is common in the HL: the normal title of Metatron in *3 Enoch* is "Metatron, the angel prince of the Presence," and one document gives directions for invoking the "prince/officer of the Presence" (*Sar Panim* §§623 39).

The "inner chamber" is the central room or holy of holies in Solomon's temple (e.g., 1 Kgs 6:5-31; 7:49, 8:6, 8; Ps 28:2; 2 Chron 3:16). The *Songs of the Sabbath Sacrifice* frequently uses this term in the singular, but sometimes also mentions multiple inner chambers (seven, if the reconstruction in VII 4Q405 7:7 is correct). It may be that each of the seven chief princes (in Song VI), along with his corresponding secondary prince (Song VII), serves in his own inner chamber. Compare the phrase "in the assembly belonging to all the gods" to "in the assembly of God" in Ps 82:1; 11Q13 ii:10; 4Q427 7i:14 and "the assembly of the gods" in 1QM i:10; 1Q22 iv:1; 4Q491^c 1:5.

The Hebrew word translated "gods" is normally used in the singular in the QL for God. It is the generic Semitic term for a god and is used in the Ugaritic texts as the name of the high god, *El.* It is the standard word for God in the QL, far more common than *Elohim.* In the HB it can be applied to God (e.g., Gen 49:25; Exod 15:2; Mal 2:10) and to pagan gods (Exod 15:11; 34:14; Ps 81:10; Mal 2:11) and perhaps angels (Ps 29:1). In the QL the plural refers to angels (e.g., 1QM i:10; 1QH^a xviii:8; 4Q511 10:11; and often in the *Songs of the Sabbath Sacrifice*). In this commentary I translate the singular form as "God" (thus not distinguishing it from *Elohim*) and the plural as "gods."

Line 5. In BH the verb "to engrave" occurs only once, in Exod 32:16, of the engraving of the Ten Commandments on the stone tablets by God. In the QL the root always refers to inscribed writing (e.g., 1QS x:6, 8, 11; 1QH^a ix:24;

1QM xii:3; 4Q511 63-64ii:3). Compare the idea of the heavenly tablets in *1 Enoch* 81:1-2; 93:1-3; 106:19; *Jub.* 3:8-14.

Line 6. The context of this line is lost, which makes its interpretation difficult. The phrase "a people of understanding" echoes Isa 27:11 ("it is a people lacking understanding"). The latter phrase is applied to the sect's opponents in CD v:16 and 1QHᵃ x:19, so it is reasonable to take it to refer to human beings in the present passage as well, especially since there is no clear case of the word "people" being applied to angels in Second Temple literature (or the HL). However, it does not follow that most of the beings encountered in the *Songs of the Sabbath Sacrifice* are really members of the sectarian community who have assigned themselves a divine or angelic identity, as has been argued by Crispin Fletcher-Louis ("Heavenly Ascent"). Although he maintains that some of the terms in the *Songs of the Sabbath Sacrifice* refer elsewhere only to human beings, many of these terms are unambiguously applied to angels in the HL, and the comments about the lowly human priesthood in II 4Q400 2:1-8 seem to distinguish it from the angelic priesthood. Yet the human community is sometimes alluded to in the *Songs of the Sabbath Sacrifice*, perhaps more often than has been recognized in the past.

Line 7. The word "sanctuary" is used in the HB of the tabernacle (e.g., Exod 25:8); the temple in Jerusalem (e.g., Isa 63:18; 1 Chron 22:19) and its attendant holy places (e.g., Jer 51:51); and Ezekiel's imagined temple (e.g., Ezek 43:21; 44:1), but not of the heavenly temple. In the QL the word can mean the temple in Jerusalem (e.g., CD i:3; 1QM ii:3; 4QMMT B 5); the eschatological temple (e.g., 11Q19 iii:11 and frequently in the *Temple Scroll*); or the celestial temple (e.g., 4Q511 35:3). The word always has this last meaning in the *Songs of the Sabbath Sacrifice*, which refers to multiple sanctuaries, as here, but also to a single sanctuary of God (e.g., VII 4Q403 1i:42). The HL uses the word for the earthly sanctuary (*Hekhalot Rabbati* §123) and a vision of the heavenly sanctuary seen by the fathers before the Second Temple was built in Jerusalem (*Sar Torah* §§297-98).

Line 12. The word "prince, officer" (שׂר) is also found in VIII 4Q403 1ii:23 and possibly in the phrase "officers of holiness" in 4Q401 6:4. It is generally applied to human officers and military leaders in the HB, but it is also used of angelic beings (e.g., Josh 5:14, 15; Dan 8:11). In the QL it refers often to human beings, but sometimes to angels (e.g., 1QS iii:20; CD v:18; 1QM xiii:10, 14), and to God in 1QHᵃ xviii:8. It is the normal term for an angelic "prince" in the HL, rather than the term translated "prince" in this chapter (נשׂיא), which is never used in the HL with this meaning (see the commentary to I 4Q400 1ii:14).

Line 13. In the HB the word "palace" (היכל) can refer either to a royal palace (e.g., 1 Kgs 21:1) or more frequently to the temple (e.g., Isa 6:1) or the nave of the temple (e.g., 1 Kgs 6:3), and sometimes to the celestial temple or palace of God (2 Sam 22:7 // Ps 18:7; Ps 11:4; 29:9). Elsewhere in the QL it is used of palaces, the temple or nave, and the heavenly temple (e.g., 1QM xii:12? // xix:5 // 4Q492 1:5; 4Q287 2:11). The Hekhalot texts are the literature that describe the heavenly "temples" or "palaces" (היכלות) and how to ascend to them in mystical visions.

Line 14. It appears from 1QSa ii:3b-9a and 1QM vii:3b-6 that good angels cannot endure the presence of cultic impurity. Compare the "pure ones" in line 15 and VI 4Q403 1i:13, and the "gods of purity" in 4Q286 7i:6. Belial and his minions are impure (1QS iv:10, 21-22; CD iv:15-18; 1QM xiii:5; cf. 4Q511 48-51ii:3; 11QPs^a xix:15). Demons are called "unclean spirits" in the NT (e.g., Matt 10:1; Mark 3:11; Luke 4:36; Acts 5:16; Rev 16:13). The book of Revelation emphasizes the purity of the one hundred forty-four thousand human beings who sing before the throne of God (14:4-5), and we are also told that nothing unclean enters the new Jerusalem that descends from heaven (21:27).

Angels are called "pure ones" in the HL (*SH-L* §188); angels who come to earth can be made impure from contact with human beings, and they must be purified by immersion in rivers of fire (*SH-L* §§181-82; cf. *3 Enoch* 36:1-2). A human being ascending through the seven palaces can be banished back to earth by the least hint of impurity (*Hekhalot Rabbati* §§226-27). *Sepher HaRazim* stresses the importance of maintaining cultic purity when adjuring angels for magical purposes.

Line 16. The phrase "who repent of transgression," from Isa 59:20, is frequently applied to the sectarian community in the QL (e.g., 1QS x:20; CD ii:5; 1QH^a vi:24; x:9; xiv:6), and thus we may take it to refer to human beings here as well (although the possibility of angelic repentance may be entertained in XII 4Q405 23i:12 and 4Q280 2:3-4). For angels as intercessors for human beings, see *T. Levi* 3:5-6; *Jos. Asen.* 15:7-8. Note also that according to CD ii:5-7, angels of destruction pursue those who refuse to repent.

4Q400 1ii:1-21

A fragment describing the angelic praise

TOP MARGIN

¹the height of [Your] kingdom [. . .] ²heights and ..[. . .] ³ornamentation of Your kingdom[. . .] ⁴in ^athe gates of the exalted heights^a[. . .] ⁵in [. . .].[. . .]..

spirit of all ..[. . .] ⁶holie[st of] holy ones [. . .] ⁷King of divinities for seven .[. . .] ⁸glory of the King BLANK .[. . .] ⁹His glory in the council of the god[s . . .] ¹⁰to the seven paths [of . . .] ¹¹for quiet judgments .[. . .] ¹²eternal [. . .] BLANK [. . .] ¹³and they exalt His glory .[. . .] ¹⁴King of princes of [. . .] ¹⁵holy ones[. . .] ¹⁶holy ones[. . .] ¹⁷gods ..[. . .] ¹⁸righteousness BLANK [. . .] ¹⁹priesthood[s . . .] ²⁰Go[d's] acts of kindness [. . .] ²¹to be sanctified by .[. . .]

BOTTOM MARGIN

Note

ᵃ⁻ᵃ שערי מרומי רום Compare the "gates of the height" (שערי המרום) in 4Q253 2:5 (line 4 of this fragment refers to a holocaust offering) and "the gate of the holy height" (שער מרֿם הקודש) in 4Q500 1:4.

Commentary

Line 9. The expression "in the council of the gods" is also found in 4Q511 10:11.

Line 11. Unfortunately the noun after "seven paths [of]" is lost, but presumably the reference is to some element of the heavenly architecture. Paths of heaven used by the angels are mentioned in *Ma'aseh Merkavah* §§545-46.

Line 14. The word translated "prince" (נשיא) is the normal term for a high angel in the *Songs of the Sabbath Sacrifice*. In the HB it refers commonly to leaders and chieftains (and to the Davidic prince in Ezekiel), but never to angels. In the *Songs of the Sabbath Sacrifice* it corresponds to the word "officer, prince" (שׂר) in the HL. The latter appears only two or three times in the *Songs of the Sabbath Sacrifice* (see the commentary to I 4Q400 1i:12), while the former is used rarely in the HL and only of human beings (e.g., *Hekhalot Rabbati* §93), although the angelic "princes of glory" appear in *Sepher HaRazim* V 4. Elsewhere in the QL the word "prince" refers to a human leader, often in an eschatological context (e.g., 1QSb v:20; 1QM iii:3, 14, 15; 11Q19 xxi:5; xlii:14; lvii:12). The messianic leader Shimon Ben Kosiba (Bar Kokhba) took this word as a title during the revolt he led in 132-135 CE (e.g., Mur 24 B:3, 9).

4Q400 3i:1-12

A fragment describing the angelic praise[a]

TOP MARGIN

[1][. . .]on behalf of the wondrous height [2][. . .]the tongue of purity [3][. . .]. divinities. Seven [4][. . .]..[. . .]. [5][. . . g]reat things [6][. . .] [7][. . .].[. . .] [8][. . .]. [9][. . .]with seven [10][. . .] [11][. . .].. [12][. . . se]ven

Note
[a]The small amount of text preserved on this fragment shows similarities to the praises of the chief princes in Song VI and of the secondary princes in Song VIII.

Commentary

Line 3. In the absence of any context, the word translated "divinities" could also be taken as a singular form and translated "God."

4Q400 4i:1-5

A fragment that mentions divinities or God

[1][. . .]. [2][. . .].. [3]. . . divinities [4][. . .] [5][. . .]

Commentary

Line 3. In the absence of any context, the word translated "divinities" could also be translated "God."

4Q400 3ii:1-7 + 5

A fragment that mentions secondary princes

TOP MARGIN

[1]His holy melodies [. . .] [2]to the secondary princes [. . .] [3]His truth. Forms[a] of
..[. . .] [4]and seven words of[. . .] [5]to bless the knowers of [. . .]. sev[en]
[6]wondrous words [. . .] BLANK [7]BLANK [. . .] BLANK

Note

[a]צורות This word is applied frequently to elements of the heavenly temple in the
Songs of the Sabbath Sacrifice, and also in *Sar Torah* §297. It is used to describe the
faces of the living creatures in *Hekhalot Rabbati* §246.

Song II

(4Q400 3ii:8-10 + 5, 2 [+ 4Q401 14])

After the opening call of the angels to psalm God, this song
praises him for the glorious chief angels, who psalm him
more wondrously than do the other divinities or the lowly
human councils and priesthood.

4Q400 3ii:8-10 + 5

Title and opening call to praise

[8]For the Sage. The s[ong of the holocaust offering of the second Sabbath[a] on
the eleventh of the first month. Psalm] the God of [9]the glorified [ones . . .]
[10].[. . .]

Note

[a]The second Sabbath of the year would have been on the eleventh day of the first
month, seven days after the first Sabbath.

Commentary

Line 9. The term "glorified ones" (נכבדים) is applied to angels in II 4Q400 2:2; 1QH[a] xviii:8; 1Q19 3:3; this usage is common in the HL (e.g., *Hekhalot Rabbati* §244, referring to the angel Anaphiel).

4Q401 14i:1-6

A fragment describing the angelic praise

¹[. . .] ²[. . .]. ³[. . .] ⁴[. . .] its exaltation is exalted above[. . .] ⁵[. . .] for You are glorified among [. . .]gods of gods to .[. . .] ⁶for the chiefs of the realms .[. . .]heavens of the kingdom of Your glo[ry]

Commentary

Line 6. The phrase "chiefs of the realms" also appears in VII 4Q403 1ii:3 and in the singular, "chief of realms," in 4Q511 2i:3 (cf. 1QM x:12 and 1QH[a] ix:11). The overall content of the *Songs of the Sabbath Sacrifice* would tend to indicate that these are heavenly realms, although according to Deut 32:8-9 and Dan 10:13-14, 20 (cf. Sir 17:17; *T. Adam* 4:6-7; *Jub.* 15:31-32; *Orig. World* NHC II, 5 105:13-16), each nation was given its own angelic ruler, and it is possible that these realms are meant. Compare 4Q511 1.3, which refers to "the spirits of her [the earth's?] realms."

In the HL the idea of the angels of the nations is made explicit in *3 Enoch* 30:1-2; in the *Hekhalot Rabbati* there is a reference to the angel Sammael, prince of Rome, who is to be hurled down from heaven along with "all the princes of the kingdoms on high," apparently the angels of the other nations (*Hekhalot Rabbati* §108). In addition, an Aramaic magic bowl mentions the benevolent demon Bagdana Aziza, "the great one of the gods, and the king, the chief of sixty kingdoms" (Naveh and Shaked, *Amulets and Magic Bowls*, Bowl 13:3, pp. 198-99, 205-6).

The common word "heavens" (שמים) is rare in the *Songs of the Sabbath Sacrifice*, appearing only here and in II 4Q400 2:4.

4Q400 2 + 4Q401 14i:7-8

The angelic priesthood

TOP MARGIN

¹to psalm Your glory wondrously among gods of knowledge and the praises of Your kingdom among the most holy of the h[oly ones.] ²They are glorified in all the camps of the divinities and are fearsome to the human councils. More wo[ndrously] ³than divinities and human beings, they recount the effulgence of His kingdom according to their knowledge and they exalt[. . .] ⁴the heavens of His kingdom and in all the exalted heights wondrous psalms according to all[. . .] ⁵the glory of the King of divinities they recount in the dwellings of their station. BLANK And [. . .] ⁶How shall we be reckoned [among] them? And our priesthood, how in their dwellings? And [our] ho[liness, how . . .] ⁷their [holy of] holies? [How] the contribution of our tongue of dust with the knowledge of god[s . . .] ⁸[. . .]to our [ch]anting, let us exalt the God of knowledge[. . .] ⁹[. . . ho]liness and His understanding more than all who kno[w . . .] ¹⁰[. . .]. holiness. Holiness of the fir[st . . .] ¹¹[. . .].. ton[gues of] knowledge .. law [. . .] ¹²[. . .]. of glor[y . . .] ¹³[. . .]...[. . .] ¹⁴[. . .]..[. . .]

Commentary

Line 1. The phrase "gods of knowledge" is also found in VII 4Q403 1i:31, 38; XII 4Q405 23i:8. Compare the "gods of purity with all eternal knowing ones" in 4Q286 7i:6. The *Songs of the Sabbath Sacrifice* refers frequently to the knowledge of the gods or angels.

Line 2. The phrase "camps of the divinities" (also XII 4Q405 20ii-21-22:13) is inspired by "a camp of divinities" or "a camp of God" in Gen 32:3, the context of which (32:2) refers to "the angels of God." The mention of angelic encampments is uncommon in the QL, although the *Hôdāyôt* hymnist complains that "mighty ones have encamped against me" in 1QHᵃ x:25, and the inscription "peace of God in the camps of His holy ones" on the clarions of the camps in 1QM iii:5 may allude to the idea. Angelic camps mentioned in the HL include "the camps of the attending angels" in *3 Enoch* 36:1; "the camps of the holy ones" in *Hekhalot Rabbati* §277; and in *Sepher HaRazim* the seven "camps of the angels" in I 5; the "princes of the camps" in IV 23; and the "chiefs of the camps" in VI 30.

Line 3. Compare "the effulgence of His kingdom" to Dan 11:21; 1 Chron

108

29:25 as well as the expressions "kingdom of effulgence and adornment" in *Hekhalot Rabbati* §251 // §260; "effulgence of kingdom" in *Massekhet Hekhalot* §15.2.

Line 5. The term "dwelling" appears eight times in the *Songs of the Sabbath Sacrifice*, always referring to the heavenly realm. In the HB the word can be a general term for a dwelling (e.g., the "lair" of jackals in Jer 9:10), but it also refers to the dwelling of God in heaven (e.g., Deut 26:15) and in the temple (e.g., Ps 26:8). In the QL it can refer to the Community as temple (1QS viii:8), or to God's heavenly dwelling (1QS x:3; 1QM xii:2; 4Q287 2:13; 4Q491ᶜ 1:13; 4Q510 1:3; 4Q511 41:1). In Jewish esoteric literature, Dwelling is the name of one of the seven firmaments (e.g., *Seder Rabba di Bereshit* §§40-41 [*SH-L* §§720-22]).

Lines 6-7. The human priesthood is compared unfavorably to the angelic priesthoods, mentioned in VIII 4Q403 1ii:20-22. For similarly self-deprecating questions, see 1QHᵃ ix:25-26; xi:23-25; 4Q511 30:4-6. For human praise as a sacrifice to God, see Heb 13:15.

According to the HL, angels are resentful of human beings who ascend to their realm, and they challenge the right of those humans to be there, sometimes objecting to their smell (e.g., *3 Enoch* 2:1-4; 4:6-9; 6:1-3). The angels also object to God's revealing the secret of the prince of Torah to human beings, since it will allow them to have spontaneous knowledge of the Torah like that of the angels (*Sar Torah* §292).

Line 8. The phrase "the God of knowledge" also appears in V 4Q402 4:12; XIII 4Q405 23ii:12; 4Q401 11:2 (cf. 1QHᵃ ix:26). Compare the similar title, literally, "the God of knowledges" (e.g., 1QS iii:15; 1QHᵃ xxii:4:15; 4Q510 1:2; 4Q511 1:7-8).

Line 11. "Tongues of knowledge" are also mentioned in 4Q503 7-9:4.

4Q401 14ii·1-8

¹[.]...[. . .] ²myster[ies of] His wondrous acts[. . .] ³a voice of chants[.] ⁴cannot[. . .] ⁵G[od] makes mighty [. . .] ⁶princes of .[. . .] ⁷They proclaim secret things [. . .] ⁸at the issue of the lips of the King .[. . .]

BOTTOM MARGIN

Commentary

Line 2. Compare the "myster[ies of] His wondrous acts" to "the mysteries of Your wondrous acts" in 1QM xiv:14. See the commentary to VIII 4Q403 1ii:27 for similar expressions.

Line 7. In the sectarian literature the "secret things" are the hidden teachings revealed to the members of the sect (e.g., 1QS v:11; CD iii:13-14).

Song III

No certain or probable fragments survive.[a]

Note

[a]No fragments from any manuscript can be placed with certainty or even high probability in Song III. It would have been sung on the third Sabbath of the first month, so its beginning probably read as follows:

> [For the Sage. The song of the holocaust offering of the third Sabbath on the eighteenth of the first month. Psalm the God of . . .]

Song IV

(4Q401 1-2; 4Q402 1)

*May have mentioned an eschatological conflict
between the angels and the forces of evil*

4Q401 1-2

Title and opening call to praise

TOP MARGIN

[1]For the Sage. The s[ong of the holocaust offering of the fourth Sabbath on the] twenty-[fifth] in the [first] m[onth.] [2]Psalm the G[od of . . .].. ...[. . .] [3]and ..[. . .] they stand before[. . .] [4]king[dom . . .]. all the chi[efs of . . .] [5]King of the divi[nities . . .] [6][. . .].[. . .]..[. . .]

110

4Q402 1

A heavenly procession or eschatological visitation?

¹[. . .].. at the entr[ance of . . .] ²[. . .] when they come with the Go[d of . . .] ³[. . .] together for all Yo[ur] set periods ⁴[. . .] their [mig]ht to mighty ones of power ⁵[. . .]. to all the councils of transgression ⁶[. . .] their ..[. . .] ⁷[. . .].

Commentary

Line 1. In BH the word translated "entrance" can mean a portal (e.g., Ezek 43:11, of Ezekiel's imagined temple) or the arrival of a person or persons (e.g., 2 Sam 3:25). The word is also used in IX 4Q405 14-15i:4-5 and XII 4Q405 23i:8-10 in both senses.

Line 2. Given the broken context, the word translated "God" could also be translated "divinities." The line may describe a procession into the heavenly temple or a future eschatological visitation.

Line 3. Given the broken context, the word translated "together" (יחד) could also be translated "the Community" (see the commentary to 4Q286 7ii:1). In BH the word translated "set period" (תעודה) is understood to be derived from the root "to witness, testify" (√עוד) and is taken to mean "testimony" (cf. 4Q216 ii:5 [*Jub.* 1:8]; vii:17 [*Jub.* 2:24]). However, in QH the word usually seems to mean a set period of time, as though derived from the root "to appoint, designate, meet" (√יעד).

Line 4. Compare the "mighty ones of power" to "mighty ones of strength" in 1QHᵃ xvi:11; xviii:34-35 as well as to "mighty ones of valor" in CD ii:17; 1QM x:6. The Hebrew word translated "mighty one" is also found in VI 4Q403 1i:2 (applied to God); VI 4Q403 1i:21; VIII 4Q405 13:5 ("mighty ones of insight"). In the HB it usually refers to human warriors (e.g., 1 Sam 16:18; 2 Sam 23:22; 2 Kgs 24:16), although it is used of angels in Ps 103:20-22.

In QH angels are called "mighty ones" in 1QM xv:14; xix:1; 1QHᵃ xi:35; xiii:21; xvi:11; xviii:34-35, although the term can also be used of human beings (e.g., 1QM xix:10; 4Q161 8-10:4, 6). Angels are often called "mighty ones" in the HL.

Line 5. The word translated "councils of" can also mean "foundations of" (*HDSS* 108-9). Given the broken context either meaning is possible.

Song V

(4Q402 2, 3; 4Q402 4 + Mas1k i:1-7)

Describes a war in heaven and praises God for his past and future works. This song may have linked the chief angel Melchizedek and the investiture of the angelic priests with the eschatological battle.

4Q402 2 + 3i

Descriptions of beings in the celestial realm[a]

[1][...].[...] [2][...] God of [3][...] glory [4][... G]od of [5]wo[nde]r and .[...] shapes[b] of [6]wonder of w[onders . . .]divinities [7][like] workmanship of colorful s[tuff][c] [...] [8]in the inner chamber of the King .[...]. [9].[ ].. .[...] [10][...]..

Notes

[a]The beginning of the fifth song is lost, but it may be reconstructed with a high degree of confidence as follows:

> [For the Sage. The song of the holocaust offering of the fifth Sabbath on the second of the second month. Psalm the God of . . .]

[b]The word "shape" (בדן) is not attested in BH. It is common in the *Songs of the Sabbath Sacrifice*, but outside it appears only in the phrase "colorful shapes" in 1QM v:6, 9. Compare the parallel phrase "colorful form" in 1QM v:14.

[c]The noun "colorful stuff" (רוקמה) is the equivalent of the BH noun רקם (cf. *HDSS* 200.26).

Commentary

Line 7. The noun "colorful stuff" appears often in the *Songs of the Sabbath Sacrifice*, as well as in 1QM v:6, 9, 14; vii:11; 4Q161 8-10:19; 4Q287 2:5; 4Q462 1:5. It seems to mean multicolored, variegated, or embroidered material (I cannot explain the use of the word in 4Q270 7i:14). Compare the phrase "colorful work" in the account of the building of the tabernacle (Exod 26:36, etc.).

The root "to be colorful" appears in a number of celestial or cosmological contexts in the HL. In *3 Enoch* 22:12 we are told that the angel KRWBY'L YWY "makes colorful the loveliness of their (the cherubim's) brightness." According to the *Hekhalot Rabbati*, the mystic who succeeds in navigating the dangers of the celestial ascent arrives before the throne of glory and breaks into song. One phrase in this song refers to God as "the One adorned with colorful song" (§252 // §261 // §974). In *Seder Rabba di Bereshit* §3 (*SH-I*, §834), God says "I made colorful" or "I used colorful materials" as one of his six acts of artisanship in creating heaven and earth.

4Q402 3ii:1-13

A fragment that refers to judgment[a]

[1][. . .] [2][. . .] [3][. . .] [4].[. . .] [5]He will judge[. . .] [6]without ..[. . .] [7]light and understa[nding . . .] [8]who removes ..[. . .] [9]on high and has divi[ded up . . .] [10]His might .[. . .] [11]divinities .[. . .] [12]to the King of the divinitie[s . . .] [13][His] glorious purpose [. . .]

Notes

[a]Qimron suggests that this fragment preserves the beginning of lines 4-13 in V 402 4 ("Review Article," 360-61), but Newsom points out that the overlap with Mas1k in lines 12-13 of frag. 4 seems to rule this join out (unless the text of 4Q402 and Mas1k was somewhat different at this point). Therefore I take frag. 3ii to preserve material from the middle of Song V.

Commentary

Line 11. In the absence of any context, the word translated "divinities" could also be taken as a singular form and translated "God."

4Q402 4 + Mas1k i:1-7

A celestial war in heaven

[1][. . .].[. . .] [2][. . .].. and He divides up knowledge[. . .] [3][. . . according to] His understanding He engraved l[aws . . .] [4][. . .] his being impure[. . .]. and not ...[. . .] [5][. . .].. and [they] shall not be [. . .].. for the Community[a] .[. . .] [6][. . . sus]tainers of [His] thought and knowledge of holi[ness . . .] [7][. . .]their [. . .] the war of God in h[oly . . .] [8][. . .] for to the God of gods belong [the

weap]ons of wa[r]fa[re . . .] [9][. . .]divinities run to His muster and the sound of tumu[lt . . .] [10][. . .]divinities in a war of heavenly clouds and there was[b][. . .] [11][. . .] wondr[ous] new acts. All these things He has done wondr[ously according to His kind purpose. Not] [12][. . . all words of knowledge.] [c]For from the God of knowledge[c] came into being all [eternally existing things. And from His knowledge] [13][and from His purposes have come about all etern]al [set periods.] He does the fir[st thi]ngs [in their times and the latter things] [14][in their appointed times, and there are none among those who know wondrous revelations] who understand before [He] a[cts. And when He acts, no divinities] [15][have insight into what He purposes. For t]hey are [of His glorious works.] Before [they existed, they were from His thoughts. BLANK]

Notes

[a]ליחד I translate "for the Community" (cf. 1QS v:5-6; 4Q181 1:2), but the word could also be construed as a Piel infinitive construct of the verb √יחד, "to unite" (cf. Ps 86:11; 1QS iii:7 // 4Q255 2:1; 1QSa i:9). It could also be construed as something like "for unity" (cf. 1 Chron 12:18). It is translated as "together" by Newsom, but this meaning is not well attested with the preposition *lamed*. It may be found in 4Q416 2iv:5, but in that broken context the sense could also be "to be united with" (cf. Isa 14:20). I am grateful to Martin Abegg for drawing the passage in 4Q416 to my attention.

[b]והיתה This verb could also be taken as *waw*-conversive and translated "and there will be." The subject is a feminine singular noun, perhaps מלחמה, "war" (cf. Rev 12:7).

[c-c]This phrase is missing in Mas1k i:2. Perhaps a scribe's eye skipped from the first appearance in line 12 of the word "knowledge" to the second, accidentally dropping the phrase in between.

Commentary

Line 4. Perhaps a reference to Belial, who is described as impure in other Qumran texts (cf. the commentary to I 4Q400 1i:14).

Line 5. This is the only possible direct mention of the sectarian community in the *Songs of the Sabbath Sacrifice*, but given the broken context the translation is open to debate. See note a above.

Lines 7-10. An eschatological battle is also envisioned in 1QM xiii:10-16; xvii:4-9, with the "luminary prince" and Michael as protagonist and Belial and the "prince of the realm of wickedness" as the enemy. Given the widespread association of the warrior angel with the eschatological war in heaven, it may be that frags. 4Q401 11, 22 belonged in this song. See "Unplaced Fragments" and the "Excursus on the Melchizedek Tradition" at the end of this chapter.

Line 7. The phrase "the war of God" could also be translated "a war of divinities." The unambiguous phrase "war of God" is found in 1QM iv:12; ix:5; xv:12, but note also "a war of mighty ones of heaven" in 1QH^a xi:35-36.

Line 10. In the absence of a clear context, the word translated "divinities" could also be taken as a singular form and translated "God." The "war of heavenly clouds" corresponds to the "war in heaven" fought by Michael and his angels against the great dragon (the devil or Satan) in Rev 12:7; the war between Melchizedek (Jesus Christ, the heavenly high priest and commander in chief of the All) and the evil archons in the *Melchizedek Tractate* from Nag Hammadi (NHC IX, lxxvi:1-14); the rescue of Sabaoth by Sophia's seven archangels when the archons "made a great war in the seven heavens" (*Orig. World* NHC II, 5 104:6-25); and the battle between the angelic "great prince" and Leviathan in a liturgical poem by Qalliri (Davila, "Melchizedek, Michael, and War in Heaven"). Compare also *Sib. Or.* 3:805-8; 5:211-13, 512-31.

Lines 10-13. These lines echo numerous passages in Deutero-Isaiah (e.g., Isa 42:9; 44:6; 45:7; 66:2).

Line 14. The word translated "in their appointed times" could also be translated as "for their festivals," but the parallelism seems to indicate the more general sense of the word

Song VI

(Mas1k i:8-21; Mas1k ii:1-6a; 4Q405 3i;
4Q403 1i:1-29 + Mas1k ii:6b-26 + 4Q404 1-2 + 4Q405 3ii)

Describes the seven sevenfold psalms of the seven chief princes and summarizes the blessings of seven words uttered by each chief prince, followed by a concluding benediction

Mas1k i:8-21

Title and opening call to praise

[8][For the Sage. The son]g of the holocaust offering of the sixth Sabbath on the ninth of the [second] [9]month. [Psalm the G]o[d] of gods, O dwellers in the exalted heights [10][... m]ost holy ones and exalt His glory [11][... kn]owledge of the

eternal gods [12][. . .]elect ones[a] of the highest heights [13][. . .]in all holiness [14][. . .] [15][. . .] [16][. . .] [17][. . .]..[ ].. [18][. . .]. [19][. . .] [20][. . .]. [21][. . .].

Notes

[a]קרואי This word comes from Num 1:16 (*ketiv* קריאי); 16:2 (*ketiv* קראי); and 26:9 (*qere* קריאי), which refer to leaders chosen for various godly or nefarious purposes during the wilderness journey. It also appears in 4Q403 2:2 and 4Q407 1:4. The terms "princes" and "chiefs," angelic titles in the *Songs of the Sabbath Sacrifice,* are also applied to these leaders in the same verses.

Commentary

Line 9. The expression "God of gods" appears often in the *Songs of the Sabbath Sacrifice,* as does a similar phrase (with *El* rather than *Elohim*), translated the same way. The latter phrase is also found in 1QM xiv:16; 4Q510 1:2; and in the HL (e.g., *SH-L* §§497, 511).

Mas1k ii:1-6a

The sevenfold psalms of the seven chief princes[a]

[Psalm of blessing by the tongue of the first chief prince] [1]to the [eternal] God [with its seven wondrous blessings. And he will bless [2]the Kin[g of all the eternal holy ones seven times with seven] [3]words of [wondrous blessings.

Psalm of greatness by the tongue of the second to the King of] [4]faithfulness and [righteousness with its seven wondrous great things and he declares great the God of] [5]all div[inities appointed for righteousness seven times with seven words of] [6][wondrous] great [things.]

Note

[a]Although the psalms and blessings of the chief princes in Song VI are fragmentary, fortunately we have four partially overlapping copies, and the text is very repetitive and formulaic. The summary of the psalms in VI 4Q403 1i:7-10 (and parallels) and the fragment of the blessings of the fourth through seventh secondary princes in Song VIII (4Q405 13) also aid the reconstruction. Overall the text of Song VI can be recovered almost completely. For details of the reconstruction, see DJD 11: 246-50, 261-63.

Commentary

The speaker in the Self-Glorification Hymn (4Q427 7i:13b–23) exhorts the angels to praise God using terminology similar to that of the angels in Songs VI and VIII. The number seven is a structuring element in the *Songs of the Sabbath Sacrifice* on many levels, just as it is in the book of Revelation and the HL (see the introduction to this chapter). Newsom notes a number of parallels to the sevenfold blessings and praises in Songs VI and VIII, including 1 Chron 29:11-12; Rev 5:12; 7:12; and the seven benedictions of the Sabbath *Amidah* in the traditional Jewish liturgy (DJD 11: 247-48).

4Q405 3i (cf. Mas1k ii:3-7; 4Q403 1i:1-2?)

A fragment that mentions the chief princes[a]

[10][. . .]greatness [11][. . .]and he declares great [12] [. . . ~~An exaltat]ion of His faith-fulness~~ <[t]o the chief princes> [13][. . . ~~with] seven~~ [14][. . . [b]and] they [ex]alt the God of[b] [15][. . . se]ven times with seven [16][. . .] <[with sev]en ac[ts of might]>

Notes
[a]This fragment corresponds to the psalms of the second and third chief princes, although its text is somewhat different from the other two fragmentary versions (one of which, 4Q403, appears to be defective), and it cannot be reconstructed to agree with either of them.

[b] [b]ורו[מ]ּמ[ו אלוהי] Note the similar phrase ורומם אלוהי, "and he exalts the God of," reconstructed below in Mas1k 3ii:8 // 4Q403 1i:1.

Commentary

See the commentary to 4Q403 1i:1-2 below.

4Q403 1i:1-29 + Mas1k ii:6b-26 + 4Q404 1-2 (ital.) + 4Q405 3ii

[Psalm of exaltation by the tongue of] [1]the third of the chief princes. An exaltation of [a]His faithfulness for the King of angels with its seven wondrous exaltations and he exalts[ab] the God of the [a]ngels of exaltation seven times with seven words of wondrous exaltations.

117

[2]Psalm of praise by the tongue of the four[th] to the Mighty One over all [divinities] with its seven wondrous mighty acts. And he praises the God of [3]mighty acts seven times with seve[n] words of [wondrous] prais[es.]

[Ps]alm of [th]anksgivings by the tongue of the fift[h] to the [K]in[g] of glory [4]with its seven wondrous than[ksg]ivings. He shall give thanks[c] to the God of glory sev[en times with s]e[ven wor]ds of wondrous thanksgivings.

[Psalm of] chanting [5]by the tongue of the sixth to [the] good God with [its] seven [wondrous] chants. [And] he chants to [the] good K[ing] seven times with s[even words of] wondrous [6]chanting. BLANK

Psal*m of [melody by the t*]ongue of the seventh of the [chief] pri[nces], powerful melody [to the Go]d of hol[iness], with [*its*] se[ven] wo[n]de[r]*ful* [7][melodies.] [*And*] *he makes melody* [to the h]oly Kin[g] seven times with [seven words of wondrous] mel[ody.]

Summary of the seven psalms of the chief princes

[Sev]en psal[ms of His blessings; sev]en [8][psalm]s *of the* greatness of [His righ-teousness; seven psalms of] the exaltation of [His] kingd[om; seven] psalms of [the praises of His glory; seve]n p[salms of the thanksgivings of] [9][His won-ders; seven psalms of the ch]an[ti]ngs of His power; seven [psalms of the melodi]es of His holiness, [d]ge[nerations of . . . of exalta]tion[d] [shall bless] [10][seven times with seven wondrous words, words of exalta]tion.

The sevenfold blessings of the seven chief princes

The first(!)[e] of the c[hief] princes [shall bless] in the name of the g[lo]ry of God to [all . . .] ... [with seven wondrous] [11][words to bless all th]eir [council]s in the sanctuary of [His holiness with sev]en wondr[ous] word[s.] [And he blesses][f] etern[al kno]wing ones.

[The second] [12][among the chief princes shall bless in] His faithful [name] all [their] sta[tions w]ith sev[en wondrous] word[s.] [And he blesses [g]with] seven [wondrous] words [13]and he blesses[g] all who exalt the] King with the seven w[ords of] the g[l]or[y of His] w[onders, all] the eternally pure ones.

The t[hird] [14][among the chief princes shall bless in the name of] His ex-alted kingdom [all the exal]ted ones of [kno]wledge with s[even] exa[lt]ed [w]ords, and all the [gods of] [15]BLANK[h] [16][His faithfu]l knowledge He shall bless with sev[e]n wondrous words. And he blesses all the ones [appointed] for righteousness [with seven] wondrous [w]ords.

[The fourth] [17]among [the chi]ef prin[ces] shall bless in the na[me] of the effulge[nce of the Ki]ng a[ll] who wal[k uprig]htly with [se]ven words of ef[fulgence and] he blesses the establisher[s of efful]gence with sev[en] [18][won-drous] word[s. And] he blesses all the go[ds drawing ne]ar to [His] faith[ful] knowledge [with seve]n words of righteousness for [His] [gl]or[ious] mercies.

The fift[h] [19]among [the chief] prin[ces] shall bless in the name of the [effulgence] of His wonders [al]l who know the [mysteries of . . .]. of purity with seven w[ords of] [His] exalted [20]faithfulness [and he blesses] all who rush after His favor with seven [*wondrous words. And he bl]es[ses*] all who give thanks to Him with seven [wor]ds of effulgence [21][for wondrous] effulgences.

The sixth among the *chief* princes *shall bless in the name of* [*mighty acts of*] *gods a*ll mighty ones of[i] insight with seven [22][wo]rds of *His wondrous[j] mighty acts. And he blesses all whose way is sound with* [*s*]*even wondrous words as a* [*co*]*ntinual sacrifice with all* coming [23][a]g[e]s *and he blesses all who wait for Him with seven wondrous word*[*s*] *for a* [*res*]*toration of* His mer[ciful] acts of kindness.[k]

[The sev]enth among the ch*ief* princes [24]*shall bless in* His holy name all holy ones who establish kno[wledge] with sev[en] words of [His] wondrous holiness. [*And he blesses*] *all who e*xalt [25]His judgments with sev[en] wondrous [wo]rds for shields of power. And he blesses all who are appoi[nted for] righteous[*ness, who ps*]*alm* the kingdom of His glory [. . .] everlastingly [26]with seven [wondrous] w[ords for] *eternal* peace.

Summary of the seven blessings of the chief princes

And all the [chief] princes [shall bless togeth]er the [G]od of gods in [His holy name with] all [27][their] sevenfold te[stimonies and] they bless those appointed for righteousness and all the blessed [. . . bles]sed fo[r]ev[er . . .] [28]to them.

Concluding benediction

Blessed be [the] Lo[r]d, Kin[g of] all, above all blessing and p[raises. And He blesses all holy] ones who bless [Him and declare Him righ]teous [29]in His glorious name, and [He bl]esses all the eternally blessed.

Notes

[a-a]אמתו למלך מלאכים ב⸌⸍שבעח רו⸌מ⸍ פלאה ורוממם This phrase is missing from the undamaged text of 4Q403 1i:1, but the text of that manuscript does not correspond to the structure of the psalms of the other six chief princes and is too short to fill the lacuna in Mas1k ii:7. I follow Newsom's schematic reconstruction of the phrase (DJD 11: 251). The original text must have been something along these lines.

119

[b]וּרוֹמֵ[ם] This is the correct reading of Mas1k ii:8. Newsom reads [ם]רוֹמֵ, "he exal[ts]," in both editions, although Qimron corrected the reading in "Review Article," 363. Note also that 4Q405 3i:14 reads "[and] they [ex]alt" (וְרוֹמֵ[מו]), although the subject should be the third chief prince.

[c]יוֹדֶה Mas1k ii:13 reads יודו, "they shall give thanks" or "they shall confess."

[d-d]The reconstruction of the end of line 9 and the beginning of line 10 is difficult, even with the help of Mas1k 1ii:22-23. Newsom reconstructs "ge[nerations of chiefs of exalta]tion" (תֹּ[ולדות ראשי רו[ם]), which may be possible paleographically but is problematic in context. Although the word תולדות is translated "generations" in English Bibles, its meaning in the HB and the QL is closer to "a genealogical listing" or "an account of a generation's actions in genealogical order" (e.g., Gen 5:1; 36:1; Ruth 4:18; CD iv:5; 1QM iii:14), which clearly does not fit here. But even if it is taken as a synonym of דורות, the normal word for "generations" (cf. 1 Chron 5:7?), the word is out of place in the context Newsom proposes since angels are immortal and are not begotten in successive generations.

[e]הראישׁון This word is missing in 4Q403 1i:10, although there is room for it in the lacuna of Mas1k ii:23. I have adopted Newsom's suggestion that it was lost by mistake in 4Q403. For the phrase לנשיאי ראש, "of the chief princes," cf. lines 1 and 6 above.

[f][ובֿרך] This word is reconstructed on the basis of the context. Mas1k ii:26 and 4Q405 3ii:1 appear to have the corrupt reading ובם.

[g-g]This phrase is unexpected, given the pattern of the other blessings of the chief princes. It may be a dittography (an accidental double copying), but it is also found in 4Q405 3ii:2, so it may be a deliberate variation, as Newsom suggests.

[h]Although line 15 is blank, it clearly does not mark a division in the text.

[i]4Q405 3ii:12 has a blank line after this word, for reasons that are obscure.

[j]פלאו 4Q404 2:3 reads פלאיו, "mighty acts of His wonders."

[k]חסדיו 4Q405 3ii:15 reads חסדו, "His merciful kindness."

Commentary

Line 1. There are seven "chief princes" in this song who correspond to the seven secondary princes in Song VIII. Presumably the inspiration for them is the seven angels in Ezek 9:1-2 and perhaps the seven archangels in later tradition (e.g., Tob 12:15; *1 Enoch* 20:1-7 in Greek; *T. Levi* 8:2; *Orig. World* NHC II, 5 104:18-19; 105:10). The book of Revelation mentions "the seven angels who stand before God" (the angels of the seven trumpets) in the heavenly temple (8:2-3, 6-13; 9:1, 13; 11:15). Later in the book, seven angels go out from the heavenly temple to pour out the seven bowls of the wrath of God (15:1, 5-7; 16:1-21). According to *Massekhet Hekhalot* §9.4, seven great princes are located in the divine throne room.

In both the HB and the QL the word "chief" can be used as the title of a leader, either by itself (e.g., Exod 18:25; Num 1:16; Judg 10:18; Mic 3:1; 1QM ii:1; iii:13; 4Q164 1:7; cf. 11Q19 xix:16; xlii:14) or combined with another term, such as "chief priest" (e.g., 2 Kgs 25:18; 1QM ii:1; xv:4; xvi:11). The title "chief" is also used of angels in the HL (e.g., *Hekhalot Rabbati* §§219-22, where the chiefs of the gates of the first five heavenly palaces figure in the narrative), and the "chiefs of the camps" appear in *Sepher HaRazim* VI 30. The phrase "chief prince" is from Ezek 38:2-3 and 39:1, where it is a title of Gog. The titles "chiefs," "princes," and "elect ones" also appear together in Numbers 1, and "chiefs," "princes," and "officers" in 1QM iii:12-14 and 11Q19 xlii:14-15. Perhaps in the *Songs of the Sabbath Sacrifice* the seven chief princes and seven secondary princes preside together over the seven priesthoods (VIII 4Q403 1ii:20, 22) in the seven sanctuaries (VII 4Q405 7:7), although the reconstructions in the last three references are not certain.

The word "angel" has the basic meaning "messenger," but it is used frequently in the HB, the QL, and the HL to indicate a divine messenger. Angels are also mentioned in VIII 4Q403 1ii:23 ("the angels of the King"); IX 4Q405 17:4 ("angels of glory"), 5 ("angels of ornamentation"); XI 4Q405 19:7; XII 4Q405 20ii-21-22:9, XII 4Q405 23i:8; 4Q407 1:3 ("angels of holiness"); XIII 11Q17 ix:9; 4Q405 49:3 ("angels of [. . .]"); XIII 11Q17 x:6 ("angels of knowledge"); 4Q405 81:2 ("angels of the ab[ode of . . .]").

Line 2. The title "Mighty One" is also applied to God in the HB (e.g., Deut 10:17; Isa 10:21; Jer 32:18; Ps 24:8), the QL (e.g., 1QM xii:9), postbiblical literature (e.g., *4 Ezra* 6:32; *2 Apoc. Bar.* 47:1), and the HL (e.g., *Hekhalot Rabbati* §§268, 271, 272).

Line 3. The phrase "the King of glory" (used often in the *Songs of the Sabbath Sacrifice*) comes from Ps 24:7-10 and is found both in the QL (1QM xii:8; xix:1; 4Q510 1:1; 4Q511 52-59iii:4) and in the HL (e.g., *3 Enoch* 2:12; *Hekhalot Rabbati* §189; *Hekhalot Zutarti* §421; *Mussekhet Hekhalot* §3.6-7).

Line 4. The various permutations of the word "thanksgiving" in this line could also be translated as analogous permutations of the word "confession." The phrase "the God of glory" comes from Ps 29:3.

Line 5. God's goodness is mentioned in the *Hôdāyôt* (e.g., 1QH^a xviii:16) and also in the Self-Glorification Hymn (4Q427 7i:23).

Line 8. The word translated "thanksgivings" could also be translated "confessions."

Line 11. The phrase "eternal knowing ones" is also found in 4Q286 7i:6 and Songs VIII 4Q403 1ii:19-20 // 4Q405 8-9:3-4.

Line 20. Compare "all who rush after His favor" with "those who rush after righteousness" in 1QH^a xiii:21-22. The word translated "who give thanks" could also be translated "who confess."

Line 22. With small variations, the phrase "those whose way is sound" ap-

121

pears often in the QL (1QS ii:2; iii:9-10; iv:22; viii:10, 18, 21; ix:2, 5, 9; CD ii:15-16; 1QM xiv:7 // 4Q491 8-10i:5; 1QH^a ix:36; 4Q510 1:9 // 4Q511 10:8; 4Q511 63iii:3), always referring to human beings, especially the sectarians. Presumably it applies to human beings here as well.

The word translated "continual sacrifice" is used as a sacrificial term unmodified in Dan 8:11, 12, 13; 11:31; 12:11 (cf., e.g., Exod 29:42; Ezek 46:15). Since other sacrificial terms are used in XIII 11Q17 ix:4-6, this may be the correct meaning here. Alternatively, the word could be used adverbially to mean simply "continually."

Lines 22-23. The phrase translated "with all coming [a]g[e]s" (cf. CD ii:9-10) could also be taken in a personal sense: "with all eternal ones," that is, the angels.

Line 23. Echoes Isa 30:18 (cf. Dan 12:12).

Line 25. The phrase "the kingdom of His glory" is found in Esther 1:4 and XIII 4Q405 23ii:11-12. Note the similar expressions in II 4Q401 14i:6; VII 4Q403 1i:32; XII 4Q405 23i:3. It is unclear whether any text has been lost in the lacuna immediately after the phrase. Compare Matt 6:13b and the phrase "blessed be the name of the glory of His kingdom forever and ever" in *SH-L* §394 // §471 // §731.

Line 26. The translation "the [G]od of gods" is more to be expected given the context, but, as Newsom notes, if this phrase is meant to be parallel to the phrase "[and] they bless those appointed for righteousness" in line 27, it should be translated "the [div]in[it]ies of the gods."

Song VII

(4Q403 1i:30–ii:17 + 4Q404 3-6 + 4Q405 4-7 + 11Q17i)

Exhorts the various classes of divinities to praise God, then calls on the architectural elements of the heavenly temple to do the same. Describes the movements of the fiery divinities in the vicinity of the tabernacle and the praise offered by the temple furnishings, the inner chambers, and the cherubim and ophannim.

4Q403 1i:30-47 + 4Q404 3-5 (ital.) + 4Q405 4-5, 6:1-8

Title and opening call to praise

[30]For the Sage. The song of the holocaust offering of the seventh Sabbath on the sixteen*th*[a] *of the mon*th. Psalm the God of exaltations, O exalted ones among all [31]gods of knowledge.

Invocations of various groups of angels

Let the holy ones of the divi*nities* declare great(!)[b] the *K*ing of glory who declares holy in His holiness(!)[c] all His holy ones.[d] O chiefs of the praises of [32]all divinities, praise the God [of] effulgent [pr]aises, for in the adornment of praises is the glory of His kingdom — in it[e] are the praises of all [33]divinities along with the adornment of [His] whole king[dom — and] exalt His exaltation on high, O divinities of the gods of exaltation, and the godhood of His glory above [34]all exalted heights, for He is [God of gods] to all the chiefs of exaltations and King of king[s] to all eternal councils. <<by the favor of [35]His knowledge>> At the words of *His* mouth a[ll gods of exaltation] *come into* being, at the issue of His lips all eternal spirits, [by the tav]*or of IIis* kno*wledge* all His works [36]in their actions.[f] *Chant, O* chanters of [knowledge, with] chan*ting among* wondrous divi*ni*ties, and recount His glory with the tongue of all recounters of knowledge, His wondrous chants [37]in the mouth of all who recount [Him, for He is] *God to all* eternal chanters <<of knowledge>> and Judge in His might to all spirits of understanding. [38]*Declare effulgent,*[g] *all gods of* effulgence, the King of effulgence, for all the *gods of knowledge* confess His glory *and all spirits of* righteousness confess His faithfulness. [39]And they make their knowledge pleasing by the judgments of His mouth, and their confessions by the return of His mighty hand for re*quiting*[h] judgments. Make melody to the God of power [40]with the best portion of spirit for [a melo]dy, with *the happiness of* God and joy among all holy ones for wondrous melodies with eter[nal] happiness.

Invocation of the celestial architecture and other spirits

[41]With these let all the fo[undations of] the most [hol]y (place) psalm the [i]load-bearing pillars[i] of the most exalted abode and all the corners of its construction.[j] Make mel[ody to] [42]G[od, fe]arsome of strength, [all spirits of knowledge and light] to [lift] up together the most [k]<<radi>> pure[k] firmament of His holy sanctuary. [43][And praise H]im, O spirits of Go[d,] for confessio[ns

forever and e]ver of the chief[1] firmament on high, all [its] b[eams] and its walls, a[l]l [44]its [constr]uction, the works of [its] struc[ture.][m] *Most hol[y spi]rits*,[n] *living divinities*, [ete]rnal holy [spi]rits *above* [45]all the hol[y ones . . . *of*[o] *wonder*, *wonderful of effulgence* and adornment. And wondrous is the God of gl]ory in the light of *perfect light(!)*[p] *of knowle[dge]* [46][. . . in all *wondrous sanctuaries*. The spirits of God surround the dwelling of the K]in[g[q] *of faithfulness* and *right-teousness. All]* [47][*its walls . . . in the holy of holies . . . light . . . structu*re . . .]

Notes

[a-a]בשש עשר One would expect the masculine form בששה עשר.

[b]יקדילו I follow Qimron's emendation of this meaningless word to יגדילו ("Review Article," 368). Newsom originally proposed the emendation יקדישו, "let them sanctify," but in DJD 11 she adopts Qimron's suggestion. Both emendations are possible, but Qimron's is more likely given the phonetic similarity of *qop* to *gimel*. Compare דקלי, written for דגלי in 4Q503 51-55:8.

[c]בקודע I follow Newsom's emendation to בקודש.

[d]קדושו The orthography of this word is defective; the plural form would normally be spelled קדושיו. Nevertheless, given the context the meaning is not in doubt. Compare the spelling לפנו for לפניו in XII 4Q405 20ii-21-22:7.

[e]בה The feminine singular pronominal suffix refers back to מלכותו, "His kingdom."

[f]במשלחם Although the root שלח√ has the meaning "to send," Newsom suggests that this word may be equivalent to the phrase משלח ידיהם, "the undertaking (literally, 'sending out') of their hands." I translate accordingly, but it should be noted that the feminine word משלחת, "mission," is found in BH (Ps 78:49) and RH (Jastrow, 855b), and interpreting the masculine word משלח here as a biform of it also yields good sense.

[g]הודו My translation takes this word as an otherwise unattested neologism derived from the root הוד√, "to be effulgent." It could also be translated "give thanks to" or "confess," from the root ידה√, but this meaning does not fit the context as well.

[h]שלומים 4Q404 4:9 reads [ש]לומם, "judgments of their [we]ll-being."

[i-i]עמודי משא The meaning of this phrase is far from clear. The word משא comes from a root whose basic meaning is "to lift" (נשא√), and the noun can mean "burden," "tribute," "that which lifts," or "oracle" in BH. Another possible translation is "oracle pillars."

[j]מבנית This word, derived from the root "to build" (בנה√), does not appear in BH but is found in QH (e.g., 4Q511 111:8). Compare the biblical word "structure" (תבנית) from the same root, also found in the *Songs of the Sabbath Sacrifice*.

[k-k]טוהר <<זו>> The scribe wrote the first two letters of the word "radiant" (זוהר), then marked them for deletion and wrote "most pure" (טוהר טהורים) instead.

[l]רוש 4Q405 6:4 reads [ר]אשי, "[ch]iefs of the."

[m]תבנית Derived from the root "to build" (בנה√), this word is used in BH to mean a copy (Josh 22:28) or pattern (Exod 25:9; 1 Chron 28:11, 18) or form (Deut 4:16-18;

Ezek 8:3). In 1QM x:14 it refers to the construction of Adam by God, and in the *Songs of the Sabbath Sacrifice* it refers to structures in the celestial realm.

[רו]חֵי] The reading is established by 4Q405 6:5 (רוחי), but note that 4Q404 5:1 reads רוח, "spirit."

°Two readings of the lost word are attested in other manuscripts, although neither is completely preserved. 4Q404 5:3 probably read [רקיﬠֵ פלא, "[firmame]nt of wonder," but 4Q405 6:6 seems to read [רקיﬠﬞי פלא, "[firmament]s of wonder." The immediately preceding word seems not to be preserved.

אורתם Pᵐ The reading in 4Q404 5:4 is אורותם. Presumably both are misspellings (or variant spellings) of אורתום, "perfect light" (see note a to VII 4Q403 1ii:1). Compare the similar expression לאור אורתום, "to light of perfect light," in 1QHᵃ xxi:14.

[מ]ל[דﬨﬞ Reading with Newsom's text (p. 269) rather than her notes (p. 271), which erroneously reconstruct [כו]ל, "[al]l," on consideration of space.

Commentary

Line 30. The seventh Sabbath falls on the sixteenth day of the second month. Note that the number of the month is not included in 4Q403 (the parallel in 4Q404 3:2 is too fragmentary for us to tell if it included a number after the word "month"). Where the other headings are preserved or reconstructable (Songs I, IV, XII), they always include the number of the month, so the word "second" may have been accidentally omitted in 4Q403.

Line 32. The phrase "the glory of His kingdom" also occurs in 4Q510 1:4. Compare "in the glory of Your kingdom" (1QM xii:7) and "blessed be the name of the glory of His kingdom forever and ever" (*SH L* §394 // §471 // §731). For similar expressions, see the commentary to VI 4Q403 1i:25.

Line 34. The title "King of kings" is found in 1 Tim 6:16; Rev 17:14; 19:16; *1 Enoch* 9:4; 4Q381 76-77:7; perhaps 4Q491 8-10:13 // 1QM xiv:16; and in the HL (e.g., *3 Enoch* 22:15; G8 1a:18-19; G23 1a:3, 9, 18; 1b:4, 7). The more common title in the HL is "the King of kings of kings" (e.g., *Hekhalot Rabbati* §217; *Maʿaseh Merkavah* §558; *Sar Panim* §631; *Merkavah Rabba* §675).

Line 35. The creation of the angels on the first day is described in *Jub.* 2:2-3. Newsom correctly notes that "works" in this context refers to created beings, since their actions are mentioned in the next line.

Line 37. According to 1QHᵃ xviii:35 and *1 Enoch* 90:20-25, God is judge of the angels.

Lines 38, 39, 43. The word translated "confess" (line 38) could also be translated "give thanks to"; likewise, "confessions" (lines 39, 43) could be translated "thanksgivings."

Line 39. Echoes Ps 105:5 and Exod 15:2.

Line 40. Newsom plausibly suggests that the phrase "with the best portion of spirit" exhorts the audience to offer God a spiritual "portion" or "offering" (often a secondary sense of the word), as opposed to a material one (cf. Heb 13:15). A heavenly sacrificial cult figures in Songs XII and XIII (see the commentary to XII 4Q405 23i:5-6). For a similar use of the word "best," normally translated "head" or "chief," see Exod 30:23.

Line 41. This line has the only mention of pillars in the surviving text of the *Songs of the Sabbath Sacrifice,* and the immediate context seems to place these in the vicinity of the heavenly sanctuary. Two pillars stood in front of the vestibule of Solomon's temple (1 Kgs 7:15-22; 2 Chron 3:15-17; cf. Ezek 40:49); presumably these are the cosmic equivalents, perhaps to be identified with the "pillars of heaven" of Job 26:11 (cf. *1 Enoch* 18:3, 11). The pillars of smoke and fire that led the Israelites through the wilderness may also be behind the image (Exod 13:21-22; 4Q470 3:5; 4Q504 6:10). *3 Enoch* 38:1 mentions "all the pillars of the firmaments and their capitals."

The word "abode" appears only here and in 4Q405 81:2 in the *Songs of the Sabbath Sacrifice.* Its root means "to be honored or princely" (cf. Gen 30:20). In the HB it is used of the temple in Jerusalem (1 Kgs 8:13 // 2 Chron 6:2), God's abode in heaven (Isa 63:15; Hab 3:11), and perhaps the abode of the dead (Ps 49:15; the text is uncertain). In the QL it refers to God's abode in heaven (1QS x:3; 1QM xii:1-2 // 4Q491 5-6:1; 1QHᵃ xi:34). In Jewish esoteric literature Abode is the name of one of the seven firmaments (e.g., *Seder Rabba di Bereshit* §§40-41 [*SH-L* §§720-22]).

Line 42. The phrase "firmaments of purity" appears in XII 4Q405 23i:6-7. Compare "heavens of purity" in 4Q262 B:5; the description of the celestial pavement in Exod 24:10; the "firmament of terrible ice" in Ezek 1:22; and the discussion of this pavement in the commentary to XI 4Q405 19:5.

Line 43. Compare the "chief firmament on high" with the "first firmament" of seven in the HL (e.g., *3 Enoch* 17:3) and in *Sepher HaRazim* I 1. In the HL the first firmament is the lowest, but in the *Songs of the Sabbath Sacrifice* the chief firmament appears to be the topmost. The beams and walls of the earthly temple are mentioned in 2 Chron 3:6-7.

Line 45. The word pair "effulgence and adornment" reconstructed here is used in descriptions of the heavenly realm in the *Songs of the Sabbath Sacrifice,* the HB, 4Q286 1ii:4, and often in the HL.

4Q405 6:9-11 (= 4Q403 1i:48-50)

A fragment mentioning (angelic?) proclamation

⁹[. . .].to God [. . .]. ends of ¹⁰[. . .]. voice ¹¹[. . .]they shall proclaim

11Q17 i (= 4Q403 1i:48-50 + ?)

A fragment referring to the architecture of the heavenly temple

⁴[. . .].. ..[. . .] the light .[. . .] ⁵[. . . its] row[sª . . .] its [row]s, construct[ion . . .] ⁶[. . .].. hol[y . . .] they [procl]aim psalms[. . .] ⁷[. . . div]inities ...[. . .]to divinities of [. . .] ⁸[. . .]and seven ..[. . .]secondary ones of .[. . .] ⁹[. . .].... .[di]vinities .[. . .]

Note

ªThe word "rows" (סדרות) in this line is used in the context of the construction of the earthly temple in 1 Kgs 6:9 (שדרת), although elsewhere in the HB the word means the ranks of an army (2 Kgs 11:8, 15; 2 Chron 23:14). In RH the word סדר means "row, order," angelic "upper ranks," "battle lines," scripture reading "portion," "order" of the Mishnah, and "colonnade" (Jastrow, 958b-59a). The last, however, is masculine, so its plural form would be different.

Commentary

Lines 7, 9. In the absence of any context, the word translated "divinities" three times in these lines could also be taken as a singular form and translated "God."

4Q403 1ii:1-17 + 4Q404 6 (ital.)

*The actions and praises of the angels, spirits,
and other beings in the celestial realms*

[*from the midst of* . . .] ¹perfect light,ª colorful mos[t] holy spirit [. . . *King of all* . . .] ²high places of knowledge and on *His foot*stool [. . . *of wonder* . . .] ³appearance of a glorious *structu*re for the chiefs of the dominions, spi[rits of . . .] ⁴His glory. And in all their turnings^b the gates of .[. . .] ⁵the going of ^csprinklers of [glo]w[ing coals of fire^c . . .].. to the chief(!)^d of the divinities of [. . .] ⁶from between them di[vin]ities run like the appearance of glowing coals of [fire . . .] ⁷walking all around. Most holy spirits .[. . .] ⁸M[os]t holy [spirits], spirits of God, an ete[rnal] appearance ..[. . .] ⁹and spirits of God, shapes of flaming fire around [. . .] ¹⁰wondrous spirits and ^ethe tabernacle of the exalted chief,^e the glory of His kingdom, the inner chamber[. . .] ¹¹and He sanctifies the seven exalted holy (places) and the voice of blessing is from the chiefs of His inner chamber [. . .] ¹²and the voice of the blessing <<is heard>> is glorified in the hearing of the divinities and the councils^f of [. . .] ¹³the blessing. And all the crafted furnishings of the inner cham[ber] hasten with psalms of wonder in the inner cham[ber . . .] ¹⁴of wonder, inner chamber to inner chamber with the sound of holy tumults. And all their crafted furnishings [. . .] ¹⁵and the chariots of His inner chamber psalm together and their cherubim and th[eir] ophannim bless wondrously [. . .] ¹⁶chiefs of the divine structure. And they praise Him in the holy inner chamber. BLANK [. . .] ¹⁷BLANK [. . .]

Notes

^aאורתום The simplest analysis of this word is to divide it into the word "light" (אור) plus the word "completeness, perfection" (תום), although some connection with the Urim and Thummim (האורים והתמים), the sacred lot kept in the high priest's breastpiece (see the commentary to XIII 11Q17 ix:6), may well be implied. The word appears here and in 1QH^a xii:26 and xxi:14, and it should probably be restored in 1QH^a xii:6 and VII 4Q403 1i:45.

^bמהפכיהם This noun, from the root √הפך, "to turn, overturn," is unattested in BH, but compare the Hitpael participle (המתהפכת) of the same root in Gen 3:24 with a similar meaning.

^{c-c}זרקי [גח]ל[י אש The first word cannot be "lightings of" (ברקי), but the reading given here fits the traces well and echoes Ezek 10:2. I interpret the word to be a Qal participle with a short spelling. This form appears twice in the HB (Lev 7:14; 2 Chron 30:16) and once in the *Temple Scroll* (11Q19 xxxiv:8), each time referring to priests carrying out sacrifices. Evidently angelic priests are pictured as sprinkling something (perhaps the glowing coals of Ezek 10:2) in the heavenly sanctuary. Another possibility is to translate the word as "darts," a meaning not found in BH but used for זרק in 1QM vi:2, 3, 16; viii:11. However, the plural there takes the feminine form זרקות.

^dEmending לדוש to לרוש. The root √דוש means "to crush," and it is difficult to think of a way to make it fit this context.

^{e-e}משכן רוש רום This phrase is difficult but may have some interesting implications. A tabernacle is also mentioned in XII 4Q405 20ii-21-22:7. The celestial tabernacle is mentioned in Heb 8:2, 5; 9:11; Rev 13:6; compare "the temple of the tent of witness in heaven" in Rev 15:5. The Hebrew word "head" (רוש) usually means an angelic "chief" in the *Songs of the Sabbath Sacrifice* (e.g., the "chief princes"), but it can also refer to the chiefmost of several objects, such as the "chief firmament on high" in VII

4Q403 1i:43. If the latter sense applies here, the meaning of the phrase would be "the exalted chief tabernacle." But two indicators point in the direction of the first translation, referring to the tabernacle of an exalted chief angel, presumably the heavenly high priest Melchizedek.

First, although multiple sanctuaries, thrones, and chariots are mentioned repeatedly in the *Songs of the Sabbath Sacrifice*, there is no reference to tabernacles in the plural (nor am I aware of a tradition of multiple heavenly tabernacles elsewhere). Second, there is a tradition of an angelic or divinized human high priest serving in the celestial tabernacle. This tabernacle is mentioned several times in the HL, almost always in association with the angelic high priest (the exception is a reference to the "tabernacle of the living creatures" in *Massekhet Hekhalot* §22.4). In *3 Enoch* 15B:1 we are told that Metatron (the divinized Enoch) has "a great tabernacle of light on high," and there are also several references to the "tabernacle of the Youth" (משכן הנער) (*SH-L* §390; §399 // §476; §488; G9 6b:35-36; for the figure of the Youth, see the commentary to XII 4Q405 20ii-21-22:6-14). According to the letter to the Hebrews, Christ also serves as high priest in the heavenly tabernacle.

ומוסדי[f] Newsom notes that one could also read ומיסדי, a Piel participle of the root סד/√, "to found," and take it as an angelic title, "founders of," or the like.

Commentary

Line 2. God's footstool is mentioned in Isa 66:1; Ps 99:5; 132:7; Lam 2:1 (apparently referring to Zion); 1 Chron 28:2. Divine footstools (plural) seem to be mentioned in 4Q286 1ii:1 (cf. *2 Enoch* 19:6?). The HL also refers to the divine footstool (e.g., *Hekhalot Rabbati* §153).

Line 3. The phrase "appearance of a glorious structure" alludes to Ezek 1:28 and also obliquely (as is typical of the *Songs of the Sabbath Sacrifice*) to the divine glory.

Another possible translation of the last phrase in the line is "for the chiefs of spi[ritual] dominions." But if the first reconstruction and translation are correct, the text may allude to the ancient idea that each nation had a chief angel assigned to it (cf. Deut 32:8-9 and Dan 10:13-14, 20). See also the commentary to II 4Q401 14i:6.

Line 4. The gates of the earthly temple are mentioned alongside the chariot in Ezek 10:19 (cf. 8:3-4) and those of Ezekiel's imagined temple in Ezek 43:1-5.

Line 5. The Hebrew infinitive translated "the going of" also appears in Ezek 1:9, 12, 17, 20 (x2), 21, 24; 10:11 (x2), 16. The "chief of the divinities" may be the same figure as the "exalted chief" in line 10.

Line 6. Compare the "glowing coals of fire" to Ezek 1:13; 10:2. This phrase also appears in 4QSecond Ezekiel (4Q385 4:12); the HL associates "glowing coals of fire" with the heavenly throne room (e.g., *SH-L* §373).

Line 7. Echoes Ezek 1:13.

Line 9. Spirits and the divine realm are represented as fiery in nature in the Psalms (Ps 104:4), apocalyptic literature (*1 Enoch* 14:11; Dan 7:9-10; Rev 4:5; *2 Apoc. Bar.* 22:6), the Phoenician tradition (Philo of Byblos, *Phoenician History* [*Praep. Evan.* 1.10.9]), and Ugaritic literature (Smith, "Biblical and Canaanite Notes," 586-87). For more fiery spirits, see Song XII 4Q405 20ii-21-22:10.

Line 11. One could possibly read "and [they] sanctify." The "seven exalted holy (places)" are presumably related to the "seven inner chambers of the priesthood[s]" (VII 4Q405 7:7); "the seven priesthoods of His interior" (VIII 4Q403 1ii:20 [cf. 22]); the "seven wondrous borders" (VIII 4Q403 1ii:21); the "seven holy councils" (VIII 4Q403 1ii:22); and the "seven most holy borders" (VIII 4Q403 1ii:27; 4Q405 44:1). The precise details and interrelationships in the cosmography are obscure.

Line 13. Compare the "crafted furnishings" to those in Exod 31:4 and the workmanship of the shields and weapons in 1QM v:6-11.

Line 15. Multiple celestial chariots are mentioned in the HB in Isa 66:15; perhaps Jer 4:13; Hab 3:8; Zech 6:1-3; Ps 68:18. In the QL they figure repeatedly in the *Songs of the Sabbath Sacrifice* and also appear in 4Q286 1ii:2. In the HL a group of them is listed in *3 Enoch* 24, and *Ma'aseh Merkavah* §§554-55 describes vast numbers of chariots, more in each succeeding palace, which sing together like those in the *Songs of the Sabbath Sacrifice*. Something of this sort may be implied in line 14 of this passage by the broken phrase "inner chamber to inner chamber with the sound of holy tumults," although this seems to refer to the resounding praise of the animate crafted furnishings of line 13. Chariots are also mentioned in *SH-L* §490; *Ma'aseh Merkavah* §585; *Massekhet Hekhalot* §12.2; 15.1; 17.1.

The cherubim are angelic beings above whom God is enthroned (see 1 Sam 4:4; 2 Sam 22:11 // Ps 18:11; cf. 4Q204 1vii:1) and who guard the entrance to Eden (Gen 2:24). They are represented as architectural motifs in the construction of the tabernacle (e.g., Exod 25:18-22; 26:31-33) and the temple (e.g., 1 Kgs 6:24-29; 1 Chron 28:18; 2 Chron 3:7, 10-14; cf. 11Q19 vii:10-12). Cherubim are often associated with the heavenly throne room in Second Temple and parabiblical literature. In the QL cherubim also appear in the *Songs of the Sabbath Sacrifice* and in 4Q511 41:2.

The "living creatures" of Ezekiel 1 are identified with the cherubim in Ezekiel 10 but are not mentioned in the surviving text of the *Songs of the Sabbath Sacrifice*. Nevertheless, the persistent association of cherubim in the *Songs of the Sabbath Sacrifice* with motifs from Ezekiel 1 seems to imply that the author accepted this identification. Strangely, Isa 6:1-3, a centrally inspirational

130

passage for the HL, is never alluded to in the *Songs of the Sabbath Sacrifice* either, which may imply that the author also took the cherubim and seraphim to be the same beings (cf. Second Ezekiel, 4Q385 4:6-7, which seems to describe the living creatures of Ezekiel 1 in terms reminiscent of the seraphim in Isa 6:2). The HL mentions the cherubim frequently, often in association with the ophannim, and always distinguishes them from the living creatures.

The word "ophannim" means "wheel" and is used of the divine chariot in Ezek 1:15-21; 3:13; 10:9-19, and 4Q385 4:10-11; and of wheels on the bronze stands in the temple, "like chariot-wheel workmanship," in 1 Kgs 7:30-33 (cf. 4Q365[a] 5i:4). In the *Songs of the Sabbath Sacrifice* they are angelic beings (XI 4Q405 20ii-21-22:3; XII 4Q405 20ii-21-22:9), as sometimes in Second Temple and parabiblical literature (e.g., *1 Enoch* 71:7; *2 Enoch* 20:1; 29:3) and always in the HL.

4Q405 7 (= 4Q403 1ii:9-16)

A fragment mentioning inner chambers of angelic priesthoods[a]

[1][. . .]...[. . .] [2][. . .] ho[ly] ...[. . .] [3][. . .]in seven ..[. . .].[ ]. kingdom[. . .] [4][. . .]chi[ef . . .]. in the sta[tion]. [. . .] [5][. . .].[ ].[. . .].[. . .] [6][. . .].. around[. . .]...[. . .] [7][. . . sev]en inner chambers of the priesthoo[ds of . . .] [8][. . .].. his [pr]iesthood and .[. . .] [9][. . .]...[. . .] [10][. . .].. work[s of . . .] [11][. . .].. ..[. . .] [12][. . .]...[. . .]

Note
[a]Most of this fragment was found superimposed on 4Q405 6, so it is one column away from frag. 6 and should correspond approximately to 4Q403 1ii:9-16. Unfortunately the latter text is badly damaged, and there is no overlap between the two fragments. Still, the placing of frag. 7 in this vicinity is very probable.

Commentary

Line 8. Could "his [pr]iesthood" refer to the priesthood of Melchizedek? Compare Ps 110:4 and VIII 4Q403 1ii:21.

Song VIII

(4Q403 1ii:18-48 + 4Q405 8-13 + 11Q17 ii;
4Q405 64 + 67 + 11Q17 iii)

> *Exhorts a second order of angels, who comprise seven priestly*
> *councils in seven territories, to praise God. Seven angels offer*
> *successive praises, each tongue louder than the previous one.*
> *After another series of seven psalms by (the same?) angels, the*
> *seven secondary princes each offer a blessing of seven words.*
> *This last section corresponds closely to the blessings of the*
> *seven chief princes in Song VI.*

4Q403 1ii:18-48 + 4Q405 8-11 + 11Q17 ii (ital.)

Title and opening call to praise

¹⁸For the Sage. The song of the holocaust offering of the *eighth* Sabbath on the tw[enty]-third [of the second month. Psalm the God of all exalted heights all holy ones of] ¹⁹eternity, second among the priests of the interior, the second council in the *wondrous dwelling*ᵃ among seve[n . . . among all who know] ²⁰[et]ernity.

Invocation of angelic princes and priesthoods

And exalt Him, O chiefs of princes with the portion of(!)ᵇ His wonders. Psalm [the God of *gods*, O seven priesthoods of His interior . . .] ²¹exaltation, seven wondrous borders by the laws of His sanctuaries ᶜ<<chiefs of princes of [a *wondrous*] prie[sthood>>ᶜ *of Melchizedek*ᵈ . . . sanctuaries of] ²²seveneᵉ pries[t-hoods] in a wondrous sanctuary for seven holy councils .[. . .] ²³the officer, the angels of the King in the wondrous dwellings and the knowledge of their un-derstanding for seven[. . .] ²⁴chief [. . .] from the priest of the interior and the chiefs of the congregation of the King in the assembly of .[. . .] ²⁵and exalted praises to the King of glory and greatness of [G]o[d . . .] ²⁶to the God of gods, the pure King and the contribution of their tongues ..[. . .] ²⁷seven mysteries of knowledge in the wondrous mystery of the seven [most] hol[y] borders [. . .]

132

The ascending praises of the seven secondary princes

f[And the tongue of the first will become mighty sevenfold by means of the tongue of the one second to him; and the tongue of his second^g will become mightier] [28]sevenfold than the one third [to him; and the ton]gue of the thi[rd will become] mightier sevenfo[ld than the one fourth to him; and the tongue of the fourth will become mighty sevenfold by means of the tongue of the one fifth to him; and the tongue of the fifth will become mighty sevenfold by means of the tongue of] [29]the one sixth to him; and the tong[ue of the sixth will become mighty sevenfold by means of the] to[ngue of the seventh to him and by means of the tongue of the seventh will become mighty^f . . . holiness of the sanctuary of . . .] [30]and according to the sevenfold w[ords of . . .] [31]with wondrous psalms, with [wo]ndrous wor[ds . . .] [32]wonder. BLANK

A summary of the psalms of the seven secondary princes

[Psalm of] blessing by [the tongue of the first . . .] [33]wonder and psalming to the Lord of all god[s of . . .] [34]the chief of His wonders for great psalming[. . .] [35]for the ones who enlighten knowledge among all gods of light[. . .] [36]praises [by] the tongue of the fourt[h . . .] [37]wonder. P[salm of thanksgiving by] the t[ongue of the fifth . . .] [38]thanks[givings . . .] [39]Ps[alm of . . .] [40].[. . .] [41][. . .] [42][. . .] [43][. . .] [44][. . .] [45][. . .]dwellin[gs . . .] [46][. . .]. with se[ven . . .] [47][. . .]...
...[. . .] [48][. . .]..[. . .]

Notes

[a]במעון The reading is במעוני, "in wondrous dwellings," in 4Q405 8-9:3 and probably in 11Q17 ii:5.

[b]במנה As it stands the text says "with the portion." Perhaps emend to במנת, as in the translation.

[c-c]The surviving words are marked for deletion with supralinear dots in 4Q403 1i:21 but not in 4Q405 8-9:5. It cannot be determined how many if any words in the lacuna in 4Q403 were marked for deletion.

[d]למלכֿי צדק The surviving text is from 11Q17 ii:7. It is tempting to restore the name Melchizedek (cf. Ps 110:4; 4Q401 22:2-3), but other restorations are possible, for example, [למלך הכבוד], "of the King [of glory]," or למלכֿ[ות], "of the king[dom of . . .]."

[e]The corresponding text of 4Q405 8-9:7 reads something different from "seven," but the word is badly damaged and cannot be deciphered.

[f-f]This passage is very difficult. I have taken לו, "to him," to indicate the order of the appearance of the various tongues with reference to the first (dative of respect); the preposition ב-, "by means of," to indicate means or instrument (this word cannot denote accompaniment); and the preposition מן, "than," to indicate comparison. The

result is not entirely consistent or satisfactory, but it appears at least to make sense grammatically.

שני[מ]‏‏‏ו[8]‏ From the context one would expect "the second" (המשנה or השני).

Commentary

Line 19. This line hints that Song VIII relates the various praises and blessings of the seven secondary princes, although the identity of the praising angels does not become explicit in the surviving fragments until we reach the blessings of the "wondrous secondary princes" in 4Q405 13.

Line 21. Presumably the "seven wondrous borders" are the same as the "seven [most] hol[y] borders" (line 27) and have some relationship with the "seven priesthoods of His interior" (line 20) and the "seven holy councils" (line 22), the "seven exalted holy (places)" (VII 4Q403 1ii:11), and are to be taken as a feature of the celestial cosmography. An angelic border is also mentioned in I 4Q400 1i:13, although any connection with this passage is less certain.

This line includes one of the three possible occurrences of the name Melchizedek in the *Songs of the Sabbath Sacrifice* (the other two are in 4Q401 11:3; 22:3). Unfortunately, all three are badly damaged and the readings are uncertain, but, nevertheless, a good case can be made that the celestial warrior-priest had a place in the *Songs of the Sabbath Sacrifice*. See the "Excursus on the Melchizedek Tradition" at the end of this chapter.

Line 24. The phrase "from the priest of the interior" is found only here (although "priests of the interior" appears elsewhere in the *Songs of the Sabbath Sacrifice;* e.g., I 4Q400 1i:8), and it seems to single out a particular angelic priest. Given the context, it may be that we should tie the phrase to the possible reference to Melchizedek in line 21.

Line 27. The "mysteries of knowledge" are also mentioned in 1QS iv:6; various permutations of the "wondrous mystery" (all in the plural) occur in II 4Q401 14ii:2; 1QS ix:18; xi:5; 1QH^a v:8; ix:21; x:13; xii:27-28; xv:27; and xix:10.

Lines 27-29. Although the grammar is somewhat obscure, this passage appears to state that the praise of each successive secondary prince resounds seven times louder than that of his predecessor. The idea is similar to the description of the praise offered by the many myriad chariots in the seven heavenly palaces in *Ma'aseh Merkavah* §§554-55 (see the commentary to VII 4Q403 1ii:15).

Line 32. The blank space in this line appears to block off a new, and unfortunately poorly preserved, section of the song (approximately lines 32b-48 + 4Q405 12, 64-67 + 11Q17 iii), which mentions a series of psalms recited by seven beings, again presumably the seven secondary chief princes.

Lines 37-38. The word translated "thanksgiving(s)" could also be translated "confession(s)."

4Q405 12 (= 4Q403 1ii:32-34?)

¹[with the t]ongue [. . . the . . . of] ²wonder .[. . .] ³and he makes great [. . .] ⁴Psalm of .[. . .] ⁵[. . .]..[ ].[. . .]

11Q17 iii + 4Q405 64 + 67 (= 4Q403 1ii:40-44?)

³[. . . of His won]der,ᵃ melody of power to [. . .] ⁴[. . .] His [won]ders to bless [. . . with seven m]elodies of won[der . . .] ⁵[. . .]. seven psalms of bl[essings . . . sev]en psa[lms of greatness] ⁶[. . .]psalms of exal[tation . . . seven . . .] ⁷[. . .] His [won]ders [. . .] ⁸[. . .]seven by se[ven . . .] ⁹[. . . L]ord of a[l]l g[ods . . .] ¹⁰[. . .] the interior in a dwel[ling . . .] ¹¹[. . .]wonder to bless[. . .] ¹²[. . . wo]nder [and] blessing to .[. . .] ¹³[. . .]...[. . .]

Note

ᵃ[פל]אות] One could also read [פל]אי, "[wond]ers of."

4Q405 66

¹[. . .]. with seven[. . .] ²[. . .]and they glorify .[. . .] ³[. . . sev]en eternal[. . .] ⁴[. . .].[ ] ... [. . .]

4Q405 13ᵃ

A fragment of the sevenfold blessings of the seven secondary princes

¹[. . .].[ ] .[wondrous] ²[words and he blesses] all the god[s who draw near to His faithful knowledge with seven wor]ds of goodness for His glorious mercies. BLANK

[The fif]th among the wondrous ³[secondary] prin[ces] shall bless in the name of [His wonders all who know the mysteries of . . .] purity with seven words of exalted purity, [and] he blesses all who rush after ⁴His faithful [favo]r

with seven [wondrous] wor[ds,] and he blesses all [who give thanks] to Him
with seven words of His glorious effulgence.

The sixth among the wondrous secondary [5][prin]ces shall bless in the
name of mig[hty acts of gods all m]ighty ones of insight with eternal knowledge, with seven words of His wondrous mighty acts. [6][And he bl]esses all
whose way is sound [with seven words of . . . wonder as a continu]al sacrifice
with all coming ages, and he blesses [al]l [who wait] for [Him] with se[ven]
[7][wondrous] [w]ord[s for a restorati]on of [His merciful acts of kindness . . .]

[And the seventh among] the [wondrous] seco[ndary] princes [. . .]

Note

[a]This passage corresponds to VI 4Q403 1i:18-23, the blessings of the chief princes,
which helps us restore the text of this fragment. See the commentary to the former
passage for additional discussion of the readings and meaning of the passage.

Commentary

Lines 2-3, 4-5, 7. The "wondrous secondary princes" may be compared to
the "secondary priests" mentioned alongside the high priest in the HB (2 Kgs
23:4; 25:18 // Jer 52:24; cf. 1QM ii:1; 11Q19 xxxi:4-5) and to the chiefs and their
seconds in the tribe of Gad (1 Chron 5:12) and among the levitical singers
(1 Chron 15:18; 16:5) and the Levites (2 Chron 31:12).

Line 4. The restored phrase "who give thanks" could also be translated
"who confess."

4Q404 11[a]

[1][. . .] with seven[. . .] [2][. . .]. with sevenfold[. . .] [3][. . .]. for glory .[. . .]
[4][. . .]knowledge [. . .]

Note

[a]This fragment has a few words that may have come from the praises and blessings
in Song VIII.

Song IX

(11Q17 iv + 4Q405 14-15i; 4Q405 17?)

Describes the brickwork, vestibules, and entryways leading into the heavenly temple, which are carved with living divinities who offer praises.

11Q17 iv

The animate celestial architecture[a]

[3][. . .].[. . . G]od of gods[. . .] [4][. . .]bri[ck]work [. . .] vestibules of the ent[rances of . . .] [5][to] their glorious [br]icks [. . .]. bricks of [. . . firma]ment [6]wondrous [appea]rances .[. . .] of pur[ity . . . miss]ions [7]with the effulgence of pra[ises . . .]in the lik[eness of . . . prai]ses. [8]Divinities .[. . . p]raises (4Q405 14-15i + 11Q17 iv) [1]. . . [sp]irit of glo[ry] . . . [2]. . . wondrous lik[en]ess of mos[t] holy spirit . . . [to]ngue of blessing and from the likeness of [3]. . . [a vo]ice of blessing to the King of exalters,[b] and their wondrous psalm is to the God of gods . . . their colorful . . . and they chant [4]. . . the vestibules of their entrances, spirits of the interior of the holy of holies in . . . eternal . . . [5][and the like]ness of living divinities is carved on the vestibules of the entrances of the King, shapes of spirit of lights . . . [K]ing, shapes of glorious li[ght], spirits of [6]. . . [in] the midst of adorned spirits are wondrous colorful works, shapes of living divinities . . . [in the in]ner chambers of glory, the construction of [7]the [mo]st holy [sanctuary] in the inner chambers of the King, sha[pes of div]in[ities and from] the likeness of . . . most holy [8]. . . [li]ving [divinities] . . .

Notes

[a]The beginning of Song IX is lost, but it may be reconstructed with a high degree of confidence as follows:

> [For the Sage. The song of the holocaust offering of the ninth Sabbath on the thirtieth of the second month. Psalm the God of . . .]

[b]מרוממים The translation interprets the form as a Polel participle. One could also take it as a Polal participle and translate "exalted ones."

Commentary to 4Q405 14-15 + *11Q17 iv*

Line 4. The "vestibule" was the entryway of the earthly temple (1 Kgs 6:3; 1 Chron 28:11; cf. Ezek 40:48). Perhaps the referent here is the multiple sanctuaries or temples mentioned elsewhere in the *Songs of the Sabbath Sacrifice*. Newsom notes the similarity to "the vestibule of the gate" in Ezekiel's imagined earthly temple (Ezek 40:7, 8, 9, 15; 44:3; 46:2, 8), pointing out that the "prince" is associated with this gate (Ezek 44:3; 46:8) (DJD 11: 332). A vestibule of the temple is also mentioned in the *Temple Scroll* (11Q19 iv:8).

The vestibule of the celestial temple is mentioned in *Sar Torah* §§297-98 in a vision of the "forms" of the temple granted to the men of the restoration before the Second Temple was built. In the *Hekhalot Zutarti* R. Akiva reports that, on his ascent to the heavenly temple, "I put more markings on the entrances of the firmament than on the entrances of my house" (§346); later he hears a heavenly voice proclaim in Aramaic, "Before YHWH made heaven and earth, He established an entrance (?) to the firmament by which to enter and to go out" (§348).

Line 5. Carvings (including of cherubim) were also part of the decoration of Solomon's earthly temple (1 Kgs 6:29, 35; 7:36; Ps 74:6; 2 Chron 3:7) and of Ezekiel's imagined temple (Ezek 41:17-20, 25). Newsom notes that Ps 24:7 inspired the notion of the animate temple praising God.

According to *3 Enoch,* names of God and the letters of creation are incised with a pen of flame on the throne of glory (39:1; 41:1-3). In the *Hekhalot Rabbati,* the visage of Jacob is incised on the throne of glory, and God kneels over his throne and embraces and kisses this image three times a day at the time of prayer (§164). God also has inscribed the likenesses of a man, an ox, a lion, and an eagle (cf. Ezek 1:10) on his throne (*Hekhalot Rabbati* §273).

4Q405 17

Celestial spirits and angels[a]

[1][. . .].[. . .] [2][. . .] wonders [ ]...[ ].[. . .] [3][. . .] their [. . .] spirits of knowledge and understanding, truth [4][. . .] purity, angels of glory with might of [5][. . . wond]rous acts, angels of ornamentation and spirits of [6][. . .]in inner chambers of holiness, dwellings of [7][. . .]. works of [8][. . .]glory [9][. . .]..

Note

[a]Newsom (*Critical Edition*, 261-64) suggests that a column might have been lost

between 4Q405 15ii-16 and 19, but in DJD 11 she notes that overlaps with the new reconstruction of 11Q17 v-vi in DJD 23 show that there is no room for the postulated missing column, so frag. 19 must come from the column immediately following frags. 15ii-16. The placement of frag. 17 is not certain, but it may well belong to the same column as frags. 15ii-16, in which case it belongs at the end of Song IX or, just possibly, at the beginning of Song X. (Note that most of the first paragraph after the transcription of frag. 17 in DJD 11: 337 has inadvertently been taken from *Critical Edition*, p. 290, unrevised and should be corrected in light of the new reconstruction.)

Commentary

Line 4. Compare "angels of glory" with "angel of His glory" (4Q511 20i:2) and "angels of His glory" (4Q511 35:4; cf. *T. Levi* 18:5). "Angels of glory" are also mentioned in *Ma'aseh Merkavah* §§564, 582.

Song X

(4Q405 15ii-16 + 11Q17 v)

Brings us to the rivers of fire, from which the curtain of the inner chamber of the King is visible. Other curtains and inner chambers are mentioned (perhaps belonging with the chariots and thrones referred to later?). The curtains seem to be embroidered with animate shapes who praise God.

4Q405 15ii-16 + 11Q17 v:1-6ª

[1]fringe of an edge [. . .] [2]and [b]rivers of fire[b] [. . .].[. . .] ...[. . .].[. . .] [3]appearances of flames of fire[. . . or]namentation on the curtain of the inner chamber of the King ..[.   ] [4]in the inner chamber of His Presence the colorful [. . .] all incised ..[ ].. shapes of divin[ities, their] works are [5]glorious from their two sides [. . .]curtains of the wondrous inner chambers and they bless [the God of all . . .] [6]their sides, they shall proclaim [. . .]. of wonder inside the scorching heat,[c] the inner chamber [at the exit of the vestibules of . . .] [7][. . .]forms of wonder [. . .] they [give tha]nks to the King of glo[ry] with a voice of chanting [. . .] [8][. . . God . . .]..[ ].. all [. . .] (11Q17 v:6-10) [6][. . .].. and forms [. . .] [7][. . .]..[. . .]. they shall proclaim [. . .] God of god[s . . .] [8][. . .]eternal thrones [. . .] [9][. . .] their [sh]apes, cherubi[m of . . .] [10][. . .]foundations[. . .].

Notes

ᵃThe beginning of Song X is lost, but it may be reconstructed with a high degree of confidence as follows:

> [For the Sage. The song of the holocaust offering of the tenth Sabbath on the seventh day of the third month. Psalm the God of . . .]

ᵇ⁻ᵇThe translation "and rivers of light" is also possible (vocalizing as אוֹר rather than אוּר).

ᶜיקדה I take this word to be the same as יקידה in RH (Jastrow, 591b), which fits the context in lines 2-3 better than "worthy place" (יקרה). The phrase "scorching fire" (אש יוקדת) is common in the HL (e.g., 3 Enoch 15:1; 22:4; 26:12; 42:1, 6; 47:4).

Commentary

Line 1. The meaning of the phrase "fringe of an edge" is unclear, but it is also found in 1QM v:5, 8, referring to ornamentation on a shield and a spear. The plural "fringes" appears in the HB in Deut 22:12 and 1 Kgs 7:17.

Line 2. The phrase "rivers of fire" is part of a long stream of tradition regarding such celestial rivers (Dan 7:10, 1 Enoch 14:19; 17:5; 71:6, etc.). In XII 4Q405 20ii-21-22:10 "streams of fire" are mentioned (cf. 4Q204 1vii:1-2). A cosmic river of fire and rivers of fire appear frequently in the HL.

Line 3. The "curtain" (פרוכת) seems to be the heavenly counterpart of the curtain concealing the holy of holies in the tabernacle (e.g., Exod 26:31-33; 36:35; Lev 16:2, 12, 15; 4Q266 5ii:7; 4Q375 1ii:7; 11Q19 vii:13-14) and in Solomon's temple (2 Chron 3:14). According to b. Yoma 72b, this curtain was woven to produce a different figure on each side. This idea may be reflected in the rest of this line and the first part of line 5 (Baumgarten, "The Qumran Sabbath Shirot," 202). The curtain of the heavenly sanctuary is mentioned (and identified with the flesh of Jesus) in Heb 10:12. In Gnostic myth there is a veil separating the material world and the seven heavens from the higher heavens of the world above (Hyp. Arch. NHC II, 4 94:9-10; 95:21-22). That veil may be an echo of the celestial curtain in Jewish tradition.

According to SH-L §372, there is a curtain of fire in the heavenly sanctuary. In 3 Enoch 45 (cf. G11 2b:2-4), Metatron shows R. Ishmael the curtain (פרגוד) of the celestial holy of holies, on which are incised the acts of all generations, past, present, and future, until the eschaton. In his ascent to the heavenly temple, R. Akiva reached "the curtain" (פרגוד) after passing the "entrances of the firmament" (Hekhalot Zutarti §346 // §673).

Line 4. The door to the nave of the earthly temple was incised with drawings (1 Kgs 6:35).

Line 5. Perhaps the phrase "from their two sides" refers to the two sides of the curtain. Compare Exod 32:15; 1QM v:12; 11Q19 xxxvii:7 (reconstructed).

Line 7. The word translated "they [give tha]nks to" could also be translated "they [con]fess."

Line 8. Given the broken context, the word translated "God" (restored from 11Q17 v:6) could also be translated "divinities."

Commentary to 11Q17 v:6-10

Line 8. An "eternal throne" of God is mentioned in *Massekhet Hekhalot* §4.11.

Song XI

*(4Q405 18 + 20i; 4Q405 19 + 11Q17 vi;
4Q405 20ii-21-22:1-5 + 11Q17 vii:1-7)*

> *Describes the living spirits engraved in the floor of the inner chambers, which may be part of the nave of the heavenly temple. The throne room is visible: the throne is mentioned, along with the priests of the interior, a seat like God's throne, multiple chariots with seats, and cherubim and ophannim.*

4Q405 18 + 20i

Angelic actions and praise in the (or an) inner chamber[a]

[1][. . .]spirits[. . .]righteousness [2][. . .]to support holy ones. The inner chamber of .[. . .] their [wond]ers [3][. . . ho]lly ones with a spirit of quiet of divinit[ies . . .]their glory [4][. . .]i[nn]e[r c]h[am]ber, they hurry at the voice of the glor[y . . .] [5][. . .] wondrous [ps]alms with a quiet vo[ice . . .] [6][. . .].[. . .]... .[. . .]

Note

[a]The beginning of Song XI is lost, but it may be reconstructed with a high degree of confidence as follows:

[For the Sage. The song of the holocaust offering of the eleventh Sabbath on the fourteenth day of the third month. Psalm the God of . . .]

According to the sectarian solar calendar, the Festival of Weeks was on the fifteenth day of the third month, the day after the eleventh Sabbath. Since the sect carried out a ceremony of covenant renewal on this day, the eleventh Sabbath would have been the prelude to the central holy day of the sectarian year. As Newsom notes, there is some evidence that Songs XI and XII draw on exegetical themes tied to Weeks in rabbinic tradition ("Merkabah Exegesis," 29).

Commentary

Line 4. Presumably it is the angels who "hurry at the sound of the glo[ry]." According to *3 Enoch* 22:16, the angel KRWBY'L, who is in charge of the cherubim, "makes them hurry with glory and power to do the will of their Creator." For "the glory," see the commentary to XII 4Q405 20ii-21-22:7.

4Q405 19 + 11Q17 vi

The animate celestial architecture

[1][. . .].[. . .] [2]and shapes of divinities, m[ost holy] spirits, praise Him [. . . chariot . . .].[ ].. [shapes of] glory, floor[a] of [3]wondrous inner chambers, spirits of eternal gods, al[l]. ..[ ] sha[pes of the inn]er chamber of the King, works of spi[rits of] a firmament of wonder, [4]purely salted, [spi]rits of faithful knowledge [and] righteousness in the holy of [h]olies, [f]orms of living divinities, forms of spirits of [5]luminaries,[b] a[l]l their [workmanship] is of h[ol]y, wondrous plates,[c] colorful [spirits], [sh]apes of the forms of divinities incised [6]around their [gl]orious bricks, glorious forms of br[ic]kwork of effulgence and adornm[ent], living divinities are all their workmanship [7]and the forms of their shapes are angels of holiness. From beneath the wondrous in[ner chambers] a quiet voice of stillness; divinities are blessing [8][. . .]... the King ...[. . . psalming continually. A]l[l . . .].[. . .].[. . .]divi[niti]es (**11Q17 vi:9-10**) [9][. . .].. in the second .[. . .] [10][. . .]wonders of effulgence and ad[ornment . . .]

Notes

[a]מדרס This word is not attested in BH but appears in RH with the meanings "treading place" and "impurity acquired by treading on" (Jastrow, 735b). The same word (מד[ר]ס]) is probably to be reconstructed in 4Q286 1ii:1, in a context that also refers to the floor of the heavenly temple.

ᵇמאורים The feminine plural form (מארות) is more common, but the masculine plural is attested in Ezek 32:8; 4Q286 1ii:3; 4Q287 1:1; *m. Ber.* 8.5. Newsom suggests that the word could also be construed as a Hiphil participle, "light-giving" (מאירים; DJD 11: 342), but this hardly seems necessary.

ᶜדּבְקִי From the root √דבק, meaning "to adhere to," the word דֶּבֶק is found in the HB only in 1 Kgs 22:34 // 2 Chron 18:33 and Isa 41:7, where it seems to mean "scale armor" and "soldering," respectively. In RH it is used to mean "glue, paste," "junction," or "nexus, cause" (Jastrow, 287a). The word דֹּבְקִים is found in a broken context in col. v:1 of the *Temple Scroll* (11Q19), referring to an upper-level structural element in the temple, perhaps to an upper chamber in the nave mentioned in xxxi:7. The reading here is damaged, but the use in the *Temple Scroll* suggests that it is correct.

Commentary

Lines 1-10. Newsom draws attention to the parallels between Song XI and *1 Enoch* 14 (DJD 11: 340). The latter describes Enoch's ascent through the nave of the heavenly temple and into the holy of holies, where God is enthroned. The floor, firmament of wonder, luminary spirits, wondrous plates, and glorious brickwork incised with forms of divinities in this fragment may correspond to the walls, mosaics, floor of crystal, and celestial ceiling of *1 Enoch* 14:10-12.

Line 3. "Firmaments of wonder" (plural) are mentioned in XII 11Q17 viii:2.

Line 4. The phrase "purely salted," also found in XII 4Q405 20ii-21-22:11; XIII 11Q17 ix:7; XIII 4Q405 23ii:10, comes from Exod 30:35, which describes a special "purely salted" incense. The verb "to salt" is used in a literal sense in Lev 2:13 and Ezek 16:4 (and presumably in Exod 30:35) as well as in 11Q19 xxxiv:10, 11, but Newsom and Strugnell are probably right to take its use here as more idiomatic, something like "purely blended." The idiomatic usage is reflected in the Hebrew of Sir 49:1 and the Aramaic translation of *Tg. Onq.* Exod 30:35 (Strugnell, "Angelic Liturgy," 340-41; DJD 11: 342).

According to the *Hekhalot Rabbati*, the mystic who succeeds in navigating the dangers of the celestial ascent arrives before the throne of glory and breaks into song. "Salted incense" is listed as one of the types of praise he offers (§251 // §260 // §974). This expression comes from the same phrase in Exod 30:35.

Line 5. Compare these luminaries to the "paths of the stars" in the ceilings of the heavenly temple in *1 Enoch* 14:11, 17. "Luminaries of His glory" are mentioned in 4Q511 2ii:8, and the phrase "host of luminaries" appears in 1QM x:11. Such luminaries figure frequently in the celestial scene of the HL: they are woven into the canopy of Metatron's throne (*3 Enoch* 10:1) and into his garment (*3 Enoch* 12:1); they glisten from the right hand of God (*3 Enoch* 48A:1);

on their heads the living creatures wear crowns made of luminaries (*SH-L* §184); and at the gate of the sixth palace the angel DWMY'L sits "on a bench of pure stone in which is the splendor of the luminaries of the firmament in the (passage on) the creation of the world" (*Hekhalot Rabbati* §233). According to *Massekhet Hekhalot* §10.4, countless luminaries are set in the gates of the palaces of the seventh firmament.

According to *Hekhalot Zutarti* §408, when the mystic arrives at the entry to the sixth celestial palace he finds that

> The sixth palace appears as though a hundred thousand of thousands and thousands and myriads and myriads of waves of the sea splash onto him. But there is not really even one drop of water; rather it is the splendorous atmosphere of the pure alabaster stones that are paved in the palace, which is a splendor more fearsome than water. And do not the attendants stand opposite him? And if he says, "What is the nature of these waters?" at once they run after him and say to him, "Fool! From now on you shall not see a vision with your eyes!"

The angels then batter the hapless mystic with iron axes. David Halperin has pointed out that there is a persistent tradition of the floor of the heavenly palace being paved with ice (*1 Enoch* 14:10; Rev 4:6; 15:2; *Life of Adam and Eve* 29:2; *Ps.-Philo* 26:8), evidently based on a combined exegesis of Exod 15:8 and Ezek 1:22. He suggests that this ice is the waters of chaos that opposed God at creation and that lapped up to the throne of God until he froze them solid. Thus the angels in the *Hekhalot Zutarti* are alarmed by the mystic's mention of water because it seems to imply, so to speak, that the cosmic refrigeration system has broken down, and they punish him for his blasphemous misstatement (Halperin, *Faces of the Chariot*, 93-100, 231-38, 247-49). It may be that the "h[ol]y, wondrous plates" are related to this tradition. Compare the "most pure firmament" of the sanctuary in VII 4Q403 1i:42 and the "firmament(s) of wonder" in XI 4Q405 19:3 and XII 11Q17 viii:5-6. According to *Massekhet Hekhalot* §9.1, the surface of the Araboth (seventh) firmament is made of precious stones and glowing coals.

Line 6. Bricks and brickwork are also mentioned in a fragmentary context in IX 11Q17 iv:4-5. The inspiration for the brickwork seems to be Exod 24:10 (cf. Ezek 1:22; 10:1), the only place in the HB that mentions bricks in the heavenly realm. The brickwork in Exod 24:10 is under God's feet, which supports the other evidence that the floor of the nave of the temple is being described. A much more ancient antecedent to the tradition of brickwork in the celestial temple is found in the Ugaritic Baal cycle (thirteenth century BCE), which mentions "bricks" *(lbnt)* among the construction materials for Baal's celestial temple (Smith, "Biblical and Canaanite Notes," 587).

Line 7. Angels of holiness are also mentioned elsewhere in the *Songs of the Sabbath Sacrifice* and often in the QL. The paradoxical idea of the quiet stillness of the heavenly liturgy alluded to in this line appears repeatedly in the *Songs of the Sabbath Sacrifice* (I 4Q400 1ii:11; XI 4Q405 18 + 20i:3, 5; XII 4Q405 20ii-21-22:7, 8, 12, 13; 4Q401 16:2) as well as in Rev 8:1. The phrase echoes the "light, quiet voice" of 1 Kgs 19:12, but other biblical references to the silence of the temple are probably also behind the idea (Hab 2:20; Zech 2:17). According to *Aristeas* 92, 95, the priests in the earthly temple ministered in silence. Allusions to 1 Kgs 19:12 in the context of the silence of the heavenly sanctuary also occur in the HL (e.g., *SH-L* §§187, 369; *Ma'aseh Merkavah* §§552-53). See also the commentary to XII 4Q405 20ii-21-22:6-14.

11Q17 vii:1-2

The celestial chariotry and its entourage

¹[. . .]..[. . .] ²[. . .]. His Presence[. . .]above the height of the throne [. . .] (4Q405 20ii-21-22:1-5 + <u>11Q17 vii:3-8</u>) ¹[they do not delay when they stand . . . inne]r chambers of all priests of the interior [. . .] ²by l[aw they are] steadfast to at[tend to . . .] a seat like the throne of His kingdom in [His inner chambers of glory They do not sit . . .] ³the chariots of His glory . . . holy cherubim, ophannim of light in the inn[er chamber . . . spirits of divinities . . . purity . . .] ⁴holiness, workmanship of [its] corn[ers . . .] dominions of seats of glory of chariot[s . . . wings of knowledge . . . wondrous might,] ⁵truth and etern[al] righteousness [. . .] the chariots of His glory when they go to [. . . they do not turn to any . . . they go straight to . . .]

Commentary to 4Q405 20ii-21-22:1-5 + <u>11Q17 vii:3-8</u>

Line 1. The word "when they stand" also appears in Ezek 1:21.

Line 2. The phrase "the throne of His kingdom" is found in Esther 1:2; 5:1 (cf. 1 Chron 28:5; 2 Chron 7:18; 2 *Apoc. Bar.* 73:1) and in *Massekhet Hekhalot* §6.1, and "a throne of an eternal kingdom" is mentioned in 4Q251 2ii + 4:7. A single throne is also mentioned in XI 11Q17 vii:2 and XII 4Q405 20ii-21-22:8 (for multiple thrones, see under XII 4Q405 23i:3).

God's throne is seen in visions in the HB in 1 Kgs 22:19; Isa 6:1; Ezek 1:26;

10:1 and is mentioned frequently in other contexts (e.g., Isa 66:1; Dan 7:9). Elsewhere in the QL, mention of the divine throne survives in Enoch's visions in 4Q202 1iii:15 (*1 Enoch* 9:4) and 4Q204 1viii:27 (*1 Enoch* 18:8).

The phrasing here is suggestive: "a seat *like* the throne of His kingdom" implies the enthronement of another figure (perhaps Melchizedek? cf. Ps 110:1) or figures (such as the chief princes of Song VI; note the multiple seats associated with chariots in line 4). This seated being is contrasted with the other angels who do not sit, in accordance with the rabbinic tradition that angels are unable to sit down (e.g., *b. Ḥag.* 15a; *Gen. Rab.* 65.21). Inasmuch as multiple thrones and chariots are mentioned in the *Songs of the Sabbath Sacrifice,* perhaps the gist of the phrase "they do not sit" is that lesser angels do not sit down, with the implication that greater ones do.

Line 3. Given the rabbinic association of Ezekiel 1 and Ps 68:18 with the giving of the Torah on Mount Sinai at the Festival of Weeks, it is interesting that Song XI, recited on the day before this festival, has a number of allusions to Ezekiel 1 and mentions heavenly chariots at least three times. "Holy cherubim" are mentioned in *Ma'aseh Merkavah* §§593, 594. Compare the "ophannim of light" here to the "ophannim of light" (the Hebrew is slightly different) in *Hekhalot Zutarti* §411.

Line 4. The HB mentions angelic wings in Isa 6:2 (of the seraphim); Ezek 1:6, 8, 9, 11, 24-25; 3:13 (of the four living creatures); 10:5, 8, 12, 16, 19, 21; 11:22 (of the cherubim, identified in Ezekiel 10 with the living creatures); and Zech 5:9? (of two women in a vision), as well as the wings of the cherubim in the earthly sanctuary (Exod 25:20; 37:9; 1 Kgs 6:24, 27; 8:6-7; 2 Chron 3:11-13; 5:7-8). Winged angels also appear, for example, in Rev 4:8; *2 Enoch* 3:1; 16:7; 19:6; 21:1; *Apoc. Elijah* 5:2; *T. Adam* 1:4, 10. The phrase "they go [st]raight" (11Q17 vii:7) echoes Ezek 1:7, 23.

Line 5. The Hebrew infinitive form translated "when they go" also appears in Ezek 1:9, 12, 17, 21, 24; 10:11. Note also the various other uses of the verbal root "to go" in Ezek 1:9-21 and 10:11-16.

Song XII

(4Q405 20ii-21-22:6-14 + 11Q17 vii:7-14; 11Q17 viii; 4Q405 23i)

After the call to praise, this song describes Sabbath worship in the heavenly tabernacle, drawing heavily on Ezekiel's merkavah vision. Various kinds of angels bless and move around the throne-chariot above the firmament of the cherubim and streams of fire. Other chariots and thrones are mentioned. Angelic troops array themselves and elements of the architecture of the temple are described, including the animate entrances and exits that bless and psalm all the angels who are sent out through them on missions.

4Q405 20ii-21-22:6-14 + 11Q17 vii:7-14

Title and opening call to praise

[6]For the Sa[ge. The song of the holocaust offering of] the twelfth [Sa]bbath [on the twenty-first of the third month. Psalm the God of] [7][won]drous [years] and exal[t] Him [ac]c[or]di[ng] to the glory in the tabernac[le of . . .][a] knowledge.

Angelic praise in the celestial throne room

The [cheru]bim fall before Him[b] [c]and they b[le]ss when they raise themselves. A voice of quiet of God [8][is heard] and tumult of chanting; at the rising of their wings, a voice of [quie]t of God.[c] They are blessing a structure of a throne-chariot above the firmament of the cherubim [9][and] they chant [the ef-fulge]nce of the firmament of light <<from>> from beneath His glorious seat, and when the ophannim go, the angels of holiness return. They go out from(!) between[d] [10]His [w]heels of glory. Like the appearance of fire are most holy spir-its all around, an appearance of streams of fire in a likeness of *hashmal*, and workmanship of [11][br]ightness with colorful glory, wondrously dyed, purely(!)[e] salted. Spirits of living [di]vinities go about constantly with the glory of [the] chariots of [12]wonder, and a quiet voice of blessing is with the tumult of their going, and they psalm (with) holiness[f] in the returning of their ways; when they raise themselves they exalt wondrously. And when (they) settle[g] [13]they [sta]nd. A voice of joyous chanting grows silent and the qui[et of] a blessing of God is in all the camps of the divinities [and] a voice of prais[es] [14][. . .]..[ ]. from be-

147

tween all their divisions on [their] side[s . . . and] all their mustered (troops) chant, ea[c]h in [his] stati[on.]

BOTTOM MARGIN?

Notes

ᵃ[ז]במשל Perhaps restore ["the God of"] ([אלוהי]; cf. II 4Q400 2:8 and Rev 13:6) with Newsom, or ["all gods of"] ([כול אלי]; cf. VII 4Q403 1i:30-31), or ["those who draw near to"] ([קרובי]; cf. I 4Q400 1i:6).

ᵇTaking לפנו as a shortened spelling of לפניו, "before Him." One could also read the word as לפני, "before," in which case the phrase should be translated "they fall before the cherubim." But see the commentary to line 7 below.

ᶜ⁻ᶜNewsom ("Merkabah Exegesis") has shown that lines 7-8 rest on an exegesis of Ezek 3:12-13 with the help of 1 Kgs 19:12, using the argument from analogy (gezerah shawah) known from rabbinic exegesis. On the basis of the widely accepted postulate that Ezek 3:12 originally read "when the glory of YHWH rose from its place" (ברום כבוד יהוה ממקומו) instead of the benediction "Blessed be the glory of YHWH from His place" (ברוך כבוד יהוה ממקומו) in the MT, she proposes that these lines interpret both variants: the wings of the cherubim raise themselves (ברומם; cf. Ezek 10:17), but they also produce a "voice" (קול) of blessing, the same sound as the "voice of a great earthquake" generated by the cherubic wings according to Ezek 3:12-13, but reinterpreted in the light of 1 Kgs 19:12, which replaces the theophanic earthquake with a "light, quiet voice."

One paragraph in the HL (SH-L §370) meditates on Ezek 3:12 in light of 1 Kgs 19:11, tying the earthquake in the former to the earthquake, wind, and fire in the latter and identifying the earthquake and wind with the sound of many waters mentioned in Ezek 1:24 (cf. Exod 15:10). It deduces that the living creatures fly because they are made of fire, which is lighter than wind. The fire is also associated with the fiery throne and river of fire in Dan 7:9-10. The conclusions differ from those of the *Songs of the Sabbath Sacrifice*, but the method of interpretation is similar.

ᵈEmending ומבין ("and from between") to מבין, even though the former reading is found in both 4Q405 20ii-21-22:9 and 11Q17 vii:12. The word echoes the word מבינות, which in Ezek 10:2, 6 has the same meaning.

ᵉEmending טוה to טוהר with Newsom. For the phrase "purely salted," see the commentary to XI 4Q405 19:4.

ᶠקוד An abstract noun used here adverbially, not "the Holy One," which would be the adjective קדוש.

ᵍבשוכן Probably a Qal infinitive construct from a root meaning "to settle" or "to abide, dwell" (√שכן), related to the word "tabernacle" (משכן). For the form compare HDSS 200.24; 311.15. This verb often has the technical meaning of God settling or dwelling in his sanctuary on earth (e.g., Exod 25:8; Deut 12:5). As Newsom notes, this word is clearly derived from Ps 68:19 (לשכן; cf. v. 17). Verses 17-20 also mention divine chariotry and the blessing of God, important themes in Song XII. The echo of Psalm 68 is further evidence of its early exegetical use in association with the Festival of Weeks.

Commentary

Lines 6-14. The Sabbath on the twenty-first of the third month would be the one following the Festival of Weeks, which took place on the fifteenth. Like Song XI, this song shows a strong interest in scriptural themes associated with the Festival of Weeks in rabbinic tradition, including exegesis of Ezekiel 1 and Psalm 68 and mention of divine chariots.

Song XII (and to some degree Song XIII) have many parallels to the Hekhalot traditions about the Youth (הנער), the celestial high priest, which appear in various forms and contexts in *SH-L* §§384-99 and parallels. The term "Youth" itself may be a title for a priestly attendant (cf. Exod 33:11; 1 Sam 3:1). The cosmographic opening of this passage describes a field of stars and lightning (cf. *1 Enoch* 14:11, 17) with doors of *ḥashmal* (cf. XII 4Q405 20ii-21-22:10), and it also mentions seal rings bearing the faces of the four living creatures of Ezekiel 1. The bands of angels stand before the Youth, who prostrates himself before God. Blessings are offered to God, including the benediction in Ezek 3:12 (cf. XII 4Q405 20ii-21-22:7-8), and the Youth goes beneath the throne of glory (cf. XII 4Q405 20ii-21-22:9) accompanied by a storm. The Youth is identified with Metatron and the prince of the Presence and is associated with twelve engraved stones "in the innermost chambers" reserved for Moses, which may have something to do with the high priestly breastpiece in the holy of holies (cf. XIII 11Q17 ix:6). One living creature descends upon the "tabernacle of the Youth" (cf. VII 4Q403 1ii:10; XII 4Q405 20ii-21 22:7) and speaks in a "light, quiet voice" (cf. XII 4Q405 20ii-21-22:7, 12) while the ophannim and angels are silent (cf. XII 4Q405 20ii-21-22:9) and other angels rush into the river of fire (cf. X 4Q405 15ii-16:2; XII 4Q405 20ii-21-22.10). The Youth places "deafening fire" into the ears of the living creatures to protect them when he recites the divine name. We are told that in "the camps of the holy ones" (cf. XII 4Q405 20ii-21-22:13) they call him Metatron, followed by a long string of magical nonsense words that are summarized as "his great name that was transmitted to Moses on Sinai," and from Moses to Joshua and the succession of elders and prophets down to Hillel, when it was lost until R. Abbahu came. (Note the allusion to the revelation at Sinai, a theme associated with the Festival of Weeks.) A quotation from Ps 68:18 supports the assertion that the Youth is prince over all the angelic princes and stands before "Him who is exalted over all gods above, on high." He goes beneath the throne of glory in a storm theophany, and we are told that his body is like the rainbow described in Ezek 1:27-29. For additional details, see Davila, "The Dead Sea Scrolls and Merkavah Mysticism."

Gnostic myth presents a similar picture of the heavenly realm created by the demiurge Yaldabaoth, a realm that contains multiple heavens, great glories, thrones, mansions, temples, chariots, virgin spirits, angelic armies, and attending angels (*Orig. World* NHC II, 5 102:11-24). In addition, his offspring, the repentant archon Sabaoth, is given control of the seventh heaven, in which he creates a mansion and before it a throne built on "a four-faced chariot called 'Cherubin'" or "Cherubim" in the form of Ezekiel's living creatures, and surrounds it with singing, ruling, and attending angels (*Hyp. Arch.* NHC II, 4 95:19-30; *Orig. World* NHC II, 5 104:31–105:12). Jesus Christ also sits on a throne in the eighth heaven, served and glorified by spirits and armies of angels (*Orig. World* NHC II, 5 105:26–106:11).

Line 7. The absolute use of the term "glory" for the divine presence is quite unusual. The "great glory" appears in heaven in *1 Enoch* 14:20; 102:3; *T. Levi* 3:4; *Ascen. Isa.* 9:37, but I am unaware of another text that refers without qualification to "the glory" for the divine presence. The normal corresponding term in the HB is "the glory of YHWH." For the association of the glory with the tabernacle, see Exod 40:35 and Ps 26:8. The glory of YHWH fills the temple in 1 Kgs 8:10-11 // 2 Chron 5:13-14; Ezek 43:4-5; 44:4; 2 Chron 7:1. For a discussion of the history of the term "glory" in the biblical and postbiblical tradition, see Newman, *Paul's Glory-Christology.*

The only other mention of a tabernacle preserved in the *Songs of the Sabbath Sacrifice* is the phrase "the tabernacle of the exalted chief" in VII 4Q403 1ii:10, which I have interpreted as a reference to the cult overseen by the angelic high priest, perhaps Melchizedek. That tabernacle may or may not be the same as this one; the nature of the latter is obscure because of the loss of the next word. See note a above for possible restorations. It may be either an angelic tabernacle, perhaps the same one as that mentioned in Song VII, or the tabernacle of God Himself in the celestial holy of holies. However, a separate heavenly tabernacle of God is not mentioned in the HL.

Compare the phrase "the [cheru]bim fall before Him" to Rev 4:10. As pointed out in note b, it is possible to translate "they fall before the cherubim," but it is extremely unusual for angels to accept the veneration of other angels in Second Temple Jewish literature. Note, however, that later on in the *Hekhalot Rabbati* the angel Anaphiel, who is one of the guardians of the seventh palace and who holds the seal-ring of heaven and earth, does receive veneration from other angels (§§241-42; cf. *3 Enoch* 18:18). For more on Anaphiel, see Dan, "Anaphiel, Metatron, and the Creator."

The phrase "a voice of quiet of God" (also line 8) echoes the description of the revelatory voice in 1 Kgs 19:12.

Line 8. The beginning of the line is restored on the basis of Ezek 10:5. The phrase "at the rising of their wings" echoes Ezek 3:12 (see above). The HL refers

150

frequently to the wings of Ezekiel's living creatures (e.g., *3 Enoch* 21:1-3; *Hekhalot Rabbati* §97; *SH-L* §§189, 368, 370; *Ma'aseh Merkavah* §596) or the cherubim (note especially *3 Enoch* 22:13, which may also echo the variant in Ezek 3:13).

The phrase "a structure of a throne-chariot" does not occur in the HB. Ezekiel mentions the throne of God but does not use the word "chariot," although Ben Sira (Sir 49:8) ties Ezekiel's vision to the chariot, and Second Ezekiel (4Q385 4:6) refers to the chariot in the context of the vision in Ezekiel 1. The phrase "the structure of the chariot" is associated with the golden cherubim located in the holy of holies according to 1 Chron 28:18. Compare also the reference to the "chariotry of God" in Ps 68:18 and to God making "the clouds His chariot" in Ps 104:3. The throne in *1 Enoch* 14:18 and Dan 7:9 is equipped with wheels, a feature that seems to presuppose the identification of the throne with the chariot. The throne-chariot is also mentioned in *3 Enoch* 46:2 and in the Gnostic treatises *Hyp. Arch.* NHC II, 4 95:19-30; *Orig. World* NHC II, 5 104:31–105:12.

Lines 8-9. The cosmography of this passage is difficult. It is unclear whether the "firmament of the cherubim" (cf. Ezek 10:1) is the same as the "firmament of light" (cf. Exod 24:10 and Ezek 1:22). The throne-chariot appears to be situated on the firmament of the cherubim (cf. *2 Apoc. Bar.* 59:3). Perhaps the name of this firmament implies that the cherubim dwell beneath the throne and on top of the firmament. The firmament of light may be the ceiling of the celestial throne room. The *Hekhalot Rabbati* places another firmament above the cherubim, ophannim, and living creatures (§100), and *1 Enoch* 14:17 associates the ceiling of the heavenly temple with stars and lightning.

Line 9. Apparently the cherubim sing praises from beneath the throne of God. In Rev 16:17-18; 19:5; 21:3 a voice from the throne is heard; in Rev 9:13-14 a voice speaks from the four horns of the golden altar; and in Rev 19:5 and 21:3 the throne of God itself appears to speak. These voices could also be those of the four living creatures (the equivalents of the cherubim in Revelation), who, according to Rev 4:6, are found both "in the midst of" and "surrounding" the throne (cf. *Hekhalot Rabbati* §§98, 173; *SH-L* §189, *2 Apoc. Bar.* 51:11; *Apoc. Abr.* 18, according to which they dwell under the throne). Compare also "His glorious seat" with "Your worthy seat" in 4Q286 1ii:1. The phrase "and when the ophannim go" echoes Ezek 1:17, 19.

Line 10. The word "wheels" (*galgalim*) is a different Hebrew word from "ophannim," but is identified with the latter in Ezek 10:2, 6, 13. It is not clear whether in the *Songs of the Sabbath Sacrifice galgalim* are the same as ophannim. The former are mentioned frequently in the HL in association with the throne of glory (e.g., *Hekhalot Rabbati* §§94, 154; G16 1b:3; *Massekhet*

Hekhalot §17.1) or the chariot (e.g., *3 Enoch* 15:1; 19:2-7; 41:2; *Hekhalot Rabbati* §160; *SH-L* §182; *Massekhet Hekhalot* §23.2). Sometimes they are identified with the ophannim (e.g., *SH-L* §373), but sometimes the two types of wheels are distinguished (e.g., *3 Enoch* 19:7; *SH-L* §182).

The phrase "like the appearance of fire" echoes Ezek 1:13, 27; 8:2. For "streams of fire," see the commentary to X 4Q405 15ii-16:2.

The word *hashmal* appears in the HB only in the phrase "like *hashmal*" (which could be interpreted to mean "like the eye of *hashmal*") and only in Ezek 1:4, 27, and 8:2. The phrasing here substitutes "in a likeness of" (cf. Ezek 8:2) for "like." The *hashmal* is mentioned frequently in the HL, usually in the singular but sometimes in the plural. It seems to be regarded as a type of angelic being or material in the heavenly temple (e.g., *3 Enoch* 36:2; *Hekhalot Rabbati* §258; *Hekhalot Zutarti* §§407, 411; *Massekhet Hekhalot* §7.2-3). The phrase "a likeness of *hashmal*" occurs in *SH-L* §371 (see the commentary to line 11 below).

Lines 10-11. The phrase "workmanship of [br]ightness" evokes the use of the word "brightness" in Ezek 1:4, 13, 27, 28; 10:4. Compare the "brightness of the chariot" in Second Ezekiel (4Q385 4:6).

Line 11. In the HB the noun "dyed material" occurs only in Judg 5:30 (x2), where its plural form refers to clothing. In RH the root means "to dip, to dye" (cloth), and the noun means "dye, color, dyed material" (Jastrow, 1259a). This word also appears in XIII 11Q17 ix:5 and XIII 4Q405 23ii:8, 9; 4Q405 49:2. Except for the last passage, whose context is broken, the word always appears within a line or two of the phrase "purely salted." In a description of the heavenly throne room in the HL with many similarities to the *Songs of the Sabbath Sacrifice*, we read "Like the likeness of both of them, sapphire and chrysolite, is the likeness of the *hashmal*, like the appearance of the fire, yet not fire but rather like the likeness of flames of fire, something like mixed dyed materials" (*SH-L* §371). The Hebrew word "(they) go about" echoes the phrase "it (antecedent uncertain) was going about" in Ezek 1:13.

Line 12. The phrase "with the tumult of their going" echoes the use of the Hebrew infinitive of the verb "to go" in Ezek 1:9, 12, 17, 19, 20, 21, 24; 10:11, 16.

Line 13. Note the reference to a camp in Ezek 1:24, interpreted by the *Tg. Ezek.* as "the hosts of the angels on high."

Line 14. The word "division" is used in Numbers 1–2, 10 to mean the banners or standards of the tribal camps, each tribe being led by a "prince." In the *War Scroll* the word means something like "military unit," perhaps because each unit would have had its own flag or standard (1QM iii:6; vi:1, 4, 5; viii:14; ix:4; cf. 4Q252 v:3). The *Temple Scroll* mentions "the princes of the divisions" (11Q19 xxi:5), evidently referring to the leaders of the Israelites in contrast to the priests and Levites, and divisions are mentioned in lvii:3 as groupings in a census. The word is used of divisions of angels in *3 Enoch* 19:6; *Seder Rabba di Bereshit* §40 (*SII-L* §773); §43 (*SH-L* §776); *Massekhet Hekhalot* §15.4. The word "their mustered (troops)," from Num 2:4, is the same word used of angelic troops in the phrase "mustered armies of princes" in *Massekhet Hekhalot* §15.4.

11Q17 viii

Wondrous firmaments and foundations

²[. . .] wonder, knowledge, and understan[ding . . .]firmaments of wond[er] ³[. . .]. with light of lights, effulgence [. . .]every structure of spirits of wond[er] ⁴[. . .]divinities fearsome of strength, all [. . .] their [wond]ers of wonders with the strength of the divinities of ⁵[eter]nity and exalting the mighty acts of Go[d . . .] from the four foundations of the firmament of ⁶wonder, they pro[cl]aim some of the voice of the oracle of God [. , .]wall,ᵃ blessing and psalming the God of ⁷gods, a tumu[lt . . .] heights[. . .]. the King of glory .[. . .]to foundations of wonder ⁸for an oracle .[. . .].. divinities[. . .] and all their supportsᵇ [. . .]holy of ⁹holie[s . .]. with the orac[le . . .] their [w]ings .,[. . .]. head[. . .] ¹⁰and [they] call [. .]stations[. . .]

Note

ᵃקיר[One could also reconstruct "[val]uable" (קיר[י]). Compare Jer 31:20 for this form rather than the much more common form יקר.

ᵇאושיהם This word is not found in BH (although cf. אשיה, "buttress," BDB, 78b), but it appears in RH (Jastrow, 35b) and QH (e.g., 1QHᵃ xi:13; xv:4) with the meaning "foundation."

Commentary

Line 2. Multiple firmaments are mentioned in XII 4Q405 23i:6 ("firma[men]ts of purity"), 7 ("firmaments of His glory"); XIII 11Q17 x:5, 8 — damaged ("firmaments of . . ."); 4Q287 2:6 ("firmaments of holiness"); and 4Q169 1-2:2; VII 4Q405 6:6 // 4Q403 1i:45 — damaged ("firmaments of wonder"?). Multiple heavens also figure in 2 Cor 12:2; *2 Enoch; 3 Apocalypse Baruch; Ascension of Isaiah; Testament of Levi; Ep. Apos.* 13; *Apoc. Paul* 21; *Hyp. Arch.* NHC II, 4 95:20; *Orig. World* NHC II, 5 102:1-2; 104:15-20, 30. The HL speaks frequently of seven firmaments, but never with any of the modifiers found in the *Songs of the Sabbath Sacrifice.*

Single firmaments are mentioned in VII 4Q403 1i:42 ("the most pure firmament"), 43 ("the chief firmament on high"); VII 4Q404 5:3 // 4Q403 1i:45; IX 11Q17 iv:4; XI 4Q405 19:3; XII 11Q17 viii:5-6 ("firmament of wonder"); XII 4Q405 20ii-21-22:8 ("the firmament of the cherubim"), 9 ("the firmament of light"). The relationship between the various firmaments is far from clear. See the introduction and the commentary to the passages cited above.

Line 5. Newsom's suggestion is plausible that the four foundations are to be associated with the four cherubim beneath the throne (*Critical Edition*, 368). Compare *Apoc. Abr.* 18:3-11. Heavenly foundations are mentioned in *3 Enoch* 22:2 and the "foundations of heaven and earth" in *Sar Panim* §629 (cf. 2 Sam 22:8).

Line 6. The word translated "oracle" also appears in VII 4Q403 1i:41 but there with the meaning "that which lifts up" or the like. Here the alternative meaning "oracle, utterance," seems more appropriate (see BDB, 672b). The word may be used in this sense in lines 8-9 and in XII 4Q405 23i:1, 5; 11Q17 x:6; 4Q405 81:3; 1Q27 1i:8; 4Q286 2:1, although the contexts are frequently broken.

4Q405 23i

Celestial thrones, offerings, and portals

[1][. . .] the[ir] oracles [. . .] [2][. . .]when they stand[. . .]rest [. . .] [3][. . .]«Your» the thrones of the glory of His kingdom and the whole assembly of the attendants of [4][. . .]. wonder, the divinities of [. . .] shall not be shaken forever [5][. . . to su]stain them, oracles of the whole, for the divinities of His whole offering [6][. . .]. His whole offering. Divinit[ie]s psalm Him [a]when they [be]gin to stand,[a] and all the s[pirits of] the firma[men]ts of [7]purity rejoice in His glory, and a voice of blessing from all its districts is recounting the firmaments of His glory, and His gates are psalming [8]with a voice of chanting. At the entrances of the gods of knowledge in portals of glory and at all exits of angels of holiness to their realm, [9]the portals of His entrance and the gates of exit proclaim the glory of the King, blessing and psalming all spirits of [10]divinities in exiting and in entering by gat[e]s of holiness. And there is none among them who oversteps a law, nor against the words of [11]the King do they set themselves at all. They do not [ru]n from the way nor do they linger away from His border. They are not too exalted for His missions. [12]They [are] n[o]t abased, for He has mercy in the

realm of the fury of the annihil[ation of] His [wra]th. He does not judge ᵇthose brought back by His glorious anger.ᵇ ¹³The fear of the King of divinities is fearsome over [al]l divinities [. . .] for [a]ll His missions in His true measure. And they go ¹⁴[. . .].[. . .]..[ ].[. . .]..[. . .]..[. . .].[. . .]

Notes

ᵃ⁻ᵃ[בתח]לת עומדם] One could also read עומדם לת[בתה], "[with the ps]alm of their station," or עומדם לת[בגבו], "[in the bord]er of their station."

ᵇ⁻ᵇכבודו אף במושבי With Qimron, I interpret the first word as a Hophal participle of the root שׁוב√, "to return, turn back" ("Review Article," 364). A Hophal or Hiphil participle of the root ישׁ√, "to dwell, abide," is also possible but difficult to make sense of in this context.

Commentary

Line 2. The word "when they stand" echoes Ezek 1:21. The word translated "rest" could also be translated "Sabbath."

Line 3. The phrase "the throne of glory" in Jer 17:21 (cf. Isa 22:23; Jer 14:21) is the closest biblical parallel to "the thrones of the glory of His kingdom" here and "the thrones of His glory" in XIII 11Q17 x:7. God's throne of glory is found in *1 Enoch* 47:3; 60:2 and is mentioned frequently in the HL. For a throne of glory that seats someone other than God, see Matt 19:28; 25:31 (the Son of Man); *1 Enoch* 55:4; 61:8; 62:5; 69:29 (the Son of Man/Enoch); *T. Abr.* 8:5, short recension (Adam); 4Q161 8-10:20 (the Davidic messiah).

The origin of the idea of multiple thrones in heaven seems to be Dan 7:9 ("*thrones* were placed") and Ps 110:1, which invites the king to sit at God's right hand. The throne of the divine king is also mentioned in Ps 45:7 (EVV 45:6). These passages were interpreted in the NT to describe the heavenly enthronement of Jesus (Matt 19:28 [with thrones for the twelve apostles]; 25:31; 26:64 // Mark 14:62 // Luke 22:69; Col 3:1; Heb 1:3, 8; 8:1; 10:12; 12:2; cf. *Sib. Or.* 2:241-44; *Apoc. Pet.* 6). In Rev 3:21; 7:17; 22:3 Jesus shares the throne with God. Other figures were also thought to sit on heavenly thrones: the Son of Man/Enoch (*1 Enoch* 45:3; 51:3); Adam (*T. Abr.* 11:4-10, long recension); Abel (*T. Abr.* 12:4; 13:2-3, long recension); Abraham, Isaac, and Jacob (*T. Isaac* 2:7); Job (*T. Job* 33:3-7; 41:5); Moses (Ezekiel the Tragedian, *Exagoge* 68-81; Aristobulus [*Praep. Evan.* 12.13.5]); the twenty-four elders (Rev 4:4); unnamed (angelic or glorified human?) judges at the eschaton (Rev 20:4); angels (*Apoc. Zeph.* A [Clement, *Stromata*, 5.11.77]; *Ascen. Isa.* 7:14, 19, 24, 27, 29, 31, 33, 35); and exalted human beings (4Q521 2ii + 4:7?; *1 Enoch* 108:12; *Apoc. Elijah* 1:8; 4:29; *Apoc. Paul*

29). In the Self-Glorification Hymn an unnamed human being is exalted to heaven and seated there on a "throne of power" in the assembly of the gods (4Q491ᶜ 1:5-6).

According to *3 Enoch* 10 and 16, Enoch was enthroned in heaven at the time when he was transformed into the angel Metatron. After the heretic R. Elisha ben Avuyah saw him and deduced that there must be two powers in heaven, Metatron lost his throne and was forced to stand like the other angels. However, *Sepher HaRazim* indicates that enthronement of angels was accepted in some Jewish circles in late antiquity: the seven overseer angels of the first firmament (I 1-2), the angels who stand on the sixth step in the second firmament (II 93-94), the three officers of the third firmament (III 2-3), and the twelve "princes of glory" (V 4-5) all sit on their own thrones. Likewise, in *Massekhet Hekhalot* §§19, 29 seven angels are seated on seven thrones, while §6.1 refers to "thrones of kingdom." The early rabbinic response to heretics who believed there to be "two powers in heaven" has been ably analyzed by Alan Segal in *Two Powers in Heaven*.

There is also a class of angels called "thrones" (Col 1:16; *2 Enoch* 20:1 [short recension]; *Apoc. Elijah* 1:11; *T. Abr.* 13:10 ms E; *T. Adam* 4:8; *Apos. Const.* 7.35.3; 8.12.8, 27), but *Songs of the Sabbath Sacrifice* gives no indication that the thrones it mentions are animate.

Lines 5-6. In the HB the term translated here as "whole offering" seems to be a synonym for "holocaust offering," a sacrifice in which the complete carcass of the animal was consumed in flames (e.g., Lev 6:15, 16; 1 Sam 7:9; Ps 51:21). This word could also be read as "His crown" (cf. 1QS iv:7-8; 1QSb iv:2; 1QHᵃ xvii:25). Angelic crowns appear in ancient apocalypses (Rev 4:4; *Apoc. Zeph.* A [Clement, *Stromata*, 5.11.77]; *T. Abr.* 13:13, short recension; *Zost.* NHC VIII, 1 58:13-24) and the HL (e.g., *3 Enoch* 12:3; 18:3; *Hekhalot Rabbati* §190), but this interpretation does not make much sense in the present context.

It is striking that terms for material sacrifices are used as though these sacrifices were carried out in the heavenly sanctuary (cf. the commentary to XIII 11Q17 ix:3-4). Compare the sacrificial altar in Rev 6:9-10 (cf. 9:13; 14:18) and the incense in 5:8; 8:3-5; the bloodless propitiatory offerings mentioned in *T. Levi* 3:5-6; and the offering of Christ as a bloody sacrifice in the heavenly holy of holies in Heb 9:11-14. In *Seder Rabba di Bereshit* §39 we read, "And Michael the great prince stands in their midst at their head as high priest, clothed with high-priestly garments, and he offers a pure offering of fire on the altar, and he offers incense on the altar of incense, and he offers a continual sacrifice of flame on the altar." (I have translated the text of *SH-L* §772, but many variants are found in the various manuscripts and editions.) In the *Baraita di Maʿaseh Bereshit* (B 321-24) Michael offers a holocaust offering on the altar of holocaust.

Lines 6-10. Newsom has pointed out that these lines echo the language of Ezek 46:1-10, which describes the comings and goings of the prince and the people through the gates, entrances, and exits of Ezekiel's imagined temple and the offerings of the priest in this temple, including the Sabbath offerings. These echoes support the contention that Song XII describes the heavenly sacrificial cult ("'He Has Established for Himself Priests,'" 112).

Lines 8-9. The word "portal" is used of the earthly temple in Ps 24:7, 9 and appears frequently in the HL for the gates to the seven celestial palaces, which are guarded by fearsome angels (e.g., *3 Enoch* 18:3-4; *Hekhalot Rabbati* §§206-29).

Lines 10-11. Newsom notes that in BH the word translated "oversteps" means simply "to leap, leap over," but in RH it can mean to skip over a passage when reading the biblical text (Jastrow, 308b). A passage in the HL reports that any angels in the heavenly choir who sing off-key or out of tempo fall into the river of fire and are burned up. But the holy living creatures always keep perfect time (*SH-L* §§186-87).

Line 11. The Hebrew word "angel" means "messenger," and angels are frequently sent on missions to earth in biblical and parabiblical literature (e.g., Dan 9:20-27; 10-12; Luke 1:11-21, 26-38; Tob 12; *4 Ezra* passim; *Jos. Asen.* 14-17; *Life of Adam and Eve* 25:2).

Line 12. Since the context deals with angels, it appears that the possibility of angelic repentance is entertained. Compare I 4Q400 1i:16 for a similar theme; see also the commentary to 4Q280 2:3-4.

Song XIII

(11Q17 ix; 4Q405 23ii; 11Q17 x)

This badly damaged song refers to heavenly sacrifices, the culmination of the Sabbath worship. Chief angels dressed in high-priestly vestments take up their positions. The last preserved bits recapitulate structural elements of the celestial temple.

11Q17 ix

The celestial sacrificial cult and priesthood[a]

[3][. . .]. favor ..[. . .]all the[ir] works [4][. . .]. for sacrifices of holy ones[. . .]. the odor of their offerings ... [5][. . .].. and the o[do]r of their libations according to the num[ber of . . .] of purity with a spirit of holi[ness] [6][. . .]eternal [. . .] with [effulgence and] adornment ..[. . . .]. wonder and the structure of breastpieces of [7][. . . c]ords of ornamentation[. . .]colorful [. . .] like [woven] wo[rkmanship . . .]purely salted, dyed things of [8][. . .] <[eff]ulgence> [and] adornment .[. . .]...[. . .].. for forms[. . .].. ephod [9][. . .]angels[. . .]...

Note

[a]The beginning of Song XIII is lost, but it may be reconstructed with a high degree of confidence as follows:

> [For the Sage. The song of the holocaust offering of the thirteenth Sabbath on the twenty-eighth day of the third month. Psalm the God of . . .]

Commentary

Line 3. The term "favor" is often associated with God's acceptance of a person, offering, or sacrifice (e.g., Exod 28:38; Lev 1:3; Isa 56:7). Compare also I 4Q400 1i:16, where it is associated with angelic or human repentance.

Lines 4-5. It is remarkable to find the word "sacrifice" associated with angelic sacrifice, since it is from a root meaning "to slaughter" (√זבח) and in the HB seems always to refer to animal sacrifices (cf. 1QM ii:5; 4QMMT B 7-11; 11Q19 lii:15, etc.). The word "offering" is a more general term. The word "odor" in the phrase "a soothing odor" (e.g., Gen 8:21; Leviticus 1; Numbers 15; 1QSb iii:1; 4Q266 11:4; 11Q18 33:1; 11Q19 xv:13) is also associated with the sacrificial cult, and the "libation" was usually offered with the holocaust offering (e.g., Numbers 28). The words "offering," "libation," and "soothing odor" occur together in 4Q220 1:9 (*Jub.* 21:9) as part of the description of the "sacrifice of wholeness," traditionally "peace offering." According to *Hekhalot Rabbati* §163, the prayers of Israel ascend before God as a soothing odor, and we are told that a "scent of splendor" rises in the heavenly throne room (*Hekhalot Rabbati* §198). For more on the heavenly sacrificial cult, see the commentary to XII 4Q405 23i:5-6.

Line 6. The breastpiece was part of the high priest's uniform and was worn with the ephod (see line 8 and XII 4Q405 23ii:5). Both are described in detail in Exodus 28 and 39. They were made of the same multicolored material. The ephod seems to have been something like an apron with an onyx stone on each shoulder set in gold filigree, each stone engraved with six of the names of the tribes of Israel. The breastpiece had twelve precious stones set in front in a four-by-three array, each stone engraved with the name of one of the twelve tribes, and it also contained the Urim and Thummim (e.g., Exod 28:30; 11Q19 lviii:18-21), evidently sacred lots used for divination. The breastpiece and ephod were held together by a blue cord (e.g., Exod 28:28). Compare the "[c]ords of ornamentation" in line 7. The plural form of "breastpiece" here and "ephod" in XII 4Q405 23ii:5 seems to indicate that multiple angels wore the high-priestly uniform.

Line 8. In *Hekhalot Rabbati* §166, the divine name appears to be identified with stones and settings of the heavenly ephod (although the passage is difficult). A still more difficult passage describes the Youth or Metatron as being inscribed with letters of cosmological import that seem to be engraved on twelve stones in an inner chamber (*SH-L* §389) — perhaps an allusion to the ephod in the heavenly holy of holies.

4Q405 23ii

The angelic priesthood

¹[ ]. ornamentation of carvings of [. . .] ²they a[pproa]ch the King when they attend be[fore . . .] ³the King and He engraved His glory .[. . .] ⁴holy ones, the sanctuary of all [. . .] ⁵their ephods. Th[ey] spread[. . .] ⁶of holies, favor [. .].[ ]...[ ].[ ]...[. . .].[ ].[ ] ⁷their holy (places).ᵃ BLANK

In their station of wonders are spirits of colorful stuff like woven workmanship, carved with forms of adornment. ⁸In the midst of the glory of the appearance of scarlet, dyed garments of light of most holy spirit take up their holy station before ⁹[the K]ing, spirits of [pure] dyed garments in the midst of an appearance of whiteness. And the likeness of the spirit of glory is like the workmanship of Ophir,ᵇ ᶜgiving ¹⁰[lig]ht,ᶜ and all their crafts are purely salted, craftsmanship like woven workmanship. These are the chiefs of the ones wondrously clothed to attend, ¹¹chiefs of ᵈdominions, dominions ofᵈ holy ones belonging to the King of holiness in all the heights of the sanctuaries of the kingdom of ¹²His glory. BLANK

Among the chiefs of contributions are tongues of knowledge [and] they, ᵉamong all the works of His glory,ᵉ bless the God of knowledge. ¹³[. . .]... their units[f] in all [. . .].[ ] hol[iness . . .] knowledge of His understanding and in the insight of His [gl]ory ...[. . .]

Notes

[a]קָדְשׁיֿהֶם This word seems to be the segholate abstract noun (קֹדֶשׁ or קוֹדֶשׁ) rather than the adjectival form (קָדוֹשׁ, pl. קְדוֹשִׁים, as in line 6), which would mean "holy ones." Compare קוֹדְשִׁים in I 4Q400 1i:14. The same noun form (קוֹדֶשׁ) is found in 4Q401 16:5, but apparently with an adverbial function.

[b]Ophir (here plural, אוֹפִירִים; usually singular, אוֹפִיר) is the land known for its fine gold in the HB (e.g., 1 Kgs 9:28; Isa 13:12; Ps 45:10; Job 28:16; 1 Chron 29:4) and is used as a name for gold in Job 22:24; 4Q374 4:2?. "Stone of Ophir" (λίθῳ ἐκ Σουφιρ) may be mentioned in Tob 13:17. An angel is girded with "gold of Ophir" (reading כתם אופיר) in Daniel's vision in Dan 10:5. The plural form in Hebrew is also found in the Self-Glorification Hymn in the phrase "I will not crown myself with gold, nor the gold of Ophir . . ." (. . . לא בפז אכתֿ[ר] לי וכתם אופירים לוא), spoken by a human being who has been exalted and enthroned in heaven (text reconstructed from 4Q491[c] 1:11 and 4Q427 7i:12).

[c-c]מאירי [או]לֿ The subject of this Hiphil participle is not entirely clear. It could be the "workmanship of Ophir," but the apparent plural form of "workmanship" is probably to be construed in the singular, as normally in the *Songs of the Sabbath Sacrifice* (cf. *HDSS* 100.34). Another possibility is that the subject is the spirits in line 9 (Fletcher-Louis, "Heavenly Ascent," 392).

[d-d]ממלכות ממלכות The repetition of this word could be a dittography, but see VI 4Q403 1i:10 for a similar construction.

[e-e]בכול מעשי כבודֿוֿ The grammar of this phrase is difficult since the verb "to bless" (√ברך), when used with God as the direct object, rarely takes the preposition -בֿ as an adjectival modifier. When it does, the preposition is used in a temporal (e.g., Ps 63:5; 145:2) or locative sense (Ps 26:12; 68:27). I take it here in the common sense of presence in a group, although I cannot find a parallel for this use. A conceivable translation of the phrase is "and they bless the God of knowledge for all the works of His glory," but the preposition על would fit this meaning better (Deut 8:10; although cf. Gen 48:20).

[f]מסרוּתֿםֿ This seems not to be used in the HB (but cf. מסרת in Ezek 20:37?). However, it is found in 1QM iii:3, 12, where it seems to mean military "units," a meaning that fits the context here. It also occurs in 1QS x:4; 4Q204 1i:19 (*1 Enoch* 2:1); 4Q209 28:2 (*1 Enoch* 82:10) with the sense of celestial "position" or "station."

Commentary

Lines 7, 10. The phrase "woven workmanship" is used of the high-priestly garments in the HB (Exod 28:32; 39:22, 27). Compare XIII 11Q17 ix:7. Fletcher-Louis plausibly suggests that the twelve engraved stones on the breastpiece are to be associated with the colorful spirits in this line and perhaps with spirits of light in lines 8-10 ("Heavenly Ascent," 391). Evidently the fabric and the stones of the heavenly breastpieces, like the temple architecture, are animate beings. According to Josephus (*Ant.* §3 214-18) and 4Q376 1ii:1-2, the earthly exemplars of these stones were known to shine with light.

Lines 8-10. Compare the description of the seven angels of the plagues in Rev 15:5-8, who come out of the heavenly "temple of the tent of testimony" (i.e., the tabernacle) wearing pure bright (white) linen and golden girdles. The Great Angel Eleleth has an appearance like fine gold and clothing like snow according to *Hyp. Arch.* NHC II, 4 93:14-15.

Line 9. "And the likeness of the spirit of glory" echoes the language of Ezek 1:28: "it is the appearance of the likeness of the glory of YHWH." A similar expression, "in the likeness of [Your] glory," seems to be used of the creation of Adam in 4Q504 8 recto 4.

11Q17 x

*Concluding praise of God and summary
of the celestial architecture?*

[2][. . .]heights of [His] gl[ory] ..[. . .] His [glo]ry in .[. . .] [3]His [rec]om[pe]nses with judgments[. . .]His mercies with the value of .[. . .] His [te]stimonies [4][and] all blessings of peace[. . . the glo]ry of His works and with lig[ht . . .]... and with the adornment of [5]His praises in all the firma[ments of . . .]. light and darkness and shapes of[. . .]the holiness of the King of [6]glory for all [His] works of truth [. . .]for [a]the angels of knowledge[a] with all ..[. . .].. oracles of holiness [7]for the thrones of His glory and for the footstool of [His] f[eet . . . the ch]ariots of His adornment and for the inner chambers of [His] ho[liness . .].. and for the portals of the entrances of [8][. . .]. with all the exits of [. . .] of its construction and for all .[. . .]for the palaces of His glory, for the firmaments of [9][. . .]for all ..[. . .]

Note
[a-a]מלאכי הדעת‎ Compare the "angels of knowledge" (מלאכי מדע‎) in *Sepher HaRazim* I 146.

Unplaced Fragments

4Q401 11 (Song V?)

The angelic priest Melchizedek?

[1][. . .]... [a][pri]est of priest[s[a] . . .] [2][. . . [b]div]inities of knowledge and pr[iests of[b]
. . .] [3][. . . [c]Melchi]zedek, priest in the assemb[ly of God[c] . . .]
[d4]BLANK [5]BLANK[d]

Notes

[a-a]I reconstruct [כו[הן כוהנ]ים]. Newsom reads the last letter of the first word as final *nun* in *Critical Edition*, 383, but as *waw* in DJD 11: 205. The photograph supports the first reading.

[b-b]I reconstruct [א[לוהי דעת וכ]והני].

[c-c][מלכי] צדק כוהן בעד[ת אל] Reconstructing with Newsom on the basis of 11Q13 ii:10 (cf. 4Q491[c] 1:5; 4Q427 7i:14). The name is probable, given the singular "priest" in this line (elsewhere only in VIII 4Q403 1ii:24).

[d-d]This fragment ends with two uninscribed ruled lines. Perhaps they indicate the end of a song.

Commentary

Lines 1-3. Most if not all of the fragments of 4Q401 seem to come from Songs I-VI. The most likely context for frags. 11 and 22 is Song V, which describes an eschatological "war in heaven" (a phrase associated with the warrior angel Michael in Rev 12:7) in V 4Q402 10. I have argued the case for this placement, which remains speculative, in "Melchizedek, Michael, and War in Heaven," especially 262-64. The angel Melchizedek is discussed in detail in the "Excursus on the Melchizedek Tradition" at the end of this chapter.

4Q401 22 (Song V?)

Dedication of angelic priests

[1][. . .]holy ones of ..[. . .] [2][. . .]. they fill their hands[. . .] [3][. . . Melc]hize-dek[a][. . .]

Note

[a][מל[כי צדק] This restoration is reasonably likely, but others are possible.

Commentary

Lines 2-3. The idiom "to fill the hands" refers to a ceremony of priestly installation (e.g., Exod 28:41; Lev 8:33; Judg 17:5, 12). In *T. Moses* 10:2 the warrior angel is consecrated by the filling of hands at the eschaton. A similar scenario may be involved here for Melchizedek and the angelic priests, in which case this fragment may belong in Song V before 4Q402 4.

4Q401 16 = 4Q402 9 (Songs III-V?)

Angelic praise and human ignorance[a]

¹[. . . God of god]s. [They] shall exalt ²[. . . th]ey shall proclaim in silence ³[. . .]holy ones of the interior ⁴[. . . His glor]y. Who understands these things? ⁵[. . .]. they praise Him in holiness ⁶[. . .].[. . .].[ ]

Note
[a]These fragments from 4Q401 and 4Q402 have overlapping texts, but there is nothing in either to indicate the exact placement of the passage. Most or all of the fragments of 4Q401 seem to come from Songs I-VI, and all of the fragments of 4Q402 seem to come from Songs III-V.

Commentary

Line 4. The confession of ignorance is probably a rare aside by the human composer (cf. II 4Q400 2:6-8). Similar sentiments are expressed in the HB (e.g., Ps 19:13; 90:11; 106:2) and the QL (e.g., 1QS xi:22; 4Q381 31:3).

4Q401 23 (Songs I-VI?)

An angelic prince[a]

¹[. . .]. prince of ho[liness . . .] ²[. . .]. heights [. . .] ³[. . .]eternal[. . .]

Note
[a]The location of this fragment is unknown, but most or all other fragments from 4Q401 belong to Songs I-VI.

Commentary

Line 1. This is the only place in the *Songs of the Sabbath Sacrifice* where the term "prince" appears in the singular. (For this term, see the commentary to I 4Q400 1ii:14.) Perhaps this prince is to be associated with the heavenly high priest; see the "Excursus on the Melchizedek Tradition" at the end of the chapter.

4Q405 46 (location unknown)

Divinities of light

[1][. . .]glory[a][ ].[ ]..[. . .] [2][. . .]divinities of lights in every lo[t . . .] [3][. . .]... from beneath His glory [ ].[. . .]

Note

[a]כבוֹד Or possibly מר[כבוֹת], "[cha]riots."

Commentary

Line 2. Compare the phrase "divinities of lights" to "gods of lights" in VIII 4Q403 1ii:35, although, given the broken context, one could also translate the first phrase "God of lights" (cf. 4Q503 13:1).

If the reading "lo[t]" (גוֹר[ל]) is correct, this is the only place this sectarian technical term appears in the *Songs of the Sabbath Sacrifice*. For its meaning, see the commentary to 4Q286 7ii:3.

Line 3. Compare XII 4Q405 20ii-21-22:9.

Excursus on the Melchizedek Tradition

Melchizedek (מלכי צדק), the non-Israelite priest-king, appears in two places in the Hebrew Bible: Gen 14:18 and Ps 110:4. His name means something like "king of righteousness," and later interpreters often refer to this meaning and develop it exegetically. In Genesis he is the king of Salem (Jerusalem?) and the priest of God Most High. Psalm 110 seems to hint that there was a priesthood of Melchizedek active in the Jerusalem temple and tied to the Davidic king.

Melchizedek is mentioned fairly frequently in Second Temple literature as a human royal figure (Josephus, *Ant.* 1 §180-81; 1QapGen xxii:13-17; Pseudo-Eupolemos [*Praep. Evan.* 9.17.6]; *Apos. Con.* 7.39.3; 8.5.3; 8.12.23) but also as a heavenly being. 11Q13 (11QMelchizedek) presents him as a warrior angel, a "god" (אלוהים; ii:10) who defeats the forces of evil at the eschaton. There is no mention of his human origin, and he is not explicitly a priest in the fragments we have, although the tantalizing assertion that the lot of Melchizedek is the Day of Atonement in the tenth Jubilee in which to atone for all the sons of God certainly hints at his function as celestial high priest, and the overall content of the surviving fragments echoes the ideas in Psalm 110, if not its language. In the Aramaic Visions of Amram (4Q544), Melchizedek's name may also have appeared in a lacuna as one of the three names of the angel of light (see Milik, "4QVisions de 'Amram," esp. 85-86). Philo of Alexandria treats Melchizedek allegorically as a high priest representing Logos or Reason, a peaceable and righteous king who is contrasted with the tyrant Mind, the Ruler of War, which leads the organism into wickedness and excessive indulgence of the passions (*Leg. All.* III 79-82; cf. *Congr.* 99; *Abr.* 235). Philo seems to be at pains to distinguish Melchizedek from the warrior angel we find in 11Q13, but his association of him with the demiurgic and divine Logos may mean that Philo accepted Melchizedek's divine status.

The Letter to the Hebrews is the only work in the NT that mentions Melchizedek directly (although Psalm 110 is the most frequently cited passage in early Christian literature). Its treatment of him is, however, enigmatic. The description in 7:1-3 includes puns on the names Salem and Melchizedek similar to those made by Josephus and Philo, but 7:3 goes far beyond what they say. Melchizedek "resembles the Son of God," but it is unclear in what sense this statement is meant. Minimally, it seems that the writer is aware of a tradition that made Melchizedek an immortal and preexistent celestial high priest and is playing off it; it is difficult to read the passage as merely allegorical. Both v. 3 and v. 8 seem to assert that Melchizedek lives eternally as a priest. The point of the chapter, of course, is that Jesus is the true celestial high priest, which makes it difficult to understand just where the celestial Melchizedek might fit into the writer's theology.

The Melchizedek legend continues to develop into late antiquity. The *Melchizedek Tractate* (NHC IX, 1), found in the Coptic Gnostic Library of Nag Hammadi, presents him as a warrior angel and eschatological high priest, a portrayal similar to that of 11Q13 with one very significant difference: Melchizedek and Jesus Christ are identified — they are one and the same being. Birger Pearson, in his edition of this tractate, argues that the work is dependent on the epistle to the Hebrews and lists parallels between the two documents, but these consist of single words or general ideas, not clear literary connections, and it seems more likely that Hebrews and NHC IX, 1 are drawing independently on Jewish traditions like those found at Qumran.

The *Second Book of Jeu* is another Coptic Gnostic text written roughly in late antiquity (but not part of the Nag Hammadi corpus). In chapters 45–46, Jesus prays to the Father for "Zorokothora Melchizedek" to "bring the water of the baptism of fire of the Virgin of Light" (presumably heavenly waters of baptism) to the disciples, and Melchizedek does so as a heavenly being with a priestly function.

Still another Coptic Gnostic text preserved outside Nag Hammadi, the *Pistis Sophia,* is a compendium of Gnostic traditions that can be divided into at least two separate works (Books 1–3 and Book 4). In both Melchizedek is a heavenly being whose job is to gather purified motes of light from the universe and deposit them in the Treasury of Light. In addition, in I 25-26; II 86; III 112, 128-29, 131; IV 139-40, Zorokothora Melchizedek has conflicts with the archons, who destroy as many souls as they can, and with the underworld goddess Hekate, who holds souls prisoner in her realm. In this compendium, all traces of the biblical Melchizedek and all eschatological elements have disappeared.

We find two versions of a strange story of Melchizedek in the Slavonic manuscripts of *2 Enoch* 71–72, a work that seems to have been translated from Greek and that contains at least some ancient traditions. Melchizedek is born posthumously of Sophanim, wife of the priest Nir, who had conceived him in her dotage without intercourse. The precocious infant looks like a three-year-old child and begins to speak immediately. He is made a priest by his family and is later taken to the Garden of Eden by the archangel Michael.

Two trajectories stand out in this long history of tradition: Melchizedek as the warrior angel and Melchizedek as the heavenly high priest. A case can be made that the *Songs of the Sabbath Sacrifice* mention him in both capacities. If the three suggested restorations of his name are correct, he is called "priest in the assemb[ly of God]" in 4Q401 11; he is associated with a priestly investiture in 4Q401 22; and there is a reference to a "wondrous priesthood of Melch[izedek]" in VIII 4Q403 1ii:21 (supplemented by 4Q405 8-9:6 and 11Q17 ii:7). The first two passages may be associated with the eschatological war in heaven in Song V (see the commentary on these fragments). Moreover, a particular angel seems to be singled out in several other passages: the mention of the "tabernacle of the exalted chief" in VII 4Q403 ii:10 may imply that the heavenly high priest had his own tabernacle, like the Youth of the Hekhalot literature. This exalted chief may be the same figure as the "chief(!) of the divinities" mentioned just before in line 5, the "priest of the interior" in line 24 (Song

VIII), and the subject of the phrase "his priesthood" in VII 4Q405 7:8. It is possible that the "prince of ho[liness]" in 4Q401 23:1 is the same angel. The reference to "a seat like the throne of His kingdom in His inner chambers of glory" (XI 4Q405 20ii-21-22:2 + 11Q17 viii:4) also seems to imply the existence of a heavenly enthroned being other than God, someone contrasted with others who do not sit in heaven. This figure may be the same heavenly high priest.

The case is not conclusive since it is based on passages that are either damaged or difficult to interpret, but the cumulative force of the evidence makes it probable that the heavenly high priest Melchizedek played a role in the cosmology and perhaps the eschatology of the *Songs of the Sabbath Sacrifice*. For more on this figure, see the bibliography on Melchizedek in the introduction to this chapter.

Times for Praising God

(4Q409)

INTRODUCTION

I. Content

This poorly preserved work invokes the praise of God and refers to some of the festivals in Israel's cultic calendar.

II. The Manuscript

4Q409 survives in four fragments (one of which has no translatable text) written in a Herodian script of the first century BCE.

III. Structure and Genre

Very little of the work survives, so correspondingly little can be said about its structure. It contains a number of verbs ("praise," "bless," "give thanks") in the imperative (command) form, so presumably it was recited. It also mentions or alludes to a number of festivals and uses terminology associated with sacrifice. God is the object of the praise, blessing, and thanksgiving. The editor, Elisha Qimron, suggests it is a hymn, and this seems likely enough.

IV. Life Situation

It is very difficult to determine when this hymn was meant to be recited. The references to several festivals seem to preclude its being meant for any one of them in particular; perhaps it was a general prayer to be recited at all of them. It seems to allude to at least one festival outside the later standardized Jewish calendar, the Festival of Wood Offering (1i:4; cf. note a to 1i:1), which is mentioned in the *Temple Scroll*. The reference to this festival may be a sign of sectarian composition, but since the Wood Offering appears in the Hebrew Bible and elsewhere outside the Qumran library (see the commentary below), this is far from certain. We do not have enough information to be sure whether or not 4Q409 is a sectarian work.

V. Literary Context

Qimron notes that a similar hymn is found in 1QS ix:26–x:17, which also praises God and mentions various festivals, although it does not invoke praise with imperative verbal forms. Moreover, he points to structural similarities in Psalms 148 and 150, which invoke praise but do not mention any festivals. The surviving fragments of the work show familiarity with the biblical passages pertaining to the festivals.

BIBLIOGRAPHY

Qimron, Elisha. "Times for Praising God: A Fragment of a Scroll from Qumran (4Q409)." *JQR* 80 (1990) 341-47.
———. "4Q409. 4QLiturgical Work A." In *Qumran Cave 4. XX, Poetical and Liturgical Texts, Part 2*, 63-67, plate iv. DJD 29. Oxford: Clarendon, 1999. (Became available to me only when this volume was at the proof stage.)

TIMES FOR PRAISING GOD

(4Q409)

4Q409 1i

[1][. . .]. . .[a][. . .] [2][. . .] new [gr]ain offering [3][. . . psal]m and bless in the days of [4][. . .]wood for the holocaust offering [5][. . .]on the day of a trumpet-blast memorial [6][. . . the Lor]d of all. Psalm [7][and bless . . . psalm and ble]ss His holy name [8][. . . psalm and bles]s the Lord of all [9][. . .]in these days [10][. . .]psalm and bless and thank [11][. . .]thank with branches of a [leafy] tree

BOTTOM MARGIN

Note

[a]Qimron restores the first line to mention "the [Da]ys of the Fi[rstfruits]" (ב[י]מֹ֫י הֹבֹ[כורים]), a phrase used in the *Temple Scroll* (11Q19 xliii:3) to refer to the Festival of Weeks (the Firstfruits of Wheat) along with two other festivals known only from Qumran: the Festival of Firstfruits of New Wine and the Festival of Firstfruits of Oil (see the general introduction to this volume). Although this reading is plausible in context, unfortunately the phrase is badly damaged and any reconstruction of it is speculative.

Commentary

Line 2. This phrase is found in the HB only in Lev 23:16 and Num 28:26, both times in the context of the Festival of Weeks (cf. 11Q19 xviii:13; xix:11).

Line 3. The imperative refrain "psalm and bless" seems to have appeared repeatedly in this hymn (cf. 1i:6-7, 7, 8, 10; ii:2, 7). This phrase does not occur in the HB, but the two roots "psalm" and "bless" appear together in Jer 4:2; Ps 145:2 (cf. 1QH[a] ix:30-31; xix:24-25; Songs VII 4Q403 1ii:15; XII 4Q405 20ii-21-22:1; XII 4Q405 23i:9).

Line 4. Perhaps a reference to the Festival of Wood Offering. This holiday is not part of the cycle of the traditional Jewish liturgy, but the *Temple Scroll* (11Q19 xxiii:1–xxv:1) and a calendar associated with 4QMMT (A v) report its observance. It is alluded to in Neh 10:35 (EVV 10:34); 13:31, as well as in Josephus, *J.W.* 2 §425 and *m. Ta'an.* 4.4-5.

Line 5. The phrase "a trumpet-blast memorial" occurs in the HB only in Lev 23:24 (cf. Num 29:1; 11Q19 xxv:3), referring to the holy convocation on the first day of the seventh month, which corresponds to the fall New Year in the modern Jewish calendar.

Line 11. Compare Lev 23:40 (the phrase here is closer to the text of the Samaritan Pentateuch than to the MT, which reads "a branch of"). This verse in Leviticus is from a passage concerning the Festival of Booths, which comes just after the fall New Year and which is presumably the subject of this line as well.

4Q409 1ii

¹...[. . .] ²psalm and bl[ess . . .] ³and lambs [. . .] ⁴.[. . .]. ⁵when burni[ng^a . . .] ⁶your Creator[. . . psalm] ⁷and bless[. . .] ⁸on the alt[ar . . .] ⁹with blowing of [the clarion . . .] ¹⁰yo[ur] God[. . .]

BOTTOM MARGIN

Note

^aThe verb קטר, "to burn," is used of burning incense or the fat of offerings; the only festival it is associated with is the Day of Atonement (Lev 16:25).

Commentary

Lines 1-10. The subject is clearly sacrifices (cf. lines 3, 5, 8), but too little of the text survives for any details to be clear.

Line 3. Lambs were routinely sacrificed during the festivals (Numbers 28–29).

Line 6. The expression "your Creator" occurs in the HB only in Isa 43:1 (but cf. the plural in Eccles 12:1).

Line 8. Presumably the festival sacrifices were offered on altars, but altars are mentioned in the context of festivals only in Exod 30:10; Lev 16:12, 18 (x2), 20, 25, 33; 2 Chron 35:16.

Line 9. Clarions were blown on festival days (Num 10:10).

4Q409 2

¹and generation[s . . .] ²forgiveness[. . .]

4Q409 3

¹[. . .]blo[wing of the clarion . . .] ²[. . .]with detested thing[s . . .]

Grace after Meals

(4Q434a)

INTRODUCTION

I. Contents

This document preserves fragments of a special liturgy of grace after meals to be used in a household mourning a recent death.

II. The Manuscript

The two fragments of 4Q434 covered in this chapter have been published by Moshe Weinfeld as 4Q434a, which he argues is a separate work from 4Q434. The manuscripts 4Q434-38 are copies of a corpus of hymns that begin "Bless, O my soul" (in Hebrew, *Bārăkî napšî*). The cumulative force of Weinfeld's arguments for regarding these two fragments as part of another work is quite strong, and I follow his analysis here almost entirely.[1] It should be noted, however, that Edward Cook translates the fragments as part of 4Q434 1 and takes

---

1. Weinfeld, "Grace after Meals."

them to be an example of the genre "songs of Zion."[2] The script can be dated roughly to the first half of the first century BCE.

III. Structure and Genre

On the basis of numerous parallels with later rabbinic texts, Weinfeld argues that 4Q434a preserves fragments of a liturgy of grace after meals for use by a family in a mourning household. Despite the damaged state of the Qumran text, it can scarcely be doubted that it anticipates on some level the later prayers for this very specific and concrete social situation. Although the order of the elements of the Qumran prayer differs from the later tradition, both echo Isa 66:13, which compares God's comforting of Jerusalem to a mother comforting her son; both connect God's defeat of the nations on Israel's behalf with mention of God's laws and Torah; both refer to God's goodness; both mention the "pleasant land" (Israel); both allude to messianic or eschatological themes; and both employ the language of blessing.

IV. Life Situation

Weinfeld has argued that liturgies for grace after meals survive in the Qumran library in two manuscripts that contain excerpted texts of Deuteronomy (4QDeut[j] and 4QDeut[n]). Both contain Deut 8:5-10, which is an appropriate text for grace after meals and was used as such in the Jewish liturgy. The layout of this passage in 4QDeut[n] even addresses indirectly a later exegetical controversy among the rabbis. The details are technical, but the point is that this manuscript places a blank line between vv. 8 and 9, supporting the view that a shorter blessing could be recited over the "fruit" of the land mentioned in v. 8 and that the full blessing mentioned in v. 10 applied only to meals that included the "bread" mentioned in v. 9.[3]

The life situation of 4Q434 is related to the ceremony behind these excerpted manuscripts but is still more specific, in that it seems to be a liturgy of grace after meals intended for households mourning a recent death.

---

2. Cook, "In Praise of God's Grace — Barki Nafshi," 394-95. However, David Rolph Seely, who is working with Weinfeld on the official publication of these manuscripts, has accepted Weinfeld's conclusions ("4Q437: A First Look," 148, 151).

3. Weinfeld, "Prayer and Liturgical Practice," 251-52; "Grace after Meals," 427-29.

V. Literary Context

Although the text echoes phrases and ideas from the Hebrew Bible, the closest parallels to its overall content come from much later Talmudic liturgical traditions about grace after meals, especially those in *b. Ber.* 46a-49a. Thus 4Q434a is another testimony to the survival of very ancient material in post-Mishnaic rabbinic literature. An early but Christianized version of the grace after meals liturgy also survives in *Didache* 10.

BIBLIOGRAPHY

Cook, Edward. "In Praise of God's Grace — Barki Nafshi." In *The Dead Sea Scrolls: A New Translation,* edited by Michael Wise et al., 394-97. San Francisco: HarperSanFrancisco, 1996.

Seely, David Rolph. "4Q437: A First Look at an Unpublished *Barki Nafshi* Text." In *The Provo International Conference on the Dead Sea Scrolls: Technological Innovations, New Texts, and Reformulated Issues,* edited by Donald W. Parry and Eugene Ulrich, 147-60. STDJ 30. Leiden: Brill, 1999.

Weinfeld, Moshe. "Grace after Meals in Qumran." *JBL* 111 (1992) 427-40.

———. "Prayer and Liturgical Practice in the Qumran Sect." In *The Dead Sea Scrolls: Forty Years of Research,* edited by Devorah Dimant and Uriel Rappaport, 241-58. STDJ 10. Leiden: Brill, 1992.

Weinfeld, M., and D. Seely. "434. 4QBarkhi Nafshi." In *Qumran Cave 4. XX, Poetical and Liturgical Texts, Part 2,* 267-86, plates xvii-xix. DJD 29. Oxford: Clarendon, 1999. (Became available to me only when this volume was at the proof stage. Weinfeld and Seely now argue that 4Q434a does belong to manuscript 4Q434.)

GRACE AFTER MEALS

(4Q434a)

4Q434a 1-2

[1]Your [ ]. Your [. . .] to be comforted concerning the mourning, afflicted (city) which .[. . .] [2]to d[est]roy nations, and He will cu[t o]ff peoples, and the wicked .[. . .]He renews [3]works of heaven and earth, and they shall rejoice. And His

glory fills [the whole earth . . . For] their [gu]ilt [4]He will atone and (the One) [a]abounding in goodness[a] will comfort them ...[. . .].. to eat its fruit [5]and its goodness. BLANK [. . .] BLANK

[6]Like a man whose mother comforts him, so will He comfort them in Jerusal[em . . . like a bridegroom] over a bride, over her [7][fore]ver He will dwe[ll . . . fo]r His throne is forever and ever and His glory .[. . .]and all nations [8][. . .]to it and there shall be in it a hos[t . . .].. and their pleasant [la]nd [9][. . .].. ornamentat[ion] .[. . .]. I will bless [10][. . .]Blessed be the name of the Most Hi[gh . . .] BLANK [11][. . .]...[. . .] Your kindness upon me [12][. . .]You have established for the Torah [13][. . .]. the book of Your laws

Note

[a-a]רב טוב Weinfeld plausibly takes this phrase not as "vast bounty" (Isa 63:7; Ps 31:20 [EVV 31:19]; 145:7; Neh 9:35) but as "abounding in goodness" on analogy with the phrase רב חסד, "abounding in kindness" (e.g., Exod 34:6; Num 14:18). The goodness of God figures in the Talmudic liturgy for grace after meals in the mourner's house (*b. Ber.* 46a-b).

Commentary

Line 1. The adjectives "mourning" and "afflicted" are in the feminine singular, since cities and city names are construed as feminine in Hebrew. The word "mourning" does not appear in the HB in the feminine singular, but it is found in the prayers for the Ninth of Av (see the introduction to 4Q501) with reference to Jerusalem (*y. Ber.* 4:3.8a). Compare also Isa 54:11. For the same theme compare 4Q179 2.

Lines 2-3. Here the text echoes Isa 65:17-18. The later grace after meals combines the ideas of God giving the land of the nations and the Torah and laws (cf. lines 12-13) to Israel in language with many similarities to 4Q434a (*y. Ber.* 1:6.3d). The Jewish grace after meals also expresses eschatological hopes (*b. Ber.* 48b), as does the corresponding prayer in *Didache* 10.

Line 3. The middle of the line is restored on the basis of Isa 6:3.

Lines 3-4. Weinfeld suggests that the reference is to the person being mourned, whose sins will be atoned for by death. The Jewish grace after meals for mourners refers to God's taking away deceased souls in justice or judgment, a related if not identical thought ("Grace after Meals," 435; *b. Ber.* 46b).

Lines 4-5. The phrase "to eat its fruit and its goodness" is found in Jer 2:7; Neh 9:36.

Line 6. Based on Isa 66:13 and taking over its unusual comparison of God with a female figure. For a similar image, but one in which the mother represents Jerusalem, see *4 Ezra* 9:38–10:28. The conventional Jewish blessings after meals in the mourner's house also draw on Isa 66:13 (Weinfeld, "Grace after Meals," 433-34).

Lines 6-7. For the phrase "over a bride" compare Isa 62:5. The only passage in the HB in which God "dwells over" someone is Deut 33:12.

Line 7. The reference to the eternal throne echoes passages concerning the king (2 Sam 7:16; Ps 45:7; Prov 29:14; 1 Chron 17:14) and God (Ps 93:2; Lam 5:19). References to God's glory are ubiquitous (e.g., Ps 24:7-10; 29:3). For the "glory" of the king, see 1 Kgs 3:13 // 2 Chron 1:11-12; Isa 22:23; Prov 25:2; Esther 1:4; 1 Chron 17:18; 2 Chron 17:5; 18:1. According to *b. Ber.* 49a, if David's kingdom is mentioned, God's should be as well.

Line 8. The nearest grammatically possible referent to "it" is "His glory" in line 7, but the referent may also be lost in the lacuna of the first part of line 8. The phrase "a pleasant land" is found in the HB in Jer 3:19; Zech 7:14; Ps 106:24 (cf. 4Q504 1-2iv:11). According to *b. Ber.* 48b, "the pleasant, good, and ample land" is to be mentioned in the grace after meals.

Lines 9-10. The language of blessing is appropriate for grace after meals. Compare the benediction to Gen 14:20; Ps 9:3 (EVV 9:2); 92:2 (EVV 92:1); 11Q14 1ii:3-4.

Lines 12-13. See the commentary to lines 2-3.

A Lamentation

(4Q501)

INTRODUCTION

I. Contents

This document laments the oppression of its reciters and calls on God to deliver them from their enemies.

II. The Manuscript

A single column of 4Q501 survives in relatively good condition. The manuscript is written in a Herodian hand from the second half of the first century BCE. A seam on the left margin indicates that at least one column followed this one. It is possible that one or more lost columns came before it as well.

III. Structure and Genre

This work is a poetic composition that addresses God, asking for his protection from the nations and perhaps from oppressors in the Jewish community. The

177

writer speaks in the first-person plural, implying that the work is meant for communal recitation. Although only one column survives, this is enough to show that 4Q501 should probably be regarded as a communal lament, a genre also known from the Psalms (e.g., Pss 44, 74, 79, 80).

IV. Life Situation

There are few clues as to when this lament was meant to be recited. It has parallels to a passage in the "Festival Prayers" (4Q509 12i-13), which might imply a setting in one of the festivals — but unfortunately we do not know which one. Lawrence Schiffman argues that 4Q501 contains similarities to the *Taḥanun* (Supplication) prayers for Monday and Thursday in the traditional Jewish liturgy, especially a common dependence on Joel 2:17.[1] However, the connection of 4Q501 with Joel 2:17 is not very striking.

The content of this lament is not obviously appropriate for the Day of Atonement since there is no confession of sin in the extant column. However, Zech 7:1-5 refers to a day of fasting and mourning in the fifth month (the month of Av), and later Jewish tradition observes the ninth of this month as a day of mourning for the destruction of the Jerusalem temple. The book of Lamentations is read on this day, and thus the connections between it and 4Q501 (see below) support the possibility that the latter was intended for recitation on the fast day mentioned in Zechariah 7. Line 1 refers to oppression by foreigners, an appropriate theme for the day.

There is nothing explicitly sectarian about the work, although nothing in it would be likely to offend sectarian sensibilities. Lines 7-8 may refer to a hostile Jewish group, but because the text is damaged and in disarray, not much can be made of this possibility. Line 9 refers to oppression of the poor, a theme associated more often with wicked Israelites than with the nations (e.g., Exod 23:6; Deut 24:14; Jer 5:28), although the nations too are sometimes charged with this sin (e.g., Ps 9:19 [EVV 9:18]; 74:21). The term "poor" is even used by the sectarians as a self-designation (e.g., 1QHᵃ x:32; 1QpHab xii:3, 6; 4Q171 1-2ii:9), although nothing in this line implies that meaning. Perhaps the most likely possibility is that the sectarians adopted this communal lament because they found elements of it appropriate for their own situation.

---

1. Schiffman, "Early History of Jewish Liturgy," 40.

V. Literary Context

The parallels with the "Festival Prayers" from Qumran have been mentioned above, as has the possible connection with the Supplication prayers in the later Jewish liturgy. This work echoes a number of biblical passages, particularly Lamentations 5.

BIBLIOGRAPHY

Baillet, Maurice. "501. Lamentation." In *Qumrân Grotte 4. III (4Q482-4Q520)*, 79-89, plate xxviii. DJD 7. Oxford: Clarendon, 1982.

Schiffman, Lawrence H. "The Dead Sea Scrolls and the Early History of Jewish Liturgy." In *The Synagogue in Late Antiquity*, edited by Lee I. Irvine, 33-48. Philadelphia: ASOR/JTSA, 1987.

A LAMENTATION

(4Q501)

TOP MARGIN

[1][. . .]. do not give our inheritance to strangers and our labor to sons of a foreigner. Remember that [2][we are those excluded] of Your people and those abandoned of Your inheritance. Remember the desolate sons of Your covenant, [3][Yo]ur dedicated [. . .] straying with no one to bring them back, broken with no one to bind them up, [4][bent over with no one to ra]ise them up. They have surrounded us — the wretched[a] of Your people — with their lying tongue and they are overturned[b] [5][. . .]. and Your bough to one horn of woman. Look and see the disgrace of the sons of [6][. . .] our skin [grows hot] and searing heat has seized us before the tongue of their revilings. Do not [7][. . .] with Your commandments and do not let their seed be [c]of ~~the sons of~~ the covenant[c] [8][. . .] to them in the tumult of Your strength and take vengeance against them. [9][. . . Y]ou, and they have not set You in front of them, and they vaunt themselves over the afflicted and poor.

BOTTOM MARGIN

Notes

ᵃחילכיא With Baillet, I take this to be a plene spelling of the same word as BH חלכה (Ps 10:8, 14; plural חלכאים in Ps 10:10), which is also found in 1QHᵃ xi:25-26; xii:25, 35.

ᵇויופכו A Hophal imperfect form of the root √הפך with elision of the *he*.

ᶜ⁻ᶜמבני־ברית According to Baillet, the indicated letters have been crossed out so as to alter the phrase to "of the covenant." The exact extent of the deletion is unclear from the photograph.

Commentary

Line 1. Compare Lam 5:2; Jer 20:5; Joel 2:17.

Line 2. With Baillet, I restore on the basis of the biblical phrase "excluded and abandoned" (Deut 32:36; 1 Kgs 14:10; 21:21; 2 Kgs 9:8; 14:26), whose meaning is unclear. The RSV translates the phrase as "bond or free," which fits the biblical contexts, but the translation given here fits the context of 4Q501 better. Compare the second clause to Lam 1:16. For the phrase "sons of Your covenant" compare 1QM xvii:8 (whose context is also one of trial); 4Q503 7-9:3; the partly deleted phrase "the sons of the covenant" in line 7 (also in *m. B. Qam.* 1.2, 3); and "the sons of His covenant" in 11QPsᵃ xxviii:11 (Ps 151:7).

Line 3. Compare Ezek 34:4, 16; 4Q509 12i-13:38.

Line 4. For the restoration of the first clause, see Ps 145:14; 146:8. The phrase "a lying tongue" is found in Ps 109:2; Prov 6:17; 12:19; 26:28; 1QHᵃ xiii:27; 4Q381 45a + b:5.

Line 5. The meaning of the first clause is not clear. The phrase "born of woman" is found in Job 14:1; 15:14; 25:4; 1QS xi:21; 1QHᵃ v:20; xxi:8-9?; xxiii:12-13; Gal 4:4 (cf. Matt 11:11 // Luke 7:28). Compare the second clause to Lam 5:1.

Line 6. Compare Lam 5:10, which also informs the reconstruction. The phrase "tongue of revilings" occurs in 1QS iv:11; CD v:11-12.

Line 7. This line seems to refer to hostile members of the Jewish community, since there would be no question of the seed of the oppressing Gentiles (line 1) being associated with the covenant.

Line 8. Compare "the tumult of His strength" in 1QHᵃ xi:34. Variations of the phrase "take vengeance against them" are found in Ezek 25:17; Ps 149:7; CD viii:11-12.

Line 9. Compare Ps 54:5 (EVV 54:3); 86:14. The phrase "to vaunt oneself over" appears in Isa 42:13; CD xx:33-34.

A Wedding Ceremony?

(4Q502)

INTRODUCTION

The document 4Q502 survives only in a single papyrus manuscript in a pitiful
state of disintegration, a factor that makes its interpretation unusually difficult.
It clearly pertains to some sort of ritual of celebration, but the exact nature of
the ceremony is elusive. It may be a wedding, or perhaps a rite for aged married
couples entering the celibate sectarian community, or even an otherwise unattested New Year celebration. All three theories have been defended, and no
doubt other solutions are possible.

I. Contents

The state of the manuscript makes exegesis of the text extremely difficult, but a
number of features are clear. The document is liturgical: various speakers recite
blessings and address one another, speaking in the first person singular and
plural. God too is blessed and addressed. Fragments of instructions for the act-
ing out of the ceremony also survive (e.g., 19:5; 24:4). The ritual seems to be
called a "festival" (מועד) in 6 + 8-10:8. It is a joyous celebration in which the
verb "to be happy" and the noun "happiness" figure prominently, as do the
roots "to bless" and "to be holy," and the noun "glory."

Men and women of all age groups in the community are involved, and

181

possibly children as well. There are repeated references to fertility and off-spring, and a married couple seems to figure in frags. 1-3. The presence in frag. 16 of a passage also found in the *Community Rule* makes it certain that this is a sectarian document. An enigmatic phrase (שמחת יחד) that appears repeatedly may be translated either "happiness together" or "the happiness of the Community." A seven-day period is mentioned in 97:2, and in 99:2 there seems to be a reference to *lulavs* (לולבים), the palm leaf wand interlaced with willow and myrtle branches that is carried by celebrants during the Festival of Booths.

II. The Manuscript

4Q502 consists of 344 papyrus fragments, the majority of which preserve no more than a few letters each. The editor, Maurice Baillet (along with C.-H. Hunzinger and J. W. B. Barnes), worked out fiber correspondences among some of the larger pieces, which, along with other visual clues, allowed them to isolate three assemblages of fragments (1-15, 16-21, and 22-24). Most of the usable information comes from these groups, although some of the small, isolated fragments have noteworthy or illuminating readings. The editors date the script to the early first century CE. I have translated most of the fragments in these three groups, along with a few of the smaller bits that preserve text of some interest.

III. Genre

Although there is no doubt that the work is a ritual of celebration, no consensus has been reached by scholars on the exact nature of the celebration. Three theories have been proposed, but no copies of Jewish works in the proposed genres survive from antiquity.

In the first edition, Baillet argues that 4Q502 is a marriage ceremony. Noting the mention of a wife and offspring in 1-3:3-4, 7 and the joyous nature of the ceremony, he draws parallels to the account of the marriage of Tobias and Sarah in the book of Tobit.

In 1983 and 1990 Joseph Baumgarten challenged this interpretation, raising the following objections. The ceremony in question seems to have a prescribed time (a קץ or מועד, if Baillet's reconstructions of the damaged words are accepted), which Baumgarten considers uncharacteristic for weddings. The references to old men and old women (19:2) and mature adult men and women (34:3) are odd if the ceremony is for a young couple. The references to "offspring" or "seed" may not be intended literally since the term is used figuratively in the sectarian texts, particularly in one passage in the *Community Rule* (1QS iv:6-7) whose immediately preceding context (iv:4-6) appears in 4Q502 16.

Baumgarten argues that 4Q502 finds its best parallels in a "popular Sukkot celebration" mentioned in *t. Sukk.* 4.2 and in the celebratory ritual of the Therapeutae described by the first century CE Jewish philosopher Philo of Alexandria (*Vit. Cont.* 64-90). The Therapeutae were an ascetic Jewish group in Egypt who lived a simple and celibate philosophical life studying the scriptures. They are similar in many ways to the Essenes. Baumgarten thinks the ritual in question might also have been celebrated in the autumn during the Festival of Booths, despite its association with a pentecontad sequence of days, which would tie it more naturally to the Festival of Weeks, or Pentecost in the late spring. His interpretation is that 4Q502 celebrates the entry of aged married couples into the celibate Essene community at Qumran.

Michael Satlow advanced a different interpretation in 1998. Accepting Baumgarten's objections to the identification of the text as a marriage ceremony but recognizing the speculative nature of his solution, Satlow proposes that 4Q502 describes a New Year and harvest celebration on the first of the month Nisan in the early spring. (The Jewish New Year is currently celebrated in the fall, but there is good evidence that in ancient times the year began in the spring.) He draws attention to possible parallels in terminology with 4Q503 49 and 4Q509 3, both of which he associates tentatively with the first of Nisan. Invoking cross-cultural generalizations advanced by Mircea Eliade, Satlow suggests that frags. 1 10 included a retelling of the Genesis creation story in roughly reverse order, because creation was tied in mythic terms to the beginning of the year, and that the presence of the whole community at the celebration brings to mind other New Year celebrations in antiquity.

None of these theories is compelling, but to my mind the first — that 4Q502 is a wedding ceremony — is less speculative and better supported than the other two. Baumgarten's objections to this reading are not persuasive. According to *m. Ketub.* 1.1 there was a preferred day of the week for Jewish weddings, and evidence from the Cairo Geniza bears this out (see the commentary to 6 + 8-10:8). We would expect the whole community, young and old, to come together for a wedding. The passage in the *Community Rule* that refers to "fruitfulness of seed" need not be explained away as figurative unless we insist on finding the idea of celibacy in the work in order to reconcile it with the classical description of the celibate group of Essenes.[1] Other interpretations are possible, and a narrow reading of the Essene hypothesis should not govern our interpretation of even the *Community Rule,* let alone a fragmentary sectarian text like 4Q502.[2]

The most that can be said of Baumgarten's and Satlow's hypotheses is that neither is impossible. However, both read a great deal into the fragments of 4Q502, and neither can point to compelling parallels to support their interpretations. I have presented additional evidence below in this introduction and in the commentary in favor of Baillet's theory, but I fully recognize that it, like the others, remains speculative.

IV. Life Situation

Unfortunately, no other Jewish wedding ceremonies survive from antiquity, but, by gathering together scattered descriptions and references to weddings from many documents of various genres composed over a long period of time (see the next section), we can work out a rough idea of what such a ceremony entailed.[3] The wedding took place only after a formal contract and betrothal were ratified (see n. 14). According to the Mishnah, the preferred day for the marriage of a virgin was Wednesday.[4] The wedding was a time of great joy in which the bride adorned herself with ornaments and fine clothing and the bridegroom wore a garland.[5] A seven-day "feast" was held,[6] in which there was

---

1. The same is true for the interpretation of "and to their seed" in 4Q171 iii 1-2 and "their seed" in 1QH[a] iv:13-15. See Baumgarten, "Qumran-Essene Restraints on Marriage," 17 and 22 n. 16.

2. For a very different reading of the *Community Rule* as a statute or constitution for a Hellenistic synagogal association, not a sectarian constitution, see Klinghardt, "The Manual of Discipline." In addition, drawing in part on 4Q502, Elder argues that the Qumran community was "ascetic" but not celibate and that it consisted of men, women, and children ("The Woman Question").

3. For another reconstruction that draws more on later material, see Archer, *Her Price Is Beyond Rubies,* 123-206. Pope compares the Song of Songs to a wide array of literature and genres (*Song of Songs,* 54-89).

4. *m. Ketub.* 1.1.

5. For example, Isa 49:18; 61:10; 62:5; Jer 2:32; 7:34; Ezek 16:10-14; Ps 45:7, 14-15; John 3:29; Rev 18:23; 19:7-8; 21:2; Bar 2:23; *Jos. Asen.* 18:5-6.

6. In BH a מִשְׁתֶּה (Gen 29:22; Judg 14:10), in Greek γάμοι or γάμος (e.g., Matt 22:2; John 2:1; Tob 11:19), and in the Mishnah a "house of feasting" (בֵּית מִשְׁתֶּה) (e.g., *m. Neg.* 3:2). The fourteen-day celebration for Tobias and Sarah is presented as a special extension in honor of the successful wedding after seven failures (Tob 8:19-20).

much eating and drinking[7] and which would go late into the evening.[8] Apparently the groom would come to escort the bride to his dwelling on the first night.[9] The details of the ceremony are obscure, although besides the feasting, wedding songs were certainly sung[10] and blessings on the couple and their private prayers are recorded.[11] On the first night the newlyweds retired to the "bridal chamber" (חפה or νυμφών) where the bride's virginity was verified when consummation of the marriage took place.[12]

Less can be said about the life situations of the rituals proposed by Baumgarten and Satlow inasmuch as the rituals themselves are hypothetical. Philo's evidence shows that there was an ascetic Jewish group in Egypt that put a special value on chastity and virginity and that carried out a liturgical celebration that involved men and women together. Whether this particular ritual took place during the Festival of Weeks in the spring or the Festival of Booths in the fall is open to debate. The first possibility seems more likely. It is even more debatable whether 4Q502 involved a similar Essene or sectarian ritual and whether aged married couples celebrated their commitment to celibacy and to the group in this ceremony.

As Satlow notes, following Eliade, numerous New Year celebrations are attested in the ancient world (e.g., the pagan Babylonian Akîtu festival),[13] and it is not impossible that 4Q502 describes a celebration of the spring New Year, although no such Jewish ceremony is attested beyond doubt elsewhere. The Babylonian New Year festival took place over eleven or twelve days of Nisan (March-April). Highlights included the recitation of the Babylonian creation epic (the Enuma Elish) on the fourth day; the ritual humiliation of the king by the high priest of the cult of Marduk (the patron god of Babylon) on the fifth day; various processions and rituals, perhaps including a sacred marriage ceremony and a cultic drama reenacting the creation myth; and a great banquet on the last day. The involvement of the whole community and the allusions to the

---

7. Matt 22:1-14; John 2:1-11; Rev 19:9.

8. Luke 12:36-38; m. Ber. 1.1.

9. Matt 25:1-13.

10. For examples, see Psalm 45 and perhaps the Song of Songs.

11. Tob 7:13; 8:4-8; 10:12; Jos. Asen. 21:4-6. Allusions to the creation story and requests for fecundity are found in these passages. Later blessings for the Babylonian Jewish wedding ceremony are found in b. Ketub. 7b-8a.

12. Ps 19:5; Joel 2:16; Tob 6:13, 17; 8:1.

13. For a discussion of the surviving evidence for details of the Akîtu celebration, see Roux, Ancient Iraq, 96-101, 365-69, and Frymer-Kensky, "Akitu." For New Year celebration customs in general, see Henninger, "New Year Festivals."

biblical creation myth offer some support to Satlow's view that 4Q502 represents a spring New Year festival.

V. Literary Context

Our information on ancient Jewish weddings must be culled from a wide variety of literary sources and genres, including narratives involving weddings (Gen 29:22-29; Judg 14:10-18; John 2:1-11; Tob 7–11; 1 Macc 9:37-41; *Jos. Asen.* 18–21); love songs (the Song of Songs); a royal wedding song (Psalm 45); proverbial sayings in prophetic oracles and elsewhere (e.g., Jer 7:34; Ps 19:5; Mark 2:19; John 3:29); parables (Matt 22:1-14; 25:1-13); and even apocalyptic visions (Rev 18:23; 19:7-9; 21:2, 9; 22:17). Jewish marriage contracts (*ketubbot* and related documents) also sometimes give background information on such matters as the obligations of the spouses to one another, the contents of wedding blessings, and rules regarding maintenance of children and inheritance.[14]

Again, literary contexts for the other interpretations of 4Q502 are difficult to establish. Baumgarten's main source for comparison is Philo's account of the Therapeutae. Satlow depends more on phenomenological parallels advanced by Eliade than on parallels in specific texts.[15]

---

14. A couple first went through an official period of betrothal in which they were under binding contract to marry but the marriage was not yet consummated (Matt 1:18-19; later legal conventions can be found in tractate *Qiddušin* of the Mishnah). Numerous legal details had to be negotiated, resulting in a marriage contract *(ketubba)* laying out the rights and obligations of both parties. A number of *ketubbot* survive from the early second century CE, a period not long after the writing of 4Q502 (Mur 20, 21; pYadin 10 = 5/6Ḥev 105), as do a few other marriage contracts dating as far back as the fourth century BCE. In addition, the Cairo Geniza has produced a number of Palestinian *ketubbot* from the tenth and eleventh centuries CE. (The Cairo Geniza is a repository for worn-out manuscripts in a synagogue in Cairo. After many centuries of use it was emptied about a century ago. The contents are still being edited by scholars.) Although evidence from these much later *ketubbot* must be used with appropriate caution, it cannot be denied that they can preserve very conservative streams of tradition. For example, Friedman discusses a case where divorce clauses found in an Elephantine papyrus of the fourth century BCE are unattested thereafter until they are alluded to but not quoted fully seven centuries later in the Palestinian Talmud, after which they appear again only after another seven centuries in *ketubbot* from the Cairo Geniza (*Jewish Marriage* 2: 315-27). Nevertheless, readers should be aware that parallels to the Cairo Geniza texts are speculative.

15. For a discussion and critique of Eliade's interpretive focus on cosmological symbolism, see Morris, *Anthropological Studies of Religion*, 174-81.

BIBLIOGRAPHY

Archer, Léonie J. *Her Price Is Beyond Rubies: The Jewish Woman in Graeco-Roman Palestine.* JSOTSup 60. Sheffield, England: Sheffield Academic Press, 1990.

Baillet, Maurice. "502. Rituel de mariage." In *Qumrân Grotte 4. III (4Q482-4Q520),* 81-105, plates xxix-xxxiv. DJD 7. Oxford: Clarendon, 1982.

Baumgarten, Joseph M. "4Q502, Marriage or Golden Age Ritual?" *JJS* 34 (1983) 125-35.

———. "The Qumran-Essene Restraints on Marriage." In *Archaeology and History in the Dead Sea Scrolls: The New York University Conference in Memory of Yigael Yadin,* edited by Lawrence H. Schiffman, 13-14. JSPSup 8. JSOT/ASOR Monograph 2. Sheffield, England: Sheffield Academic Press, 1990.

Elder, Linda Bennett. "The Woman Question and Female Ascetics Among Essenes." *BA* 57 (1994) 220-34.

Friedman, Mordechai Akiva. *Jewish Marriage in Palestine: A Cairo Geniza Study.* 2 vols. Tel Aviv and New York: Jewish Theological Seminary of America, 1980-81.

———. "Babatha's *Ketubba:* Some Preliminary Observations." *IEJ* 46 (1996) 55-76.

Frymer-Kensky, Tikva. "Akitu." In *Encyclopedia of Religion,* edited by Mircea Eliade, vol. 1, 170-72. New York: Macmillan, 1987.

Henninger, Joseph. "New Year Festivals." In *Encyclopedia of Religion,* edited by Mircea Eliade, vol. 10, 415-20. New York: Macmillan, 1987.

Klinghardt, Matthias. "The Manual of Discipline in the Light of Statutes of Hellenistic Associations." In *Methods of Investigation of the Dead Sea Scrolls and the Khirbet Qumran Site: Present Realities and Future Prospects,* edited by Michael O. Wise et al., 251-70. Annals of the New York Academy of Sciences 722. New York: New York Academy of Sciences, 1994.

Kramer, Ross S. "Monastic Jewish Women in Greco-Roman Egypt: Philo Judaeus on the Therapeutrides." *Signs* 14 (1989) 342-70.

Lapin, Hayim. "Palm Fronds and Citrons: Notes on Two Letters from Bar Kosiba's Administration." *HUCA* 64 (1993) 111-35.

Morris, Brian. *Anthropological Studies of Religion: An Introductory Text.* London: Cambridge University Press, 1987.

Pope, Marvin H. *Song of Songs: A New Translation with Introduction and Commentary.* AB 7C. Garden City, N.Y.: Doubleday, 1977.

Roux, Georges. *Ancient Iraq.* 2nd ed. New York and London: Penguin, 1980.

Satlow, Michael L. "4Q502: A New Year Festival?" *DSD* 5 (1998) 57-68.

———. "'One Who Loves His Wife Like Himself': Love in Rabbinic Marriage." *JJS* 49 (1998) 66-86.

Schuller, Eileen. "Women in the Dead Sea Scrolls." In *Methods of Investigation of the*

Dead Sea Scrolls and the Khirbet Qumran Site: Present Realities and Future Prospects, edited by Michael O. Wise et al., 115-31. Annals of the New York Academy of Sciences 722. New York: New York Academy of Sciences, 1994.

————. "Women in the Dead Sea Scrolls." In *The Dead Sea Scrolls after Fifty Years: A Comprehensive Assessment,* edited by Peter W. Flint and James C. VanderKam, vol. 2, 117-44. Leiden: Brill, 1999.

Weinfeld, Moshe. "Prayer and Liturgical Practice in the Qumran Sect." In *The Dead Sea Scrolls: Forty Years of Research,* edited by Devorah Dimant and Uriel Rappaport, 241-58. STDJ 10. Leiden: Brill, 1992.

Yadin, Yigael, et al. "Babatha's *Ketubba.*" *IEJ* 44 (1994) 75-103.

A WEDDING CEREMONY?

(4Q502)

Group I

4Q502 1-3

A ritual involving a married couple[a]

TOP MARGIN?

[1]. . . [m]an is acquainted with [. . .] when adding [. . .] [2][. . .]. the law of God [. . .] to remove [. . .] [3][. . . [b]the man] and his wife[b] for [. . .] . . . [4][. . .] to produce offspring [. . .]..[. . .]. these [. . .] [5][. . .].. which [. . . ho]ly ones, he gives thanks to God [. . .] [6][. . .].. from being hol[y . . .]. to him, a daughter of truth and ...[c][. . .] [7][. . .] his darling wh[o . . .] she has insight and understanding in the midst of [. . .] [8].. fat[hers?].[. . . to]gether to become [. . .] [9][. . .]. conjugal duty[d] of ..[. . .].. and he atones [. . .] [10][. . .]. to sons of right[eousness[e] . . .] on this day .[. . .] [11][. . .].[. . . A]aron [. . .]

Notes

[a]Frags. 1 and 2 have a fiber correspondence in line 7; frags. 1 and 3 probably have traces of a top margin.

[b-b]וֹאשתוֹ [האדם] Baillet's plausible restoration on the basis of Gen 2:25; 3:8.

188

ᶜ]ומתה Baillet reads [מתהלל]כת, presumably translated "and she walks," although he gives no translation. The damaged letter might be a *lamed*, but it is impossible to be sure.

ᵈעונת Possibly "iniquity of," but contrast the spelling ע]וֹונתם[with two *waws* in frag. 19:7 (as is normal in QH), which tends to confirm that we have a different word in this context.

ᵉלבני צד]ק[One could also reconstruct [לבני צד]וק, "for the sons of Zad[ok]." Compare line 11, which refers to Aaron, and see the commentary to line 10 below.

Commentary

Line 3. Compare the reference to "[the man] and his wife" (or "[Adam] and his wife") with the prenuptial prayer and blessing in Tob 8:6-7. The story of the creation of Adam and Eve is tied to wedding benedictions in *b. Ketub.* 8a.

Line 4. The production of offspring (here literally "seed") is a great blessing according to biblical thought (e.g., Gen 1:28; 13:16; Isa 48:19; Ps 127:3-5; cf. 4Q287 5:12; *Jub.* 21:25 [4Q219 1ii:31-34]), a blessing invoked in association with weddings (e.g., Gen 24:60; Ruth 4:11-12; Ps 45:17; Tob 8:6; 10:12; *Jos. Asen.* 21:5-6). The *ketubbot* lay out explicit provisions for children (e.g., 5/6Hev 10 recto 12-16; Mur 20 recto i:8-9, 13; Mur 21 recto ii:10-15; KCG 1:25-28). See also 4Q502 14:6; 20:3; 163:3. There is no need to take this phrase as figurative, contra Baumgarten and Satlow (see the introduction to this chapter).

Line 5. The term "holy ones" normally refers to angels in Jewish literature of this period (see the commentary to Songs I 4Q400 1i:2). Various forms of the root "to be holy" appear about seventeen times in 4Q502, unfortunately usually in badly broken contexts.

Line 6. Although the phrase "daughter of truth" is otherwise unattested, the term "sons of truth" is used by the sectarians as a self-designation in 1QS iv:5, 6 (paralleled here in frag. 16) and elsewhere. Presumably "daughter of truth" has the same sectarian connotation.

Line 7. The word translated "darling" (רעיה) is attested only in the Song of Songs, referring to King Solomon's beloved (Cant 1:9, 15; 2:2, 10, 13; 4:1, 7; 5:2) and always in the form "my darling." The reference to "his darling" here seems to indicate that a couple figured in this line, presumably the same couple as in line 3.

Satlow interprets frags. 1-3 and 6-10 to involve a retelling of the creation story in reverse order, beginning with a mention of Adam and Eve in line 3 above and concluding with a reference to "the waters of its (the earth's) abysses" (cf. Gen 1:7). He takes the woman's insight in this line to be an echo of Gen 3:6 (Satlow, "4Q502: A New Year Festival?" 64), an odd verse to invoke in any ceremony unless the woman is being contrasted with Eve; he then ties these echoes of the creation story to a New Year celebration, which is possible. Weinfeld, however, also points out that the creation of humankind is a theme in the traditional marriage ceremony benediction ("Prayer and Liturgical Practice," 250-51).

Line 8. The word translated "together" (יחד) appears about nine times in 4Q502; it is unclear in many cases whether it should be translated "together" or "Community." For the technical use of this term, see the discussion in the commentary to 4Q286 7ii:1.

Line 9. The word translated "conjugal duty" (עונה) appears in Exod 21:10, referring to one of three things a man may not reduce for his first wife when he takes a second (the other two are her food and clothing). Although the meaning of the word in the biblical passage is uncertain, the rabbinic literature understands it as translated here (*m. Ketub.* 5.6), while the *ketubbot* often refer to these three obligations of the future husband (e.g., 5/6Hev 10 recto 7; KCG 4:9-11; cf. Friedman, *Jewish Marriage* 1: 167-78). This word also appears with the meaning "a period of time" in RH (Jastrow, 1054) and QH (e.g., 4Q177 5-6:13).

Line 10. The phrase "sons of righteousness" is a self-designation for the sectarians in 1QS iii:20. The alternative reconstruction, "the sons of Zadok," is used of the priestly leadership in the sectarian texts (e.g., 1QS v:2, 9; ix:14; CD iv:3) since the Aaronid priests came from the family line of Zadok (whence comes the title Sadducees).

Line 11. The context of the name Aaron is lost, but the sectarians had a priestly leadership and Aaron and the sons of Aaron are mentioned frequently in the sectarian texts (e.g., 1QS v:21; viii:5-6; 1QSa i:15-16, 23; CD v:17-18).

4Q502 4

A fragment that mentions happiness[a]

¹[. . .].[. . .] ²[. . .] his [fa]ther .[. . .] ³[. . . ha]ppiness tog[ether . . .] ⁴[. . .]. . .[. . .] ⁵[. . .].[. . .]

Note
   [a]Baillet places this fragment a short distance below frag. 1 (and therefore to the right of frag. 5 and perhaps above it).

Commentary

Lines 1-2. Conceivably the first line could refer to the father of the groom (cf. frags. 15:1; 108:3), and the second (with a frequently repeated phrase) to the anticipated wedded bliss of the couple; but given the damaged state of the text this is no more than speculation.

Line 2. Another possible translation is "[hap]piness of the Comm[unity]" However, this phrase never occurs elsewhere in the QL. It does appear in frags. 105 + 106:2 and is possibly to be reconstructed several more times in 4Q502. In addition, the root "to be happy" appears about seven more times in this manuscript. Both weddings (e.g., Isa 61:10; 62:5; Jer 7:34; John 3:29; *Jos. Asen.* 20:7-8; *b. Ketub.* 8a) and the festivals (Deut 16:11, 15; 26:11; 2 Chron 30:21-27; 11Q19 xxi:8-9; *m. Pesaḥ.* 10.5-6; *m. Sukk.* 4.8; 5.1, 4; *m. Ta'an.* 4.8) were considered times of great joy and happiness.

4Q502 5

A fragment that mentions happiness[a]

¹[. . .] their .. to..[. . .] ²[. . . wh]o has commanded [us . . .] ³[. . .].[happin]ess together for[. . .] ⁴[. . .].. he walks[. . .]

Note
[a]Baillet places this fragment below frag. 2.

4Q502 7

A fragment that mentions happiness[a]

¹[. . .]Is[rael . . .] ²[. . .]thank[sgiving . . .] ³[. . . happi]ness together [. . .]

Note
[a]Baillet places this fragment either above or below the complex of fragments formed by frags. 6 + 8-10 (see below).

4Q502 6 + 8-10

Individual and communal liturgies[a]

*A man recites a joyful psalm that alludes
to the creation story*

[1][. . .]...[. . .] [2][. . .]God of Israel and he answers and s[ays] [3][. . .][b]. of happiness[b] to psalm His name [4][. . .].[. . .] their adults[c] and youths [5][. . .].[. . .] their ..., [l]ambs and g[oats . . .].. among our cattle, and it creeps [6][. . .]...[. . . cree]ping thing in our shadow. And the fowl [. . .] our [. . .] and our land and all its produce [7][. . .]...[. . .]. fruit of its trees, and our waters [. . .].. and the waters of its abysses. All of us [8][. . .]. the name of the God of Israel [d].[. . . fes]tival[d] for our happiness, and also [9][. . .].[. . .]. the testimony of the .[. . .] in the midst of righteous adults [10][. . .]. in peace .[. . . I am? . . .].. giving thanks to God and boasting [11][. . .]... brothers to me, adults [12][. . . they are bles]sing in our midst. BLANK

A liturgy recited by a group

[13][. . .]holiness [. . .] most [ho]ly adults [14][. . .]day, I [. . . bless?] the God of Israel [. . .]. [15][. . . a]dults of .[. . .]his ..[. . .] glo[ry].. [16][. . .] and ..[. . .] we [are happ]y in the test[imony . . .] to become [17]... because of [. . .].[. . .].. [18][. . .]...

Notes

[a]On the basis of a fiber correspondence, Baillet places frag. 6 to the right of frags. 8-10 and suggests that the former belonged to the preceding column. It contains a small amount of untranslatable material from three successive lines. The relationships between frags. 8-10 are established by fibers tying frag. 8 to frag. 10 and frag. 10 to frag. 9. Fragment 8 (lines 5-10) is above frag. 10 (lines 13-16), and both are to the right of frag. 9 (lines 1-18).

According to Baillet, frags. 11-13 go just below frag. 9. Frags. 11 and 12 have a corresponding fiber. All three are too badly damaged to give any connected sense.

[b-b]Baillet reads שמחה קֿ[ץ], "[peri]od of happiness," but the last letter of the first word is damaged and could be either a ṣade or a taw, and thus his reconstruction is speculative.

[c]The word "adults" (אשישים), which appears about eight more times in 4Q502, is difficult. Baillet originally translated it as *gâteaux*, "cakes," taking it as the noun אשישה, which appears with both masculine and feminine plurals in BH (2 Sam 6:19 // 1 Chron 16:3; Hos 3:1; Cant 2:5); but in DJD 7 he notes that this translation does not fit the contexts of its usage in 4Q502 and in 1QpHab vi:11. The word appears as the plural of "man" (איש) in Isa 16:7. A connection with the root having to do with old

age (ישש√) is also possible, and thus the meaning "adults" fits the context here as well as anything.

d-dIn the lacuna Baillet reconstructs אָ[שר נתן לנו מ[וֹ]עד, "w[ho gave to us a fest]ival," but this is speculative. His reading of the last word is possible, but the *waw* is too badly damaged for the reading to be certain.

Satlow compares the phrase "[fes]tival for our happiness" (מֹ[וֹעד לשמחתנו]) here to the similar phrase "fes[tivals of] our [happ]iness" (מֹוֹ[עדי שמ[חתנו) in 4Q503 48-50:5, which he follows Baillet in ascribing to Passover ("4Q502: A New Year Festival?" 58-59). But the latter reading is a speculative reconstruction that (contra Satlow) is not identical to the phrase in frags. 8-10:8, and its connection with Passover is unlikely (see the commentary to 4Q503 48-50).

Commentary

Line 2. This line probably continued with a blessing of God.

Line 3. See the commentary to line 8 below.

Lines 4-7. This passage echoes Gen 1:7, 12, 20-21, 24-27, 30; 9:2-3; Ps 148:7-12.

Line 8. As noted in the introduction to this chapter, Baumgarten and Satlow argue that the proposed application of the words "period" in line 3 and "festival" in this line to the ritual of 4Q502 makes it unlikely that the ritual was a wedding ceremony, since both words imply a festival with a set or appointed time. Even if Baillet's reconstructions of the damaged readings in lines 3 and 8 are granted (see notes b-b and d-d), the argument against their referring to a wedding does not hold up, since early Jewish tradition (*m. Ketub.* 1.1) assigned a particular day of the week for the wedding of a virgin (Wednesday) and of a widow (Thursday). (The ostensible reason for prescribing that the wedding of a virgin be held on a Wednesday was to make it convenient for the groom to go straight to the courts the next morning if he had found her not to be a virgin!) The much later *ketubbot* of the Cairo Geniza show a preference for Thursday as a wedding day, which indicates that, although local traditions varied, the principle held well into the Middle Ages (Friedman, *Jewish Marriage* 1: 98-102). Compare "on this day" in frags. 1-3:10 above. Festivals are also mentioned several more times in 4Q502.

Line 9. The word translated "testimony" (תעודה), which appears about five times in 4Q502, could also be translated with the technical sectarian meaning "set period." See the commentary to Songs IV 4Q402 1:3.

Line 11. In the HB the word "brother" could mean a literal brother (e.g., Gen 4:2), a male relative (Gen 14:14, 16) or merely a fellow Israelite (Deut 15:12). The early Christians addressed and referred to one another as "broth-

193

ers" and "sisters" (e.g., 1 Cor 1:26; 7:15; 9:5; 1 Tim 5:1; James 2:15). The followers of the messianic revolutionary Shimon Bar Kosiba (Bar Kokhba) seem to have used the same form of address; in one letter (5/6Hev 12:4) Bar Kosiba rebukes two of his followers for not being concerned about their "brothers." Following the usage of the HB, the sectarian texts sometimes refer to the members as "brothers" (e.g., CD vi:20-21). Since the context is lost we cannot say whether this line refers to sect members or literal family members. See also the commentary to frags. 19:2-3 and 96:1.

Line 12. The theme of blessing is important in this document. The root "to bless" occurs about eighteen more times in 4Q502, unfortunately mostly in badly broken contexts.

Line 15. The word "glory" appears about nine more times in this document, unfortunately always in badly broken contexts.

4Q502 14

A fragment that addresses God[a]

¹[. . .]...[. . .] ²[. . .]... ... .[. . .] ³[. . .] testimoni[es] and al[so . . .].[. . .] ⁴[. . .]. the God of Israel who commanded the sons of [Israel[b] . . .] ⁵[. . .].[. . .]. Your glory ... and the love of the kindness of [. . .] ⁶[. . .]. of sons and dau[ghters] <...>[c][. . .] ⁷[. . .]. also .[. . .] ⁸[. . . I]srael [. . .]

BOTTOM MARGIN

Notes
[a]Baillet places this fragment above frag. 13, but he is unsure where exactly it goes.
[b]For this restoration compare Lev 7:38; 24:1-2; Num 28:1-2; 34:1-2; 35:1-2.
[c]Baillet reads the smeared supralinear text as]כבֿוֿ, perhaps to be taken as the word "glo[ry]."

Commentary

Line 5. This line seems to address God and refer to his glory.
Line 6. Compare the commentary to frags. 1-3:4.

4Q502 15

A fragment that mentions a father[a]

¹[. . .]his father [. . .]

BOTTOM MARGIN

> **Note**
> [a]The fragment is at a bottom margin. According to Baillet, it belongs below the left side of frag. 9.

Group II

4Q502 16

*A passage about the "sons of truth," which is
also found in the Community Rule*[a]

¹[and a spirit of knowledge in every plan of] action, [and zeal for righteous judgments and a holy plan] ²[with a settled purpose, and an abundance of] acts of kindness tow[ard all the sons of truth, and pure glory that abominates all] ³[defiled idols, and] proceeding [mode]stly in prudence [regarding everything, and concealing the truth - mysteries of knowledge. These are spiritual counsels] ⁴[for the sons of truth of the inhabited wo]rld [and a muste]ring of all [who walk in it for healing . . .]

> **Note**
> [a]Baillet places this fragment above frag. 18 (a small piece with three lines whose only readable word is "His glory" in line 1). Fragment 16 is restored on the basis of 1QS iv:4b-6. The reconstructed lineation is schematic, and it is not certain that the wording in frag. 16 was exactly the same as in 1QS, but the use of this passage on the two spirits confirms that 4Q502 is a sectarian document.

Commentary

Lines 1-4. The material in this fragment is also found in similar form in

195

1QS iv:4-6, which is part of the unit iv:2-8 marked off by blank spaces in 1QS. This passage describes the "counsels of the spirit for the sons of truth," and its larger context is the "Treatise on the Two Spirits" (iii:13–iv:26), a unit that describes the work of the angelic prince of luminaries and the angel of darkness, the two spirit leaders of the sectarians and of their enemies, according to sectarian theology. Baillet suggests that the excerpt in 4Q502 is a part of the wedding ceremony that invites the couple to conduct themselves according to the way of light.

4Q502 19

A liturgy involving men and women of all ages[a]

A ritual in a council

[1]and he sits with him in the council of [b].[. . .][b] [2]seed of blessing, elder men and eld[er women . . . [c]choice youths] [3]and virgins,[c] young men and youn[g women . . .] [4]there,[d] all of us together. [e]And I .[. . .][e]

A communal blessing

[5]And afte[rward] the men of [. . .] shall speak [. . .] [6][and they answer] and say, Blessed be [Go]d [. . .] [7]their [ini]quities .[. . .] [8][. . .]..[. . .]

Notes

[a]Baillet places this fragment to the left of frag. 9 at the level of lines 4-11. It is the right side of what seems to be the column that immediately follows frag. 9.

[b-b]Baillet reconstructs [וֹדשים]קֹ סוד, "the council of the h[oly ones]" (cf. Ps 89:8; 1QH[a] xii:25; lxiii:2), or [וֹדש קודשים]קֹ סוד, "the council of the m[ost holy ones]" (cf. 1QS viii:5-6), but the reading is very unclear; an earthly council would fit the overall context better.

[c-c][בחורים] וֹבתולותֹ] A common word pair. Compare Deut 32:25 (singular); Ps 148:12; Isa 62:5 (singular); Jer 51:22 (singular); Amos 8:13; 1 Esdr 1:53 (singular).

[d]Surely read שם, "there," not (with Baillet) עם, "with."

[e-e]Baillet reconstructs [ואני תֹ]רנן לשוני, "and as for me, [my tongue] wil[l chant]," inspired by 4Q511 63iii:1. His reconstruction is possible but speculative.

Commentary

Line 2. Compare the "seed of blessing" to Gen 28:4; Isa 44:3; 61:9; 65:23; Ps 37:26; *Jub.* 21:25 [4Q219 1ii:31-34], all of which refer to literal offspring, and to the promise of "fruitfulness of seed with all everlasting blessings" in 1QS iv:7, which makes perfectly good sense if read literally. Baumgarten suggests that the male and female elders in frag. 19:2 are the referent to the seed ("Golden Age," 128). This is possible, but the fragmentary state of the passage precludes certainty. See in addition the commentary to frags. 1-3:4.

Elders had a leadership role in ancient Israelite and Jewish society (cf., e.g., Deut 21:19; Ruth 4:2-9; Jth 6:16, 21; 8:10) and in the sectarian texts (e.g., 1QS vi:8; CD ix:4). In 4Q502 they are mentioned six times altogether. The Cairo Geniza *ketubbot* sometimes quote Ruth 4:11-12 (KCG 1 verso 3; 21:2-3; 44:2) and Ezra 6:14 (KCG 14:1; 21:1; 22:1; 23 verso 3) as opening blessings. Both passages refer to elders.

The feminine plural of this word, "elder women" or "old women," is found in the HB only in Zech 8:4 in the phrase "old men and old women," in a passage that uses both terms in a general sense. Thus the same phrase reconstructed here may refer simply to elderly members of the group. Fragment 24:4, however, seems to mention female elders alongside a council of male elders, which implies that both are titles of offices. (The feminine plural does not occur elsewhere in the QL or in the Mishnah.)

Lines 2-3. Baumgarten seems to take these virgins (the word is grammatically feminine) to be the "aged virgins" among the Therapeutae who chose a contemplative celibate life over marriage and children. He also compares 1 Tim 5:1-16, which refers to "elder women" who are enrolled as widows in a formal process; younger men (cf. the "adult men" in 4Q502) who are to be regarded as brothers (cf. frags. 6 + 8-10:11); and younger women who are to be regarded as sisters (cf. frag. 96:1) ("Golden Age," 131-33). Given the damaged state of the text, his interpretation cannot be disproved. However, it seems simpler to read these passages as references either to participants in a communal festival such as a New Year celebration (Satlow, "4Q502: A New Year Festival?" 65) or, better, to the family and friends of the bride and groom at a wedding ceremony. Compare *Jan. Jamb.* 26a 1-3, which mentions "men and brothers" in a broken context having to do with a wedding; see also the commentary to frags. 6 + 8-10:11 and 96:1.

Line 4. The phrase translated "all of us together" could also be translated "all of us, the Community."

4Q502 20

A blessing?[a]

[. . .]. ..[. . .] [2][. . . leng]th of days [. . .] [3][. . .] his [. . .].. [b]for the fruit of the
w[omb[b] . . .] [4][. . . orna]ment,[c] [d]and [you] have spread out [[d]. . .]

Notes

[a]Baillet places this fragment below frag. 19, at the level of lines 14-17 of frag. 9.

[b-b][טן]בֿ לפרי This reconstruction is probable. One could also read "the fruit of
ca[ttle]" ([המה]בֿ לפרי), but the latter phrase is found only three times in the Hebrew
Bible (Deut 28:4, 11, 51) and always in the immediate context of the phrase "fruit of
the womb."

[c]מֿ[כו] Baillet's reconstruction of this word is possible but far from certain.

[d-d]והוצעתֿ From the verbal root √יצע. As it stands, the word addresses a woman:
"you (feminine singular) have spread out . . ." However, one could also reconstruct
[ה]והוצעתֿ, in which case it would address a man.

Commentary

Line 2. The phrase "length of days" (cf. frag. 102:1) also appears in 1QS
iv:7 and brings to mind Tobias' prenuptial prayer that he and his bride might
grow old together (Tob 8:7).

Line 3. The phrase "fruit of the womb" appears fairly frequently in the HB
(Gen 30:2; Deut 7:13; 28:4, 11, 18, 53; 30:9; Isa 13:18; Mic 6:7; Ps 127:3; 132:11;
cf. *4 Ezra* 10:12) and is also found in the QL (1QpHab vi:11-12; 4Q502 163:3;
4Q503 183:1; 221:2). Note also "womb, belly" (בטן) in frag. 180:2 and "his
fruit" in frag. 50:2. This phrase offers some support to Baillet's contention that
4Q502 is a marriage ceremony. Baumgarten argues that it could be used figuratively since it is interpreted "as a designation for the disciples of the Teacher of
Righteousness" in 4Q173 2:1-2 ("Golden Age," 132). However, his reading depends on a questionable reconstruction of the small fragment (the phrase in
question does not appear on the leather), and in any case the text is explicitly
marked as a *pesher*, or spiritual interpretation. There is no need to assume such
a figurative usage here.

Line 4. The word reconstructed and translated as "ornament" seems to
mean some sort of golden ornament (Exod 35:22; Num 31:50; Sir 32:5). The
context in Numbers involves idolatry, and the word means an objectionable ornament (perhaps a fertility charm) in RH (*b. Shab.* 64a), but there is nothing
negative about the contexts in Exodus or Sirach.

Our sources mention the ornaments worn by a bride at her wedding (e.g., Isa 49:18; 61:10; Jer 2:32; Ezek 16:10-13), as well as presents given to her by the bridegroom at betrothal (e.g., Gen 24:53; KCG 1:12; 34:8; 50:16-17) and jewelry or finery included in her dowry (e.g., *Jos. Asen.* 18:5-6; KCG 1:14-20; 2:20-29; 4:22-24; 5:19-30). As far as I can determine, however, this word is never used in these cases.

The noun "couch, bed," derived from the verbal root "to spread out," is used of the marriage bed in Gen 49:4 (cf. 4Q252 iv:5) and 1 Chron 5:1. The verb used here is from the same root and can mean "to make a bed" (e.g., in *m. Ketub.* 5.5, where this act is listed as one of the duties a wife owes her husband).

4Q502 21

An unidentified fragment[a]

[1]God in every ..[. . .] [2]God. BLANK
. . . [3]together in the midst of . . . [4]Israel and .[. .] [5]his inheritance in ..[. . .]

Note
  [a]Baillet places this fragment below frag. 20.

Commentary

Line 5. Matters of inheritance are of great interest in the *ketubbot* (e.g., 5/6Hev recto 12-16; Mur 20 recto i:13; 21 recto i:13; KCG 1:25-27; 4:25-30, 33-36).

Group III

4Q502 22

A fragment that mentions glory and happiness[a]

[1][. . .]..[b] ..[. . .] [2][. . .]..[. . .]. their glory .[. . .] [3][. . .]...[c] for the happiness of[d] [. . .]
[4][. . .] this [. . .] to become .[. . .] [5][. . .] strength[e] [. . .]

Notes

^aAccording to Baillet, Group III belongs to the left of frag. 9 and perhaps of Group II. Baillet places lines 2-4 of frag. 22 at the level of lines 1-3 of frag. 9.

^bLine 1 seems to contain a final *kaph*, which might be a pronominal suffix "your," addressing a woman.

^cThe word preceding לשמחת can be restored either as "[judgm]ents" (משפ[טים]) or "[you]ths" (ז[עטו]טים). The latter word seems also to be found in frag. 28:4 (ז[עטוטי]ם]) and frag. 311:1 (ז[עטו]טי᷌ם). It is not used in BH but appears in 1QM vii:3; 4Q266 8i:8; 4Q491 1-3:6, and in RH (Jastrow, 407).

^dPerhaps restore "for happiness together" or "for the happiness of the Community" (לשמחת [יחד]).

^eכֿחֿ I have translated these two letters as though they were a word. They are, however, exceptionally large, and Baillet suggests they may represent the number 28. In the postbiblical era it became standard practice to write numbers in Hebrew letters, and this may be an early instance of this usage (although it does not seem to be attested elsewhere in the QL). But if so, the reason for putting the number 28 in this spot is obscure.

Commentary

Line 2. Conceivably a reference to angelic glory, but equally likely to human glory.

4Q502 23

A fragment that mentions a council^a

¹[. . .]..[. . .] ²[. . .]..[. . .] ³[. . . a]dults of .[. . .] ⁴[. . .] they [dw]ell in the counc[il of . . .] ⁵[. . . w]eek^b[. . .]

Notes

^aBaillet places this fragment above the left side of frag. 24.

^b[ש]בֻֿעֿ] According to Baillet, this reading is based on the old photograph PAM 41.989. All but the tips of the last two letters are lost in the photograph published in DJD 7, plate xxix. However, this fragment is not actually found on PAM 41.989, and I cannot find another photograph showing the reading that Baillet gives.

Commentary

Line 5. Compare the commentary to frag. 97:2.

4Q502 24

A liturgy in which God, a woman, and a man are blessed before a council of elders[a]

[1][...].[...]..[... a]ll festivals [...] [2][...] [b]<[...]. the man, the thanksgivings:>[b] Blessed be the God of Israel who help[ed ...] [3][...]... your life[c] in the midst of an etern[al] people [...] [4][...] she stands in a council of elder me[n], elder wo[men[d] ...] [5][...] your days[e] in peace and [...] [6][...]... eld[ers[f] ...]

Notes

[a]Baillet places this fragment at the level of lines 14-19 of frag. 9.

[b-b]The difficult Hebrew phrase ‏[ה הודות‏ ‏איש‏ ‏ה‏[is written above the line over the first two words. It could be understood as "the man, the thanksgivings" (‏האיש‏ ‏ההודות‏) or "the woman, thanksgivings" (‏האשה הודות‏[with a plene spelling of "the woman"). Baillet suggests that the phrase is part of a rubric preceding the prayer that begins in line 2, but neither interpretation of the phrase gives a clear meaning.

[c]‏חייֹךָ‏ Addressing a woman. Baillet suggests the phrase be reconstructed "you have [multi]plied your life" (‏הר[בֹת חייֹך‏]), although he gives no parallels for the expression. Another possible reading of the second word is ‏חית‏, with an unusually large taw, but this reading yields no good sense. Baillet's comparison with the Phoenician equivalent of the name Eve (Hebrew ‏חוה‏) is implausible.

[d]‏זקנֹ[ם]ֹ זקנֹ[ות]‏ Baillet's reconstruction is reasonable, although since the last two letters are missing, the second word's gender is uncertain.

[e]‏ימיֹכֹה‏ Addressing a man.

[f]‏זקן[נים]‏ Baillet reads the letters preceding this word as "[in] the midst of" (‏ב]תֹוֹך‏]), but the traces are very uncertain.

Commentary

Line 2. A blessing of God, perhaps to open a ceremony or part of a ceremony. If the supralinear text is a rubric, its meaning is obscure.

Line 3. A speaker addresses a woman (the bride?), perhaps wishing her long life among her people.

Line 4. A woman (the bride?) stands in a council of elders as part of the ceremony. For the title "elders," see the commentary to frag. 19:2. Note that, assuming the reconstruction is correct, both male and female elders seem to be present in this council.

Line 5. A speaker addresses a man (the groom?), wishing him a peaceful life.

Other Fragments

4Q502 27

A fragment of a hymn?

[1][. . .] eternal spirits ...[. . .] [2][. . .] a<. . . to You always>a [ev]ening and morning ..[. . .] [3][. . .] with all divisionsb of ..[. . .] [4][. . .] with a star [. . .] [5][. . .]your ... [. . .]

Notes

a-a<לכֹּה תמִׄיד °[> The supralinear phrase is damaged and very difficult to read.

bFor the range of meaning of the word translated "division" (דגל), see the commentary to Songs XII 4Q405 20ii-21-22:14 and the introduction to 4Q503. Note also the beloved's enigmatic statement "and his banner (?) over me is love" (ודגלו עלי אהבה) in the love song in Cant 2:4.

Commentary

Line 1. The phrase "eternal spirits" is also found in Songs VII 4Q403 1i:35. Compare "eternal holy spirits" in Songs VII 4Q403 1i:44 and "spirits of eternal gods" in Songs XI 4Q405 19:3. All these terms in the *Songs of the Sabbath Sacrifice* refer to angels.

4Q502 31

A blessing for fertility?

[1][. . .] blessed be [. . .] [2][. . .] and may He ble[ss]a [. . .] 3[. . .] twin girlsb[. . .] [4][. . .]. Leahc[. . .] [5][. . .].[. . .]

Notes

[a]ויבר[ך] Or "and may he ble[ss]," or, reading ויבר[כו], "and may th[ey] ble[ss]," etc.

[b]תאמות[This word is difficult. Baillet reconstructs מו[תאמות], [*ju*]*melées*, "twins," "double," but the sense of the Pual passive participle of the root תאם√ here is not clear (cf. Jastrow, 1642, which gives the meaning "compartments," and the phrase קלמרין המותאמות, "the double inkstand," in *m. Kelim* 2.7). One could take the word as it stands and interpret it as "twin girls," but in that case one would expect the spelling תאומות or even תומות (cf. Gen 25:24; 38:27). Likewise, we could reconstruct תאמות[מ] and take it as a Hiphil participle, "women who bear twins," but again we would expect the spelling מתאימות (cf. Cant 4:2; 6:6). For possible interpretations, see the commentary below.

[c]לאה Though I interpret this word as the name Leah, it could also be the beginning of a damaged word such as לאה[בה], "for love," or לאה[רון], "for Aaron."

Commentary

Line 1. The word "blessed be" refers normally to God.

Line 2. I have taken this line as a fragment of a rubric expressing a wish that God will bless someone (perhaps the bride), but other interpretations are possible (see note a).

Line 3. A blessing on the new bride might well express a hope for fertility. In the patriarchal narratives Rebekah (Gen 25:24) and Tamar (Gen 38:27) both gave birth to twin boys, so twins might be a symbol of fertility. The blessing in this passage may have expressed the hope that the bride should bear both twin boys and twin girls, or perhaps that she should be among women who bear twins.

Line 4. The marriage blessing invoked over Ruth mentions Rachel and Leah, the matriarchs of the tribes of Israel, and also Tamar and one of her twin boys, Perez (Ruth 4:11-12). If the surviving word is the name Leah, perhaps a similar blessing is given here. The passage from Ruth is quoted at the beginning of some of the *ketubbot* from the Cairo Geniza (KCG 1 verso 3; 21:2-3; 44:2).

4Q502 34

A fragment of a communal recitation

[1][. . .]. withheld[. . .] [2][. . .].[. . .].. and here we are[a] [. . .].[. . .]..[. . .] [3][. . .] adult males and women, and (we are?) bl[essing . . .] [4][. . .]... ...[. . .]

Note

^aוְהִנֵּנוּ Or "and here I am" (reading הִנְנִי).

4Q502 94

A fragment that involves communal singing

¹[. . . i]n the house of the [. . .] ²[. . .] and they are psalming [. . .] ³[. . .]happiness [. . .] ⁴[. . .] he who comes into ..[. . .] ⁵[. . .]. ...[. . .] ⁶[. . .].[. . .]

4Q502 95

An unidentified fragment

¹[. . .] who cherishes [. . .] ²[. . .].. of glory [. . .]

BOTTOM MARGIN

Commentary

Line 1. The verb חבב√, "to cherish" (cf. frag. 96:6), occurs only once in the HB (Deut 33:3). Satlow notes that it is used several times in RH to mean the passionate sexual desire of a man for a woman ("One Who Loves His Wife Like Himself," 70, 72).

4Q502 96

A fragment that involves individual recitation

¹[. . .]for sisters ²[. . .]Blessed be God ³[. . .]. to arise ⁴[. . .] and he answered ⁵[. . .] with happiness ⁶[together][. . .]. to cherish

Commentary

Line 1. As noted above in the commentary to frags. 6 + 8-10:11 and 19:2-

3, "sister" can mean "fellow Israelite woman" in the HB and "fellow Christian woman" among the early Christians. I am not aware of the term being used in this way in the sectarian texts from Qumran, but given that the *Damascus Document* does seem to use the words "father" and "mother" as titles of offices (4Q270 7i:13-14), I would not rule out the possibility. In the Song of Songs, the king calls his bride "my sister" as a term of endearment (Cant 4:9, 10, 12; 5:1, 2), but one would not expect this usage in the plural. The fragment could also, of course, refer to literal sisters.

4Q502 97

A fragment that mentions seven days

[1][. . .], to them [2][. . .]seven day[s] [3][. . .] mos[t ho]ly [4][. . .] most [hol]y [5][. . .]. His holiness

Commentary

Line 2. The context of the seven days is lost, so any interpretation is speculative. However, it seems reasonably likely that the phrase refers to the length of the celebration described in the text. There is a long and consistent tradition that wedding feasts lasted seven days (Gen 29:22-29; Judg 14:10-18; Tob 11:19; *Jos. Asen.* 21:8; *Jan. Jamb.* 26a 1-2; *m. Neg.* 3:2).

The phrase "seven days" appears in the HB in reference to the Festivals of Passover or Unleavened Bread (e.g., Exod 12:15, 19; cf. 11Q19 xvii:11-12) and Booths (e.g., Lev 23:34, 36, 39-42; cf. *m. Sukk.* 2.9); the ordination of the high priest (e.g., Exod 29:30, 35, 37, cf. 11Q19 xv:4, 14); the feast for the dedication of Solomon's temple (2 Chron 7:8-9); the period for dedicating Ezekiel's imagined temple (Ezek 43:25-26); various periods of uncleanness or purification (e.g., Lev 12:2; 13:4; Num 12:14-15; 19:11; 31:19; Ezek 44:26; cf. 4Q266 6i:11; 6ii:3, 5; 4Q272 1ii:8; 11Q19 xlix:6, 7; l:12, 13); and to other seven day periods in narrative passages (e.g., Gen 31:23; 1 Sam 10:8; 1 Kgs 16:15; Ezek 3:15-16). As Baumgarten notes ("Golden Age," 131), the rites of Philo's Therapeutae are celebrated "after seven sets of seven days" (*Vit. Cont.* 65), a phrase whose meaning is uncertain.

4Q502 98

A fragment that involves happiness and a blessing

[1](...)...[. . .] [2][. . .]. before him al[1 . . .] [3].[. . .]. for happiness [together . . .]
[4][. . .] the blessing of the name [. . .] [5][. . .]. to keep .[. . .]

4Q502 99

A fragment that mentions lulavs

[1][. . .]...[. . .] [2][. . .]*lulav*[*s*[a] . . .] [3][. . .]peace [. . .] [4][. . .].. ...[. . .] [5][. . .]glory [. . .]
[6][. . .]..[. . .]

Note

[a][מ]לולבי[The first *lamed* is very uncertain.

Commentary

Line 2. If the reading is correct, this line appears to mention *lulavs,* the traditional name of palm branches with willow and myrtle leaves attached, which, along with citrons, were carried by celebrants in the Festival of Booths. (The object is described in Lev 23:40, but not by the name *lulav,* which never appears in the HB.) The word is mentioned in the Mishnah, especially in trac-tate *Sukkot,* but as far as I am aware the earliest attestation is in one of the letters of Shimon Bar Kosiba during the Bar Kokhba revolt of 132-35 CE, in which Bar Kosiba orders the recipient to send "the camp" a supply of palm fronds (ללבים), citrons, myrtles, and willows, evidently for the celebration of Booths (pYadin 15). A Greek letter found in the same bundle gives a similar order per-taining to "[t]he festival" (pYadin 3).

The word *lulav* tends to confirm Baumgarten's theory that 4Q502 has to do with the Festival of Booths, although his connecting the rites of the Therapeutae to those of Booths is ad hoc speculation ("Golden Age," 131). However, Baillet's view is not excluded. Palm branches were carried during other times of celebration (Jth 15:12; John 12:13). Moreover, Weinfield has pointed out that much later marriage customs involved bringing myrtle to the bridal chamber ("Prayer and Liturgical Practice," 250-51).

4Q502 102

A fragment of a blessing wishing someone long life?

¹[. . .] his days [shall be] full so as to en[te]r into .[. . .]

BOTTOM MARGIN

4Q502 108

*A fragment that addresses God and mentions
the father of a young woman*

¹[. . .].[. . .] ²[. . .] Your [glo]ry with thanksgi[vings . . .] ³[. . . ªthe fat]her of the
young womanª and [. . .] ⁴[. . .]

Note

ª ª[א]בֹּי הנערה The *bet* in the first word is damaged but is not in doubt.

Commentary

Line 3. The phrase "the father of the young woman" appears in Deut
22:16, 19 (in which a father must defend his daughter against the accusation
that she was not a virgin on her wedding night); 22:29 (which rules that a man
who rapes an unmarried woman must pay her father a fine and marry her); and
Judg 19:3-4, 6, 8-9 (in which a father supports his daughter's reconciliation
with her common-law husband). Since in the HB the phrase always has to do
with the father's involvement in matters pertaining to his daughter's marital situation, it may well have been used in a similar context here.

4Q502 163

A fragment that mentions the fruit of the womb

¹[. . .] and Israe[l . . .] ²[. . . the goo]d and the upright[. . .] ³[. . .]. ªby the fruit of
the wo[mbª . . .]

Note

ª-ª בפרי בטֹ[ן] The second letter of the second word could be a *tet* but cannot be a
he, so the reading "wo[mb]" is virtually certain (cf. note b-b to frag. 20).

Daily Prayers

(4Q503)

INTRODUCTION

Time is an important factor in the human social construction of reality. People in different cultures divide and organize time not only on the basis of recurring elements of the natural world (such as solar, lunar, and seasonal cycles) but often according to intricate social relationships within the culture in question.[1] As noted in the general introduction, there were competing calendars within the Jewish world of the Second Temple period, and disagreements over calendrical reckoning seem to have created friction between the Qumran sect and other forms of Judaism. The collection of "Daily Prayers" covered in this chapter is thus of interest not only for its content but also because it links two methods of calculating the month — that of the lunar and that of the solar calendar.

---

1. The Balinese reckoning of time is a good example. It includes a lunar-solar calendar, but the ten "permutational" cycles of days, with each cycle of a different length and none tied directly to the natural celestial year, are more important in daily life and are linked with other important aspects of Balinese culture such as names and kinship relationships. See Geertz, "Person, Time, and Conduct in Bali," in *The Interpretation of Cultures*, 360-411.

I. Contents

This document contains a liturgy of evening and morning prayers for a single month of the year, probably either the first or the seventh month according to the version of the Jewish calendar that begins the year in the spring.

II. The Manuscript

The papyrus manuscript that contains 4Q503 is written on both sides (the technical term is "opisthograph"). The work on the other side is 4Q512, "Purification Liturgies." 4Q503 is written in a script that can be dated to roughly the early first century BCE. The manuscript survives in some 225 fragments, most of which contain only a few letters. Fortunately, the calendrical nature of 4Q503 gives us some help in reconstructing the manuscript as a whole, and the content of 4Q512 also offers some clues. 4Q503 covers the morning and evening prayers for a single month, with each prayer taking up from four to six lines. Hints in the larger fragments allow us to place many of them in their proper order, although the location of many others cannot be recovered. Some top, bottom, and side margins also survive, which in principle ought to help us reconstruct the overall contours of the manuscript. In practice, the problems in the way of a full reconstruction are nearly intractable. Corrections to the original editor's placement of frags. 1-3 have rendered impossible his reconstruction of thirteen columns with twenty-one to twenty-four lines. Depending on whether we take frags. 1-3 to form a column by themselves or in combination with frags. 29-30, we may reconstruct columns with either sixteen to seventeen or twenty-eight to twenty-nine lines each. Neither reconstruction is straightforward, however, and both require secondary assumptions. For this reason I have presented as many fragments as possible in their probable original order but have refrained from attempting to assign them to columns. Various aspects of the reconstruction of the manuscript in this chapter are provisional — and debatable — but a complete reconstruction and its defense are beyond the scope of this volume. The beginnings of paragraphs in this manuscript are indicated not only by their content but also by a special mark in the margin.

III. Structure and Calendrical Technicalities

The basic structure of 4Q503 is self-evident: the (presumably) thirty days of the month are each assigned a prayer for the evening and a prayer for the morning (the day is reckoned to begin at sundown rather than sunrise; cf. Gen 1:5). Evening prayers begin with either "And on the nth of the month in the evening" or "And on the nth day of the month in the evening"; morning prayers begin with the phrase "And when the sun rises." The evening prayers seem always to continue with a blessing on God, as do many if not all of the morning prayers. There is no indubitable case of additional explanatory material or extra prayers being inserted into the schema, although the text is too badly damaged to rule such additions out.

Numerous chronological cycles inform the calendrical texts from Qumran, ranging from the cycle of the lunar month to a multiple grouping of Jubilee periods that encompasses nearly three centuries. 4Q503 follows both a twenty-eight-day lunar month and a solar calendar. A solar calendar, presumably the same one, was favored by the sectarian community and is also known from the Enoch literature, especially the Astronomical Book preserved in *1 Enoch* 72–82 and in a longer Aramaic version in the Qumran library (see the general introduction to this volume).

Three technical terms tie these two systems together in 4Q503. First, according to the morning prayers, each day has a set number of "gates" (שער) of "light" or "glory" that correspond to the date of the month, that is, to the number of times the sun has risen during the month. Second, we find "lots" (גרול) of "night," "darkness," and "light" in both morning and evening prayers, evidently corresponding to the incremental illumination and darkening of the moon's face as it waxes and wanes. The moon has a total of fourteen lots divided between light and darkness that shift by one each day: thus on the first day of the lunar month it has fourteen lots of darkness and none of light, whereas on the fifteenth it has fourteen lots of light and none of darkness, and on the twenty-eighth it has one lot of light and thirteen of darkness. Third, there are "divisions" or "flags" (דגל) of "light" or "night," which seem also to come in a certain number of units per day, but the surviving contexts of the word are too fragmentary for us to determine whether these divisions pertain to sunlight or moonlight.

IV. Life Situation

Although it can scarcely be doubted that 4Q503 was used by a Jewish community and indeed by the sectarians who collected the Qumran library, it is much less clear who composed the work. It contains little if any sectarian technical terminology, and such formal similarities as there are to sectarian prayers are generic and do not prove sectarian composition. 4Q503 ties the lunar cycle to the rising and setting of the sun, which may indicate an interest in the solar calendar, but both cycles are taken for granted and there is no hint of polemic. The work may have been composed outside the sectarian community but adopted by it. We do not know why only one month of the year is represented. If other manuscripts gave daily prayers for the other eleven months, they are now entirely lost.

Evidently these daily prayers were uttered communally each evening and morning. The traditional Jewish liturgy includes a daily morning prayer, afternoon prayer, and evening prayer, and there are early references to the custom of daily prayer at these times (e.g., Dan 6:10), although the evening prayer has no basis in the sacrificial schedule of the temple. Philo notes that the Therapeutae offered communal prayers at sunrise and sunset (*Vit. Cont.* 27-28; see also the introduction to 4Q502) while Josephus mentions that the Essenes did the same at sunrise (*J.W.* 2 §128-29).

V. Literary Context

The prayers in this work frequently echo scripture, particularly Genesis 1, with its description of the creation of the world and of the heavenly bodies that determine seasons and natural cycles. If 4Q503 does pertain to the first month, as seems likely, the prayers for the fourteenth day, and perhaps some later prayers, can be seen to draw on biblical traditions and prescriptions about the Festivals of Passover and Unleavened Bread. There is also a relationship between 4Q503 and the efforts of the Enochic Astronomical Book (*1 Enoch* 72–82) to reconcile the lunar and solar calendars, especially the traditions found in 4QEnastr[h] (4Q209). It is not clear, however, that the composer of 4Q503 knew the Enoch literature directly.

BIBLIOGRAPHY

Abegg, Martin G., Jr. "Does Anybody Really Know What Time It Is? A Reexamination of 4Q503 in Light of 4Q317." In *The Provo International Conference on the Dead Sea Scrolls: Technological Innovations, New Texts, and Reformulated Issues*, edited by Donald W. Parry and Eugene Ulrich, 396-406. STDJ 30. Leiden: Brill, 1999.

Baillet, Maurice. "503. Prières quotidiennes." In *Qumrân Grotte 4. III (4Q482-4Q520)*, 105-36, plates xxxv, xxxvii, xxxix, xli, xliii, xlv, xlvii. DJD 7. Oxford: Clarendon, 1982. References in the notes and commentary to Baillet, with no other information, are to the relevant places in this work.

Baumgarten, Joseph M. "4Q503 (Daily Prayers) and the Lunar Calendar." *RevQ* 12/47 (1986) 399-407.

Charlesworth, James H., et al. *The Dead Sea Scrolls: Hebrew, Aramaic, and Greek Texts with English Translations*, vol. 4A: *Pseudepigraphic and Non-Masoretic Psalms and Prayers*, 235-85. Tübingen: Mohr Siebeck; Louisville: Westminster/John Knox, 1997.

Falk, Daniel K. *Daily, Sabbath, and Festival Prayers in the Dead Sea Scrolls*. STDJ 27. Leiden: Brill, 1998.

Geertz, Clifford. *The Interpretation of Cultures*. N.p.: HarperCollins, 1973.

Glessmer, Uwe. "Calendars in the Qumran Scrolls." In *The Dead Sea Scrolls after Fifty Years: A Comprehensive Assessment*, edited by Peter W. Flint and James C. VanderKam, vol. 2, 213-78. Leiden: Brill, 1999.

Milik, J. T., with Matthew Black. *The Books of Enoch: Aramaic Fragments of Qumrân Cave 4*. Oxford: Clarendon, 1976.

Nitzan, Bilhah. *Qumran Prayer and Religious Poetry*. STDJ 12. Leiden: Brill, 1994.

Pfann, Stephen. "4Q298: The Maskíl's Address to All Sons of Dawn." *JQR* 85 (1994) 203-35.

Tov, Emanuel. "Scribal Markings in the Texts from the Judean Desert." In *Current Research and Technological Developments on the Dead Sea Scrolls*, edited by Donald W. Parry and Stephen D. Ricks, 41-77. STDJ 20. Leiden: Brill, 1996.

Weinfeld, Moshe. "Prayer and Liturgical Practice in the Qumran Sect." In *The Dead Sea Scrolls: Forty Years of Research*, edited by Devorah Dimant and Uriel Rappaport, 241-58. STDJ 10. Leiden: Brill, 1992.

DAILY PRAYERS

(4Q503)

4Q503 4-6

A prayer for the morning of the fifth day of the month[a]

¹ᵇ[and when the sun] ris[es[b] . . .] ²the numb[er of . . .] ³because to[da]y . . . ⁴festivals of gl[ory . . .] ⁵it shall complete [its] glo[ry . . . ete]rnal [. . .] ⁶Israel[. . .] BLANK [. . .]

A prayer for the evening of the sixth day of the month

⁷ᶜand on the sixth of the mo[nth in the evening they shall bless and answer and s]ay, Ble[ssed be the God of] Israel[c] [. . .] ⁸a night which i[s . . .] before Him [. . .].. ...[. . .] ⁹we are His holy people [. . .] in it fiv[e . . .] ¹⁰fiv[e lo]t[s of . . .] ¹¹and ..[. . .]

A prayer for the morning of the sixth day of the month

¹²and when [the sun rises . . .]

BOTTOM MARGIN

Notes

[a]Baillet includes frags. 1-3 in the same column as frags 4-6, but I have placed them later as part of the prayers for the fourteenth and fifteenth days of the month. A few letters of a preceding column are preserved on frag. 4. It is likely but not certain that frags. 5-6 belong with frag. 4. Each prayer is consistently four to six lines long, so it is possible to reconstruct either two columns preceding this one (for a column length of sixteen or seventeen lines) or one column preceding this one (for a column length of twenty-eight or twenty-nine lines).

[b-b]The normal opening of a morning prayer in 4Q503. See, for example, frags. 10:1; 1-3:1; 33ii + 35:1 for the reconstruction.

In Hebrew idiom the sun "goes out" (√יצא) when it rises (e.g., Gen 19:23) and "comes in" (√בוא) when it sets (e.g., Lev 22:7).

[c-c]The evening prayers in 4Q503 begin with the date and this benediction. See, for example, frags. 1-3:6; 42-44:4.

Commentary

Line 4. The phrase "festivals of glory" does not appear in the HB but is found in CD iii:14-15; 4Q286 1ii:10; 4Q503 1-3:13; 4Q508 13:2. Note also "glorious pilgrimage-festival" in frag. 36:4.

Line 9. The phrase "holy people" is applied to Israel in the HB (e.g., Deut 7:6; 14:2; Isa 62:12; and elsewhere in the QL).

Line 10. The sixth day (line 7) of the lunar month has five lots of light according to the system described in the introduction to this chapter. In the HB the word "lot" (גורל) usually refers to lots cast to make decisions, divide up property, or assign responsibilities (e.g., Prov 18:18); but it can also mean the share or thing allotted (e.g., Num 36:3). The calendrical sense seems to have evolved from the latter meaning: the moon is allotted a certain number of shares of light and darkness for each month. For the technical use of the word "lot" by the Qumran sectarians, see the commentary to 4Q286 7ii:3.

4Q503 7-9

More of the prayer for the morning of the sixth day of the month

TOP MARGIN

[1]..[. . .]the light of daytime[a] for our knowledge[. . .] [2][. . .]. in six gates of lig[ht . . .] [3][. . .]sons of Your covenant. We will psal[m . . .] [4]with all the divisions of [. . . al]l tongues of knowledge. He has blessed ...[. . .] [5]light of peace [. . . li]ght. BLANK

A prayer for the evening of the seventh day of the month

[6]On the seventh of [the month in the evening they shall bless and they answer and sa]y, Blessed be the God of Is[rael . . .] [7]righteousness [. . . al]l [th]ese things we know by[. . .] [8][ ]...[. . .] Blessed be [the G]od of [Israel . . .]

Note

[a]היומם This word can function as either an adverb, "by day," or an abstract noun, "daytime." The latter meaning is indicated here by the definite article. The phrase אור יומם, "light by day," is used in the HB in Isa 60:19; Jer 31:35.

214

Commentary

Line 2. According to the system described in the introduction, the sixth day of the month would have six "gates" of sunlight.

Line 4. The basic meaning of the word translated "divisions" is "flags," but it is used in 4Q503 to refer to units of "light" and "night" that relate somehow to the course of the month. The phrase "tongues of knowledge" also appears in Songs XIII 4Q405 23ii:12 (cf. Prov 15:2).

Line 7. The phrase "these things we know" is also found in 4Q504 4:5 and 4Q506 131 + 132:10 (cf. 1QM x:16).

4Q503 10

A prayer for the morning of the ninth (?) day of the month

TOP MARGIN

[1][And when] the sun [rises] to give light upon the ear[th . . .] [2]with divisions of light. And t[o]d[a]y .[. . .] [3][. . .]daytime. N|i|n|e . . .]

Commentary

Line 1. The phrase "to give light upon the earth" comes from Gen 1:15, 17.

Line 3. Apparently a reference to the nine gates of sunlight accruing to the ninth day.

4Q503 11

*The end of a prayer for the morning of the
eleventh day of the month*

[1][. . .].. BLANK

A prayer for the evening of the twelfth day of the month

[2][On the tw]elfth[a] of the month in the evening(!)[b] [. . .] [3][. . .]... [c]and we, His holy people, are exalted to[n]ig[h]t[c][. . .] [4][. . .]us and witnesses with us at the station of daytime [. . .] [5][. . .].[. . .].[. . .] BLANK [. . .]

215

Notes

[a]בשני[ם] עשר] "Twelfth" is the only number from eleventh to nineteenth whose first word in its Hebrew form ends in *mem*.

[b]Read בערב, "in the evening," for the unintelligible בערם in the text.

[c-c]Or, reading the last word as הלולי[ו] rather than הלילה, translate this line as "and we are His holy people who exalt [His] psalm[ings]." This word is found in Lev 19:24; Judg 9:27; 11Q19 lx:4; and in RH (Jastrow, 346a).

Commentary

Line 4. The witnesses appear to be angels. See the commentary to frags. 15-16:11, 14; 65:2-3.

4Q503 1-3

A prayer for the morning of the fourteenth day of the month[a]

TOP MARGIN

[1]And when [the sun] rises [. . .] the firmament of the heavens, they shall bless and they answ[er and say,] [2]Blessed be the Go[d of Israel . . .].[. . .]. and this day He re[ne]wed [. . .] [3]in four[teen . . .] for us a realm [. . .] [4]-teen[b] divis[ions of . . .]... [c]heat of the [sun[c] . . .] [5]when He passed over [. . . by the stren]gth of [His] mighty hand [. . . Peace be upon you,] [6]<Israel.>

A prayer for the evening of the fifteenth day of the month

[6]On the fif[teenth of the month in the ev]ening they shall bless and they answer [and s]ay, Blessed be the Go[d of Israel] [7]who closes [up[d] . . .]. before Him in every allotment of its glory. And tonight[. . .] [8][. . . for]ever to thank Him [for] our redemption in the beginn[ing] [9][. . .] revolution<s>[e] of vessels of light. [And t]o[da]y fourte[en] [10][. . .] the light of daytime. P[eace be upon] you, Israel. [11][. . .] BLANK

A prayer for the morning of the fifteenth day of the month

[12][And when the sun rises . . .] to give light upon the earth, they shall bless and they answer(!)[f] [and say,] [13][Blessed be the God of Israel . . .] which belongs to

216

pilgrimage-festivals of happiness and festivals of g[lory] [14][. . . f]ifteen gate[s of . . .] [15][. . . i]n the lots of the night[. . .]

Notes

[a]Baillet placed frags. 1-3 (which in his interpretation cover the morning of the fourth and all of the fifth day) above frags. 4-6, but Baumgarten ("4Q503 [Daily Prayers]," 401) has argued convincingly that frags. 2-3 belong in a later column, and Falk (*Daily, Sabbath, and Festival Prayers*, 29-35) has extended the argument to include frag. 1. A number from ten to nineteen is found in line 4, the number fourteen is found in line 9, and there is a reference to fifteen gates (of sunlight) in line 14, so it can scarcely be doubted that lines 1-5 pertain to the morning of the fourteenth day of the month and lines 6-15 to the fifteenth day. My reason for concluding that frags. 21-28 are not likely to have come between frag. 20 and frags. 29-32 is given in note a to frags. 21-28 below, in the section of "Unplaced Fragments." Frags. 1-3 begin with a top margin but have only fifteen lines of text, so either the columns were about sixteen lines high or frags. 29-30, which follow with no more than one line missing, must be part of the same column as frags. 1-3, in which case the columns were at least twenty-eight or twenty-nine lines high.

[b]עשר This number could be anything from ten to nineteen, since part of it may be lost at the end of the previous line. This day would have fourteen gates of light and thirteen lots of light.

[c-c][שמש]ה חום Restoring with Baillet (cf. Exod 16:21; 1 Sam 11:9; Neh 7:3). One could also restore [היום]ה חום, "the heat of the [day]" (cf. Gen 18:1; 1 Sam 11:11, 2 Sam 4:5).

[d]הסותﬦ In the HB this verb is usually used of stopping up a spring of water (e.g., Gen 26:15). The context may indicate a reference to astronomical phenomena; in *y. Sanh.* 10:28c the verb is used (in the Piel stem) of the attending angels closing the windows of heaven.

[e]I have adopted Baillet's suggestion that the form תסובות comes from a noun תסובה, "revolution," derived from the root סוב√ (a variant of סבב√), analogous to the pattern תקופה from קוף√.

[f]ועו] Correct this reading to [ו]ועני.

Commentary

Line 1. The phrase "the firmament of the heavens" appears in Gen 1:14, 15, 17, 20.

Line 3. There are fourteen gates of sunlight on the fourteenth day of the month.

Line 5. The verb "to pass over" is used of Passover in Exod 12:13, 23, 27; *m. Pesah* 10.5. Passover occurs on the fourteenth day of the first month (Lev 23:5), so this line gives us some evidence that 4Q503 covers the first month of the year (March-April), although it is possible that this verb is used in an (otherwise unattested) technical calendrical sense here. Compare "the strength of His mighty hand" to 1 Chron 29:12; 2 Chron 20:6.

Line 6. This reference to the fifteenth day of the month shows that according to the reckoning of this document the day begins at sundown. The fifteenth of the first month marks the beginning of the seven-day Festival of Unleavened Bread (Lev 23:6), and the fifteenth of the seventh month marks the beginning of the seven-day Festival of Booths (Lev 23:34).

Line 7. The "allotment" seems to have to do with the phases of the moon, but its exact import is unclear.

Line 8. The word "redemption" is associated with the plagues brought against Egypt in Exod 8:19 (EVV 8:23) (cf. Ps 111:9), and the verb "to redeem" is connected with the Exodus in Deut 7:8; 9:26; 13:6 (EVV 13:5); 15:15; 24:18; 2 Sam 7:23 // 1 Chron 17:21; Mic 6:4; Ps 78:42. Redemption is also associated with Passover in *m. Pesaḥ* 10.5-6, but a different Hebrew word is used. Perhaps "the beginning" refers to the beginning of the nation of Israel at the Exodus.

Line 9. Perhaps a reference to the fourteen lots of moonlight on the fifteenth day of the month.

Line 10. Compare the phrase "peace be upon you, Israel" to Ps 125:5; 128:6; 1 Chron 22:9.

Lines 12-13. Baillet reads the end of line 12 together with frags. 4-6:2 and line 13 and reconstructs "and sti[ll] the number of days [. . . are eleven] to the happy pilgrimage-festivals and festivals of g[lory]." However, as Baumgarten notes, this reconstruction ignores the number "fourteen" in line 9 and the "fifteen gates" in line 14; there are ten days between the fifth and fifteenth of the month, not eleven; the syntax is awkward (one would expect "until the pilgrimage-festivals"); and there is no clear motivation for counting ahead from the fifth day to the holiday on the fifteenth ("4Q503 [Daily Prayers]," 401).

Line 13. The word translated "pilgrimage-festival" refers to the three festivals that involved pilgrimages to Jerusalem: Passover, Weeks, and Booths (e.g., Exod 23:14-16). The word translated "festival" is a more general term whose basic meaning is an appointed time or event, but often it is used of festivals or holy days, including the Sabbath (cf. Lev 23:1-3; 2 Chron 8:13). The festivals are associated with joy and happiness (see the commentary to 4Q502 4:2).

Line 14. "Fifteen gates" of sunlight would correspond to the fifteenth day of the month.

Line 15. This is the first surviving reference to the "lots" of lunar darkness, whose count would be reduced to zero on the fifteenth of the month. Perhaps this line also mentioned that they would begin to accrue again on the next day.

4Q503 29-30

*The end of the prayer for the morning
of the fifteenth day of the month*

[1]And the peace of [God be upon you, Israel . . .]

A prayer for the evening of the sixteenth day of the month

[2]On the six[teenth of the month in the evening they shall bless and they answer and say, Blessed be the God of Israel who] [3]sanctified for Himself[. . .] [4]and to-night .[. . .]. people ..[. . .] [5][. . .]... to us. Pe[a]ce[. . .] [6][. . . Go]d will bless Jeshuru[n . . .]

A prayer for the morning of the sixteenth day of the month

[7][And when the sun rises to give light up]on [the ea]rth, [th]ey shall ble[s]s [and they answer and say, Blessed be the God of Israel] [8][. . .].[. . .]light and they are happy .[. . .] [9][psa]lming Your name, God of ligh[t]s, who have renewed .[. . .] [10][. . .] gates of light. And with [us] in the chantings of Your glory .[. . .] [11][div]isions of night. The peace of God be [up]on you, Israel, when [the sun] rise[s . . .]

A prayer for the evening of the seventeenth day of the month

[12][On the s]eventeenth of the mo[nth in the] evening they shall bless and they answer [and say, Blessed be the God of Israel who] [13][. . .] to [ps]alm [. . .].[. . .]

Commentary

Line 6. The poetic name "Jeshurun" is sometimes used for Israel as a people or a place in the HB (Deut 32:15; 33:5, 26; Isa 44:2). It is derived from a root meaning "to be upright" and seems to have the meaning "the upright one," although the formation of the noun is unclear.

Line 10. Since this is the sixteenth day, presumably the text mentioned "[sixteen] gates of light."

4Q503 31-32

A prayer for the morning of the seventeenth day of the month

¹[And when the sun rises to give light upon the earth, they shall bless and they answer and say, Blessed be the God of Israel] ²[. . . our hap]pi[n]e[s]s [. . .] ³[. . .]divisions of night[. . .] ⁴[. . .] we tod[ay . . .] ⁵[The peace of God be upon you, Is]rael, in all the fes[tivals of . . .]

A prayer for the evening of the eighteenth day of the month

⁶On the ei[ghteentha of the month in the evening] they [shall] bless and they answer and say, B[lessed be the God of Israel] ⁷[. . . holy of ho]lies.b And to-night .[. . .] ⁸[. . .]...[. . .]

> **Notes**
> ªI have followed Baillet in placing these fragments together, but it is uncertain whether frag. 31 (which contains the partial date) belongs with frag. 32.
> bOne could also omit the restored word in brackets and translate "[ho]ly ones" (i.e., angels).

Frag. 33i

A prayer for the morning of the nineteenth (?) day of the montha

TOP MARGIN

¹[. . . the ligh]t of daytime ²[. . . exa]lting ³[. . .] holiness ⁴[. . .] festivals of . . . ⁵[. . .]...

A prayer for the evening of the twentieth (?) day of the month

⁶[On the twentieth of the month in the evening they shall bless and they answer and say, Blessed be the God of Isra]el who ⁷[. . . gl]ory and the night ⁸[. . .]to do-minions of ⁹[. . .]round aboutb ¹⁰[. . .]Pe[ac]e ¹¹[be upon you, Israel . . .]

> **Notes**
> ªFragment 33i begins the column that immediately precedes 33ii. The latter begins with the prayer for the morning of the twenty-first, and thus 33i probably begins with

the prayer for the morning of the nineteenth. But if so, this column must have contained nineteen to twenty-three lines, which would not fit either reconstruction implied by frags. 1 3 and 29-30 (see above). It may be that some of the prayers in the second half of the manuscript contained more than six lines.

[b]במסבב Baillet suggests that the word מסב means "circuit," although this meaning is attested only in modern Hebrew. His suggestion is speculative given the lack of a context, although the meaning adopted in my translation is not attested with the preposition -ב, "in." The word could also be translated "on the couch of" (cf. Cant 1:12; see also Jastrow, 803b).

4Q503 33ii + 35

A prayer for the morning of the twenty-first day of the month

TOP MARGIN

[1]And when the sun ri[se]s upon the [earth, they shall bless and they answer and say, Blessed are You, God, who] [2][have] renewed our happiness with light[. . .] [3]our ..[. . .] ..[. . .]like the day of[. ,] [4]with his happiness (they are) st[an]ding [. . .] [5]Peace be upon you, Israel[. . .]

A prayer for the evening of the twenty-second day of the month

[6a][On] the tw[enty-seco]nd [day] of[a] the [month in the evening, they shall bless and they answer and say, Blessed are] [7]Y[ou, G]od, wh[o . . .] [8]..[. . .]..[. . .] [9] [. . .]. Isr[ael . . .]

A prayer for the morning of the twenty-second day of the month

[10][And when the su]n [rises] upon the [earth . . . they shall bless and they answer] [11][and say, Bles]sed be God w[ho . . .] [12][With tw]enty[-two gates of . . .] [13][. . , Peace be] upon you, I[srael . ,]

A prayer for the evening of the twenty-third day of the month

[14][On the] twe[nty-third day of the month in the evening they shall bless and they answer and say,][b]

221

Notes

a-a[שרים וע]שני ם [ביום] The date is badly damaged, but given the surviving letters, this is the only possible reconstruction.

bBaillet includes frag. 36 as part of lines 20-24 of this column. For the reasons why this is impossible, see the notes to this fragment under "Unplaced Fragments," below.

Commentary

Lines 6-13. According to Lev 23:26, the twenty-second day of the seventh month was a "holy convocation" and day of rest immediately following the Festival of Booths.

Line 12. The twenty-second day of the month would have twenty-two gates of sunlight.

4Q503 37-38

The end of a prayer for the morning of the twenty-fourth day of the month

¹[et]ernal [. . .] BLANK [. . .]

A prayer for the evening of the twenty-fifth day of the month

²On the ª[twenty]-fifth dayª [of the month in the evening they shall bless and they answer and say, Blessed be] ³the God of all holy[ones . . .] ⁴holiness and repose for u[s . . .] ⁵from the lot of its realm [. . .] ⁶[. . .].[. . .]

A prayer for the morning of the twenty-fifth day of the month

⁷[And when the sun rises upon the earth, they shall bless and they answer and say, Blessed be the God of all] ⁸[ho]ly ones ...[. . .] twenty- ⁹[five] gates of [. . .] ¹⁰[ps]alming with us .[. . .] ¹¹our glory. Peace [be upon you, Israel . . .]

A prayer for the morning of the twenty-sixth day of the month

¹²And on the [twenty]-sixth day [of the month in the evening they shall bless and they answer and say, Blessed are] ¹³ᵇ[You, Go]d ofᵇ ...[. . .]

[BOTTOM MARGIN]^c

Notes

a-aSince the number of gates of light is always the same as the day of the month, this number and the damaged date in lines 8-9 together complete the restoration of one another.

b-bל[אתה א] I propose this reconstruction, which fits the lacuna and is paralleled in frags. 34:5; 33ii-35:6. I can read none of the other letters in this line.

cThe verso (4Q512) shows that this fragment comes from the bottom of a column.

Commentary

Lines 3, 8. For the "holy ones" (angels), see the commentary to Songs I 4Q403 1i:2.

Line 4. According to the solar calendar, the twenty-fifth day of the first month was a Sabbath. For the association of "repose" with the Sabbath, see the commentary to frags. 24-25:5.

Line 5. I take "its realm" to be that of the moon, but one could also understand this phrase as "his realm," referring to an angel. See the commentary to Songs II 4Q401 14i:6.

Lines 8-9. The twenty-fifth day would have twenty-five gates of sunlight.

Line 10. Perhaps a reference to the angels celebrating the Sabbath in the celestial temple, as in the *Songs of the Sabbath Sacrifice*.

4Q503 39ᵃ

A prayer for the evening or morning of the
twenty-eighth or thirtieth day of the month

¹[...], [...].[...]...[.]. ²For ᵇ‹it is the night of [...] until ...›ᵇ thirte[en] lots of darkness [...] ³[divi]sions of evening and morning ,.. our peace. Peace be upon you [Israel ...]

BOTTOM MARGIN

Notes

aOn the verso, frag. 39 overlaps two columns of 4Q512, perhaps the first two — in which case frag. 39 may preserve the end of 4Q503, and we should reconstruct a blank space of papyrus to have followed it.

b-bThis phrase is written above the text of line 2 and is very difficult to read. The word after "until" (°°אתתב) may be a form of the verb √חבא, "to hide" ("I am hidden"?).

Commentary

Line 2. "Thirteen lots of darkness" would accrue to the evenings of the twenty-eighth and the thirtieth.

Line 3. "Divisions of evening and morning" are mentioned only here. If this fragment pertains to the thirtieth day rather than the twenty-eighth, one might speculate that it refers to the fact that the lunar cycle begins anew on this day.

Unplaced Fragments

4Q503 13, 14, 15-16, 19?, 20?[a]

Frag. 13

A fragment of a prayer?

TOP MARGIN

[1][. . .] God of lights[. . .] [2][. . .].. of light and witness[es . . .]

Note

[a]A possible reconstruction of the verso (see the appendix to the chapter on 4Q512) would indicate that frags. 13-16 form a single column next to frags. 1-3. This would cohere with the numbers in frag. 16:7-8, which would fit the thirteenth day. Baillet also places frags. 19-20 in the same column as frags. 13-16. However, it is very difficult to divide the first twenty or so lines of this column into the usual sections of morning and evening prayers. Given that frag. 13 has a top margin and frags. 1-3 begin a column with the prayer for the morning of the fourteenth, the column comprising frags. 13-20 may have contained the prayers for the morning of the twelfth through the evening of the fourteenth. However, one would expect these prayers to take up no more than twenty-four lines, whereas this column has at least twenty-seven.

Commentary

Line 1. The same title appears in 4Q405 46:2. For similar phrases see Isa 2:5; Ps 44:4 (EVV 44:3); 136:7.

Line 2. The witnesses may be angels. See the commentary to frags. 15:2, 5; 65:2-3.

Frag. 14

The end of a prayer that mentions daytime

¹[. . . the lig]ht of daytime [. . .] ²[. . .] Your [na]me, God of Israel, in a[ll . . .] ³[. . .] BLANK [. . .]
⁴...[. . .]...[. . .]

Frag. 15

Prayer material that mentions the light of daytime

¹[. . .].. .[. . .] ²[. . . ho]ly ones on hig[h] ³[. . .] His holy [na]me ⁴[. . .]... and glory in holi[ness] ⁵[. . .]. and witnesses for us in the holy(!)ª of holies. ⁶[. . .]in the realm of the light of daytime. Blessed be ⁷[. . . P]eace be upon you [Israel . . .]

Notes
ª בקוד Emend to בקודש, "in the holy of," with Baillet

Commentary

Line 2. A reference to angels. See the commentary to Songs I 4Q400 1i:2.

Line 5. Given the context, it is likely that angelic witnesses are intended (cf. frag. 65:2-3). According to the *Songs of the Sabbath Sacrifice*, angels carry out sacrifices in the heavenly temple that correspond to those in the earthly one.

Line 6. Compare Gen 1:16; Ps 136:7-9; 1QS x:1 for similar language.

Frag. 16

Prayer material that mentions the night

[1][. . . Bless]ed be the God of Isr[ael] who does wond[rously] [2][. . .]earth and the night ..[. . .] [3][. . .]to a[d]d to u[s . . .] [4][. . .] its whole allotment to it [. . .]

A prayer for the morning of the thirteenth of the month?

[5][. . .] God of Israe[l] [6][. . .]Your holiness. [7][. . .]with th[i]r- [8][teen][a] . . .]twelve [. . .] [9][. . . I]srael

The beginning of another prayer?

[10][. . .]Israel [11][. . .] Your [holin]ess

Note

[a][עשר] שׄה [ו]בשלׄ[ב] One could also read "with th[r]ee," or "on the third," which would place this fragment in the third day (with twelve lots of darkness).

Commentary

Line 4. Perhaps a reference to the allotment of light and darkness to the moon.

Lines 7-8. The word "with th[i]r[teen]" may refer to the number of gates of sunlight for this day, which always corresponds to the date of the month. There would be twelve lots of moonlight on the thirteenth day of the month.

Frag. 19

A fragment of a prayer[a]

[1][. . . and] they [sa]y, [Bl]e[s]s[ed] be[. . .] [2][. . .][b][-t]een gates of light[b] [. . .]

Notes

[a]Baillet tentatively places this and frag. 20 in the same column as frags. 14-16.

[b]אור שערי שר [ע] This phrase could refer to anything from ten to nineteen gates of light, which would correspond to the day of the month.

Frag. 20

A fragment of a prayer

¹[. . .]...[. . .] ²[. . . at]tendants [. . .] ³[. . .].[ ]. His dwelling[. . .]

Commentary

Line 2. The word "attendants" probably refers to angels. See the commentary to 4Q286 3:2 and Songs I 4Q400 1i:4.

Line 3. The word "dwelling" is used frequently to refer to God's habitation in heaven. This seems to be a fragment of a prayer that spoke of the celestial realm.

Frag. 17

A fragment from the same column?

¹[. . .] they [shall ble]ss and they answer [and say, Blessed be . . .] ²[. . .]the [ge]nerations[a] of the[. . .] ³[. . . tw]elve[. . .]

Note
[a]The word תולדות, "generations," means a genealogical account of someone or a genealogy. Its meaning in this damaged context is uncertain.

Commentary

Line 1. Part of an opening benediction for an evening or a morning prayer.

Line 3. The number "twelve" could refer to the day of the month (cf. frag. 11:1) or the lots of light on the thirteenth (cf. frags. 16:7-83) or seventeenth day of the month, respectively.

4Q503 21-28

These may have formed a single column,
perhaps including a Sabbath

Frags. 21-22

A fragment of a prayer[a]

TOP MARGIN

[1][. . .]by the light of His [gl]ory. And He has made u[s] rejoice [. . .] [2][. . .].[. . .] saying to us [. . .]

Note
   [a]Baillet takes frags. 21-28 to come from between frags. 15-19 (his col. vi) and frags. 29-32 (his col. viii). However, this is possible only if frag. 16 does not contain the prayer for the morning of the thirteenth day of the month, since if it does, frags. 1-3 must come directly after it.

Commentary

Line 1. Compare "the light of His glory" to Ezek 43:2, where the earth shines with God's glory.

Frag. 23

A fragment of a prayer

[1][. . . holy of]holies [. . .] [2][. . .] BLANK [. . .] [3][. . .]. .[. . .]

Commentary

Line 1. One could also omit the restored material in brackets and translate "holy ones" (i.e., angels).

Frags. 24-25

The end of an evening prayer[a]

¹[. . .]. .[. . .] ²[. . .]...[ ] .[. . .]

A morning prayer

³[And when the sun rises to give light] on the earth, they shall bless [and they answer and say, Blessed be] ⁴[the God of Israel w]ho cho[se] us from all [the] nations .[. . .] ⁵[. . .]. for a fest[ival of] repose and d[e]l[i]g[h]t[. . .] ⁶[. . . rejoi]cing .[. . .] ⁷[. . .]...[. . .]

Note

[a]If frags. 24-25 pertain to a Sabbath, they may refer to the first Sabbath on the fourth day (before frags. 4-6), the second Sabbath on the eleventh day (above frag. 11), or the third Sabbath on the eighteenth day (between frags. 31-32 and 33i), but they cannot apply to the fourth Sabbath on the twenty-fifth day, which is covered in 37-38:2-11.

Commentary

Line 4. Compare Deut 7:6; 14:2. Baumgarten notes that the keeping of the Sabbath is associated with the chosenness of Israel in *Jub.* 2:19 ("4Q503 [Daily Prayers]," 402). Weinfeld also points out that this theme is present in the Jewish liturgy in the *Amidah* prayer for the Sabbath and the festivals ("Prayer and Liturgical Practice," 244).

Line 5. Baillet connects this phrase with the rejoicing of the Festival of Unleavened Bread, but Baumgarten argues that it fits better with the Sabbath ("4Q503 [Daily Prayers]," 401-2). Compare the use of the verb "to delight" in Isa 58:13-14 and the use of the root "to rest, have repose" in Exod 20:11; 23:12; Deut 5:14. Note also that the Sabbath is associated with "repose" in *m. Tamid* 7.4 and with "repose and delight" in *m. Ta'an.* 4.3.

Frag. 26

A fragment of a prayer

¹[. . .]..[. . .] ²[. . . ac]tions[. . .] ³[. . .]...[. . .] ⁴[. . .].[. . .]

Frag. 27

A fragment of a prayer

[1][. . .].[. . .] [2][. . .] heaven and [. . .] [3][. . .]. He reckoned for it [. . .] [4][. . .]they shall bless [the . . .] [5][. . . hol]y of h[olies . . .]

Frag. 28

A fragment of a prayer

[1][. . .].[. . .] first[. . .] [2][. . .] He [cr]eated them, evening and [morning . . .] [3][. . .] eternal [. . .] [4][. . .] Israel and .[. . .] [5][. . .] we ..[. . .]

Commentary

Line 1. Baillet suggests that the reference is to the first day of the Festival of Unleavened Bread, but this interpretation is unlikely on other grounds (see the commentary to frags. 24-25, above), and many other meanings are possible.

4Q503 34

The end of a morning prayer

[1][. . .] [a]we [st]and up for [our] lo[t[a] . . .] [2][. . .].[. . .]

An evening prayer

[3][On the . . . of the] month in the [eve]ning they shall bless and they answer and sa[y, Blessed be . . .] [4][. . .].[ ] and tonight is for us the head of the realm of .[. . .] [5][. . . Bless]ed are You, Go[d of I]srael, who have established[. . .] [6][. . .] in all the festival[s of] the night. ℭ[b] BLANK [. . .]

BOTTOM MARGIN

Notes
[a-a]This reconstruction is suggested by Baillet on the basis of Dan 12:13.

^bThe Old English ℭ represents a sign after the last word in line 6. Baillet takes it to be a numerical sign for 21, but this is surely wrong. The sign is clearly a *taw* written in the so-called Cryptic A script, (Pfann, "4Q298," 221), not a number. Tov has shown that letters in this script are often used as scribal marks in the Qumran Scrolls, although their meaning (as in this case) is usually obscure ("Scribal Markings," 56-61).

On the basis of his interpretation of this scribal mark as the numeral 21, Baillet deduces that this passage refers to the twenty-first day of the month and thus belongs in column x of 4Q503. Without this number, the date of the passage becomes uncertain, as does its place in the manuscript. However, the shape of frag. 34 is very similar to the shape of frag. 39, and it seems likely that it preserves the bottom of the column immediately preceding or following frag. 39, depending on whether the latter belongs to the twenty-eighth or thirtieth of the month (see above). It is tempting to speculate that this letter *taw*, the last of the Hebrew alphabet, might refer in some way to the thirtieth being the last night of the solar month.

Commentary

Line 3. Presumably God is the object of the blessing, as elsewhere in this work.

Line 4. Baillet reads "the head of the realm of d[arkness]" (possible, but uncertain) and suggests that the line refers to the fact that after the night of the twenty-first, the moon will no longer be more than half full. If so, the word "head" would have the connotation "beginning," which is a possible meaning (cf. Judg 7:19). Indeed, this meaning would be quite appropriate if the phrase refers to the beginning of the lunar month on the night of the thirtieth.

Line 5. Perhaps the lost object of the verb was "the covenant" (cf. Ps 105:8-10) or "the Passover" (cf. 1 Chron 30:5).

Line 6. Or "and in all the appointed times of the night." Compare Ps 104:19.

4Q503 36

A prayer fragment pertaining to a pilgrimage-festival^a

¹[. . .] sixth [da]y ²[. . . rig]hteousness ³[. . .]Blessed be God ⁴[. . .] ^bin a glorious pilgrimage-festival^b ⁵[. . .]. ..[. . .]

[BOTTOM MARGIN]^c

Notes

[a]Baillet assigns this fragment to lines 20-24 of his col. xi, the morning of the twenty-third and the evening of the twenty-fourth days of the month. Although the physical evidence of the verso (4Q512) would seem to support this identification (see note a-a to 4Q512 36), Baumgarten has pointed out that the twenty-fourth day of the first month is not a pilgrimage-festival day (nor is that of the seventh month) ("4Q503 [Daily Prayers]," 402-3). The proper placement of this fragment is uncertain.

[b-b]בחג כבודו One could also read בחג כבוד[ו], "in His glorious pilgrimage-festival." For this idea, compare *m. Sukk.* 4.8.

[c]The verso (4Q512) shows that this fragment comes from the bottom of a column.

Commentary

Line 1. The sixth day of the week is Friday (Gen 1:31; Exod 16:5, 22, 29; *m. Ḥag.* 3.7). Num 29:29 gives instructions for the sixth day of the Festival of Booths, which, according to the solar calendar, would fall on a Monday. In this broken context, the meaning of the phrase is very difficult to determine. Baumgarten suggests it could refer to the sixth day of Passover, which is, however, a half-holiday, or to the sixth day of the *Omer,* which in Pharisaic practice is the same as the final day of Passover ("4Q503 [Daily Prayers]," 402-3). If Passover and Unleavened Bread are counted as one festival (cf. Deut 16:1-8, 16; Mark 14:12; *Ps.-Philo* 13:4), the nineteenth of the month would be the sixth day of this festival, and frag. 36 would therefore belong at the bottom of the column immediately preceding frag. 33i.

Line 4. If the other indicators that 4Q503 covers either the first month or the seventh are correct, the pilgrimage-festival in question would be either Passover or Booths.

4Q503 frags. 40-41

col. ii[a]

A fragment of an evening prayer

[TOP MARGIN?][b]

[1]and its sign[c] [. . .] [2]and in the real[m . . .] [3]the name of the God of [. . . Peace be upon you, I]srael, in all the f[estivals of . . .]

232

A morning prayer

[4]And when [the sun] rises [to give light upon the earth . . .]the third[d] [. . .] to
..[. . .] [5]our glory [. . .]repose of holiness [6]and they praise .[. . .]. and psalmed is
the name of[. . .] [7]all the hol[y ones . . .] holy ones ..[. . .] [8]glory [. . .]..[. . .]

Notes

[a]The final letters of lines 2-6 of the first column of this fragment survive, but no
words can be reconstructed. The association of frag. 40 with frag. 41 is assured due to
overlaps between the text of 4Q512 on the verso and 4Q414.

[b]The other side (4Q512) preserves a top margin, so line 1 of this side of the fragment was probably the first line of the column.

[c]ואותו Baillet translates "et lui," that is, "and to him," evidently taking the word
אות to be the marker of the definite direct object. However, it would be very unusual
for this marker to have a conjunction before it, and the word "sign" is spelled the same
way and could fit well in an astronomical or calendrical context (cf. frags. 51-55:14;
Gen 1:14; Jer 10:2) or refer to the Sabbath (Exod 31:13, 17).

[d]It is unclear how this word can be integrated into the normal opening of the
morning benediction. One would expect the phrase "they shall bless and they answer
and say, Blessed be . . ." somewhere in line 4.

Commentary

Line 2. For angelic realms, see the commentary to Songs II 4Q401 14i:6.

Line 4. Although "the third" could conceivably refer to the third night of
the month, in which case frags. 40-41 would belong to col. i, or to the third Sabbath of the month (the eighteenth), the physical parameters of the manuscript
seem to rule out both possibilities.

Line 5. The mention of "repose" supports the possibility that this passage
pertained to a Sabbath, perhaps the first one on the fourth day of the month.

Line 6. Compare Ps 113:3.

Line 7. For the holy ones (angels), see the commentary to Songs I 4Q400
1i:2.

4Q503 42-44, 45-47[a]

Frags. 42-44

The end of a morning prayer

¹[. . .]...[ ].[. . .] ²[. . .] night ...[. . .] ³[. . . Peac]e be upon yo[u, Israe]l, in the mouth of all to[ngues of . . .]

An evening prayer

⁴On[the . . . of the] month [in the] evening they shall ble[s]s and they answer and sa[y, Blessed be . . .] ⁵[. . .] us ..[. . .]the weeks of His glory. And [to]n[ig]ht is to us[. . .] ⁶[. . . ni]ght ..[. . .]..[. . .] ⁷[. . .].[. . .]

Note

[a]Frags. 42-43 have a small break between them but make good sense on both recto (4Q503) and verso (4Q512) when combined. The placement of frag. 44 with them (at the beginnings of lines 5-6) is possible but speculative. Baillet suggests that frags. 45-47 belong in the same column, presumably because their content is somewhat similar.

Frags. 45-47

The end of a prayer

¹[. . .]..[ ].[. . .] ²[. . .]in the festivals of [. . .] ³[. . .]... ...[. . .] ⁴[. . .].. of glory . . . ⁵[. . .] BLANK [. . .].[. . .]

The beginning of a prayer

⁶[. . . they shall bless] and they answer [and say, Bl]essed be [. . .] ⁷[. . .].[. . .]

4Q503 48-50

The end of a morning prayer

¹[. . .]...[. . .] ²[. . . Peace be upon you, Is]rael. BLANK [. . .]

An evening prayer

³[On the . . . of the month in the evening they shall bless and they answer and say, Blessed be] the God of Israel wh[o] ⁴[. . .] our happiness and [our] j[oy]ᵃ ⁵[. . . t]hird [. . .] in ..[. . .] our [happ]iness. And You [. . .] ⁶[. . .] Your salv[ati]on. Peace be u[pon you, I]srael. BLANK

A morning prayer

⁷[And when the sun rises to give l]ight upon [the] earth, they shall bless and they answer and s[ay], Blessed be the God of Is[rael] ⁸[. . .].. who [. . .]. sons of righteousness. And righteousness [. . .]God over a[ll]

Note

ᵃ[שונו]שֹׁו Reconstructing speculatively on the basis of Esther 8:17 (cf. Ps 51:10; Isa 22:13; 35:10; 51:3, 11).

Commentary

Line 5. Baillet suggests that this line refers to the third night of a festival of happiness. If this is a liturgy for the first month, the only possibility would be the third night of Passover, on the sixteenth. However, this reconstruction would link this assemblage with frags. 29-32, where it would not fit.

4Q503 frags. 51-55

A fragment of a morning prayer

¹[. . .]. [. . .] ²[. . .]11ᵃ lots of [. . .].. ..[. . .] ³[. . .] declarationᵇ of thanksgivings[. . . et]ernal [. . .] ⁴[. . .] us [. . .] ⁵[. . .]-teenᶜ gates of glo[ry] <[. . .]the light of daytime. Peace be upo[n you, Israel.]>

An evening prayer

⁶[On the . . . of the month in the evening they shall bless and they answer and s]ay, Blessed be the God of Is[rael] ⁷[. . .]..[. . .]..[. . .] ⁸[. . .]. divisionsᵈ of lig[ht . . .] ⁹[. . .] You have [made kn]own to us in the psalms of Your glory [. . .] ¹⁰[. . .]festivals of night. Peace be upon you, [Israel.] ¹¹ [. . .] BLANK [. . .]

A morning prayer

[12] [And when the sun rises upon the earth, they shall bless and they answer] and say, Blessed be the God of Israel [13][. . .] He has [mad]e known to us in the gr[eat] plan of His understanding [14][. . .] lots of light in order that we may know of the sign[s of] [15][. . . God of Isra]el wh[o . . .]...[. . .] [16][. . .] BLANK [. . .]

An evening prayer

[17] [On the . . . of the month in the evening they shall bless the God of Isra]el and they answer [and say] [18][. . .] His [gl]ory [. . .] [19][. . . fi]fth [. . .]

Notes

[a]אי‎ The first letter is damaged but might well be a *yod*. Baillet suggests that the two letters represent the numeral 11, as they would in the later Hebrew system of letters representing numbers. I have followed his suggestion in the translation, although it is quite speculative.

[b]אחות‎ Baillet proposes that this is an Aramaic noun from the root חוה√, "to declare," a noun that appears elsewhere in Hebrew only in Job 13:17.

[c]עשר‎ The number could be anything from ten to nineteen.

[d]דקלי‎ An irregular spelling of דגל with a *qop* where we would expect a *gimel*. Compare the spelling יקדילו for יגדילו ("they declare great") in Songs VII 4Q403 1i:31.

4Q503 62

A fragment that mentions Sabbaths

[1] [. . .] God of Is[rael . . .] [2][. . .]on the Sabbaths [. . .] [3][. . .]. holy to [. . .]

Commentary

Line 1. Perhaps part of a blessing of God at the beginning of a prayer.

Line 3. Perhaps a reference to the holiness of the Sabbath (cf. Exod 16:23; 31:14; 35:2), although many other referents are possible (see, e.g., Num 18:8-10; 28:25; Jer 2:3; Zech 14:20, 21).

4Q503 65

A morning prayer?

¹[. . . they shall bless an]d they answer and say, B[lessed . . .] ²[. . .]hosts of gods[. . .] ³[. . . l]ight and witnesses wi[th us . . .] ⁴[. . . the s]un. Blessed be the God of [Israel . . .] ⁵[. . . Peace be up]on you, [Israe]l [. . .]

Commentary

Line 1. From the first line of a prayer.

Line 2. The title "Lord of hosts" contains the best-known biblical reference to the angelic armies of heaven. Angels or "gods" are sometimes called the heavenly "host" elsewhere (e.g., Deut 4:19; Josh 5:14-15; 1 Kgs 22:19; Isa 24:21; 34:4; Ps 103:21). Angels are also called "gods" in the HB and the QL (see the commentary to Songs I 4Q401 1i:4).

Line 3. Given the context, it is likely that angelic witnesses are intended (cf. the commentary to frags. 15:5).

4Q503 67

A fragment of an evening prayer?

¹[. . . ᵃBlessed be the God of Is]rael whoᵃ [. . .] ²[. . .]eighth division[. . .] ³[. . . n]i[g]ht to confirm[. .]

Note

ᵃ⁻ᵃOr "[Blessed are You, God of Is]rael, who. . ."

Commentary

Line 1. The beginning of a prayer, probably for the evening (cf. line 3).

Line 2. The divisions come in numbered units, but their significance is unclear.

4Q503 69

The end of a Sabbath prayer?

[1][. . .] tranquil qu[iet . . .]

The beginning of a prayer

[2][. . . they shall bless and they answer and sa]y(!),[a] Blessed be the God of Isra[el . . .] [3][. . .]. festival[. . .]

Note

[a]I emend the broken word רֹמֹו[to [וא]מרו, "and they say," assuming that the *mem* and *resh* have accidentally been transposed.

Commentary

Line 1. The closest parallels to this phrase in the HB are in Ezek 16:49; 1 Chron 4:40. The phrase might be appropriate for a Sabbath prayer.

Line 2. If my emendation is correct (see note a), this line begins a new prayer.

4Q503 76

An evening prayer

[1][On the . . . of the month in the even]ing [they sh]all bl[ess and they answer and say,] [2][Blessed be the God of Israel] who has made known to us[. . .] [3][. . .] this night to us [. . .] [4][. . . l]ots of darkness[. . .]

The Words of the Luminaries

(4Q504, 4Q506)

INTRODUCTION

I. Contents

The "Words of the Luminaries" is a liturgical work consisting of prayers of supplication to be recited on each day of the week. The prayers survey biblical history from Adam to the writer's present and request God's mercy and help. The Sabbath prayer (or prayers) praises God for his creation.

II. The Manuscripts

The composition survives in two, possibly three, manuscripts. The oldest, 4Q504, is written in a Hasmonean script that the editor, Maurice Baillet, dates to the middle of the second century BCE. This copy is well preserved for a manuscript from Cave 4. All together forty-eight fragments survive. Fragments 1-2 preserve most of the text of the prayers for the fifth and sixth days of the week and some material for the Sabbath, while the smaller pieces contain much of the rest of the work. Originally it probably consisted of twenty columns of about twenty-two lines each. The last two columns were written on the back of the scroll (part of the last column survives), and the title was written on the back of frag. 8. Baillet did not attempt a full reconstruction of the manuscript. I follow the reconstruction of Émile Puech in his review of DJD 7, but with attention to refinements by Esther Chazon and Daniel Falk.[1] The manuscript has an unusually large number of scribal corrections, and various editor's marks are written in the margins, but their meaning is generally uncertain or unknown.

4Q506 is written on the verso of a papyrus manuscript that also bears a copy of a version of the *War Scroll* (4Q496). Its recto contains a copy of the "Festival Prayers" (4Q509 + 4Q505?; see below). The Herodian script is dated by Baillet to the first century CE. Forty-nine fragments, most of them tiny, contain text from the "Words of the Luminaries." Connected text that overlaps with 4Q504 is underlined in the translation.

Baillet also identified the ten fragments he called 4Q505 as part of a copy of the "Words of the Luminaries," but this identification has rightly been called into question by Florentino García Martínez and Falk:[2] the few suggested overlaps with 4Q504 are not very close; it is unclear why someone would copy a work onto the back of a much older manuscript already containing the same work; and the material on the backs of the fragments indicates that those passages that parallel 4Q504 are ordered differently, which is unlikely in such a highly structured work. I therefore follow García Martínez and Falk in treating 4Q505 and 4Q509 together as a single copy of the "Festival Prayers."

III. Structure and Genre

It is very rare for the title of a work to survive on a Qumran manuscript, but we are fortunate to have it in this case. However, the meaning of the title "Words of the Luminaries" (דברי המארות) is not immediately clear. In the Hebrew Bible the word "luminaries" refers to the heavenly bodies that regulate times and seasons (Gen 1:14-18; cf. 1QS x:3), but the Qumran literature also uses the word to mean angels (1QM x:12; 1QH[a] ix:11). Various interpretations are possible, but the most likely seems to be that of Chazon: these prayers are words to be recited

---

1. Puech, Review of DJD 7, 407-9; Chazon, "*4QDibHam:* Liturgy or Literature?" 448-50; Falk, *Daily, Sabbath, and Festival Prayers,* 63-68.
2. García Martínez, Review of DJD 7, 161-62; Falk, *Daily, Sabbath, and Festival Prayers,* 60.

at the times marked out by the celestial luminaries — in this case the sun and the stars, which divide the individual days of the week.[3]

The basic structure of the work is clear: it consists of a prayer for each day of the week from Sunday to Saturday, perhaps with multiple prayers for the Sabbath, or at least a prayer with multiple stanzas. The use of "we" throughout tends to indicate that it was meant for public rather than private recitation. However, the deeper structures are more complex and show that it is probably a unitary composition rather than an unredacted collection of prayers from various sources. The historical allusions begin with the story of Adam in the prayer for the first day, then proceed in chronological order to the events of the postexilic period in the prayer for the sixth day. Chazon has also shown that the individual prayers share linguistic patterns and patterns of scriptural citation.[4]

It is interesting to note that the Greek translation of the Psalter sometimes assigns a given Psalm to a specific day of the week: Psalm 24 (LXX 23) to the first day, Psalm 38 (LXX 37) to the Sabbath, Psalm 48 (LXX 47) to the second day, Psalm 93 (LXX 92) to the sixth day, Psalm 94 (LXX 93) to the fourth day. Both the Hebrew and Greek titles assign Psalm 92 to the Sabbath. Thus the custom of assigning a prayer to a particular day of the week is not unparalleled.

If we can generalize from the surviving fragments, it appears that each prayer began with a title (those for the fourth and seventh days survive). The prayers for the first six days open with a request for God to remember his past wondrous acts. A summary of some aspect of Israel's history comes next, followed by a request for God's deliverance and mercy (these two elements are sometimes difficult to separate). A closing benediction invokes a blessing on God, and the prayer ends with a double amen. The prayer (or prayers) for the Sabbath differs substantially from the others, containing no historical summary or petitions. Rather than addressing God, it praises him for his creation and calls on the angels to share in this praise. These features are typical of Sabbath prayers known from Qumran and later Jewish tradition.

The prayers for the first six days seem to correspond to the genre "communal lament," known from the book of Psalms (e.g., Pss 44, 80) Chazon divides them into two subtypes: requests for physical deliverance (Tuesday, Wednesday, Friday) and requests for spiritual strengthening (Sunday, Thursday).[5]

---

3. Baillet, "Un recueil liturgique de Qumrân Grotte 4," 249; Chazon, "*Dibre Hamme'orot:* Prayer for the Sixth Day," 24.

4. Chazon, "*4QDibHam:* Liturgy or Literature?"

5. Chazon, "*Dibre Hamme'orot:* Prayer for the Sixth Day," 23; cf. Falk, *Daily, Sabbath, and Festival Prayers,* 69-70.

IV. Life Situation

There are no explicitly sectarian literary characteristics in the text of the "Words of the Luminaries," but neither is there anything in the content that would have been unacceptable to the members of the Qumran community. Given the early date at which 4Q504 seems to have been copied, it seems likely that this is a presectarian composition adopted by the sectarians and used by them for a very long time. Beyond this, the specific life situation of the work or context in which it was used is difficult to specify. It was clearly composed for use in the daily public prayer life of a Jewish group. The fact that copies of it were made over a period of as much as two centuries makes it likely that it was put to use by the sectarians, although there is no assurance that it was used in the way intended by its author. Falk suggests two possibilities: first, that it was meant originally as a liturgy for Levites (the assistants to the priests in the temple), or second, that it was used in the *ma'amadot* service (a pre-Mishnaic institution in which delegations of lay representatives would participate in the temple sacrificial services for a week at a time). Neither possibility can be proven at this stage.[6]

V. Literary Context

The "Words of the Luminaries" draws heavily on, indeed is completely immersed in, biblical literature and tradition. Overall the text is a collage of scriptural quotations and allusions, with different scriptural passages frequently connected by "catchwords," words found in both passages. The work also draws on Jewish tradition from outside the canon (e.g., in frag. 8:4, the tradition of Adam's glory before the Fall).

It also shares themes with other Sabbath prayers (see section III, "Structure and Genre," above) and with material from the later Jewish liturgy, especially the *Amidah* and the *Tanḥanunim*.[7] However, such parallels are very general, are often based on biblical models, and show merely that many themes in the later liturgy already existed during the Second Temple period.[8]

---

6. Falk, *Daily, Sabbath, and Festival Prayers*, 90-92.

7. The *Amidah* is a series of benedictions recited as part of the liturgy of daily prayers. The *Tanḥanunim* are private supplicatory prayers recited immediately after the *Amidah*.

8. Lehman, "A Reinterpretation"; Weinfeld, "Prayer and Liturgical Practice," 248-50; Nitzan, *Qumran Prayer*, 108-11; Chazon, "Is *Divre Ha-Me'orot* a Sectarian Prayer?" 9-13; Falk, *Daily, Sabbath, and Festival Prayers*, 73-78.

BIBLIOGRAPHY

Baillet, Maurice. "Un recueil liturgique de Qumrân Grotte 4: 'Les Paroles des Luminaires.'" *RB* 68 (1961) 195-250, plates xxiv-xxvii.

———. "504. Paroles des Luminaires (premier exemplaire: DibHam^a)." In *Qumrân Grotte 4. III (4Q482-4Q520)*, 137-68, plates xlix-liii. DJD 7. Oxford: Clarendon, 1982.

———. "506. Paroles des Luminaires (troisième exemplaire: DibHam^c)." In *Qumrân Grotte 4. III (4Q482-4Q520)*, 170-75, plates xviii, xx, xxiv. DJD 7. Oxford: Clarendon, 1982.

Charlesworth, James H., et al. *The Dead Sea Scrolls: Hebrew, Aramaic, and Greek Texts with English Translations*, vol. 4A: *Pseudepigraphic and Non-Masoretic Psalms and Prayers*, 107-53. Tübingen: Mohr Siebeck; Louisville: Westminster/John Knox, 1997.

Chazon, Esther G. "*4QDibHam*: Liturgy or Literature?" *RevQ* 15/57-58 (1991) 447-55.

———. "Is *Divre Ha-Me'orot* a Sectarian Prayer?" In *The Dead Sea Scrolls: Forty Years of Research*, edited by Devorah Dimant and Uriel Rappaport, 3-17. STDJ 10. Leiden: Brill, 1992.

———. "On the Special Character of Sabbath Prayer: New Data from Qumran." *Journal of Jewish Music and Liturgy* 15 (1992-93) 1-21.

———. "Prayer from Qumran: Issues and Methods." In *SBLSP* 32, 758-72. Atlanta: Scholars Press, 1993.

———. "*Dibre Hamme'orot*: Prayer for the Sixth Day (4Q504 1-2v-vi)." In *Prayer from Alexander to Constantine: A Critical Anthology*, edited by Mark Kiley et al., 23-27. London and New York: Routledge, 1997.

———. "'Words of the Luminaries' (4QDibHam): A Liturgical Document from Qumran and Its Implications." Unpublished Ph.D. diss., Hebrew University, 1992. Forthcoming in STDJ, Brill. This work was not available to me.

Falk, Daniel K. *Daily, Sabbath, and Festival Prayers in the Dead Sea Scrolls*. STDJ 27. Leiden: Brill, 1998.

García Martínez, Florentino. Review of DJD 7. *JSJ* 15 (1984) 157-64.

Lehman, M. R. "A Reinterpretation of 4Q Dibrê Ham Me'oroth." *RevQ* 5/17 (1964) 106-10.

Nitzan, Bilhah. *Qumran Prayer and Religious Poetry*. STDJ 12. Leiden: Brill, 1994.

Puech, Émile. Review of DJD 7. *RB* 95 (1988) 404-11.

Weinfeld, Moshe. "Prayer and Liturgical Practice in the Qumran Sect." In *The Dead Sea Scrolls: Forty Years of Research*, edited by Devorah Dimant and Uriel Rappaport, 241-58. STDJ 10. Leiden: Brill, 1992.

THE WORDS OF THE LUMINARIES

(4Q504, 4Q506)

4Q504 8 verso

The title of the work

The Words of the Luminaries

Commentary

For possible interpretations of the title, see the introduction to this chapter.

4Q504 8 recto

The prayer for the first day of the week (Sunday)

[1][. . . Rememb]er, L[o]r[d], that ...[. . .] [2][. . .] You have [. . .]. us and You live fore[ver . . .] [3][. . .]. wondrous acts of old[a] and fearsome acts[. . .]

The story of Adam and the Fall

[4][. . . Adam] our [fat]her You formed in the likeness of [Your] glory [. . .] [5][. . . the breath of life] You [br]eathed into his nose, and understanding and knowledge [. . .] [6][. . . in the Gar]den of Eden which You planted You made [him] ru[le . . .] [7][. . .]. and to walk around in the land of glory ..[. . .] [8][. . .] he did [no]t keep, and You put him under obligation not to tu[rn aside . . .] [9][. . .] he is flesh and to dust .[. . .] [10][. . .].. And You know [. . .]

The story of the Flood?

[11][. . .] to eternal generations[. . .] [12][. . .] living God and Your hand[. . .] [13][. . .]mankind in the ways of[. . .] [14][. . . to fill] < [the e]arth> [with vio]lence and to she[d . . .] [15][. . .].[. . .]

Note

ªמקדם Although the meaning "of old" is clear in this context (cf. Ps 77:6 [EVV 77:5]), this word may be an echo of Gen 2:8, where it means "to the east."

Commentary

Lines 1-3. The request that God remember his own mighty acts appears to be unique to this document (cf. frags. 6:6-7; 1-2ii recto 11-12).

Line 1. Compare this badly damaged line to frag. 5ii:3. The phrase "Remember, Lord" occurs in Ps 89:51 (EVV 89:50) (cf. "Remember, Yahweh" in Ps 132:1; 137:7; Lam 5:1).

Line 2. Compare Deut 32:40; Dan 12:7; 6Q18 2:5.

Line 4. Here the story of the creation of Adam (Gen 1:26; 5:1) is associated with the glorious figure of a man (the same word as Adam) in Ezek 1:28. The word "in the likeness of" is found in all three passages and serves as a catchword to connect them. However, God "creates" Adam in Genesis 1 but "forms" him in Gen 2:7. Compare the "glory of Adam" in 1QS iv:23 and CD iii:20, and Adam's loss of the "glory of God" in *3 Apoc. Bar.* 4:16 (Greek). A rabbinic midrash teaches that Adam and Eve were clothed with "garments of light" before the Fall, based on a pun that changes one letter of "garments of skin" in Gen 3:21 (*Gen. Rab.* 20.12). The same tradition seems to lie behind *Apoc. Mos.* 20-21.

Line 5. The first clause echoes Gen 2:7. The second clause may allude to Gen 3:5-6 (cf. Sir 17:7; Ezek. 28:4).

Line 6. Inspired by Gen 1:26, 28; 2:8, 15. Compare 4Q287 4:2; 4Q381 1:7 for the verb "to make rule" in a similar context.

Line 7. Or "to walk around in the land. The glory of." Perhaps a reference to Satan's wanderings as he came to tempt the first couple (cf. Job 1:7; 2:2), "Glory" is sometimes associated with the land of Israel (1 Sam 4:21-22; Ezek 43:2; Ps 85:10 [EVV 85:9]; 1QM xix:4). There is a legend in *3 Enoch* 5:1-6 that God's visible manifestation of glory in the form of the Shekhinah dwelt in the Garden of Eden until the idolatry of the generation of Enosh (cf. *2 Enoch* 31).

Line 8. Presumably a reference to the disobedience of the first couple in the garden. For the idiom "to put one under obligation," see Esther 9:21, 31. The phrase "not to turn aside" is found in Deut 17:20; Josh 23:6; Jer 32:40.

Line 9. An echo of Gen 3:19.

Line 10. Compare Ps 103:14 (which also expresses the sentiment found in line 9 above).

Line 11. The phrase "eternal generations" also appears in frags. 1-2ii:11;

vi:9; 7:3; Gen 9:12; Tob 13:12; *Jub.* 4:26; 1QH^a vi:6; xiv:11; 4Q158 1-2:9; 4Q422 ii:10-11; iii:7; 4Q507 3:2 (cf. 4Q213a 3-4:7 in Aramaic); compare Isa 51:9; 1QH^a ix:15-16. Here, perhaps a reference to the covenant with Noah.

Line 14. Probably a reference to the violence and bloodshed that led up to the Flood; cf. Gen 6:11, 13; 9:6; *1 Enoch* 9:1; *2 Enoch* 70:5; *Sib. Or.* 1:154-56; *Jub.* 7:22-25.

4Q504 6

God's guidance in the wilderness

^{1}[. . .].. ..[. . .] ^{2}[. . .]. and fruit of the thought of ..[. . .] ^{3}[. . .]. to gain understanding of every law[. . .] ^{4}[. . .].. its produce to ...[. . .] ^{5}[. . .]... ..[ ]. in Your deeds always [. . .] ^{6}[. . . Reme]mber, please, that all of us are Your people and You bore us wondrou[sl]y ^{7}[on wings of] eagles, and You brought us to You, and "as an eagle fans its nest [over] ^{8}[its fledglings and h]overs, spreads its wings and takes and bears them on [its pinions]" ^{9}[. . .].. his [dwe]lling solitary and among the nations unreckoned and .[. . .] ^{10}[. . .].You were in our midst ^{a}in a pillar of fire and cloud^a .[. . .] ^{11}[. . .] Your [hol]iness going before us and Your glory in [our] midst [. . .] ^{12}[. . .]the face of Moses [Your] ser[vant . . .] ^{13} [. . .]because You .[. . .] ^{14}[. . .]. and <by no means> do You declare innoce[nt . . .] ^{15}[. . .]as a man disciplines [his son] ^{16}[. . . hol]y ones and pure [ones . . .] ^{17}[. . . which] a man [shall do] and live by them ..[. . .] ^{18}[. . . oa]th which [You] sw[ore . . .] ^{19}[. . .]... in Your presence [. . .]...[. . .] ^{20}[. . .] Blessed be the Lord[. . .] ^{21}[. . .]we [cannot] search out Your great acts [. . .] ^{22}[. . .]spirit of all [l]i[f]e[. . .]

Note

$^{a-a}$4Q506 126:2 reads "[in a pil]lar of cloud in a pi[llar of]." Line 1 of this fragment is illegible, but line 2 reads "[in] our [mids]t," so the fragment may correspond to 4Q504 6:10-11, even though the text is slightly different.

Commentary

Line 2. Compare Jer 6:19.
Line 6. The phrase "all of us are Your people" also appears in Isa 64:8.
Lines 6-7. These lines invoke God's promise of support in Exod 19:4.
Lines 7-8. A nearly exact quotation of Deut 32:11 with minor variants,

mostly of spelling. This verse picks up the comparison of God to an eagle in Exod 19:4.

Line 9. This line echoes Balaam's description of Israel in Num 23:9.

Lines 10-11. These lines echo Num 14:14 (cf. Exod 13:21-22; 14:24).

Line 12. Perhaps a reference to Exod 34:35. Moses is called God's servant frequently in the HB (e.g., Exod 14:31; Num 12:7, 8; Deut 34:5; Josh 1:1; cf. 4Q378 22i:2; 4Q504 1-2v recto 14; *Apos. Const.* 8.12.25).

Line 14. A phrase from the liturgical pronouncement in Num 14:18 (cf. Exod 34:7; Nah 1:3).

Line 15. Compare Deut 8:5 and frag. 1-2iii recto 5-7. In both cases Israel is the recipient of the discipline.

Line 16. The referents of the adjectives are lost, but angels are frequently called both "holy" and "pure" in QL. For a tradition that angels were present during the revelation of the Torah at Sinai, see *Jub.* 1:27-29; Acts 7:38, 53; Gal 3:19.

Line 17. Restored on the basis of Lev 18:5; Ezek 20:11, 13, 21; Neh 9:29; CD iii:15-16. The subject is always the laws of God.

Line 18. God's promise to give Abraham the land of Israel (Gen 12:7) is frequently described as an oath that God swore (e.g., Gen 26:3; 50:24; Exod 13:5; Num 14:23; Deut 7:8; Jer 11:5; Ps 105:9).

Line 21. The negation is reconstructed on the basis of Ps 145:3; Job 5:9; 9:10.

4Q506 131 + 132:1-6

[1][. . .] ..[. . .] [2][. . .]. we .[. . .] [3][. . .]woman [. . .] [4][wor]ks of hands .[. . .] [5]You have [gi]ven us ...[. . .] [6][a m]an born in .[. . .]

1Q504 4 + 4Q506 131 + 132:7-14

[1][. . .].,[ ]..[. . .] [2][. . .].. You showed favor [to] generations[a] of[. ,] [3][. . . the] land and service of all ...[. . . You have given to him] [4][in the goodness of their heart, fo]r You are the God of knowledge [and] every though[t . . .] [5][before You.] These things we know, inasmuch as You have granted [us] [b]h[oly] spirit.[b] [Have mercy on us] [6][and "do not reme]mber against us the iniquities of the primeval ones,"[c] with all their ev[il] recompense, [and that] [7][they stiffened] their neck. You, ransom us and forgive [please] our iniquities and [our] s[ins] [8][according to] Your [righteou]sness.

The revelation of the Torah

The Torah that [You] comma[nded] [by the h]and of Mose[s . . .] [9][. . .].[. . .]. which ..[. . .] in a[l]l[. . .] [10][. . . "a dominion of] priests and a holy nation" [ ].[. . .] [11][. . . wh]ich You have chosen. Circumcise the foreskin[s of our heart . . .] [12][. . .].. .. again strengthen our heart to do[. . .] [13][. . . to] walk in Your ways [. . .]

Conclusion

[14][. . . Blessed be] the Lord who has made kno[wn . . .] [15][. . .]Amen. Amen. BLANK [. . .]

The prayer for the second day of the week (Monday)

[16][. . . Blessed,] O Lord, be Yo[ur] holy name and [17][. . .]... on account of You and because of [. . .] [18][. . .]... ..[ ]. ...[. . .] [19][. . .].. transgression[. . .]...[. . .] [20][. . .] the spirit of [. . .] [21][. . . bu]rning, thanking[. . .] [22][. . .].. to take ..[. . .]

BOTTOM MARGIN

Notes

[a][לְ]דוֹרוֹתֵֿ] 4Q506 131 + 132:7 reads הָיֹו[(translation uncertain).

[b-b][שׁוד]קֹֿ רוּח 4Q506 131 + 132:11 reads הֿקוּדשׁ, "the holy [spirit]."

[c]רשונים 4Q506 131 + 132:12 reads אבותינֿוֹ הרשונים, "our primeval fathers."

Commentary

Line 2. Ps 44:4 (EVV 44:3) seems to express a similar thought.

Line 4. To be "good of heart" in biblical idiom means merely to have a good time (Judg 19:9; 2 Sam 13:28), but here the idea seems to have a moral sense. The phrase "God of knowledge" (literally "of knowledges") is also found in 1QS iii:15; 1QH[a] xxii:4:15; 4Q379 22i:6 (cf. 4Q510 1:2; 4Q511 1:7-8). The phrase "every thought" is also found in 1QS iv:4; xi:19.

Line 5. God's granting of the spirit is also mentioned in 1QH[a] vi:25.

Line 6. A quotation from Ps 79:8. The phrase "the iniquities of the primeval ones" is also found in 4Q512 23:2, albeit in a broken context. The term "primeval ones" (literally, "the first ones") also occurs in Lev 26:45; Deut 19:14.

Line 7. The "stiff neck" (stubbornness) of Israel at the time of the Exodus is proverbial (e.g., Exod 32:9; 33:3, 5; 34:9; Deut 9:6, 13; cf. 1QS iv:11; vi:26). Compare the rest of the line to Exod 34:9; Jer 36:3.

Line 8. An echo of Neh 9:14; compare 4Q381 69:5.

Line 10. A quotation from Exod 19:6.

Line 11. The first phrase may refer to God's choosing of Jerusalem as the place of his sanctuary (cf. Deut 12:5, passim). Compare the second clause to Deut 10:16; Jer 4:4; 1QpHab xi:13; 4Q509 287.

Line 12. Compare 1-2vi recto 9.

Lines 14-15. A concluding benediction and the double amen bring the prayer for the first day of the week to an end. For the double amen, see the commentary to 4Q286 5:8.

Line 16. An opening benediction in the prayer for the second day of the week. Compare 4Q287 3:1.

4Q504 26

The rebellion of Israel during the Exodus

[1][. . .]...[. . .] [2][. . .] Your [. . .] [3][. . .] Your [won]drous acts [4][. . .]nations [5][. .]firstborn [6][. . .] Your land [7][. . .] to anger [ ]..[ ] [8][. . .]the imprecations[a] [9][. . .] You have [. . .]...

Note

[a]האלות[In the translation I interpret this word as a feminine plural noun (see the commentary below), but it could also be a Hiphil infinitive construct, "to put under oath" (cf. 1 Kgs 8:31).

Commentary

Lines 1-9. The text is badly damaged, but the surviving words would fit an account of the early part of the Exodus, picking up the theme in the first prayer. Compare, for example, Psalm 106, especially vv. 7, 22, 24, 29, 32, 38, 40-41.

Line 5. Perhaps a reference to Israel, who is called God's firstborn in Exod 4:22 (cf. frag. 1-2iii recto 5-6). It is also possible that the word refers to the destruction of the firstborn in Egypt (cf., e.g., Ps 78:51).

Line 7. Compare Deut 9:18; 32:16; Ps 106:29.

Line 8. Or "the covenant oath." This word is used to describe the ratification of the Sinai covenant and its covenant curses in Deut 29:11, 13, 18, 19, 20 (EVV 29:12, 14, 19, 20, 21).

4Q504 17ii[a]

[1][ ]..[. . .] [2][. . .]and from all[. . .] [3][ ].. us and ..[. . .] [4]in the ways of the .[. . .]
[5]uprightness. Amen. [Amen . . .] [6]...

Note
[a]According to the reconstruction followed here, frags. 17i, 20, and 14 come after
frag. 26 and before frag. 17ii. They contain no translatable text.

Commentary

Line 5. The double amen ends the prayer for the second day of the week.

4Q504 5i

The prayer for the third day of the week (Tuesday)

[1][. . .]...[a] [2][. . .]. You have done [3][. . .]eternal name and to se[e] [4][. . .] Your
[. . .]... to generations of [. . .] [5][. . .] BLANK?[b] [. . .] [6][. . .].. You in the he[avens
and on ear]th [7][. . .]... .[. . .] You have [. . .] [8][. . .]...

BOTTOM MARGIN

Notes
[a]Baillet reads this badly damaged word as שֶׁ֫לְמֹנִ֫כֹ֫ה, "Your present." He takes it to
be the same as the word שִׁלְמֹן, which appears elsewhere only in Isa 1:23 with the apparent meaning "present, gift, bribe." The reading is very doubtful.
[b]Either a blank space at the end of a line (although not marking the end of a
prayer) or an unusually wide space between lines (in which case the next three lines
should be labeled 5-7).

Commentary

Line 2. The phrase "eternal name" is also found in Isa 56:5; 63:12; Sir 15:6;
1 Macc 2:51; 6:44; 13:29; 1QM xi:14.
Line 6. Restored on the basis of 1QM x:8; 1QH[a] viii:3.

4Q504 5ii + 4Q506 124:1-5

ᵃ[. . .You every . . . and You chose]ᵃ ¹their seed after them to .[. . .] ²holiness standing before Y[ou . . .] ³[Reme]mber, O Lord, that ..[. . .] ⁴ᵇ[. . .]. and in Youᵇ we celebrate [our] redempt[ion . . .] ⁵in our transgressions and to seek out [. . . not to do] ⁶what is evil in Your sight. [You] have commanded[. . .] ⁷and according to what is in [Your] soul [. . .] ⁸to Your understanding and .[. . .]

BOTTOM MARGIN

Notes

ᵃ ᵃThe bracketed line is restored on the basis of 4Q506 124:1 and Deut 10:15.

ᵇ⁻ᵇובך Two or three letters preceded this word, but only part of the last letter (a final *kaph?*) survives. Perhaps the word was written, deleted, and rewritten as it stands now.

Commentary

Line 2. Compare the phrase "standing before You" to Exod 17:17 (Moses addressing the Israelites at Meribah and Massah) and 1QHᵃ xii:21; xv:31 (God's worshipers before him).

Line 3. Compare frag. 3ii:5 and Ps 89:51 (EVV 89:50).

Line 4. The basic meaning of the verb is "to celebrate a pilgrimage-festival," but it can mean more generally "to celebrate, throw a party" (e.g., 1 Sam 30:16).

Line 5. The QL uses the verb "to seek out" (BH "to spy on"; e.g., Num 13:17) in the sense of seeking out evil to do (CD ii:16; iii:11-12; 1QHᵃ xii:15).

Lines 5-6. Compare Ps 51:6; 1QHᵃ vi:18.

Line 7. Compare 1QHᵃ iii:11:9.

4Q504 3i

¹⁴[. . .].. ¹⁵[. . .] our[. . .].. ¹⁶[. . .] our[. . .].. ¹⁷[. , .].. to do ¹⁸[. . .]... ¹⁹[, . .].

[BOTTOM MARGIN]

4Q504 3ii + <u>4Q506 125 + 127</u>

[1][. . .]..[. . .] [2][. . .].. Blessed be the Go[d] who gave us rest .[. . .] [3][Amen.] Amen. BLANK [. . .] [4]BLANK [. . .]

The prayer for the fourth day of the week (Wednesday)

Title

[5][Prayer on] the fourth [da]y.

Opening supplication

Remember, Lord[. . .] [6]Your [. . .]... is declared holy in glory[. . .] [7][. . . eye] to eye You are seen in our midst[. . .] [8][. . .]. and [we] have heard Your holy words [. . .] [9][. . .].. on our faces in order not to ..[. . .] [10][. . .] Your grea[t name of] [ho]liness [. . .] [11][. . . the] earth ...[. . .] [12][. . .]and because we believe .[. . .] [13]forever.

The covenant with God at Horeb

And You made a covenant with us at Hor[eb . . .] [14]concerning all th[ese] l[a]ws and customs [. . .] [15]and the good [ones . . .]... and holy ones ..[. . .] [16]which [You spoke by the hand of] Moses and ... [17]in all [. . .] <u>face to face</u> <[You] <u>spoke></u> <u>wi</u>[th him[a] . . .] [18]glor[y . . .]<u>You were pleased with him</u>. And th<u>ey</u> found [fa<u>vor</u> <u>in</u> Your sight . . .] [19][. . . <u>al</u>l] their [. . .] in his hand in our sight[. . .]

BOTTOM MARGIN

> Note
> [a][תו]אֹוֹ 4Q506 125 + 127:3 reads [ו]עֹמֹ, also translated "with [him]."

Commentary

Lines 2-4. A concluding benediction and the double amen bring the prayer for the third day of the week to an end.

Line 5. Titles of the prayers are preserved only for the fourth and the seventh days (1-2vii recto 4). This prayer opens with "Remember, Lord" (also found in frag. 5ii:4 and Ps 89:51 [EVV 89:50]).

Line 6. Compare Exod 29:43 and 1QSb iii:4.

Line 7. An echo of Num 14:14 and perhaps of Isa 52:8.

Line 8. The closest parallels to the phrase "Your holy words" are in Jer 23:9; Ps 105:42.

Line 10. Compare Ezek 36:23; Ps 99:3.

Lines 12-13. Compare Exod 19:9.

Line 13. Compare Deut 5:2. The wording of the Hebrew is slightly different.

Line 14. Compare 2 Chron 33:8. "Laws" and "customs" are favorite terms of the book of Deuteronomy (e.g., Deut 4:1, 45; 5:1; 6:1; 12:1).

Line 15. Perhaps a description of the laws and customs (cf. Neh 9:13), but see also the commentary to frag. 6:16, above.

Line 16. Reconstructed on the basis of 1QM x:6; 1QH[a] iv:12. See also the commentary to line 17.

Line 17. Compare Exod 33:11 (and Gen 32:31; Num 12:8; Deut 5:4; 34:10; Judg 6:22; Ezek 20:35).

Line 19. Compare Ezek 37:20. Baillet plausibly suggests that this line refers to the tablets of the law given to Moses.

4Q504 7

[1][. . .].. straightening [2][the . . . won]ders that You have done [3][. . .]<[I]srael> for eternal generations to recount [4][. . .]the works of Your hands [5][. . .].. for Your glory [6][. . .]it is not shortened [7][. . . not inacc]essible to You. All [8][. . .].. it [9][. . .]You have put a treasure[a] [10][. . .]. and do not forsake us [11][and do not abandon us. . .]. . and by Your mercies [12][. . .[b]]... we encountered[b] [13][. . wh]ich You forgave [14][our fathers . . . des]ert where they rebelled [15][against Your command . . .] and they libated it and they found You [16][. . .]. they did n[ot] believe [17][. . .]. they saw.. [18][. . .].[. . .] eyes [19][. . .]... [20][. . .].

Notes

שימה With Baillet, I take this to be a word attested in RH (Jastrow, 980b, 1563b). However, one could also translate "You have placed what is set" (cf. 2 Sam 13:32).

b-b קדמנו[°וֹת Perhaps reconstruct מֹות קדמנו] [מקושׁי, "we encountered the [snares of de]ath" (cf. 2 Sam 22:6 // Ps 18:6 [EVV 18:5]).

Commentary

Lines 2-3. Compare Judg 6:13; Ps 78:3-4, 6.

Line 6. Compare Num 11:23; Isa 50:2; 59:1. The subject is probably the hand of the Lord (although it could also refer to his spirit not being impatient; cf. Mic 2:7).

Line 7. For this restoration compare Gen 11:6; Job 42:2.

Lines 10-11. For this restoration compare 1 Kgs 8:57 and Ps 27:9.

Lines 13-15. Restored on the basis of frag. 1-2ii recto 7-8.

Line 16. This phrase is used of the unbelieving Israelites (2 Kgs 17:14; Ps 78:22; 106:24; 1QpHab ii:3-4) and of the inhabitants of the earth who thought Jerusalem invulnerable before the Exile (Lam 4:12).

4Q504 18

¹[. . .]... ....[. . .] ²[. . .] You have [give]n to them a he[art to know . . .] ³[. . . and eyes] to see and ear[s to hear . . .] ⁴[. . .] last and You will seal [their eyes] shut [. . .] ⁵[. . .]a traveler ..[. . .] ⁶[. . .]. ...[. . .]

Commentary

Lines 2-3. Reconstructed on the basis of Deut 29:3.

Line 4. Reconstructed on the basis of Isa 6:10.

4Q504 1-2i recto

Conclusion

⁷[. . .]Amen. Amen.

The prayer for the fifth day of the week (Thursday)

References to the Exodus from Egypt

⁸[. . .]. wondrous acts ⁹[. . .]. from Egypt ¹⁰[. . .de]sert

Commentary

Line 7. The double amen concludes the prayer for the fourth day of the week.

Lines 8-10. The prayer for the fifth day of the week begins with allusions to the Exodus. Compare Ps 78:12, 15, 32; 106:7, 9, 14, 22; Neh 9:9-10, 17-18, 21.

4Q504 1-2ii recto

*Petition for God's forgiveness as during
the rebellion in the wilderness*

⁶[. . .].[. . .].[. . .]...[. . .]..[. . .].[. . .] Your [. . .] ⁷Please, [Lo]rd, [a]ct, please according to Yourself, according to the greatness of Your strength [w]he[n You for]gave ⁸our fathers when they rebelled against Your command and You were incensed with them to the point of destroying them. But You had compassion ⁹on them because of Your love for them and for the sake of Your covenant — for [M]oses atoned ¹⁰for their sin — and for the sake of the knowledge of Your great strength and Yo[ur] abundant loyalty ¹¹to eternal generations. Please let Your anger and Your wrath turn back from Your people, Israel ⟨regarding all [their] si[n]⟩ and remember ¹²Your wondrous acts that You did in the sight of nations, for Your name is called over us ¹³[. . .]ªt[o make] us [ret]urnª with the whole heart and the whole soul and to plant Your Torah in our heart ¹⁴[. . .]from right and left, for You have healed us from madness ⟨and blindness⟩ and bewilderment of ¹⁵[heart . . .] we have been sold [for] our [in]iquities, but even in our transgressions You called us ¹⁶[. . .].. and You have saved us from sinning against You ¹⁷[. . .].. and to make us understand the testimonies ¹⁸[. . .]... You have made them ¹⁹[. . .].. and their deed

Note
ª⁻ªReading ל[הש]⁸בנו. Other restorations are possible.

Commentary

Line 7. The phrase "please, Lord" is also found in 1-2vi recto 10; Dan 9:4; Neh 1:11 (cf. 1:5). The phrase "according to the greatness of Your strength" appears in 1QHª vi:23.

Lines 7-8. An echo of Num 14:19.

Line 8. In the HB the Israelites are warned or rebuked several times for re-belling against God's command (Deut 1:26, 43; 9:23; 1 Sam 12:14). The next clause echoes Deut 9:8.

Lines 9-10. An echo of Exod 32:30 and, less directly, Num 14:13-19 (note especially vv. 18, 19). Compare also Deut 7:8; 2 Kgs 13:23; 2 Chron 21:7.

Line 11. An echo of Dan 9:16.

Lines 11-12. Compare Ps 78:4; 96:3; Neh 9:17; 1 Chron 16:12. Compare also the last clause in line 12 with Deut 28:10; Dan 9:18-19; Bar 2:15; 4Q380 1i:5.

Line 13. Compare the phrase "with the whole heart and the whole soul" with 2 Kgs 23:3; 1QS v:8-9; CD xv:12, all of which refer to keeping the stipula-tions of the Mosaic law. Compare the last clause to Isa 51:7; Jer 31:33; Ps 37:31; 4 Ezra 9:31, 36; *Apos. Const.* 7.26.3.

Line 14. For the general sense of the first clause, compare Deut 17:20; Josh 23:6.

Lines 14-15. An echo of Deut 28:27-28, referring to curses to be brought on Israel if the nation breaks the covenant with God.

Line 15. Based on Isa 50:1.

Line 16. For this sentiment compare Ps 39:9 (EVV 39:8); 79:9.

Line 17. Given the context, the word translated "testimonies" (תעודה) probably has the biblical meaning of "custom, teaching" (Isa 8:16, 20; Ruth 4:7) rather than the Qumran sectarian sense of "set period." For the latter sense, see the commentary to Songs IV 4Q402 1:3.

4Q504 1-2iii recto

God's election of Israel

[1]...[. . .].[. . .]. [2]..[ ]...[. . .]..[. . .]reckoned [. . .].[ ]. behold, [3]all the nations [are as though they are n]ot, compared to You, [less than] the void and nothingness before You <[they] are reck[oned].> [4]Only Your name [have] we [invo]ked and for Your own glory You created us and made us [5]sons for Yourself in the sight of all the nations, for You called [6][I]srael "my firstborn son" and You discipline us as a man disciplines [7]his [so]n. [a]And You multiplied us[a] in the years of our gen-erations [8][. . .]severe illnesses and hunger and thirst and plague and a sword [9b][executing the venge]ance of Your covenant,[b] for it is we You have chosen for Yourself [10][as a people from the whole] earth.

The covenant curses

Therefore You have poured out Your rage on us [11][. . .] Your [. . .]. with all the wrath of Your anger, and there has clung to us [12c][all] Your [bl]ows[c] which Moses wrote, and Your servants [13]the prophets wh[om] You [se]nt, in order for evil to [mee]t us in the last [14]days, for[. . .] [15]and our kings, for[. . .] [16]to take the daughters of[. . .] [17]and they acted corruptly ..[. . .] [18]Your covenant and .[. . .] [19]the seed of Israel[. . .] [20]You are righteous ...[. . .] [21]and ..[. . .]

Notes

[a-a]Corrected by the scribe from תברנו ("You made us fat" or "You created us"?) to תרב אותנו ("You multiplied us").

[b-b]נק[מת ברית]כה[I take the first word to be a feminine singular participle of the verb √נקם, "to avenge," and the second word to be the construct form of the noun נקמה, "vengeance." Compare חרב נקמת נקם ברית, "a sword executing the vengeance of the covenant," in Lev 26:25; CD i:17-18.

[c-c]את כול מכ[ותיכה] Reconstructing on the basis of Deut 28:61. Alternatively, one could reconstruct את כול אל[ותיכה], "[all] Your [imprec]ations," on the basis of CD i:17.

Commentary

Line 3. Based on Isa 40:17.

Line 4. An echo of Isa 43:7.

Lines 4-5. For the Israelites as God's sons, see Deut 14:1; Hos 2:1 (EVV 1:10); *Jub.* 1.24. This idea is picked up in the NT and applied to Christians (John 1:12; Rom 8:14, 19, 23; Gal 4:5-6; Heb 12:7-8; 1 John 3:1-2).

Line 5. The phrase "in the sight of all the nations" is found in Isa 52:10; 2 Chron 32:23.

Line 6. The quotation is from Exod 4:22 (cf. Exod 4:23; Hos 11:1; *4 Ezra* 6:58; *Jub.* 2:20; *Pss. Sol.* 18:4).

Lines 6-7. Based on Deut 8:5. The idea is applied to Christians in Heb 12:7-11.

Line 7. Compare the promise to Abraham in Gen 17:2, etc., and to Israel in Lev 26:9, etc. Expressions similar to "the years of our generations" occur in Deut 32:7; Joel 2:2.

Line 8. Inspired by the covenant curses in Deut 28:48, 59 (cf. Ezek 5:17; Bar 2:25). Perhaps the lost beginning of this line read something along the lines of ["yet You also multiplied"]. Compare Deut 28:63 for the general sentiment.

Lines 9-10. Compare 1QM x:9; 1QH[a] vii:27.

Lines 10-21. The author breaks out of historical sequence here to make the point that the covenant curses were not an idle threat; according to the prophetic theology accepted by the writer, the nation had suffered from them up to the present day. Otherwise the traditional historical sequence of events is followed closely throughout the week.

Line 10. Restoring with Baillet on the basis of Deut 7:6 // 14:2; 1Q34bis 3ii:5.

Line 11. According to 1QS ii:15 and CD i:17, the covenant curses "cling" to the unfaithful Israelites.

Lines 12-13. Compare 1QS i:3.

Lines 13-14. These lines are difficult, but I follow Baillet's reconstruction and interpretation, based on Deut 31:29. Originally the phrase "the last days" referred to the prophetic idealized future in the HB (e.g., Deut 31:29; Hos 3:5), but in later literature it took on the overtones of apocalyptic eschatology (e.g., Dan 10:14; 1QpHab ix:6; Acts 2:17; 2 Pet 3:3).

Line 15. The first reference to the monarchical period. Baillet suggests this line may be part of an enumeration of those responsible for the sins of Israel (cf. Jer 44:17; Dan 9:6, 8; Ezra 9:7; Neh 9:32, 34; Bar 1:16; 2:1, 19; 4QMMT C 23).

Line 16. Baillet suggests that the reference is to the problems of intermarriage facing the restoration community in the time of Ezra and Nehemiah (Ezra 9–10; Neh 13:23-27). The surviving phrase could also refer to the miscegenation between the sons of God and the daughters of men (Gen 6:2) or to Solomon's marriage to numerous pagan women (cf. Deut 17:17; 1 Kgs 3:1; 11:1-8), but the context supports Baillet's interpretation (cf. Deut 7:3).

4Q504 1-2iv recto

The covenant with David and the united monarchy

[1][. . .]. [2]Your t[aber]nacle [. . . r]e[p]ose [3]in Jerus[alem, the city which] You [cho]se from the whole earth [4]for [You]r [name] to [b]e [th]ere forever, for You have loved [5]Israel more than all the peoples, and You chose the tribe of [6]Judah and You established Your covenant for David to be [7]l[ike] a shepherd,[a] a ruler over Your people, and he sat on the throne of Israel before You [8]all the days. And all the nations saw Your glory, [9](by) which You were sanctified in the midst of Your people, Israel. And to Your great [10]name <<and>> they brought their offering — silver and gold and precious stones, [11]along with everything desirable of their land — to glorify Your people and [12]Zion, Your holy city, and Your or-

namented house. "And there was no adversary ¹³or evil smiter," but rather peace and blessing ..[. . .] ¹⁴and they a[t]e and were satisfied and grew fat[. . .] ¹⁵[. . .]. and ...[. . .]ᵇ

Notes

כרעיa Perhaps read **מֹרֹעִי**, "f[rom being a sh]epherd" (cf. 2 Sam 7:8). The form **רעי** (normally **רעה**) for the word "shepherd" is also found in Isa 38:12; Zech 11:17.

ᵇPresumably the prayer ended with a benediction and the double amen, as do the surviving endings of the other prayers.

Commentary

Line 2. Probably a reference to David's bringing of the ark of the covenant to Jerusalem (2 Samuel 6; Psalm 132; 1 Chronicles 15–16). The word "tabernacle" may refer to the "tent" of 2 Sam 7:2 (cf. also 1 Chron 15:1; 16:1) or to the "dwelling place" of the ark (the same word in the plural) mentioned in Ps 132:5, 7. The "repose" or "resting place" of God is the dwelling place of the ark in Jerusalem (Ps 132:8, 14).

Line 3. Restored with Baillet on the basis of 1 Kgs 11:32; 2 Chron 6:34 (cf. 4QMMT B 60-61). However, the "Words of the Luminaries" puts the election of Jerusalem in the context of the whole earth, not just the tribes of Israel.

Line 4. Compare the first clause to 1 Kgs 8:16; 2 Chron 6:6; 7:16.

Lines 4-5. God's love for Israel is a persistent theme in the HB and Jewish tradition; compare, for example, Deut 7:8, 13; Isa 43:4; Hos 11:1; Mal 1:2; 2 Apoc. Bar. 21:21; Jub. 1:25; Pss. Sol. 18:3.

Lines 5-6. Compare Ps 78:68.

Line 6. God's covenant with David is mentioned explicitly in, for example, 2 Sam 23:5; Isa 55:3; Jer 33:21; Ps 89:4-5 (EVV 89:3-4); 132:12.

Line 7. For David as shepherd and ruler, compare Ps 151:1, 7 (11QPsª xxviii:4, 11). Compare the rest of the line to 1 Kgs 8:20 // 2 Chron 6:10, which, however, refer to Solomon. But lines 8-14 fit Solomon's reign better than David's, and it may be that the subject is the golden age of the united monarchy under both David and Solomon.

Line 8. For the revelation of God's glory to the nations, see Ps 72:17-19 (of the reign of Solomon); Isa 60:1-3; 62:2; 66:18-19; Hag 2:7-9. The last four references speak of eschatological revelations.

Line 9. Compare Lev 22:32.

Lines 10-11. Compare 1 Kgs 9:26-28; 10:2, 10-11, 14-15, 23-25; Isa 66:12, 20; Hag 2:7-8.

Lines 11-12. Compare Isa 60:7. The word translated "to glorify" can also have the meaning "to honor" or "to enrich."

Lines 12-13. A quotation from 1 Kgs 5:18 (EVV 5:4), again concerning the time of Solomon, whose reign was proverbial for its peace (1 Kgs 5:4 [EVV 4:24]; 5:26 [EVV 5:12]; Ps 72:7; 1 Chron 22:9; *2 Apoc. Bar.* 61:3) and blessings (2 Sam 7:29; Ps 72:15, 17; 4QMMT C 18).

Line 13. An echo of the covenant blessing in Deut 31:20, but also of the general situation remembered of Israel during Solomon's reign (1 Kgs 4:20; 5:5 [EVV 4:25]; Ps 72:3, 16).

4Q504 1-2v recto

The prayer for the sixth day of the week (Friday)

The exile and restoration

[1][. . .].. ...[. . . they abandoned] [2]the source of living water .[. . .].[. . .].. ... [3]and they served a foreign god in their land and also their land [4]was desolated by their enemies, for Your wrath [was pour]ed forth, [5]and Your rages of anger with the fire of Your jealousy, so as to eradicate it [6]of anyone passing by or returning. [a]In all this[a] You did not reject [7]the seed of Jacob, and You have not loathed Israel [8]to the point of annihilating them, so as to break Your covenant with them. For You [9]alone are the living God and there is none beside You, and You remembered Your covenant [10]by which You brought us out in the sight of the nations. And You did not abandon us [11]among the nations, and You were gracious toward Your people Israel among all [12][the] lands where You had driven them, in order to bring it back [13]into their heart to return to You[b] and to listen to Your voice; [14]all that You commanded by the hand of Moses Your servant. [15][Fo]r You have poured out[c] Your holy spirit on us [16][to b]ring Your blessings to us as Your visitation, when we are so troubled [17][as to mut]ter at the outpouring of Your discipline. And we come into troubles [18][and stro]kes and tests in the wrath of the One who pours out, for also [19]we [have wea]ried <God> with our iniquities, we have enslaved the Rock to [our] si[ns.] [20][And You have not ensl]aved us to profit [d]from [our] ways,[d] in the w[ay] [21]in [which we walk, and] we have not[e] listened t[o Your commandments.]

Notes

[a-a]בכול זואת Replacing ואף גם זאת (Lev 26:44) with a more readily comprehensible postbiblical expression.

[b]עודך or עידך In BH the form would be עדיך (perhaps cf. *HDSS* 200.26).

[c]יצקתה, "You have poured out," from the root √יצק, "to pour out." In line 17 I have translated the difficult word צקון as "outpouring" on the assumption that the word comes (or was taken by the writer to come) from either the same root or the root √צוק II, which has the same meaning. The form המציק in line 18, which appears twice in Isa 51:13, is usually taken to mean something like "the oppressor" (from the Hiphil stem of the root √צוק I, "to constrain, oppress"). This translation is possible here, but the obvious play on the similar words in lines 15 and 17 may mean that the writer derived the word from √יצק as well. Hence, I have translated it "the One who pours out."

[d-d]מדרכי|נו] I follow Baillet in analyzing this word as the preposition מן, "from," and the suffixed plural of the noun דרך, "way, road." However, the MT spells and vocalizes the word as מַדְרִיכֶךָ, "who leads your way" (a Hiphil participle), in Isa 48:17. But the spelling of the word here, in 1QIsa[b], and in 1QH[a] xiv:20 (based on the same passage) supports Baillet's interpretation.

[e]לוא|ן] I have translated this word as though it were the simple negation לוֹא, but the MT vocalizes it לוּא in Isa 48:18. If the writer of the "Words of the Luminaries" had this vocalization in mind, we should translate "Would that we had . . ."

Commentary

Lines 1-2. Restored on the basis of Jer 2:13; 17:13, the only places in the HB where the phrase "source of living water" appears. The phrase "living water" is an idiom for running water (e.g., Gen 26:19; 11Q19 xlv:16), but it can be used in the metaphorical sense of spiritual refreshment or the like (1QH[a] xvi:16; John 7:38).

Line 3. Similar phrases are found in Josh 24:20; Jer 5:19. The phrase "foreign god" (using *El* rather than *Elohim*) appears only in Deut 32:12, Ps 81:10.

Lines 3-4. Compare Lev 26:32-33; CD iii:10. Desolation of the land is a covenant curse invoked frequently in the HB against disobedient Israel (e.g., Zech 7:14)

Lines 4-5. In the HB "wrath" is frequently "poured forth" (e.g., Lam 2:4). The word "rage" almost always occurs in the phrase "the rage of Your anger" (e.g., Zeph 3:8), and in the plural only in Ps 88:17 (EVV 88:16); the phrase "rages of Your anger" never appears in the HB. The "fire" of God's jealousy is mentioned in Ezek 36:5; Zeph 1:18; 3:8; Ps 79:5.

Lines 5-6. Inspired by Zeph 3:6 (which in tandem with 3:8 connects most of the words and phrases in lines 4-6). The phrase "of anyone passing by or returning" comes from Zech 7:14 (cf. lines 3-4 above); 9:8.

Lines 6-8. Based on Lev 26:44 with 2 Kgs 17:20 (cf. Jer 31:37).

Lines 9-10. Based on Lev 26:45.

Lines 11-12. The Hebrew is nearly identical to Dan 9:7.

Lines 12-13. An echo of Deut 30:1 (which in turn is linked with Dan 9:27 by the verb "to drive" as well as the general sense).

Lines 13-14. An echo of Deut 30:2. The phrase "by the hand of Moses Your servant" appears in Neh 9:14. Compare the commentary to frag. 6:12 above.

Line 15. Compare Isa 44:3, which, however, refers to God's "spirit" rather than "holy spirit." The latter phrase is uncommon in the HB (only Isa 63:10, 11; Ps 51:13), but it does appear in Second Temple Jewish literature (e.g., Sus 45; *Pss. Sol.* 17:37), in the New Testament and early Christian literature (e.g., Luke 11:13; Rom 1:4; Eph 1:13; 4:30; 1 Thess 4:8; *Ascen. Isa.* 3:16, 27; *Odes Sol.* 6:7; 11:2; 14:8), and the QL (e.g., 1QS viii:16; ix:3; CD ii:12; 1QH^a xx:12; 4Q270 2ii:14). The idea of the holy spirit as a person in the Godhead is a much later development in trinitarian Christian theology.

Line 16. The mention of blessings echoes both Deut 30:1 and Isa 44:3.

Lines 16-17. An echo of Isa 26:16, a passage whose meaning is quite unclear.

Line 18. Compare "Your tests and Your strokes" in frags. 1-2vi recto 7. The phrase "the wrath of the one who pours out" (or "of the oppressor") appears twice in Isa 51:13, although not, apparently, referring to God.

Line 19. Based on Isa 43:24, shifted into the third person and with the clauses reversed.

Line 20. The phrase "and You have not enslaved us" echoes Isa 43:23.

Lines 20-21. Based on Isa 48:17-18.

4Q504 1-2vi recto

[1][. . .] [2][. . .].[and You have cas]t fr[om up]on [u]s all o[u]r transgressions, and You [have pur]if[ie]d us [3]of our sin for Your sake. To You — You, <Lord> — belongs righteousness, "for [4]it is You who did all these things."

Israel's response to God's mercy

And now, on this very day [5]when our heart is humbled, we have made amends for our iniquity and the iniquity of [6]our fathers when we were treacherous and when we walked obstinately. And we have not rejected [7]Your tests and Your strokes. Our soul has not loathed (You) so as to break [8]Your covenant, even with all the distress of our soul, for You <who sent our enemies against us> [9]have strengthened our heart <<and>> in order that we may recount Your might to eternal [10]generations. Please, Lord, since You do wondrous acts from of old

and forever and ¹¹ever, let Your anger and Your wrath turn back from us, and
see [our] a[ffliction] ¹²and our labor and our oppression, and save Your people
Isr[ael out of all] ¹³the lands near and far w[here You have banished them.]
¹⁴Everyone written in the book of life[. . .] ¹⁵to serve You and to give thanks
t[o . . .] ¹⁶from all their persecutors^a[. . .] ¹⁷<who> cause to stumble^b ..[. . .]
¹⁸...[. . .] ¹⁹.[. . .]

Notes

^aצורריהמה This word appears first to have been miswritten צורעיהמה, which
would presumably mean something like "their lepers." But the reading has been corrected to "their persecutors," which makes much better sense in the context.

^bה<מכשׁילים> The translation takes this word as a Hiphil participle of the root
כשׁל√ (cf. 4Q174 1-2:8; 4Q177 10-11:7). It could also be read as the noun מכשׁול, in
which case it should be translated "the stumbling blocks" (cf. Ezek 21:20).

Commentary

Line 2. The first clause has been restored on the basis of Ezek 18:31.

Lines 2-3. Compare the phrase "You have purified us of our sin" to "purify me from my sin!" in Ps 51:4 (EVV 51:2). Note also the catchword "transgressions" here and in Ps 51:3, 5 (EVV 51:1, 3). Compare "for Your sake" with
Isa 43:25.

Line 3. An echo of Dan 9:7, which in turn is echoed by Bar 1:15; 2:6.

Lines 3-4. The last clause quotes Jer 14:22.

Lines 5-8. These lines rework and reorder Lev 26:40-44 freely, by implication calling on God to fulfill the promise in these verses to revoke the covenant
curses if Israel truly repents of its sins.

Line 9. Compare Josh 11:20.

Lines 9-10. The closest parallel is 1QH^a xiv:11 (cf. 4Q504 1-2ii recto 11).
No biblical passage has closely similar wording, but the same general ideas are
expressed in passages like Ps 71:18; 78:3-4, 6; 79:13; 145:4.

Lines 10-11. Compare Ps 136:4; 1QH^a vi:23; xiv:11.

Line 11. Compare frags. 1-2ii recto 11; Dan 9:16; Ezra 10:14; 2 Chron
29:10.

Lines 11-12. Based on Deut 26:7 (cf. Ps 44:25 [EVV 44:24]).

Lines 12-14. An echo of Dan 9:7, with modifications drawn from Ezek
22:4-5.

Line 14. The expression "the book of life" appears in the HB only in Ps
69:29 (EVV 69:28), but the same idea seems to be expressed in Exod 32:32; Mal

3:16; Dan 12:1. Second Temple Jewish and early Christian literature likewise mention the "book of life" (e.g., *1 Enoch* 108:3; *Apoc. Zeph.* 3:7; *Jub.* 30:22; 36:10; Phil 4:3; Rev 3:5; 13:8; 17:8; 20:12, 15; 4Q381 31:8). This line also echoes Josh 23:6; Isa 4:3; Jer 25:13.

4Q504 1-2vii recto

Conclusion[a]

[1][. . .]...[ ].. was [. . .] [2]who has saved us from all trouble. Ame[n. Amen . . .] [3]BLANK [. . .]

Prayers for the Sabbath day (Saturday)

Title

[4]Thanksgiving hymns[b] on the Sabbath day.

A Sabbath prayer

Give than[ks to . . .] [5]His holy name always ..[. . .] [6]all the angels of the holy firmament and .[. . .] [7]to the heavens, the earth and all i[ts] depths[c][. . .] the great [8][abyss] and destruction and the waters and all that is [in them . . .] [9]all His creatures continually, forever [and ever. Amen. Amen.] [10]BLANK

Another Sabbath prayer

[. . .][d] [11]His holiness. Chant to God ..[. . .] [12]glory ..[ ]...[. . .]

Notes

[a]At least one column appears to have been lost after this one.

[b]הודות This noun is unattested in the HB. The plural form here looks the same as the Hiphil infinitive of the root √ידה, "to praise, give thanks"; the closest analogue in BH is the noun תודה, "thank offering" or "thanksgiving." The word does appear as a noun in QH (e.g., 1QM xv:5; 4Q510 1:1) and in RH (הודאה or הודיה; Jastrow, 337).

Traces survive of a word written (then erased?) above the line, which may have been part of the title. Puech reads it as שיר, "song" (Review of DJD 7, 409). Compare the title to Psalm 92 and also 11QPs[a] xxvii:7. The titles of the thirteen *Songs of the Sabbath Sacrifice* also include the word "song."

מחשביה For this word, see the commentary to 4Q286 5:1.

[d]The supralinear addition to vi:8 has pushed this line down. The surviving first part of line 10 is blank, but presumably the first words of the next prayer came in the lost end of the line. Perhaps the end of line 10 and the beginning of line 11 read something along the lines of "[Bless] His holy [name]."

Commentary

Lines 2-3. Compare 1 Sam 26:24; Ps 54:9 (EVV 54:7). A damaged concluding benediction and the double amen bring the prayer for the sixth day of the week to an end. A blank line separates the end of this prayer from the prayers for the Sabbath.

Line 4. The apparent plural form may indicate that the section for the Sabbath included more than one prayer, or multiple stanzas (perhaps seven). Compare the title and opening line to Ps 92:2 (EVV 92:1), another Sabbath hymn. Unlike the weekday prayers, the Sabbath prayers in the "Words of the Luminaries" and other Qumran texts avoid petitionary prayer. Rabbinic tradition discourages petitionary prayer on the Sabbath (e.g., *m. Ta'an.* 3.7; *y Šabb.* 15.15b).

Line 6. Angels and heavenly firmaments also figure frequently in the *Songs of the Sabbath Sacrifice;* compare Songs XI 4Q405 19:3; XII 4Q405 20ii-21-22:8-9; XII 23i:6-8.

Lines 7-8. Compare 1QH[a] xi:31-33; 4Q286 5:9-12. The phrase "great abyss" is found in the HB in Gen 7:11 (cf. 4Q252 1i:5); Isa 51:10; Amos 7:4; Ps 36:7; and in the QL in 1QH[a] xi:31-32. (The two words come in reverse order in the Hebrew phrase.) For the word "destruction," see the commentary to 4Q286 7ii:7. The end of the line is restored on the basis of Neh 9:6.

Line 9. I follow Baillet's restoration here, which assumes that the prayer ended with a double amen, although this may not be the case for the Sabbath prayers.

Line 10. Compare Ps 81:2 (EVV 81:1).

4Q504 1-2vii verso

Another(?) Sabbath prayer[a]

[1][. . .] willing ones [2][. . .] they shall exalt [3][. . .].. glory [4][. . .] since all [5][. . .]and He created [6][the . . .]... .. .. [7][. . .]. .. .. their holiness [8][. . .]. His holiness and He lifted up [9][. . .]His covenant and He sat [10][. . .]. their psalms

Note

ᵃApparently the scribe ran out of room on the scroll and had to turn it over and finish copying the work on the back. It is unclear whether the text continued beyond line 10.

Commentary

Line 1. This word can either mean "willing" (e.g., 2 Chron 29:31; 1QM x:5) or function as a leadership title, roughly "noble" (e.g., 1 Sam 2:8). Those entering the Community are called "willing ones" in 1QS i:7, 11.

Line 8. The Hebrew word translated "He lifted up" could also be translated "He forgave" (cf. frags. 7:13; 1-2ii recto 7).

Line 9. The verb could also be translated "and He returned."

Purification Liturgies

(4Q512, 4Q414)

INTRODUCTION

Ritual boundaries have always been exceedingly important in Judaism (see the general introduction to this volume for a discussion of the concept of ritual purity). The Hebrew Bible, especially the books of Exodus through Deuteronomy, presents these boundaries as mandates from God, and they have been commented on from the time of their composition to the present. Indeed, much of the biblical material itself is essentially commentary and adaptation of earlier biblical and prebiblical traditions. The text of the "Purification Liturgies" is an early but regrettably fragmentary part of this stream of commentary and adaptation of the biblical rules for ritual purification.

I. Contents

This document is a collection of liturgies and instructions for rituals used to purify people from ceremonial uncleanness. Although the concern with ritual purification is clear, most of the surviving text is too badly damaged for us to determine exactly which rituals were involved. Fragments 1-3 dealt with the use of the ashes of the red heifer for purification from corpse defilement (cf. Numbers 19), and frags. 29-30 with holocaust offerings associated with purification rites (cf. Lev 12:6, 8; 14:22, 31; 15:15, 30; Num 6:11). These two passages may have originally formed a single column. There is also a brief summary of the liturgical occasions requiring ritual purity in frags. 33 + 35. Other fragments refer to ritual ablutions and purification from unclean bodily discharges. The most notable element of this text is the inclusion of liturgies to be recited during the rituals and sacrifices, something almost entirely absent from the corresponding biblical texts.

II. The Manuscripts

4Q512 is a rare example of an "opisthograph," a manuscript with writing on both sides. The other side contains 4Q503, "Daily Prayers." The papyrus manuscript is written in a scribal hand that can be dated to the first part of the first century BCE, and it is preserved in approximately 225 fragments, most of them tiny. Very little of the text survives. Thanks to the better-preserved and highly formulaic text of 4Q503, the order of many of the fragments of 4Q512 can be determined. Sometimes the two documents help reconstruct one another. For more details, see the appendix to this chapter and the introduction to 4Q503.

4Q414 is also an opisthograph (the verso contains 4Q415 or 4QInstruction[a]). This parchment manuscript is written in a Herodian hand and survives in thirty-six mostly small fragments. Nevertheless, it preserves some interesting material and sometimes aids the reconstruction of 4Q512, even though the two manuscripts may not preserve identical recensions of the work.

III. Genres and Structure

The poor condition of both manuscripts prevents a thorough analysis of the genres and structures in the work. The surviving material consists mostly of instructions for carrying out rituals and the texts of liturgical recitals to go with these rituals. The ritual instructions are generally brief, functioning mainly as rubrics for the recitals. The recitals are often introduced by the phrase "he shall bless and he answers and says, Blessed are You, God of Israel." They seem usually to be recited by the person being purified rather than the officiating priest. The prayers ask God for mercy and purification, sometimes mention details of the ritual in passing, and sometimes condemn sinners. The biblical penitential psalms (e.g., Psalm 51; Ezra 9; Nehemiah 9) provide some literary parallels.

IV. Life Situation

Leviticus gives no instructions for music or texts of prayers to be recited during the rituals and sacrifices it describes (although it mentions the formal confession of sins in 5:5), and such material is rare in Numbers (cf. Num 5:19-22; 6:23-27). Yet music and prayer were central elements in the temple traditions of the ancient Near East, and the Chronicler refers to their use in the Jerusalem temple (e.g., 1 Chronicles 25; 2 Chron 5:11-13; 7:6). 4Q512 has a reference to the sanctuary in a fragmentary context in 56:1 (not translated here), and it is possible that this document preserves liturgical material that was actually used in the temple during the Second Temple period. The content is not overtly sectarian, although 33 + 35:1-3 may allude to the solar calendar (see the general introduction to this volume).

V. Literary Context

The main inspiration for this work is the ritual prescriptions for purification in the Hebrew Bible, especially those in Leviticus and Numbers. There is some evidence for exegesis of these prescriptions: the terminology of 1-3:1-12 is somewhat different from Numbers 19, on which it is based, and the "Purification Liturgies" seems to add an additional ablution on the third day of the ritual, one that may be implied in the biblical text but is not made explicit. The same ablution is attested in the *Temple Scroll* (11Q19 xlix:18). Overall, however, the text of the "Purification Liturgies" is too fragmentary for its exegesis to be recovered. The *Damascus Document*, 4QMMT, and the *Temple Scroll* are concerned with many of the same issues alluded to in the "Purification Liturgies," as are some other fragmentary Qumran texts such as 4Q274-79 and 4Q513-14. Later rabbinic texts also show sustained interest in problems regarding ritual purity. The earliest rabbinic treatments of these matters can be found primarily in the Mishnaic tractates *Nega'im, Para, Niddah,* and *Zabim.*

BIBLIOGRAPHY

Baillet, Maurice. "512. Rituel de purification." In *Qumrân Grotte 4 III (4Q482-4Q520),* 262-86, plates xxxvi, xxxviii, xl, xlii, xliv, xlvi, xlviii. DJD 7. Oxford: Clarendon, 1982. References in the notes and commentary to Baillet, with no other information, are to the relevant places in this work.

Baumgarten, Joseph M. "The Purification Rituals in DJD 7." In *The Dead Sea*

Scrolls: Forty Years of Research, edited by Devorah Dimant and Uriel Rappaport, 199-209. STDJ 10. Leiden: Brill, 1992.

————. "The Laws about Fluxes in 4QTohora^a (4Q274)." In *Time to Prepare the Way in the Wilderness: Papers on the Qumran Scrolls,* edited by Devorah Dimant and Lawrence H. Schiffman, 1-8. STDJ 16. Leiden: Brill, 1995.

————. "The Purification Liturgies." In *The Dead Sea Scrolls after Fifty Years: A Comprehensive Assessment,* edited by Peter W. Flint and James C. VanderKam, vol. 2, 200-212. Leiden: Brill, 1999.

Eshel, Esther. "4Q414 Fragment 2: Purification of a Corpse-Contaminated Person." In *Legal Texts and Legal Issues,* edited by M. Bernstein et al., 3-10. Leiden: Brill, 1997.

————. "4Q414. 4QRitual of Purification A." Forthcoming in *Qumran Cave 4: Halakhic Texts,* edited by Joseph M. Baumgarten, 135-53, plates xi-xii. DJD 25. Oxford: Clarendon, 1999. I am grateful to Dr. Eshel for making this chapter available to me before its publication.

Levine, Baruch A. *The JPS Torah Commentary: Leviticus.* Philadelphia and Jerusalem: Jewish Publication Society, 1989.

Milgrom, Jacob. *The JPS Torah Commentary: Numbers.* Philadelphia and Jerusalem: Jewish Publication Society, 1990.

————. "4QTOHORA^a: An Unpublished Qumran Text on Purities." In *Time to Prepare the Way in the Wilderness: Papers on the Qumran Scrolls,* edited by Devorah Dimant and Lawrence H. Schiffman, 59-68. STDJ 16. Leiden: Brill, 1995.

Schiffman, Lawrence H. *Reclaiming the Dead Sea Scrolls: The History of Judaism, the Background of Christianity, the Lost Library of Qumran,* esp. Part IV, "To Live as a Jew," 243-312. Philadelphia and Jerusalem: Jewish Publication Society, 1994.

PURIFICATION LITURGIES

(4Q512, 4Q414)

I. 4Q512

4Q512 39i

An unidentified passage[a]

¹[. . .].. ²[. . .]after

BOTTOM MARGIN

Note
[a]This fragment probably preserves parts of the first two columns of this work.

4Q512 39ii

A fragment of a purification liturgy

¹atoneme[nts[a] and] I will psalm [Your] n[ame[b] . . .] ²for You have pu[ri]fied me and You will bring me into [. . .]

Notes
[a]The plural of the abstract noun is found in the HB (Exod 29:36; 30:10, 16; Lev 23:27, 28; Num 29:11) and also in the QL (e.g., 1QS iii:4; 1QpHab xi:7).
[b]Compare 4Q414 2-4ii:10; Sir 51:11; 1QH[a] xx:3; 11QPs[a] xix:8.

Commentary

Line 1. The Hebrew root √כפר *(KPR)*, translated "to atone" (best known from Yom Kippur, the Day of Atonement), has the basic meaning "to cover over." In Gen 6:14 it is used in the Qal (basic) stem, referring to the covering of Noah's ark with pitch. Normally, however, it appears in the Piel stem with the meaning "to cover over, atone." In the Jewish ritual system, sacrifices were offered to atone for moral failings, ritual defilements, and inadvertent sins. All three categories are alluded to in this document.

4Q512 37-38

A fragment of a ritual and liturgy[a]

[1][. . .] his clothes and [. . .] [2][. . .].. all tongues of [. . .] [3][. . .]. to You councils of me[n . . .] [4][. . .] BLANK [. . .]

A fragment of a liturgy?

[5][. . .].[. . .] [6][. . .]. you from all nake[dness of[b] . . .]

BOTTOM MARGIN

Notes

[a]For my reasons for not associating frag. 36 with frags. 37-38, see note a-a to frag. 36 and note a to 4Q503 36.

[b]ערו[ת] Baillet's reading is plausible but not certain. One could also read, for example, ערי, "cities of."

Commentary

Line 1. Probably a reference to the washing of the clothes as part of a purification ritual (cf., e.g., Lev 11:25; 13:6; 14:8, 9; 15:5; Num 19:7; 4Q272 1ii:6; 11Q19 xlv:8, 9, 15; xlix:17, 20; l:8, 13-15; li:3, 5). However, it is also conceivable that the subject of this passage is a priestly installation, which involves a special set of clothing (see Exod 28:40-43; Lev 8:2, 30).

Line 2. The phrase "all tongues" (i.e., languages) appears in Zech 8:23, but there is no way of knowing if the context in this fragment is similar. The image of angelic tongues giving praise to God figures frequently in the *Songs of the Sabbath Sacrifice*, especially in Songs VI and VIII. However, compare also CD xiv:10 and the commentary to line 3 below.

Line 3. The phrase "council of men" is also found in CD xiv:10.

Line 6. Note the reference in Exod 28:42 to covering the nakedness of the priests with sacred garments. The "you" here does not seem to refer to God. Although usually the recitations are apparently meant to be spoken by the person being purified, this one may have been recited by the officiating priest address-ing the purificant.

4Q512 33 + 35

Occasions requiring ritual purity

¹[. . .] and for the festival of the Sabbath, in the S[abbath]s for all the weeks of ²[. . .]festiv[al . . .]four festivals of[a] ³[. . .] festival of ha[rve]st <and summer fruit> and the beg[inning of mo]nth 1[b] ⁴[. . .] BLANK [. . .] BLANK [. . .] BLANK[c]

A sanctification ritual and liturgy

⁵[. . .]with water[. . .]to sanctify oneself ⁶[. . . w]ho shall [bless and he answers] and says, Blessed are You, ⁷[. . .] for [Your] merci[es . . .] Your [. . .] ⁸[. . .]... and .[. . .].. ⁹[. . .]... in defile[ment . . .] ¹⁰[. . .]. pure[. . .] ¹¹[. . .]...[. . .]

Notes

[a]Perhaps restore "memorial" (זכרון) as suggested by Baillet, on the basis of *Jub.* 6:23.

[b]The letter א may represent the numeral 1 here, as it does in the later system that expresses numerals with Hebrew letters.

[c]Line 4 seems to have been completely blank. Evidently it separates two units of text in the work.

Commentary

Line 1. The Sabbath is called a "festival" or "appointed time" in Lev 23:2-3. The reference to "weeks" may have to do with reckoning the seasons of the year.

Lines 2-3. The "four festivals" mentioned in these lines may be the open-ing days of the four seasons in the sectarian solar calendar (cf. *Jub.* 6:23-31), the first day of the first, fourth, seventh, and tenth months, respectively. For the major festivals in the biblical period, see the general introduction.

Line 3. Compare "the festival of harvest to summer fruit" mentioned in 1QS x:7.

Lines 5-11. A new unit that appears to be a liturgy for ritual purification.

Line 5. The words "with water" and "to sanctify oneself" appear in 1QS iii:9, a passage that speaks of the sanctification of sect members through ritual purification.

4Q512 31-32

A fragment of a liturgy involving righteousness and judgment

¹[. . .]..[ ].[. . .] ²[. . .]. and..[. . .] ³[. . .] my sin .[. . .] ⁴[. . .]. righteousness and [. . .] ⁵[. . .] You leave unpunished until judgment[. . . I]srael wh[o . . .]

The beginning of a benediction

⁶[. . . Blessed are Y]ou, God of Is[rael . . .]for a[t]onement[. . .] ⁷[. . .]...[. . .]

Commentary

Line 5. The verb "to acquit, find innocent" can also mean "to leave unpunished" (Exod 20:7 // Deut 5:11; 1 Kgs 2:9; Jer 30:11 // 46:28). Such a meaning fits with the following phrase, "until judgment." Compare "until the appointed time of judgment" in 1QS iv:19-20.

4Q512 29-30

A benediction associated with purification[a]

¹[. . .B]l[e]s[s]ed [are] Y[ou, God of Israel . . .] ²[. . .] hol[y] people[. . .] ³[. . .].[. . .] error[b] [. . .] ⁴[. . .]water[c] .[. . .]...[. . .]

A benediction associated with purification and the holocaust offering

⁵[. . .] he shall bless [d][His] name[d] [. . .] ⁶[. . .]before You in the fest[ival . . .] ⁷[. . .] You have [. . .] me for purification of[. . .]

Another benediction associated with purification and the holocaust offering

[8][. . .]. and his holocaust offering. He shall bless and he answ[ers] and says, Blessed are You[. . .] [9][. . . al]l my transgressions, and may You purify me from indecency of defilement <and may You atone> for entry [. . .] [10][. . .] pure [. . .]. and the blood of the holocaust offering of Your favor and a sooth[ing] memorial [. . .] [11][. . .] Yo[ur] holy censer[and] Your [soo]t[hi]ng favor[. . .]

Notes

[a]It is possible to assemble frags. 1-3, 14i, 15i, 16i, and 29-30 together in a single column, although this assembly creates some difficulties for the overall reconstruction of the manuscript. See the appendix to this chapter for the proposed reconstruction.

[b]מִשְׁגֶּה This word for "error" is found in the HB only in Gen 43:12 (the normal synonym is שְׁגָגָה) but also in CD iii:5; 1QH[a] x:19; 4Q174 1-2i:9; 4Q184 i:9. Since the present context is lost, the word could also be taken as a Hiphil participle of the root שׁגה√, "to go astray, err" (Deut 27:18; Job 12:16; Prov 28:10), in which case it should be translated "he (or she) who leads astray."

[c]מִים[The translation "[d]ays" (מִים[י]) is also possible.

[d-d]שֻׁמָּ[ו] Baillet suggests that the word שָׁם, which I read as שֻׁמָּ[ו], be taken as the word "there" (cf. Gen 32:30; 2 Chron 20:26; 4Q158 1-2:10; 1QM xiv:3; xix:13). Yet the reading and interpretation adopted here fit the traces better and are also paralleled frequently in the HB and QL (Ps 96:2; 100:4; 145:2, 21; Neh 9:5; 1QS x:13; 1QM xviii:6; 1QH[a] x:30; xix:6; 4Q511 63-64ii:2; 63iv:2).

Commentary

Line 2. The phrase "holy people" is also found in Isa 63:18; Dan 12:7; 1QM xii:1; xiv:12; 4Q171 1, 3-4iii:7-8.

Line 8. Holocaust offerings were offered in purification rites, according to Lev 12:6, 8; 14:22, 31; 15:15, 30; Num 6:11.

Line 9. "Indecency" (literally "nakedness") and "defilement" occur together in the HB with reference to sexual intercourse during a woman's menstrual period (Lev 18:19) and to adultery between a man and his sister-in-law (Lev 20:21). Perhaps the phrase "for entry" refers to the petitioner's hope of being admitted into the sanctuary after purification (cf. Ps 65:3-5 [EVV 65:2-4]). The sanctuary is mentioned in a badly broken passage (not translated here) in frag. 56:3.

Lines 10-11. Compare 1QM ii:5; 11QPs[a] xviii:9. Neither the phrase "soothing memorial" nor "soothing favor" appears in the HB; the word "soothing" is found there only in the phrase "a soothing odor."

Line 10. The phrase "blood of the holocaust offering" is found in 2 Kgs 16:15; 11Q19 xxxii:15; *m. Zebaḥ* 10.2. Holocaust offerings are presented for God's favor (or not) in Lev 22:18-19; Isa 56:7; Jer 6:20.

Line 11. The word "censer" is found only in Ezek 8:11; 2 Chron 26:19; 1QM ii:5.

4Q512 1-3[a]

Instructions for the third day of the ritual for purification from defilement through contact with a corpse

TOP MARGIN

[1]And on the third day [. . . he shall ble]ss and he answers and sa[ys, Blessed are] [2][Yo]u, [God of] Israel [. . . ti]mes to purify oneself fr[om uncleanness][b] [3][. . .]soul with atone[ment . . .]holy ashes [. . .] [4]..[. . .]... with the water of c[lea]n[sing[c]. . .]. [d]on ete[r]n[a]l tablets[d] [. . .] [5]and water of bathing for purification of times[. . .] his [cl]othes. And after [. . .] [6]the waters [of] <spri[nkl]ing> to purify him and all[. . .]

A *liturgy for the ritual*

[7]And a[fter] his [sp]rinkling with water[s of sprinkling he shall bless and he an-swers and says, Blessed are You,] [8] God [of Israe]l, who have given to[. . .] [9]and from defilement of impurity. And today [. . .] [10]defilement to sanctify oneself for You and [. . .] [11][. . .]defilement and he is not abl[e to . . .] [12][. . .]the prime-val ones .[. . .]

Notes

[a]The reasons for placing frags. 1-3 together at this point in the manuscript are ex-plained in note a to 4Q503 1-3, but they also make good sense together on this side of the manuscript. For the possible reconstruction of a column consisting of frags. 1-3, 14i, 15i, 16i, and 29-30, see the appendix to the present chapter.

[b][טמאת]מָ Restored on the basis of 4Q414 2-4ii:4 (cf. Lev 14:19).

[c][י]דֹוֹכֹ The reading is very doubtful, but it is supported by the phrase במי דוכי, "with waters of cleansing," in 1QS iii:9. I take this word, translated "cleansing," to come from the Aramaic root √דכי, "to be clean," but note also the Hebrew word דכי, which occurs only in Ps 93:3 and which seems to mean something like "splashing"; perhaps the phrase should be translated "with waters of splashing."

[d-d]עֹוֹלֹם בלוחות Baumgarten ("Purification Rituals," 207) proposes to read בליחות עולם, "in perennial streams" (cf. *m. Para* 8.9; *Sib. Or.* 4:165). See the commentary for other interpretations.

Commentary

Lines 1-12. These lines pertain to the use of the ashes of the red heifer, which are made in a special ritual and then mixed with water for a purification solution (Numbers 19; 4Q269 8ii:3-6 // 4Q271 2:10-13; 4Q276-77; 4QMMT B 13-16; *m. Para*).

Line 1. The person who acquired impurity by touching a corpse had to be purified by having a ceremonially pure person sprinkle him on the third and seventh day with water mixed with the ashes of the red heifer. This line appears to mention the purification of the third day (see Num 19:12, 19; 11Q19 xlix:18), along with a blessing uttered by the purificant (the blessing is not mentioned in the biblical text).

Line 3. The word "soul, being" is used in Num 19:11, which says that anyone who touches "the dead (body) of any human being" shall be unclean for seven days. A similar reference is possible here but does not obviously fit the immediate context, and many other interpretations are possible. Baillet tentatively suggests reconstructing the end of line 2 and the beginning of line 3 "to purify oneself o[f defilement of the flesh and the] soul," offering Deut 12:23, Isa 10:18; 2 Macc 7:37; 14:38; 15:30; Matt 10:28; 1 Thess 5:23 as parallels. However, this interpretation seems to invest the word "soul" with a Hellenistic sense foreign to the Hebrew word. The "holy ashes" are the ashes of the red heifer (see Num 19:9, 10; Heb 9:13).

Line 4. Compare "water of c[lea]n[sing]" with "water of pur[ity]" in 11Q19 1 2, a passage that also deals with purification from corpse defilement. According to Num 19:19, the recipient of purification washes his clothes on the seventh day after being sprinkled. The one who gathers the ashes of the red heifer must also wash his clothes afterward (Num 19:10). However, according to 11Q19 xlix:17-20, one who enters a house contaminated with corpse impurity must be sprinkled with the "water for defilement" (see the commentary to line 6 below) on the third day and bathe and wash his clothes, then repeat the procedure on the seventh day. This passage in 4Q512 seems to have the same more thorough arrangement. (In the *Temple Scroll*, the purificant must also bathe and wash his clothes on the first day. See the commentary to 4Q414 2ii-4:2 for evidence that this procedure may also have been prescribed in the "Purification Liturgies.")

The "eternal tablets" may correspond to the "eternal law" of the red heifer ritual (see Num 19:10, 21), although heavenly tablets are also sometimes mentioned in nonbiblical texts (e.g., *1 Enoch* 106:19; *Jub.* 6:17).

Line 5. The phrase "water of bathing" may imply that the purificant underwent a ritual immersion before being sprinkled with the "water of cleansing." Compare the "water of bathing" in frags. 42-44:5; 4Q414 13:7.

Line 6. The "waters of sprinkling" correspond to the "water for defilement" in Num 19:9, 13, 21 (cf. on lines 9-10, below in the appendix). The corresponding phrase in the Mishnah (especially tractate *Para*) is "waters of the sin offering" (cf. Num 8:7). The verb "to sprinkle" is used, for example, in Num 19:4, 18, 19, 21; 4QMMT B 14, 16; 11Q19 xlix:18, 20; l:3, 14, 15. The noun "sprinkling" is found in RH (Jastrow, 341b) but never in BH.

Line 9. The phrase "her defilement of impurity" occurs in Lev 18:19, with reference to menstrual impurity.

Line 12. For "the primeval ones," see the commentary to frag. 23:2.

4Q512 10

TOP MARGIN

¹[. . . ªfro]m his unclean dischargeª [. . .] ²[. . .].[. . .]

Note

ª⁻ªReading מֹזוב, although the identification of the first letter is in serious doubt. Compare Lev 15:30, which has the same phrase referring to a woman (מזוב טמאתה).

Commentary

Line 1. The rules regarding a man or woman with various kinds of discharges are given in Leviticus 15 (cf. 4Q266 6i:14-16; 6ii:1-4 // 4Q272 1ii:3-18; 4Q274; 4Q277 1:1-13; 11Q19 xlv:15-17; xlvi:18; xlviii:15; *m. Zabim*).

4Q512 11

A purification ritual

¹[. . .]...[. . .] ²[. . .]. for him the seven days of [his] pur[ification . . .] ³[. . .]he washes his clothes ªwith w[ater and bathesª . . .] ⁴ᵇand he puts on his clothesᵇ ᶜand kneels o[n his kneesᶜ . . .

The beginning of a liturgy for the ritual

And he answers and says, Blessed are You,] ⁵God of Isr[ae]l [. . .]

278

Notes

a-a[ורחץ במ]מֹים Restoring on the basis of Lev 15:5 and passim; 17:15; Num 19:19. Baillet adds [את בשרו], ["his flesh"], based on Num 19:8 and Lev 14:9; 16:26, 28; Num 19:7.

b-bוכסה את בגדיו Literally, "he covers his clothes" — an unusual expression paralleled only by Jonah 3:6: ויכס שק, "and he put on sackcloth."

c-cוברך ע]ל ברכיו] Restored with Baillet on the basis of 2 Chron 6:13.

Commentary

Line 2. Compare Lev 12:2; 15:13, 19, 24, 28; 19:11-12, 14, 16, 19; 4Q274 1i:4-6?; 11Q19 xlv:15; l:13-15. The purificant is a man. His seven-day purification period might be the result of a discharge of his own or exposure to a discharge of someone else, to menstrual impurity, to birth impurity (of a male child), or to corpse impurity.

These passages refer to seven-day purification periods for discharges, exposure to menstrual impurity, and exposure to corpse impurity.

Line 3. Compare Lev 15:13, 21-22, 27; 11Q19 xlv:8, xlix:17; l:8, 13; li:3, 5, 14-15.

Line 4. This line seems to direct the purified man to offer a blessing recited on his knees, a detail missing in Leviticus 15.

Line 5. Compare Ps 41:14; 106:48; 4Q503 4-6:7, etc.

4Q512 7-9

*Instructions for the purification of a man
who recovers from a discharge*

TOP MARGIN

¹all the w[ords . . .] ²when he is purified from [his] dis[charge^a . . . pu]rification of Is[rael . . .] ³to eat and to d[rink . . . cit]ies of [their] residence[s . . .] ⁴to be with [his wife^b . . .] BLANK [. . .] ⁵[. . .] BLANK [. . .] whi[ch . . .]

Notes

a[ומז]מ Restored plausibly with Baillet on the basis of Lev 15:13, 28.

bFollowing Baumgarten's restoration ("Purification Rituals," 202) rather than reading "to be with [a holy] people," with Baillet.

Commentary

Lines 3-4. Compare 4Q414 7:8-9.

Line 3. Baillet notes that "to eat and to drink" is a common word pair (2 Sam 11:11; 1 Kgs 18:42; Jer 16:8; Job 1:4; Ruth 3:3; Eccles 5:17; 8:15; Neh 8:12). Eating and drinking are also mentioned in the context of ritual purity in 4Q514 7:8.

The expression "city of residence" is found in Ps 107:4, 7, 36. Baillet suggests that the sense of the line might have been related to Lev 7:26, which orders the Israelites not to consume blood in any of their residences. However, the passage seems to deal with purification rites for discharges, not dietary laws, so perhaps this line was part of an admonition to keep ritual uncleanness under control in the cities of Israel (cf. Lev 15:31).

Line 4. Presumably indicates that once the man is purified from his discharge, he is free to resume sexual relations with his wife.

4Q512 4-6

A fragment of a liturgy regarding atonement and defilement[a]

[1][. . .]...[. . .] [2][. . . e]tern[al . . .] because [3][. . . the da]ys of Your glory[b] [4]and ..[. . .] their guilt and concerning [their] s[in] [5]all .[. . .]... .[. . .]. and You will sanctify him [. . .] [6]atonement[s of] Yo[ur] favor [. . .] their [. . .].. and You shall abominate them for .[. . .] [7][. . .]. ..[. . .] their works and [. . .] [8][. . .] with a stroke of defilement so as to be separated [. . .] [9][. . .]. isolated[c] [. . .]

BOTTOM MARGIN

Notes

[a]Baillet associates frags. 1-3 with frags. 4-6, and they do seem to make sense in this context, but the reconstruction on the obverse (4Q503) and the overall physical evidence show that they do not belong here.

[b]The phrase "the days of Your glory" is reconstructed on the basis of similar but not identical expressions in CD iii:14-15 (cf. 4Q503 4-6:4); 1QM xiii:8; and 1QH[a] xx:22. In a private communication, Martin Abegg has suggested to me the reconstruction [רח]מי כבודכה, "Your glorious [merc]ies," on the basis of Songs VIII 4Q405 13:2.

[c]מנודדה appears to be a Pual participle of the root √נדה, "to retreat, depart." The Pual stem for this root is unattested in BH, but this form is used in RH to mean some-

one such as a mourner who is excommunicated or isolated because of cultic impurity (e.g., *m. Mid.* 2.2; *m. Neg.* 14.2; cf. Jastrow, 878b).

Commentary

Lines 1-9. A difficult fragment whose general drift seems to concern God's gracious atonement for sinful actions and his condemnation of the wicked in Israel. The surviving text mentions no specific sins, but ritual defilement figures in lines 8-9.

Line 6. The ideas of God's favor and atonement are found together in Lev 1:3-4. Part of the same phrase seems to survive in 4Q414 8:4 (not translated here). Note also the similar phrase "atonements of favor" in 4Q513 13:2. Songs I 4Q400 1i:16 asserts that the angelic priests "propitiate His favor" on behalf of all who repent of transgression.

The words "to abominate" or "abomination" are used in the HB chiefly of acts that violate cultural taboos, such as male homosexuality (Lev 18:22), worship of idols (Deut 7:25), and forbidden eating customs (Gen 43:32; Deut 14:3), although the verb can have a somewhat broader meaning, roughly the same as "to abhor" in English (e.g., Amos 5:10; Ps 5:7 [EVV 5:6]; 106:40; 107:18; 119:163).

Line 8. For separation of the wicked Israelite from the people, compare Num 16:21; Deut 29:20 (EVV 29:21). The phrase "stroke of defilement" is also found in frag. 34:5.

Unplaced Fragments

4Q512 14i, 15i, 16i[a]

Frag. 14i

An unidentified fragment

[1][. . .]...[b]

Notes

[a]Fragments 13-16 each overlap two columns (no text of the first column survives on frag. 13), and it is likely although not certain that they belong together. Fragments

15 and 16 seem nearly to connect to one another. For a possible reconstruction of a column containing frags. 1-3, 14i, 15i, 16i, and 29-30, see the appendix to this chapter.
[b]No translatable text survives on this fragment.

Frag. 15i

A fragment of a ritual

[1][. . .]. iniquity of guilt [2][. . .]in the waters of [3][. . .] and he bathes [4][. . .] to him in three [5][. . .].[. . .]

Frag. 16i

A fragment of a liturgy

[1][. . .] all [2][. . . righte]ous to fill [3][. . .]. [4][. . .] the pure [. . .].. [5][. . .] iniquity [6][. . . he bles]ses the name of [7][. . .] I have [pu]rified [8][. . .].. And after [9][. . .].[. . .]

4Q512 13, 14ii, 15ii

Frag. 13

An unidentified fragment

TOP MARGIN

[1].[. . .]

Frag. 14ii

A fragment of a ritual?

[1]female[. . .] [2]by His favor[. . .] [3]truth .[. . .]

Commentary

Line 1. Compare 4Q414 7:11. On the basis of the word "female" (cf. Lev 15:33), Baillet suggests that this section dealt with sexual purifications corresponding to those in Leviticus 15. Yet other contexts are possible; see, for example, Lev 3:1; 4:28; 12:5, 7.

Frag. 15ii

The end of a liturgy?

¹righteousness [. . .]

The beginning of a ritual?

²And after [. . .] ³pure[. . .]

4Q512 17

A fragment mentioning "festivals of peace"ᵃ

¹[. . .]... ..[. . .] ²[. . . fes]tivals of pea[ce . . .] ³[. . .].. to you .[. . .]

Note
ᵃBaillet places this fragment in the vicinity of frags. 13-16, based on the content of its other side (4Q503).

Commentary

Line 2. Compare "o[ur] festival of peace" in 4Q509 3:2.

4Q512 18

A fragment about mourning rites for the dead?

¹[. . .]... [. . .] ²[. . .] his [clot]hing and he cov[ers his lip . . .] ³[. . .]with happiness[. . .]

Commentary

Line 2. The surviving text of this line resembles Lev 13:45, which describes the steps a leper is required to take to warn others of his unclean state. However, the reference to "happiness" in line 3 does not seem to fit such a context. It is more likely that this fragment refers to mourning rites for the dead, which included the rending of one's clothing (e.g., Lev 10:6; 1 Sam 4:12; 2 Sam 1:11; Job 1:20) and the covering of the lip (Ezek 24:17, 22) and were ceremonially defiling (Lev 21:1-5).

Line 3. It is difficult to see how happiness fits in with either scenario just proposed. Perhaps the line alludes to the putting aside of joy and happiness for mourning. Compare Jer 48:33, 37-38; Joel 1:13, 16; Eccles 3:4.

4Q512 21-28ᵃ

These may have formed a single column

4Q512 21-22

A ritual fragment?

TOP MARGIN

¹[. . .].. ᵇand setting his [ha]nd toᵇ .[. . .] ²[. . .]ᶜin [his] fulfill[ment ofᶜ . . .]

Notes

ᵃFor possible placement of some or all of frags. 21-28, see note a to 4Q503 21-22 and note a to 4Q503 24-25.

ᵇ⁻ᵇThe phrase "and setting his hand to" includes a rare independent use of the infinitive absolute (נתון), perhaps prescribing an action as in Isa 58:6. Baillet notes that this phrase is used of committing oneself to an agreement (rather like the idiom "to shake hands on it" in English) in 2 Kgs 10:15; Ezek 17:18; Ezra 10:19; 2 Chron 30:8.

ᶜ⁻ᶜ[לו ת[במילא] Baillet proposes this reconstruction here and in frags. 11:2; 27:1, based on the use of the same phrase in 1QS vi:18, 21b (cf. the similar phrases in 1QS vi:17, 21a; viii:26). It is uncertain in all of the places he reconstructs it.

Commentary

Line 2. Baillet suggests that the phrase ["the seven days of his purification"] may have followed (cf. 11:2). This is the period of isolation imposed on a person being examined for leprosy (Lev 13:4-6, 21, 26-27, 31-34; 4Q266 6i:4, 10-11; 4Q272 1i:6-7). The reconstruction is reasonably likely if one grants the proposed reading on the papyrus of this line.

4Q512 23

A liturgical fragment?

[1][. . .]...[. . .] [2][. . . the iniq]uities of the primeval [ones . . .] [3][. . .]...[. . .]

Commentary

The phrase "the iniquities of the primeval ones" is also found in 4Q504 4:6 and Ps 79:8, both times in the context of a plea that God not remember the sins of Israel's forefathers. The term "primeval ones" (literally, "the first ones") also occurs in Lev 26:45; Deut 19:14.

4Q512 24-25

A fragment of a liturgy

[1][. . .] Your [. . .]. [. . .] [2][. . .] their [. . .]... for abundance[a] ..[ ].[. . .] [3][. . .]. Your name with happiness[. . .]

The beginning of instructions for a ritual

[4][. . .]. And after th[ese] thin[g]s [. . .] [5][. . .].[. . .] ..[. . .]in his hair[. . .]

Note

[a] לרוב The reading לריב, "to dispute" or "as a dispute," is also possible.

Commentary

Lines 1-3. The surviving material seems to be part of a liturgy of praise or thanksgiving.

Line 3. Compare 1QM xiv:4. The phrase clearly addresses God.

Line 5. Assuming the reading and interpretation of this word is correct, Baillet may be right in associating it with the priestly examination of the hair of potential victims of skin disease in Leviticus 13 (or the rules for their purification in Lev 14:1-9). One could also read the word as "in its gate" or "in the gates of," in which case it may refer to daily units of sunlight, as in 4Q503.

4Q512 27

A ritual fragment[a]

[1][...and i]n [his] [fu]l[f]i[l]l[m]ent of[b][...] [2][... [c]he shall bathe] his flesh and he pu[ts on his clothes[c] ...] [3][... and he stan]ds[d] at [his] station [...] [4][...]...[...] [5][...]..[...]

Notes

[a]Fragment 26 does not contain any translatable text.

[b]For this restoration, see note c-c to frags. 21-22.

[c-c]See the notes and commentary to frags. 11:2-3 for parallels and discussion.

[d]וֹ[עמד] Following Baillet's restoration on the basis of Dan 8:18; 10:11; Neh 13:11; 2 Chron 30:16; 34:31; 35:10.

Commentary

Line 2. The reference to "his flesh" offers some support to Baillet's idea that this column covered the rules concerning skin diseases in Leviticus 13–14, although the indicators are far from compelling.

4Q512 28

A liturgical fragment

¹[. . .].. ...ᵃ[. . .] ²[. . . my] tongue confesses [. . .] ³[. . .]. before You .[. . .]
⁴[. . .]my sin offeringᵇ ..[. . .] ⁵[. . .]to show oneself[. . .]

Notes
ᵃBaillet reads and restores [עבֿדכה]נ֗י עבֿ[א], "I, Your se[rvant]," but I see what looks like a *yod* or a *waw* before the *'ayin* in the photograph and read]נ֗י ועבֿ[. I cannot suggest a translation, although the second word is likely to be a form of the root √עבד, "to serve," or the root √עבר, "to cross, transgress."

ᵇOr "his sin offering."

Commentary

Line 2. The word translated "confesses" (מודה) could also be translated "gives thanks."

Line 4. Compare Lev 14:19, 22, 31.

Line 5. The infinitive "to show oneself" or "to be seen" may be a reference to the requirement that one afflicted by or cured of a skin disease must be shown to the priest for evaluation (Lev 13:7, 14, 19, 57; 14:35; cf. Mark 1:43-44 and parallels).

4Q512 34

A liturgy of supplication?ᵃ

¹[. . .]..[. . .].[. . .] ²[. . .]midst of His people [. . .] ³[. . . I] ask favorᵇ concerning all the secret th[ing]s of gui[ltᶜ . . .] ⁴[. . .]. the Righteous One in all Yo[ur] wo[rks . . .] ⁵[. . .].. from the stroke of defilement [. . .].. [b]e[ca]u[s]e[. . .]

BOTTOM MARGIN

Notes
ᵃSee note b to 4Q503 34 for a discussion of the problems with placing this fragment.

ᵇתֿחנך[א] I follow the reconstruction suggested by Baillet. This imperfect form of the verb "to be gracious" (√חנן) does not seem to be in the Qal stem, since it would

take a direct object, not a preposition. Only the Hitpaël is attested with the preposition
עַל, "concerning" (Esther 4:8; 1QHᵃ iv:18).

ᶜ[ה]מֹשֶׁא Alternative reconstructions are [תי]מֹשֶׁא, "my guilt," or אֲשֶׁר, "which."

Commentary

Line 2. Perhaps a reference to the presence or holiness of God in the "midst of His people" (cf. Exod 25:8; Lev 22:32; Ezek 39:7).

Line 3. For sins committed unwittingly, see Lev 4:27-28; 5:17-19; Ps 19:13.

Line 4. For similar phrases couched in the third person singular, see Dan 9:14; Bar 2:9.

Line 5. Compare frags. 4-6:8; 11QPsᵃ xxiv:13.

4Q512 36

¹[. . .]...[. . .] ²[. . .] ᵃour [fl]esh toᵃ .[. . .]

BOTTOM MARGIN

Note
ᵃ⁻ᵃAlthough the text of line 2 is a plausible continuation of 4Q512 38:2, a fragment that is also followed by a bottom margin and is physically similar to frag. 36, the text on the recto of frag. 36 precludes it from belonging to the same assemblage; see note a to 4Q503 36. The reference to "flesh" might link it to frags. 21-28.

4Q512 40-41 + 4Q414 27-28

The end of a ritual fragment?ᵃ

TOP MARGIN

¹[. . .]...[. . . which becomes] impure in him.

A liturgical fragment

²[and it sh]all be when a <[ma]n or woman> arrives [. . . and he shall bless] and he answers and says, ³[Ble]ssed <are You,> God of Isr[ael . . . You dist]inguish

for us between ⁴the impure and the pure[. . .].. to You ⁵[with] a purification of righteousness[. . .] and with the favor of ⁶Y[o]u[r goodn]e[ss]ᵇ i[n] r[igh]t[eous]ne[ss . . .] BLANK

The beginning of a new unit?

⁷[. . .].

Notes

ᵃThe overlap of the two manuscripts confirms Baillet's suggestion that 4Q512 40-41 belong in a single assemblage.

ᵇבכה [טו] Or read [ע]מֹכֹֿה, "Y[o]u[r peo]p[le]" (cf. Ps 106:4).

Commentary

Line 2. In the HB the phrase "man or woman" is found in Exod 21:29; Lev 13:29, 38; 20:27; Num 5:6; 6:2; Deut 17:2; 29:17; and in the QL in 11Q19 lv:16. The passages most likely to be connected to the general content of 4Q512 are Lev 13:29, 38 (on diagnosis of skin diseases) and Num 6:2 (on the Nazirite vow).

Lines 3-4. Compare Lev 10:10; 11:47; 20:25; Ezek 22:26; CD vi:17; xii:19-20; 4QMMT B 56-57.

4Q512 42-44ii + 4Q414 2ii-4:5-7ᵃ

The end of a unit

¹. . .

A liturgy of purification

²And after he enters [the water . . . he shall bless and he answers] ³and says, Blessed [are Yo]u, [God of I]s[rael . . . for from the issue of] ⁴Your mouth the purification of everything has been clearly defined [. . . men of defilement according to their guilt.] ⁵They shall [no]t be purified with the water of bathing. And I [to]d[a]y[. . . the ways of Your favor . . .] ⁶[. . .]...[. . .].[ ]...ᵇ hand[s], thenᶜ ..[. . .]

Notes

[a]For additional text before this assemblage, see the parallel assemblage in 4Q414. According to Baillet's reconstruction frags. 45-47 belong under frags. 42-44, with frag. 47 coming from the column that preceded the other fragments. The only certain word in frags. 45-47 is "to Your people" (לעמכה) in 46:1.

[b]רוֹשׁ[ ]° It is likely that this damaged word was a form of the root פרשׁ√, "to spread out" (cf. Isa 1:15; Jer 4:31).

[c]אז Baillet reads this rare word here (cf. Ps 124:3, 4, 5; 11QPs[a] xxviii:13; Mur 42:5), but the reading and its meaning are very uncertain.

Commentary

Line 5. For the "water of bathing," see frags. 1-3:5 and compare 4Q414 13:7.

4Q512 frags. 48-50

The end of a liturgy

[1]...[. . .] [2]and he answers[a][. . .] [3]a hol[y] people [. . .] [4]and who is it who st[ands when he appe]ars[b][. . .]

The beginning of a liturgy that takes place at sunset

[5c]And after [the] sun [sets] today .[. . .].[. . .] [6]when You [took][c] us for Yourself as a people [. . .]. .[. . .] [7][. . .]..[. . .]

Notes

[a]Perhaps restore ["and says, Blessed are You, God of Israel"] or the like (with Baillet).

[b]Following Baillet's restoration on the basis of Mal 3:2.

[c]Following Baillet's restoration on the basis of Exod 6:7.

Commentary

Line 5. Compare Lev 22:7; Deut 23:12.

II. 4Q414

4Q414 1i

An unidentified fragment

¹[. . .].. ²[. . .] fresh [. . .]. ³[. . . BLA]NK? ⁴[. . .]..

Commentary

Line 2. Eshel suggests that this passage dealt with the rule that Nazirites could not eat fresh grapes (Num 6:3). No other biblical passage using this word seems to offer a context that could plausibly fit this document.

4Q414 1ii-2i

A fragment of a liturgy involving purification for a festival

¹[. . . and he shall bless and he answers and] says, Blessed ²[are You, God of Israel . . .] those pure for His festival. ³Your light[. . .] Your [. . .] and to atone for us ⁴by Your favor [. . . to be] pure before You ⁵alw[ay]s[. . .] I have [. . .] in every matter ⁶[. . .]. to purify oneself before ⁷[. . .].[ ] You have made us ⁸[. . .].[. . .]

Commentary

Line 2. A state of ritual purity was required for participation in the festivals (Num 9:6-13; 1 Sam 20:24-26; 1 Chron 30:17-19; John 11:55).
Lines 3-4. Compare 4Q512 4-6:6.

4Q414 2ii-4 + 4Q512 42-44ii^a

A fragment of a liturgy of purification

¹And You will purify us according to [Your] holy laws [. . .] ²for the first, for the third, and for the se[venth . . .] ³by the truth of Yo[ur] covenant [. . .] ⁴to purify oneself from impurity[. . .]

291

A liturgy to follow an immersion

[5]And after he enters the water[. . . he shall bless] [6]and he answers and says, Blessed are Y[ou, God of Israel . . .] [7]for from the issue of Your mouth [the purification of everything] has been [clearly defined . . .] [8]men of defilement according to [their] g[uilt. They shall not be purified with the water of bathing. And I today . . .] [9][the w]ays of [Your] favor [. . . hands, then . . .] [10]I shall psalm Your name .[. . .] [11][. . .].. ..[. . .]

Note

[a]See also the notes and commentary to 4Q512 42-44ii.

Commentary

Line 1. Holy laws are also mentioned in CD xx:30 and 4Q512 64:6.

Line 2. Eshel suggests that this line refers to the more rigorous course of purification known from the *Temple Scroll* and 4Q512 1-3:1-2 (see the commentary to the latter passage). This proposal makes sense, but it is odd that this line speaks of something "for" these days rather than "on" them, as in the other two passages.

Line 3. The phrase "the truth of Your covenant" is also found in 1QH[a] viii:15.

Line 8. Compare the similar phrase "human defilement" in 1QS xi:14-15.

Line 10. Compare 4Q512 39ii:1.

4Q414 7

A fragment of a liturgy

[1]soul ..[. . .] [2]that [. . .] [3]to You for a pu[re] people [. . .] [4]and also I ...[. . .] [5]today which[. . .] [6]in festivals of purity .[. . .] [7]together. BLANK [. . .]

A fragment of a ritual?

[8]With the purification of Israel to e[at and to drink . . .] [9][re]siden[ces . . .] [10]and it shall be on [that] day [. . .] [11]female and the menstru[ant . . .] [12][. . .]. .[. . .]

Commentary

Line 1. See the commentary to 4Q512 1-3:3.

Line 7. The word translated "together" could also be translated "the Community," but without a context the proper translation is uncertain.

Lines 8-9. Compare 4Q512 7-9:3-4.

4Q414 13

A fragment of a liturgy

¹For You have made me .[. . .] ²Your fav[o]r to purify oneself befo[re You . . .] ³and He established for Himself a law of atonement[. . .] ⁴and to be in a purification of rig[hteousness . . .]

Instructions for immersion and sprinkling

⁵And he ba[th]es in water and sprinkles o[n . . .] ⁶[. . .].. And afterward he shall return ..[. . .] ⁷cleansing his people with the waters of bathing[. . .]

A second liturgy in the same ritual

⁸[. . .]. a second time at his station and he an[swers and says, Blessed are You, God of Israel] ⁹[wh]o have pu[rif]ied by Y[our] glory [. . .] ¹⁰eternal [generations. And toda[y . . .]

Commentary

Line 1. Compare the Greek translation of Ps 39:10 (LXX 38:10 [EVV 39:9]), which reads "You are the One who made me."

Line 4. Restored on the basis of 4Q512 40-41:5.

Line 5. Compare 4Q512 27:3.

Line 7. Compare the "water of bathing" in 4Q512 1-3:5; 42-44ii:5.

Line 9. Compare "purification of glory" in 1QS iv:5.

4Q414 27-28

See 4Q512 40-41 above

293

APPENDIX: A PROPOSED RECONSTRUCTION
OF A COLUMN OF 4Q512

4Q512 1-3, 13i, 14i, 15i-16, 29-30[a]

*Instructions for the third day of the ritual for purification
from defilement through contact with a corpse*

TOP MARGIN

[1]And on the third day [. . . he shall ble]ss and he answers and sa[ys, Blessed are]
[2][Yo]u, [God of] Israel [. . . ti]mes to purify oneself fr[om uncleanness]
[3][. . .]soul with atone[ment . . .]holy ashes [. . .] [4]..[. . .]... with the water of
c[lea]n[sing. . .]. on ete[r]n[a]l tablets [. . .] [5]and water of bathing for purification of times[. . .] his [cl]othes. And after [. . .] [6]the waters [of] <spri[nkl]ing>
to purify him and all[. . .]

A liturgy for the ritual

[7]And a[fter] his [sp]rinkling with water[s of sprinkling he shall bless and he answers and says, Blessed are You,] [8]God [of Israe]l, who have given to[. . . fro]m
iniquity of guilt [9]and from defilement of impurity. And today[. . .] by means of
waters for [10]defilement to sanctify oneself for You and [. . .]

More instructions for the ritual

and he bathes [11]. . . defilement and he is not abl[e to . . .]to him in three
[12][days . . .]the primeval ones .[. . .].[. . .] [13][. . .].[. . .] all

A benediction associated with purification

[14][the . . . B]l[e]s[s]ed [are] Y[ou, God of Israel . . . righte]ous to fill
[15][. . .]hol[y] people [. . .].[. . .] [16][. . .].[. . .] error [. . .] the pure [.·.]. [17][. . .]wa-
ter .[. . .]...[. . .]iniquity

*A benediction associated with purification
and the holocaust offering*

[18][. . .]he shall bless [His] name[. . . he bles]ses the name of [19][. . .]before You in
the fest[ival . . .] I have [pu]rified [20][. . .] You have [. . .] me for purification
of[. . .]

294

Another benediction associated with
purification and the holocaust offering

And after [21][his . . .]. and his holocaust offering, he shall bless and he answ[ers] and says, Blessed are You, [God of Israe]l, [who] [22][. . . al]l my transgressions, and may You purify me from indecency of defilement <and may You atone> for entry [. . .] [23].[. . .] pure [. . .]. and the blood of the holocaust offering of Your favor and a sooth[ing] memorial [. . .] [24][. . .] Yo[ur] holy censer [and] Your [soo]t[hi]ng favor[. . .]

Note
[a]The proposed assemblage produces a text that offers good sense throughout, a fact that argues strongly in its favor. It also produces a column on the recto (4Q503) that seems overly long given the physical parameters that govern the reconstruction of that text. See note a to 4Q503 1-3 for additional discussion. Baillet also assigns lines 19 and 20 to this column. Fragment 19 has the end of a line with the word "he bathes" or "bathing," and line 20 ends a line with some indecipherable letters. For additional notes and commentary, see the separate fragments covered earlier in this chapter.

Commentary

Line 8. The phrase "iniquity of guilt" is found in Lev 22:16, in a discussion of who may eat the priestly food; in 1QS v:15, which relates the dangers of associating with fallen members of the sect; in 1QpHab vii:12, which describes the avarice of the Wicked Priest; and in 11Q19 xxxv:8, which refers to improper priestly service in the temple.

Lines 9-10. The expression "waters for defilement" corresponds to the nearly identical phrase "water for defilement" in Num 19:9, 13, 21; 1QS iii:4, 9; 4Q272 1ii:15; 11Q19[a] xlix:18. Along with the text of lines 8-9, its occurrence here incidentally confirms the relationship between frag. 2 and frags. 15-16.

Lines 10-17. Again, the expression "in three [days]" (or "on the third [day]"; cf. the Hebrew of Exod 19:15) in lines 12-13 confirms that frags. 15-16 belong with frags. 1-3. Additional confirmation comes from other terms also found in frags. 1-3, such as the word "he bathes" or "bathing" (line 11); "pure" (line 16); and "I have [pu]rified" (line 19).

Index of Modern Authors

Index of Scripture References

298

Index of Dead Sea Scrolls

Index of Other Ancient Writings